Behind the Blue Lamp

Policing north and east London

By

Peter Kennison

David Swinden

Printed and published by

Coppermill Press
1 Cranham Farm
Upminster
Essex
RM 14 3YB
Tel/fax 01708 641868

Distributed by

John Barrett
60 Skypearls Road
Woodford Green
Essex
IG8 9NF
www.policegifts.co.uk

First published 2003

ISBN 0-9546534-0-8

British Library Cataloguing-in-Publication data
A catalogue record for this book is available from the British Library.

All photographs/illustrations are reproduced courtesy of the Metropolitan Police Museum with the exception of the following;

Peter Kennison 1, 4, 6-9, 13, 17, 26-27, 32, 34 - 35, 45, 47-49, 55-59, 67, 73-74, 77, 80, 86, 89, 95, 96, 112-116, 119, 123, 124-125, 129-132, 136, 138-141, 144-148, 154-155, 157, 160-168, 174-175, 180-182, 186-187, 191, 196, 199-200, 203, 205, 208, 210-211, 216, 225-226, 235-237, 240-241, 245, 254, 265, 279, 284-286, 289-290, 296
Victor Wilkinson, 5, 12, 18, 19, 22, 282.
Ken Batson 30-31.
David Swinden 15, 36, 38, 69, 120, 183, 188, 193, 197, 212, 218, 222, 227-228, 250, 255, 260, 264, 271, 276, 299.
Metropolitan Archives 39.

Dedicated to the men and women of the Metropolitan Police (both past and present) who risk their lives in the protection of the public.

Shoot and take away our civil liberties.

Acknowledgements.

The authors are particularly indebted to friends and colleagues who advised, directed and discussed the research, yet still remained interested. Particular gratitude and thanks are also extended to;

Ken Batson
S. Barson
Maggie Bird MPS Records Management Branch
Bernard Brown (Metropolitan Police retired)
John Barrett BEM (Metropolitan Police retired)
Dr. Melvyn Brooks, Israel
Professor Linda Clarke University of Westminster
Bill Davidson, Surveyor Metropolitan Police,
Betty Donaldson
Jack Edwards
Bryn Elliott (Metropolitan Police retired)
Steve Earle, Metropolitan Police Service, Museum Charlton,
Fred Feather, Essex Police Museum (Essex Police retired)
John Havers, Devon.
Neville (Spike) Hughes, (Metropolitan Police retired)
Andrew Kinch, Metropolitan Police
London Metropolitan Archives
Nick Mackay
David Mander Hackney Borough Archivist
Jeremy Pearce (Metropolitan Police retired)
Ray Seal, Metropolitan Police Service, Museum Charlton,
Pam Taylor of the Old Enfield Charitable Trust
Kenneth Venables MBE (Metropolitan Police retired)
Sarah Ward, Essex Police Museum Curator
Victor Legender Wilkinson (Metropolitan Police retired)
Julieanne Young, Librarian MPS Architectural Library,

To our wives to whom we owe our biggest debt of gratitude. To Valerie Swinden, for her continuous support, characteristically efficient copy-editing and constructive suggestions to our draft manuscripts. To Julie Kennison for her unceasing tolerance, advice and support during the past years.

List of illustrations   page no.

CONTENTS

Metropolitan Police Stations and Offices in the North and East London

BEHIND THE BLUE LAMP

INTRODUCTION

In 1829 the Metropolitan Police were established in London to control the streets of the Metropolis. They were one of the largest employers, at the time, and later they became one of the largest landlords in the country. They had highly regulated and disciplined work practices, which led to distinct work patterns that changed the nature of employment. This had far reaching repercussions for society at large mainly because of daily contact between the police and public[1].

Since that time much has been written about the police in terms of enforcement, however little has been done to tackle the institutional [2] nature of policing and to show the social side of the police organisation. This book aims to fill that void.

A large number of general police histories have been written which tell the story of how the police evolved from early times, yet they omitted the day to day functions and duties of constables apart from riots, murders, and the strange or outrageous. The histories of the stations, section houses and other police buildings, which housed our police in London were also left out.

A great deal of the recent comment on the police has been critical, but it is easily forgotten that the British police represent an admirable balance between liberal and authoritarian control. The increase in the pace of life, improvements in communication and advances in technology are all issues of the moment, and are matters which the police must consider in their daily tasks. Yet in many quarters we seem to expect more from our police than we do from any other profession. Many people, these days, only see the police when a uniformed police officer attends an incident out on the streets, or when a police vehicle passes them either on patrol or answering an emergency call. Lack of resources have always kept the police 'low on numbers' a fact which led to the old adage that 'you can never find a copper when you want one'. This, together with the fact that the majority of people never see the inside of a police station except perhaps when portrayed on television, attracts accusations from some quarters that the police are a secretive, covert and biased organisation. This book looks at the police culture from its very beginning through its organisation, buildings, equipment, work practices and social groups. It portrays the police at work and play.

Many of the older police stations have disappeared, and new ones have been built to keep pace with the increases in population and new technology. Police stations, like hospitals and schools, add to our sense of community, and it threatens our security when police decide to close them for ever and also generates a sense of loss for those living nearby.

The gradual increase in manpower, changing work patterns and the implementation of new technology have all created demands for more space. Although many of today's police stations have been rebuilt on the same original sites, many details, photographs and plans of the original buildings have long since disappeared. Our research has involved collecting material from a variety of sources including the archives of the Metropolitan Police Museum, the National Archives (formerly the Public Records Office) and many Local Authority Libraries.

We have examined and documented details from existing records in the north and north east of London, and have included stations which have at some time either been within, or are no longer in, the Metropolitan Police Area.

We hope the book will be of interest to a wide variety of people, and particularly those who enjoy police history and also those serving and retired police officers, special constables and civilian support staff, who want to remember some of the police stations where they once served or were posted to. This book may also be useful to those who have an interest in family history and want to add more detail to their family tree of ancestors who were, and may still be, police officers. A list of the names of almost five hundred police officers mentioned in this book is shown in the Appendix.

This book is an opportunity to look behind the 'blue lamp' in a socio/historical way, and to tell the stories of the people who have lived and worked in these police stations. It reveals how police culture developed historically, socially and institutionally. The book is organised so that the police history is set within each of the borough boundaries. The social aspects of policing have been introduced throughout the text. With the exception of three chapters –'The Early days of Policing', 'Epping Forest District Council' and 'Thames Division' the book has been structured geographically into the north and the north-east boroughs of

London. Chapter One relates to the early history, Chapter Two to Barking and Dagenham, Chapter Three to Camden, Chapter Four to Enfield, Chapter Five to Epping Forest, Chapter Six to Hackney, Chapter Seven to Haringey, Chapter Eight to Havering, Chapter Nine to Islington, Chapter Ten to Newham, Chapter Eleven to Redbridge, Chapter Twelve to Thames Division, Chapter Thirteen to Tower Hamlets and Chapter Fourteen to Waltham Forest.

A large number of references have been made throughout this book and these are located at the end of each chapter. This will assist those who wish to do further study on any particular aspect of this book or use it as a basis for continued research. Many references have been made to the Metropolitan Police Orders. These are internally published confidential documents sent out from Force Headquarters to all police stations, giving instructions to the Force on operational and administrative matters. It also gives joining and leaving details of police officers within the Service, and in recent years has included the details of civilians working for the Force. It also contains promotions and discipline punishments. It was originally published daily, but is published twice a week now.

This book covers the eleven boroughs of London and two District Councils plus the Thames Division, which patrols the waterways. It will be for others to trace the police history of the remaining London boroughs. This subject is a continuing story and therefore suitable for expansion and further research. The authors have tried to be as accurate as possible with the information contained in this publication, and any errors must be theirs.

David Swinden
Peter Kennison

---

[1] Shpayer-Makopv, H. (2002) The making of a Policeman. Ashgate Press, Aldershot
[2] Ibid p7.

Chapter One

THE EARLY DAYS OF POLICING

The origins of the Police date back as far as the 9th century when the duty of apprehending criminals was placed on the community. Although interrupted and weakened by the Norman Conquest in 1285, the Statute of Westminster revived much of the old system and set the tone of law for the next five hundred years.

In 1361 Justices of the Peace (JP's) were introduced to keep the peace in the shires. These were Lords; men who were learned in law. The justices could not pursue criminals personally, so constables were established to assist them, starting with volunteers, and then by workers and merchants. Gradually people paid others to undertake their duties as a constable, rather than perform the duty themselves.

The power of the Justices diminished under Cromwell and the Civil War, but when Charles II returned to England he re-instated them. However, during the Restoration the judicial positions fell into disrepute because of the appointment of 'Charlies' or watchmen by the City of London. These were old persons who were infirm or incapable of keeping order or those who were too young or more interested in committing crime, rather than preventing it.

In 1673 an Act was passed authorising JP's to appoint Petty Constables thus statutorily authorising a custom which had been in practice for some time. By the mid 1730`s, Colonel Sir Thomas de Veil, a London JP, set up a Justices Office at Bow Street (Covent Garden). The office was very efficient, and set the trend for sweeping changes in the policing system.

Henry Fielding, the novelist, entered the judicial scene after a short political career that had not only rendered him to poverty but also gave him ill health and many enemies. In 1748 he accepted a position as Justice of the Peace at Bow Street and he became a very efficient and energetic magistrate.

Fielding tried to understand the criminal mind and the root causes of crime. He formed a band of special constables who were called Bow Street Runners. They were largely unpopular, although they were very experienced at breaking up the criminal gangs. There was a suspicion that some Runners incited people to commit crime so they could apprehend the criminal and pocket the reward.

Henry Fielding produced pamphlets regarding his view of crime and would surely have had a great impact on crime had he not died in 1754. He was succeeded by his blind half-brother John, and together with another magistrate, Saunders Welch, they put into practice some of the ideas developed by Henry Fielding.

By the 1770's crime in London was increasing dramatically and a series of committees were set up to consider the state of the policing system. London was the greatest town in the world but it was also the most lawless. In fact the whole of Britain had many criminals, and by 1819 had the harshest criminal code, with 223 capital offences.

In the forty years prior to the introduction of a uniform police force there were no less than seventeen Parliamentary Select Committees which tried to find an answer to the problem of crime and the criminal.

THE FORMATION OF THE METROPOLITAN POLICE

The Metropolitan Police was established in London by the Metropolitan Police Act 1829. With its introduction, Sir Robert Peel, the Secretary of State for the Home Department and its main sponsor, immediately set about finding suitable leader(s) for the new police. It was his wish to appoint two Commissioners in the first instance. He found two very good candidates, a forty-six year old Army Officer, Colonel Charles Rowan, and a young Irish Barrister, Richard Mayne who was some thirteen years Rowan's junior. The two Commissioners started their work at the Home Office in July 1829. Premises for the new headquarters of the police were found at 4, Whitehall Place, which backed onto a narrow lane to the east of Whitehall, called Scotland Yard. They moved into these new premises in August that year. Peel wrote to the Commissioners outlining the initial established strength of the new police force;

8	Superintendents
20	Inspectors
88	Sergeants
895	Constables.

Recruitment

When the Metropolitan Police was formed in 1829 the Commissioners faced a variety of problems. Recruiting and retaining suitable staff was difficult, given the standards which had been imposed by Sir Robert Peel. Having recruited the officers, the issues of concern then became pay, uniform and service conditions.

When the first thousand police were recruited, it was found that a large number of the original watchmen were not physically capable of performing the new duties required, and were, therefore not retained. In the Borough of Poplar the old watchmen were presented with their greatcoats and a weeks pay when they lost their jobs.[1] Consequently, the new Force had to be built up from scratch. The Commissioners recruited young men of limited education who then received no formal training other than drill instruction.

In 1829, it was the policy to recruit men from the agricultural community, not because of the superior physique and health of the rural worker, but because these country people had no experience of town life, and it was suggested that they made more trustworthy policemen and were easier to train.[2] Londoners knew too much about their town and its ways. After the first thirty years the Force was still accepting people from the same social classes. A Home Office Report pointed out that,

> "Constables are recruited principally from the class of daily labourer and lower class of artizan"[3]

It is interesting to note that one third of the recruits in 1829 were married and by 1833 the proportion had risen to two-thirds with 2531 married constables and only 864 bachelors.[4]

The only ranks above Sergeant were Inspector and Superintendent. These posts were nearly all held by former Sergeant Majors from the Guards or the Cavalry, who had been selected for their ability to enforce discipline.

There were a large number of applicants to join the Force, and the Commissioners personally interviewed each candidate.[5] They had to be less than thirty-five years of age, except in cases where they might be fit to be sergeants, and at least five feet and eight inches tall.[6] The minimum height was reduced by one inch in 1855, but later it was increased to five feet and eight inches again,[7] and this remained in force until 1990 when all height limits were removed. Candidates were also examined by the Police Surgeon to ensure they were 'free from any bodily complaint'[8]

The Commissioners carefully enquired into the character and qualifications of each candidate.[9] The names of those persons selected were submitted to Sir Robert Peel, the Home Secretary, for approval.[10] Three thousand, two hundred and forty seven men had been recruited during the period from September 1829 to March 1830.

Each officer, on joining the Metropolitan Police, is given an individual warrant number which remains with that officer throughout their service. Starting at number 1 in 1829 the current warrant numbers of officers joining the service in the year 2003 exceeds 203000[11]. Women Police have a separate warrant number, which reached 26563 before the separate recording of women officers was abolished by Robert Mark in 1973. This means that over a period of nearly 174 years that nearly 230,000 persons have joined the Metropolitan Police.

The speed at which the police organisation was founded and organised, although many Londoners thought that it would not last, caused Peel to say to his wife,

"I have been busy all morning about my police. I think it is going very well. The men look smart and a strong contrast to the old watchmen"[12].

Whilst recruiting was underway, the urgent problem of framing the instructions of the new police was the next most important task. These instructions became known as the primary objects of police and these are still as applicable today as they ever were. The main principle was;

"It should be understood at the outset, that the principle object to be attained is the prevention of crime. To this great and every effort of the police is to be directed. The security of person and property, the preservation of public tranquillity and all other objects of the police establishment will thus be better effected than by detention and punishment of the offender after he has succeeded in committing the crime"[13]

By Saturday 26th September 1829 sufficient numbers of men had been recruited and they were sworn in "en masse" by the Commissioners Rowan and Mayne in the grounds of the Foundling Hospital, Holborn. They were each given a parcel containing their uniform, their conditions of service were read aloud to them and they were given lodging instructions. That evening they were shown, but not posted to, their beats. At 6pm on Tuesday 29th September 1829, just over two months after the act became law; the new police were marched out and posted to their beats. Instantly, Londoners regarded them with hostility and derision, nicknaming them 'Peelers' or 'Bobby' after Sir Robert Peel.

Peel was desperate for his new police to become accepted by the people, but the early 1830s saw the Reform Bill riots and calls for the abolition of the police in favour of a return to parish policing. Rumours and inflammatory comments still continued in an effort to denounce the new Police. In August 1830 the first murder of a police officer, on duty occurred. Constable John Long was stabbed to death in Grays Inn Road, Holborn.[14]

Discipline and Complaints

Discipline in the force was strict and the punishment imposed was arbitrary, leading to a great many dismissals. The new Commissioners tirelessly investigated the complaints against police, which flooded into Scotland Yard. Complaints were handled and investigated personally by them.

Complaints of misconduct were diligently and expeditiously dealt with, which was quite some undertaking bearing in mind that there were only two Commissioners investigating these matters. A comprehensive set of rules were developed and issued outlining the role and functions of each rank; however these rules were frequently altered or changed. These rules or instructions defined police misbehaviour and were published and promulgated through Police Orders issued from Scotland Yard. It was a requirement of each police officer to keep himself abreast of each police order and instruction.

Within a short time the Commissioners experienced great difficulty investigating their complaints because of the sheer numbers being reported. They examined ways that would be more efficient and effective. One of the problems they experienced was that many of the complainants could not identify the alleged errant constable. Although they supplied each constable with collar numbers many complainants failed to take the details. This led the Commissioners to issue another order on 11th October 1829 stating;

> "Any man reported for endeavouring to conceal his number, or refusing to show or tell it when properly asked, will be dismissed, as such concealment or denial can only be caused by having done something he is ashamed of." [15]

When the uniform was changed in 1863 the constables' divisional number was also displayed within the helmet plate badge. Another difficulty experienced by the Commissioners related to what constituted 'off duty' with respect to complaints. The instructions required constables to wear their uniform at all times, even when off duty, which caused difficulties when it came to 'on duty' behaviour witnessed by a member of the public. Clearly the public could not easily distinguish between a police constable who was on or off duty. This lead to problems of supervision, especially as constables lived and worked in the community. It caused the Commissioners to issue another order on 8th March 1830 to the effect that;

> 'In issuing to the Police Force a new badge to be worn when men are on duty, the Superintendent will fully explain that the object in view is to prevent the constant complaints that would be made by the public on seeing those of the Police Force who are not on duty walking, or talking together, which they will now be able to do without that unpleasant consequence, the badge will be worn on the left arm, just above the cuff. [16]'

The duty arm band became an everyday part of a police officers uniform but was phased out in the mid 1960s having lasted for over 130 years.

The harsh discipline also extended to the private lives of the police. For example the regulations stated that;

> "All men of the force who shall associate, drink, or eat with any civilians without immediately reporting that same to the Superintendent, will be dismissed from the force" [17]

The Commissioners would attend a station house for the purpose of inspection, to ensure their instructions were being carried out. A lack of supervision by Superintendents, Inspectors and Sergeants was a grave offence, which invariably resulted in dismissal. Superintendents, who were in charge of each station/station house, would ensure the Inspectors were doing their job of supervising the Sergeants, who in turn would check up on the constables for the same reasons.

Another grave offence against discipline was to idly gossip or hold conversations with anyone in the street, and another instruction was issued in October 1830 to the effect that constables would be reported and the matter brought to the attention of the Commissioners. Judging by the number of defaulters and by the level of dismissals and other punishments awarded, the Metropolitan Police had significant numbers of unsuitable candidates. Drunkenness was the most common weakness not only amongst police, but also throughout the population in general. It was a hard struggle to enforce the high standards. Each day brought dismissals for drunkenness and a first offence against discipline was always their last. Between 300-400 police officers were dismissed, on average, each year, and after Christmas in those early years large numbers of police officers were sacked without recourse to defence or appeal.

The first signs of a gradual and begrudging acceptance of the new police came in an instruction issued in November 1830 some thirteen months after the new police was formed;

> 'The Commissioners have much satisfaction in acquainting the police, that they have received numerous representations, from gentlemen and respectable persons, of the courage and steady good conduct of the Police when assaulted, in different quarters, on Tuesday last: and the Commissioners have communicated this information to the Secretary of State for the Home Department, who has directed the Commissioners to express to the Police Force the satisfaction which this report of good conduct has given him'[18]

It followed therefore that gradually the new police spread throughout England and Wales, although pockets of the parish constable system did remain in existence for some time. The people accepted the police, although the cost of such a force of men, especially to some county ratepayers, was always a problem. There was a high turnover of manpower especially in the Metropolitan Police and of the first 100,000 police constables one third would be dismissed, one half would resign prior to pension and of the remainder 4,000 died in service, leaving the residue.[19]

Throughout the Victorian era the high standards and conditions of service were blamed for the high wastage of police officers. One such problem, which was an issue, was that of corruption in the mid 1870s involving the Criminal Investigation Department of the Metropolitan Police. Some critics argue that these problems stemmed from the harsh conditions of service, the authority and office of constable and his particular relationship within the law. From time to time Royal Commissions were ordered to enquire into the conduct of police to ease public disquiet and dissatisfaction. These took place in 1855, 1906, 1929, 1960 and 1993, and very often were followed by legislation.

Conditions of Service

In the early days the facilities were much different from those of today. Unmarried officers lived in accommodation provided at police stations and station houses. They had common rooms and a kitchen. The officers frequently returned to the station, after their duty patrol, wet and exhausted. There were no facilities for drying clothes or even having a hot bath. A Home Office Committee in 1868 visited one station house and found the boots of the men were kept in a place open to the air. In winter the boots were frozen stiff[20].

The married officers had to find private lodgings on their Division. It was not easy to find accommodation at a price they were willing to pay. Often they would be cramped into a single room where they were forced to try and dry their clothes in front of the rest of their family. These and other issues led the Home Office Committee[21] to recommend that quarters be built for married constables, with proper facilities to ensure the health and well being of the men. Police married quarters were situated all over the Metropolitan Police District and it is only in recent years that they have sold many of these premises to increase revenue and reduce their building stock.

Uniforms

The uniforms were chosen to look as unmilitary as possible. Each man was supplied with a greatcoat and cape, a body coat, two pairs of trousers, two pairs of boots, a hat and an oil skin cover, a stock, an embroidered collar, a button brush and a stick[22]. Each man paid for his own uniform. The body coat was £1. 7s. 6d, his greatcoat £1. 15s., his trousers 12s. 6d., his hat 12s., his boots 12s., - the total amount being £4. 19s. 3d. Two shillings a week was deducted from his pay to cover the cost of his uniform. It would take him almost a year to pay off this debt.

The quality of the uniform in those days was poor, as greatcoats for example did not protect the officers in the wet weather. Their boots were also of an inferior quality[23]. The hat was strengthened with cane supports to protect the head from injury, and as it weighed 18 ounces it would have been extremely uncomfortable to wear.

As early as August 1830, the Commissioners decided that the quality of the uniform should be improved. The constables were to have cloth of better quality; the Sergeants were to wear the style of uniform previously worn by the Inspectors who would then wear the same pattern previously worn by the Superintendents. It is interesting to note that the Superintendents' clothes were to be enhanced and decorated with the acorn and laurel leaf embroidered in silver on the collar, and the collar and cuffs would be edged with narrow silver lace. At the same time the inscription on the button was to be altered; instead of 'Police Force' it was to be 'Metropolitan Police'. The hat and uniform then remained virtually unchanged for a number of years although eventually the hat was replaced in 1864 by the now classically styled helmet[24].

Constable Smith circa 1856 with top hat

Pay

At first pay was twenty-one shillings a week. By July 1830 the men were allowed nineteen shillings a week, but the Commissioner paid for their uniform. The typical hours of duty for a constable were eight hours night duty from 10pm until 6am, and day duty was from 6am to 9am and then again from 3pm to 10pm. Meals were taken on the beat, usually in the form of snacks.

It was estimated that on average the constable walked sixteen miles on night duty and twenty miles on day duty[25]. During the day in that period which should have been his rest time, he would often be required to attend Court as a witness, and on occasions he would be directed to practise foot drill. He sometimes had to walk a considerable distance to and from the drill ground. He worked seven days a week although he was worked 'less severely on a Sunday. In 1868 an increase of 1000 men allowed him one day off every fourteen days. It was thought in those early days that if the constable was given a day off he would spend his time drinking and wasting time. In 1910 the officer was given one days rest each week.

By 1914 the average pay of a constable was still only £1.10s per week, and some of this money came from local council rates. Whilst police pay stayed the same during the First World War, the cost of living almost doubled placing them in great financial hardship. The police had no unions and were not allowed to strike.

In 1919, serious disorder was prevented by the government who appointed a Royal Commission (The Desborough Committee). The Royal Commission considered methods of recruiting, conditions of service, rates of pay, pensions and allowances. Better pay and conditions were awarded to the police in recognition of their unusual position in society, and for the first time the professional status of policing was formally acknowledged. With this came Police Regulations and Discipline Code, which formalised the rights, responsibilities and accountability of individual police officers, their wives and family.

Health

The health of the people of London during the early part of the nineteenth century has a direct relationship to the police officers working in London. The pay was only just sufficient for a married officer to live on, but his accommodation and lifestyle put him amongst the poor persons of London. As the health of the population suffered, so did the health of the officers and their children. Many officers resigned during those early years of the Metropolitan Police, some probably to return to the cleaner rural areas of the country[26].

The sanitary conditions in London during the early part of the nineteenth century were lamentable, and in 1846 there were still 200,000 undrained cesspools in London. The death rate was high. From 1838 – 1840 the average mortality rate in London was 37.4 per thousand population, and in some slum districts was as high as 60 per thousand.[27] These figures were much higher than the average for England and Wales, which for this same period had an average of 23 deaths per thousand population.[28] However the accuracy of these figures is often questioned. It is difficult to arrive at mortality figures when they are set against unreliable population figures.[29] Drinking water was contaminated and disease was ever present, particularly typhoid and cholera. One cholera epidemic in 1832 killed over 5,000 Londoners; another in 1849 caused the deaths of 14,000.

An examination of the Metropolitan Police Register [30] which recorded the deaths of police officers shows that in 1832 there were 35 deaths of serving officers and thirteen of them died of cholera. Eleven of those thirteen died between 20th July – 18th September 1832, during a particularly hot summer. A similar picture emerged for the year 1849 when 27 officers died of cholera from a total of 62 deaths. 1849 was identified as a 'peak for deaths' when looking at the relationship between the total number of deaths against the total average strength of the Force.

Many of the police officers who died of cholera lived and worked in the area south of the Thames. It wasn't too healthy either living to the east of London. The difference between areas of west London compared with south and east London is marked. The west side of London obtained safe water upstream whereas the east side had drinking water fouled by both the west Londoners and themselves. Water was supplied to the Eastenders by the Lambeth Company and Southwark Water Works. Until 1854 they took their water from below Westminster Bridge and near London Bridge respectively. [31]It should be noted that between 1838 and 1854 the average age of death for males in England and Wales was 39.9 years.[32]

There were also many severe outbreaks of influenza, which caused a large number of deaths in London. The worst years were 1833, 1837 and the winter of 1847/8 which saw about 50,000 deaths.[33]

The first Medical Officer appointed to the staff of the Metropolitan Police was John Fisher. Initially his duties were vague and undefined apart from examining recruits at headquarters and attending sick constables. In a letter to the Home Office in 1839 he wrote that his duties had increased enormously. He had a staff of thirty part-time Divisional Police Surgeons to assist him, but he had also examined sixty thousand candidates for the Force during the previous ten years[34].

The Divisional Structure.

Outside the City of London, local government was the responsibility of the parish vestries. The formation of the Metropolitan Police in 1829 was the first London wide body, which had the responsibility for maintaining law and order across 88 parishes, liberties and hamlets.

Later, in 1855 the Metropolitan Board of Works was established to look after the roads and sewers. It was not until 1889 when the London County Council (LCC) was set up to govern London, and 28 metropolitan districts replaced the old parish vestries.

In 1965 the Greater London Council (GLC) replaced he LCC, and absorbed all of Middlesex as well as parts of Essex, Hertfordshire, Kent and Surrey. Thirty-two new London Boroughs were created. The GLC was abolished in 1986, although the London Boroughs remained in place. In April 2000 the Greater London Authority (GLA) came into being, and the boundary of the Metropolitan Police was adjusted to coincide with the new GLA boundary. Certain police station areas were then absorbed into various County Constabularies.

Peel envisaged that the new police would be initially policing the inner area of the metropolis with the formation of six Divisions. The final stage was policing the remainder consisting of 120 miles, with a population of nearly one and half million people.

Six letters of the alphabet A, B, C, D, E, and F   identified the first Divisions. The Divisions were formed on the following dates:-

29th September 1829

      "A" or Whitehall Division operated from The Metropolitan Police Office at Great Scotland Yard.
      "B" or Westminster Division operated from New Way, Tothill Street
      "C" or St. James Division operated from Vine Street Police station, Piccadilly.
      "D" or Marylebone Division operated from Marylebone Lane Police Station.
      "E" or Holborn Division operated from George Street, St. Giles.
      "F" or Covent Garden Division operated from Bow Street, Covent Garden.

19th December 1829
      "M" or Southwark Division operated from Southwark Bridge Road.

10th February 1830
      "G" or Finsbury Division operated from Bagnigge Wells, Clerkenwell.

"H" or Whitechapel Division operated from Chapel Yard, Spitalfields.

"K" or Stepney Division operated from Arbour Square, Stepney.

"L" or Lambeth Division operated from Tower Street, Waterloo Place.

12th February 1830

"S" or Hampstead Division operated from Albany Street, Regents Park.

10th April 1830

"N" or Islington Division operated from The Old Watch House, Islington Green, Islington.

May 1830

"P" or Camberwell Division operated from Park House, Walworth.

"R" or Greenwich Division operated from Blackheath Road.

"T" or Kensington Division operated from Brook Green, Hammersmith.

"V" or Wandsworth Division operated from the Plain, Wandsworth

Furthermore "W", "X" and "Y" Divisions were formed on 21st October 1865, "J" Division on 28th July 1886

By June 1910 the Metropolitan Police had grown to 22 Divisions and Thames Division, which covered 699 square miles, together with the Dock Divisions.

The strength of the Force in 1910 was now 19045 officers made up as follows:-

1	Commissioner
4	Assistant Commissioners
5	Chief Constables
32	Superintendents
600	Inspectors
2509	Sergeants
15894	Constables

The final two divisions to be set up were, "Z" Division on 28th February 1921 and "Q" Division on 1st April 1965.

The District/Area Structure

As the Metropolitan Police Divisions grew, there was a need to develop a supervising structure between Superintendents and the Commissioners. Prior to 1903 the Divisions were allocated and supervised by Chief Constables as follows:-

No. 1 District. "H" "J", "K", "M", "N", "R", and Thames Divisions.
No. 2 District. "D", "E", "F", "G","S", "X" and "Y" Divisions.
No. 3 District. "A", "B", "C", "L", "P", "T", "V" and "W" Divisions.
The Criminal Investigation Department was also supervised by a Chief Constable.

In 1903 the Metropolitan Police Area was divided into four Districts. The Chief Constables continued to supervise their Districts from Scotland Yard. :-

Northern District.   "D","E","S","X" and "Y" Divisions.
Eastern District   "G","H","J","K","N" and Thames Divisions
Southern District   "L","M","P","R", "V" and "W" Divisions.
Western District   "A","B","C","F", and "T" Divisions.
The Criminal Investigation Department retained a Chief Constable post.

Between 1903 and 1918 the District structure changed from four to five Districts. In 1918 the direction and supervision of the Districts from Scotland Yard was abolished. Arrangements were made for each Chief Constable to work from an office situated within his District[35]. Divisions were allocated to Districts as follows:-

No.1 District. "A","B","C","D","E" and "T".   (Office at Ixworth Place)
No.2 District. "F","N","S","X","Y".   (Office at Paddington)
No.3 District. "G","H","J","K" Thames.   (Office at Hackney)
No.4 District. "L","M","P","R","V","W".   (Office at Camberwell)

This structure remained in place although the offices moved to different buildings within the Districts. In 1969 Divisions were renamed 'Districts', and the four Districts known as 'Areas'. Each Area was supervised by a Deputy Assistant Commissioner and covered the same geographical area as before. In 1986 the Metropolitan Police was divided into eight Areas. In 1995 under the Service Restructuring exercise Areas

14

were reduced to five and regraded the officer in charge to Assistant Commisioner[36].The Area/District Structure disappeared when two Assistant Commissioners were appointed from Headquarters to supervise the North and the South of the Thames. The current structure is designed around the London Boroughs each of which has its own Borough Commander, a Superintendent, who reports on most operational matters to an Assistant Commissioner (Territorial Policing).

POLICE BUILDINGS

The Receiver

The Secretary of State for the Home Office was the police authority for the Metropolitan Police District when the Force was established in 1829. In addition to the two Commissioners being appointed, there was also a person appointed to receive all sums of money in respect of the Force. His full title was 'The Receiver for the Metropolitan District', and he was responsible, amongst other matters, for paying the salaries and eventually the pensions of the retired officers. He was also responsible for the funds provided to build police stations. This was laid out in The Metropolitan Police Act 1886, which gave power to the Receiver with respect to construction of buildings and the purchase of land.

> "The police receiver from time to time may provide, by building or otherwise, a central office and such police stations, offices, houses, and buildings as are required for the purposes of the metropolitan police force,...............and may improve, enlarge, fit up, and provide proper access, yards, and other appurtenances for, any offices, stations, houses and buildings...............may purchase by agreement..........take on lease and hold.......any land."[37]

The approval of the Secretary of State was necessary for all purchases and loans made by the Receiver.

Police Architects and Surveyors

When the Metropolitan Police Force was established in 1829 the Receiver, John Wray, took on the responsibility for about seventy old watch houses[38]. The larger buildings were known as 'police stations' and the smaller buildings were the 'station houses'. The Surveyor General of

Prisons had the overall responsibility for all those buildings used by police. If work needed to be done it was supervised by an outside 'consultant' surveyor, who was paid for each job completed. By 1842 the fees payable for these professional services became exorbitant. It was decided by the Secretary of State that there should be appointed a 'Surveyor of the Police Establishment' who would remain under the control of the 'Surveyor General of Prisons'. The salary would be £150 per year with an allowance for coach and cab hire when visiting buildings on the outer limits of the Police District. The first appointed surveyor lacked 'zeal and regularity' and left within the year, as did the second appointee[39].

The third Surveyor to be officially appointed was Charles Reeves who took up his post in November 1843. He was responsible for listing all police buildings. He was also tasked with the inspection of all premises, making sure that they were in good repair. By this time there were 125 buildings within the Metropolitan Police District. Many of these properties were old watch houses and other rented properties. Reeves reported in 1845 that much of the police accommodation was poor and there was serious overcrowding. He introduced the 'Surveyors Book' to be kept at each police building. The Police Inspector at each station was responsible for entering details of work that needed attention[40].

In 1845 Reeves' post was removed from the control of the 'Surveyor General of Prisons' and placed under the control of the Commissioner of Police. In 1847 the first building was actually purchased for police use, instead of renting or leasing a property. During the next 23 years he was responsible for the building and opening, for operational purposes, of twenty-nine new police stations in north and north-east London.

In 1852 the Common Lodging Houses Act imposed upon Reeves the responsibility for the measuring and examination of the fitness of each house. This was followed by the Dangerous Structures Act in 1853 which added to his responsibilities. In 1853 a new post was created of Assistant Surveyor to help Reeves with this increase in work[41]. By 1855 Reeves was now the 'Surveying Inspector of Common Lodging Houses and Surveyor of Dangerous Structures'[42].

By 1857 he was appointed as Chief Surveyor with a salary of £200 per year. The early period of police buildings is interesting because of the sheer volume of police stations that needed to be built during those early years. This increase in work meant that in 1861 staff were increased to a Deputy Surveyor and two Assistant Surveyors[43]. The average cost of building a police station in 1857 was about £2500, but by 1900 the cost had risen to about £10,000.

Reeves spent much time looking at ways of improving the design of police stations. There was a need to provide cells, office space and living accommodation for police officers. Whilst he toured the police area he became concerned about the poor conditions in which he found police officers working, particularly those still working out of old watch houses. In 1863 he prepared a report concerning police officers at an old watch house on the Isle of Dogs. He said, 'only one small room for police business, indifferent cells which open into a charge room, all unfit for the purpose'. The constables were living in private lodgings, about half a mile away from the station.

Reeves made proposals that there should be eleven rooms in his new station, including a day room, a charge room, a drying room, a coal store, three water closets for the 'comfort of officers', three cells and a separate stable block. This was to become the standard format of police stations over the next few years[44].

In November 1866 Reeves wrote to Sir Richard Mayne indicating that his health was poor and that medical advice suggested that he needed six months rest in the country air away from London. His letter mentioned that during the forthcoming year there were further new police stations and other buildings to be erected and that he needed some additional help to supervise this work. The police buildings were at Bedfont, Harrow, Enfield, Lea Bridge Road, Hanwell, Uxbridge, Church Street, Spitalfields, Enfield Highway, Bagnigge Wells and Poplar. There were also to be additions and alterations to King Street Police Station.

At the time he was being helped by Frederick H. Caiger, Assistant Surveyor, who had been in his post since starting as a young 24-year-old in 1850. He was the Surveyor of Dangerous Structures and Common Lodging Houses in London[45]. In 1857 John Butler, who later became the Surveyor in 1881, was working for Reeves as 'Clerk of Works'.

Sadly, Reeves died suddenly in December 1866, within a few weeks of asking for a six months rest. There were a number of applicants for the vacant post including one from Caiger. However, in January 1867 Thomas Charles Sorbey was appointed as Surveyor of the Metropolitan Police and Police Courts[46]. During his first year in the post he designed two police stations – East India Road and Lea Bridge Road.

Sorbey resigned in 1868, after a short period in post. He later emigrated to Canada and carried on designing both residential and commercial buildings. He died in 1924 at the age of 88.

In November 1868, Caiger, who had been the Deputy Surveyor, became the new Surveyor, and John Butler became the Deputy Surveyor[47]. At the same time as the new building programme was running they were also converting suitable buildings into police stations. A good example of this is the one at Barkingside which opened in 1869. Ten new police stations were opened in north and northeast London during his period of office. Caiger held the post until 1881 when John Butler followed him. Butler was by then 50 years old[48] and was a very experienced architect and surveyor.

By 1878 the Surveyor had the responsibility for ensuring the maintenance of 150 police stations, seventeen section houses, nine separate married quarters, seven stables and six offices.

Twenty-one new police stations were opened in north and northeast London during John Butler's time as Surveyor between 1881 and 1895. His son, John Dixon Butler, already an established Architect and Surveyor, followed his father into the post as Surveyor of the Metropolitan Police, and remained there from 1895 until he died in November 1920. Whilst in his post he designed over 200 police stations and courts.

The holder the Police Surveyor post had some difficult issues to resolve within the command structure in the early days. He reported to the Receiver for all the financial issues in respect of police buildings, but directly to the Commissioner for Dangerous Structures and Common Lodging Houses. This sometimes caused a conflict of interest.

The post still exists within the Metropolitan Police and is known as the Director of Property Services. The post holder has a direct responsibility to the Commissioner for the maintenance of all the 200 or so police stations in London. The post also has the responsibility for major office buildings, warehouses, training establishments and the residential estate. The Department has about sixty architectural staff, both trainees and qualified personnel[49].

POLICE RANKS

Since the formation of the Metropolitan Police there have been a number of different titles used for various ranks within the structure. As the size of the Force increased it was necessary to increase the number of supervisors. The Constable rank supports all those ranks above in the hierarchal structure. The history of the rank structure is as follows:-

Constables/ Detective Constable

This is the basic rank at the front line of policing within the police service. Before the establishment of the Metropolitan police in 1829, constables were the local magistrates. Local householders also served for a period of twelve months as the parish constable. There were a number of different classes of constable, each being paid extra money as they moved up through the grades. The constable can be recognised by a number and divisional letter (or two letters which show a station designation) which are shown on either shoulder. In 1951 an open neck tunic was introduced that showed the divisional letter and numbers on epaulettes[50] however the ceremonial No. 1 dress uniform tunic was still in existence and showed the identification around the collar.

Sergeant/ Detective Sergeant (2nd Class)

The next rank above that of Constable is Sergeant. It is the first supervisory level in the command structure. This was the only military title adopted in 1829. The badge of rank is that of triple chevrons on the sleeves. They are also known as Section Sergeants, as they supervised eight to ten Constables. From 1872 until 1875 there existed the post of Schoolmaster Sergeant. The post was created due to the high rate of illiteracy in the Force. Whilst today sergeants perform a range of duties within their rank there have been divisions within the sergeant rank. Sergeants perform Custody Officer Duty when they are attached to charge rooms and Custody Suites. They can also be Section Sergeants, which requires them to perform duty out on the streets or section of the sub-division. Sergeants can also be attached to the Criminal Investigation Department (CID) but they wear no overt badge of rank because they operate mainly in plain clothes. Their identity and rank can be verified by disclosure of their warrant cards. Constables can become acting sergeants on a temporary basis and wear two stripes on each arm or epaulette.

Station Sergeant /Detective Sergeant (1st Class)

In 1868, owing to a lack of Inspectors at that time, the senior sergeant was

known as the Station Sergeant/clerk sergeant and deputised for the Inspectors who were in charge of stations on the Division. When the Chief Inspector rank was created in 1869 on the Division the Inspectors became 1st Class and 2nd Class inspectors and then in 1878 station sergeants became 3rd class inspectors. The rank of Clerk Sergeant was created to be responsible for administrative work on a Division. Originally the sergeants added an extra bar to the three chevrons making a four bar sergeant however this was phased out in 1921 when a Tudor crown replaced the

Station Sergeant pre 1921

fourth bar. The picture above shows a sergeant with four bars on each upper arm dated 1902. The picture at right shows the badge of rank post 1921.

From 1890 until 1973 the rank of Station Sergeant was unique to the Metropolitan Police and replaced the short-lived rank of Sub-Inspector. The badge of rank was three chevrons with a crown above the chevrons.

Station Sergeant post 1921

In 1950 a chromium plated badge of four stripes was allowed on epaulettes for bush type shirts (1961) and raincoats (1962)[51].

Inspector/Detective Inspector/Junior Station Inspector/Station Inspector/Sub-Divisional Inspector

This was introduced in 1829 as the next supervisory level above that of a Sergeant[52]. At that time the next level above the Inspector was the Superintendent who was in charge of the Division. In 1841 Inspectors had an embroidered double crows toe containing the divisional letter sown onto the coat collar. The most able Inspectors were promoted to Superintendent and the best Sergeants to Inspector.

By 1868 there were insufficient Inspectors so the rank of Station Sergeant was created between that of Sergeant and Inspector. In 1869 Inspectors were graded in classes from one to four. In 1878 Station Sergeants were appointed for a short period of time as 3rd class Inspectors[53]. The picture at left shows an Inspector with Victorian helmet and plate together with silver lace on both sleeves.

Victorian Inspector in ceremonial dress with sword

The Inspector was responsible for the proper and efficient running of a police station. Inspector's wore the standard service pattern helmet, but instead of a number and division the centre of the plate contained a large divisional letter instead as shown in the illustration above.

The picture right shows an ordinary uniform Inspector with Kepi hat (introduced in 1865)[54] without badge or any indications of rank on the jacket collar, but with medals and ceremonial gloves. The medals are the 1887 Silver Jubilee, the 1897 bar, and the 1901 Coronation medal. It appears that the picture was taken in a station yard outside the parade room.

Kepi hats were withdrawn from wear in 1908. Inspector's had a better standard of uniform than constables and sergeants, with one inch black braid on the cap and four rows of black cord with drop loops on the shoulders on ceremonial uniforms[55]. The dark blue

Inspector circa 1906

caps with ventilation holes shown below were introduced in 1906[56].

21

Inspector with flat hat without black braid peak

From 1916 all Inspectors, Chief Inspectors and Sub-Divisional Inspectors wore a crown badge on the cap, although a simple metal crown had been unofficially worn prior to this date[57].

By 1919 the senior Inspector was known as the Station Inspector. Both Superintendents and Inspectors replaced their braid for two stars (sub-divisional Inspectors) and one star (Inspectors) in 1921. In 1922 all Inspectors badge of rank was required on mackintosh epaulettes and greatcoats[58]. Lord Trenchard introduced the rank of Junior Station Inspector for the graduates from the newly formed Hendon College, but the rank was abolished in 1939. In the 1960's Temporary Inspectors wore only one star during their probationary period. The picture at left shows an Inspector with ordinary plain flat cap without badge.

The picture at right shows a Sub-Divisional Inspector in normal daily uniform plus spurs and a ceremonial sword. It shows him with a star located on each side of the collar and a hat badge on his cap. Inspectors would generally be accomplished horsemen because supervision at the turn of the century was often done on horseback especially in the outer Divisions. They therefore had riding equipment as shown in the photograph. This Inspector is also displaying his service medals starting at left with the 1897 Jubilee, the 1901 Coronation and the 1911 Coronation medals. This meant that he took an active part in the celebrations and was on duty almost certainly as part of a serial of officers policing the event. It is

Sub- Divisional Inspector circa 1916

hard to judge whether the picture was taken for ceremonial purposes, although this is doubtful otherwise he would have worn his more ornate ceremonial tunic with embellishments.

The current badge of rank for an Inspector is two stars and this is worn on the shoulders. The Inspector's flat cap shows black braid on the peak (as shown on the cap of the Sub-Divisional Inspector above).

Chief Inspector/Detective Chief Inspector

CHIEF
INSPECTOR

The rank of Chief Inspector was introduced first in the CID in 1868. In 1869 the rank was introduced to Divisions. The Inspector's uniforms, caps, kepi's and other items of clothing remained the same for Chief Inspectors. Mackintoshes were issued to Chief Inspectors in outer divisions in 1904 and inner divisions in 1914[59]. The badge of rank is three stars. The Chief Inspector is the last inspecting and federated rank before the Superintendent Ranks.

Superintendent/ Detective Superintendent

Superintendent Grade
1 - Pre 1953

The Superintendent rank in 1829 was the highest rank below the two Commissioners. The title used by them was seen as non-military and the same as used by orphanages, schools etc.

Superintendent circa 1916

Between 1830 and 1843 a small piece of silver lace on the coat or the greatcoat collar denoted the badge of rank for Superintendent[60]. Later the badge of rank became a Tudor crown. When the Metropolitan Police District was extended in 1840 to cover an area of just under 700 square miles (about six times its former size) an Inspecting Superintendent was appointed. His job was to travel around the District and save the Commissioners a great deal of routine supervision[61].

In 1872 Superintendents wore kepi style caps, which differed from the Inspectors because it had a smaller peak. The picture above shows a Superintendent with cloth crown on the collar showing his rank. The cap also shows a black peak and small metal cap badge.

SUPERINTENDENT

Prior to 1953 there were three grades of Superintendent. Although designated by the Police Act 1964, which introduced two grades of Superintendent, these grades had been in force since 1953[62]. These were termed Class I and Class II and the same badge of rank was worn i.e. the crown. Class I Superintendents in the Metropolitan Police were often called Chief Superintendents (see below). In 1959 Superintendents were required to remove the crown in favour of the St. Edwards crown pattern. The Metropolitan Police Superintendents Class I wore a crown and bath star later known as Chief Superintendents[63].

Chief Superintendent/Detective Chief Superintendent

The first time the term Chief Superintendent was used in the Metropolitan Police was in January 1866 when the Superintendent on 'A' Division was recognised as the senior Superintendent and officially designated Chief Superintendent. The term only lasted until February 1869 when it was discontinued[64]. In 1949 the rank of Chief Superintendent was reintroduced initially to take charge of Divisions, which later became Districts. Divisions were divided into Sub-Divisions. It was phased out in 1995 as a formal rank although it is currently used as recognition of seniority. The badge of rank is a crown above a star.

This senior officer of the Metropolitan Police is wearing his ceremonial uniform

Divisional Chief Superintendent
Circa 1936

together with a sabre. His helmet shows the 1911-1935 Senior Officer's ornate helmet plate together with a braided chin strap. His ornate ceremonial uniform befits the rank of Chief Superintendent. It was

CHIEF
SUPERINTENDENT

probably taken around 1935 for the Jubilee celebrations. Additionally he is wearing three medals, which from left to right are the Order of St. John of Jerusalem medal, the 1911 silver Coronation medal and the 1937 Coronation medal. One noteworthy point from this photograph is the fact that he does not have a moustache or beard which was common at the time for most police officers.

The Superintendent on the right is John Michael Mulvany KPM. He joined 'H' Division of the Metropolitan Police as warrant number 54255 on 29th May 1871. He later rejoined 'H' Division as Divisional Superintendent on 8th November 1895 and retired on 2nd September 1911 aged 61 years and with forty years service. He was awarded the King's Police Medal on 5th January 1912 after he retired for distinguished service. This picture of Mulvany shows him wearing a flat cap introduced in 1906[65].

John Michael Mulvaney
'H' Divisional Superintendent

Today, Borough Police Commanders hold the rank Superintendent Grade I but wear the crown and star attributed to the Chief Superintendent - a rank which was phased out in 1995. The additional star is to denote seniority over Superintendents (Grade II).

Chief Constable

This rank was created in 1886 and in rank order is between Superintendent and Assistant Commissioner. It was given to the four District Superintendents placed in charge of all the Divisions in 1869. In 1889 the first Chief Constable was appointed within the CID. The post holders were based at Scotland Yard until 1918 when they were required to work from an office within their own District[66]. The creation of the rank of Deputy Assistant Commissioner in 1928 was seen as more senior than the rank of Chief Constable and finally abolished within the Metropolitan Police in 1946.

Deputy Commander

Deputy Commander

The post was created in 1946 when the rank of Chief Constable was abolished, as a deputy to the new rank of Commander[67]. The badge of rank for Deputy Commander was crossed tip staves in a Bay Leaf Wreath which were later used for Commanders. When the re-grading took place in the late 1960's most Deputy Commanders were regraded as Commanders. The rank was abolished when those not regraded retired.

Commander

The rank is between Chief Superintendent and Deputy Assistant Commissioner. It is the lowest rank of Chief Officer, conferring membership of the Association of Chief Police Officers (ACPO). It was introduced in 1946 to take charge of the four Districts of London. It is held to be the equivalent to Assistant Chief Constable rank.

Commander

COMMANDER

When the rank was introduced the badge of office was similar to Deputy Commander but with the cloth star later used for Deputy Assistant Commissioners. In the late 1960's the Divisions were renamed Districts and the majority of the Chief Superintendents were promoted to Commander. The four original Districts were renamed Areas, and a Deputy Assistant Commissioner was placed in charge of each. The badge of rank for a Commander is cross batons on a laurel wreath[68].

Deputy Assistant Commissioner

The rank was introduced in 1919[69] and was used to head departments at New Scotland Yard. In 1925 the silver star was added to the crossed batons[70]. In 1933 the four Chief Constables in charge of each of the four districts were replaced by four Deputy Assistant Commissioners (DAC's). The DAC's rank was seen as a grade senior to the Chief Constable rank it replaced. In March 1946 on each of the four Districts of the Metropolitan Police, the title of DAC was changed to Commander and that of Chief Constable to Deputy Commander[71]. Then in 1969 the DAC's replaced the Commanders in each area and the DAC's deputy, a Commander, took on an inspectorial role over the Districts, which were now commanded by Commanders. In 1976 the DAC's took over more of an operational and administrative role[72]. In 1995 it was considered that that it was not necessary for there to be the two ranks, DAC and Commander, to occupy the position between Superintendents and Assistant Commissioners. Although the title has been given to some Commanders to reflect higher responsibilities. The badge of rank is cross batons on a laurel wreath and one bath star.

DEPUTY ASSISTANT COMMISSIONER

Assistant Commissioners

The rank was first authorised in 1856[73]. The number of Assistant Commissioners was originally two but it was increased to three in 1884[74]. The number of Assistant Commissoners were further increased to four in 1909[75] and to five in 1933[76].

Deputy and Assistant Commissioners circa 1946

Assistant Commissioner

The Assistant Commissioners were in charge of major headquarter departments at New Scotland Yard. In recent years some of the Assistant Commissioners have been moved from New Scotland Yard and put into operational command positions. The badge of rank which has remained consistent (save for the crown) is the cross batons on a laurel leaf and a crown. The illustration at left is the current badge of rank introduced in 1953 and up until 2000 was also used for the Deputy Commissioner.

Deputy Commissioner

The fifth Assistant Commissioner post was created in 1933[77] and allowed the Force to use one of the Assistant Commissioners as a Deputy to the Commissioner. Until 2000 the post holder wore the badge of rank of an Assistant Commissioner but now has Cross Batons on a laurel wreath, and small stars and a crown.

Commissioner

COMMISSIONER

The Crown appoints the Commissioner. When the Metropolitan Police was first formed there were two Commissioners but only one from 1856[78]. The badge of rank is Cross Batons on laurel wreath, one crown and a bath star.

CURRENT STATUS

Currently the term 'police station' refers to a police building to which members of the public have a twenty four hour a day front office counter service. Each London Borough now has at least one police station with this service. Whereas, a 'police office' now refers to a police building which has restricted hours of opening.

In April 2000 the boundaries of the Metropolitan Police District were aligned with the Greater London Authority. This meant that in the north and northeast of London the following Metropolitan Police stations/offices, although included in this book, have been transferred to County Constabulary Police Forces.

Cheshunt Police Station to <u>Hertfordshire Constabulary</u>

The following Police Stations/Offices were transferred to Essex Police.

Debden Police Office
Limes Farm Police Office
Loughton Police Station
Waltham Abbey Police Station
Chigwell Police Station. (This station has since been demolished and new residential accommodation built on the site)

[1] Thompson H.M. Keeping the Peace in Poplar 100 years ago in 'Books to Read' Spring/Summer 1939.
[2] Moylan J (1929) Scotland Yard and the Metropolitan Police. Putnam & Co. p114
[3] Home Office Departmental Report dated 6th May 1868, p12. The report makes a number of recommendations relative to pay and conditions. The Home Office Committee Report was signed by James Fergusson, Henry Thring and George Everest .
[4] Palmer. S.H. (1988) Police & Protest in England & Ireland 1780-1850 Cambridge: Cambridge University Press. p303. See also Reith.C.(1943) British Police and the Democratic Ideal. Oxford. Oxford University Press . p62.
[5] PRO MEPO 2/5796 Evidence given by Colonel Rowan to the Night Watch committee at Guildhall on 15 July 1830 as cited in Swinden D.R.(1992) Policemen in London during the Early 19th Century (1829-1850) University of London – Unpublished.
[6] Ibid
[7] Floud. R. et al (1990) Height, health and history. Cambridge. Cambridge University Press. p.155
[8] Home Office Departmental Report, dated 6th May 1868. p12.
[9] The word 'Qualifications' was not defined, although Ascoli.D.(1979) in Queen's Peace. Hamish Hamilton p.89 mentions that one of the standards set was to test candidate's ability to read and write. This would have limited the number of candidates considerably for Rule.J (1986) The Labouring classes in early Industrial England (1750-1850) Longman. p234., states that in 1830 barely 30% of the workers in South-East Lancashire could write their own names. It is clear that literacy was a problem in recruitment during the early nineteenth century.
[10] PRO MEPO 2/38 Letter from Sir Robert Peel written to the Commissioners on 10 December 1829, as cited in Swinden D.R.(1992) Policemen in London during the Early 19th Century (1829- 1850) University of London – Unpublished
[11] Metropolitan Police Orders dated April 2003
[12] Op cit
[13] Laugharne, A. (1985) The Principles of Policing and Guidance of Professional Behaviour. Metropolitan Police Service
[14] Some historians attribute the first police murder to have occurred 7 weeks before Constable Long. On 29th June 1830 Constable Grantham stepped between two drunken Irishmen quarrelling over a woman in Somers town. They turned on him instead knocked him down where he received a kick to the temple and died within a few minutes.
[15] The Police and Constabulary Review 1844 p110
[16] Ibid p104
[17] Critchley T. (1978) The History of the Police in England and Wales.
[18] The Police and Constabulary Review 1844 p110
[19] PRO MEPO 4/2 Register of he Deaths of Serving Metropolitan Police Officers (1829 – 1889).

[20] Home Office Departmental Report dated 6th May 1868. p.23.

[21] ibid.

[22] PRO MEPO 2/5796 Evidence given by Colonel Rowan to the Night Watch Committee at guildhall on 15th July 1830.

[23] Home Office Departmental Report dated 6th May 1868 p.26.

[24] Moylan.J., (1929) Scotland Yard and the Metropolitan Police. Putman & Co. p.170.

[25] Home Office Departmental Report dated 6th May 1868 pp 12-13.

[26] Swinden D.R. (1992) Policemen in London during the early 19th Century, University of London (Unpublished).

[27] Seaman. L.C.B. (1973) Life in Victorian England Batsford. p35. Also referred to in Cruickshank,R..J. (1946) Roaring Century (1846-1946) Hamish Hamilton. p.161.

[28] Tranter, N.L. Population and Society (1750 – 1940). Longman. 1985. p.46. See also Mitchell B.R. and Deane. P., Abstract of British Historical Statistics. Cambridge University Press. 1962.

[29] Drake.M. The Census, 1801 – 1891, cited in Nineteenth Century Society, ed. Wrigley E.A. Cambridge University Press. 1972. p.13.

[30] PRO MEPO 4/2 Register of the Deaths of Serving Metropolitan Police Officers.

[31] Smith F.B., (1979) The People's Health (1830-1910) Weidenfeld & Nicolson. London. p.231

[32] Ibid p.197.

[33] Ibid p.323.

[34] Reith C., (1943) British Police and Democratic Ideal. Oxford University Press. p.228.

[35] Metropolitan Police Orders dated 16th & 20th November 1918.

[36] Fido, M. and Skinner, K. (1999) The Official Encyclopedia of Scotland Yard. Virgin, London. P12

[37] s.2. Metropolitan Police Act 1886

[38] Barson S., (1986) London Police Station Architecture, MA Thesis. (Unpublished)

[39] Police Museum Document – photstat page 95. Source document unknown.

[40] Ibid

[41] Ibid

[42] PRO MEPO 2/14 Letter dated 22nd November 1855

[43] Police Museum Document – photstat page 95. Source document unknown.

[44] Barson S., (1986) London Police Station Architecture, MA Thesis. (Unpublished

[45] PRO MEPO 2/14 Letter dated 23rd November 1866.

[46] PRO MEPO 2/14 Letter dated 4th January 1867

[47] PRO MEPO 2/14 Letter dated 2nd November 1868

[48] PRO Census 1881.

[49] Fleming R., & Miller.H. (1995) Scotland Yard. Signet. p.497.

[50] Fido, M. and Skinner, K. (1999) The Official Encyclopedia of Scotland Yard. Virgin, London

[51] Fairfax, N and Wilkinson, V. (1969) Uniforms of the Metropolitan Police (unpublished) Metropolitan Police Museum, Charlton

[52] Ibid

[53] ibid

[54] Fairfax, N and Wilkinson, V. (1969) Uniforms of the Metropolitan Police (unpublished) Metropolitan Police Museum, Charlton

[55] Ibid

[56] Ibid

[57] Ibid

[58] Ibid

[59] Ibid

[60] Ibid

[61] Heron F.E., (1970) A Brief history of the Metropolitan Police. P.17 (Unpublished)

[62] Fairfax, N and Wilkinson, V. (1969) Uniforms of the Metropolitan Police (unpublished) Metropolitan Police Museum, Charlton

[63] Devlin, J. D. (1966) Police Procedure, Organisation and Administration. Butterworths, London

[64] Ibid

[65] Fairfax, N and Wilkinson, V. (1969) Uniforms of the Metropolitan Police (unpublished) Metropolitan Police Museum, Charlton

[66] Metropolitan Police Orders dated 16th November 1918

[67] Metropolitan Police Orders dated 15th March 1946

[68] Fido, M. and Skinner, K. (1999) The Official Encyclopedia of Scotland Yard. Virgin, London

[69] s11 Police Act 1919

[70] Fairfax, N and Wilkinson, V. (1969) Uniforms of the Metropolitan Police (unpublished) Metropolitan Police Museum, Charlton

[71] Heron F.E. (1970) A Brief history of the Metropolitan Police. P.17 (Unpublished)

[72] Metropolitan Police Orders dated 2nd July 1976

[73] s2 Metropolitan Police Act, 1856

[74] s2 Metropolitan Police Act, 1884

[75] s3 Police Act 1909

[76] Metropolitan Police Act, 1933

[77] Ibid

[78] s1 Metropolitan Police Act, 1856.

Chapter Two

The London Borough of Barking & Dagenham

The London Borough of Barking is situated north of the Thames, and about nine miles east of the centre of London. It covers the areas of Dagenham and Barking. One of the most famous buildings in the borough is Barking Abbey, which is the second oldest Saxon Abbey in the country. It was founded in 665 AD, but very little remains standing now. The borough's name is believed to have derived from the earliest settlements in Essex. The ancient name given to Barking means 'Berica's' people and to Dagenham means 'Daecca's' people[1].

The fishing industry was an important part of life in Barking from the 14th to the mid 18th century. In 1887 the riverfront at Dagenham was developed into a major dock area. One of the largest industries in the area is the Ford Motor Company which bought land from Samuel Williams in 1924 and built a factory between 1929-1931. This car production plant at Dagenham has been a major employer in the Borough. It also provides a location for some of Europe's leading shipping container and warehousing companies[2].

When the Metropolitan Police District was extended in 1840 it began policing the areas of Dagenham and Barking and was situated on "K" Division.

Barking Police Station.

A watch house was erected near the Whalebone cross roads in 1643 to protect the constable and watchmen as they looked out for highwaymen and footpads on the (Chadwell) Heath. It was 1837 before a night watch was established in Barking[3]. Prior to 1840, and the introduction of the Metropolitan Police to the town, there were two old-style police officers who worked from Vine Cottage in Tanner Street [4]. Barking Police Station should not be confused with Barking Road Police Station which is nearer Canning Town and Plaistow than Barking old town.

Barking Police
Station Lamp

The first Barking Police Station was built on land bought in 1848 for £144. This new purpose built station house was erected in 1849 in North Street at the cost of £942[5]. By 1864 there were two Sergeants and eleven Constables at the station[6]. The station was small and built with a charge room and 2 cells, which were frequently insufficient for the needs of the station. A 2-stall stable was also erected - with a hayloft above. The officers of the station could rest in the mess room or the library, both situated on the ground floor[7]. The station had a total of eleven constables and two sergeants in 1864. A mounted officer and his horse were also located there[8]. Instructions were also given that the Inspector from Ilford Police Station should make periodic visits to the station to ensure the officers were correctly carrying out their duties[9].

Metropolitan Police Star pattern Helmet plate 1875 -1902

In 1881 Thomas LAMB, aged 50 years old from Aldworth near York, was the Inspector in charge of the station. He resided there with his 41 year old wife Mary and their 17 year old son. The station's six single constables lived in the section house[10].

The photograph at left was taken at Calverts Photographers, near Barking Police Station, and shows Constable 420K William Cook dressed in the 1875 uniform with a helmet having a black star pattern plate, similar to the item at above.

The picture was taken before the end of 1901 as the helmet plate bears the Victorian crown. Cook was born at Bromley-by-Bow in Middlesex and his previous occupation was shown as hammerman in an iron foundry.

Constable 420 'K' William Cook

Records also show he was 5ft 11 inches tall, and had joined the service on 9th May 1892 at the age of 23 years. His warrant number was,

77645 and after initial training he was posted to "E" Division (Constable 278 "E"). The Training of constables took place at Kennington Lane Section House as Peel House[11], Pimlico did not open until 1907[12]. This was a barracks and school of instruction where recruits had to undertake a course lasting between three to five weeks[13]. Within a year Constable Cook had transferred to "K" Division however on 18th January 1902, he suddenly died [14]. Death in service is a sad event at any time, not only for relatives but also for colleagues. This would, under normal circumstances, resulted in a police funeral, paid for by the police service and attended by all of his family, friends and fellow officers.

By 1890 two inspectors, Thomas Dixon and George Allen, three sergeants and twenty-six constables were posted to the station[15]. In 1892 more building work created accommodation for six single police officers. They were each charged one-shilling (£3.06) [16] a week for their lodging. The station call sign was Bravo Kilo (BK) in 1893[17].

In 1891 an inspection of the station found that the sewer was leaking into the station's water supply from underneath the kitchen. Urgent work was completed to correct the fault. The well and cesspool were cut off, and arrangements were made with the South Essex Water Company to lay on and supply mains water. The cells and rooms were also lit[18]. The picture

Barking Police Station
83, North Street, Barking, Essex.
1849 – 1910

below shows Barking Police station in 1872. The station lamp above the front door was issued in 1861, lit with gas and had blue glass[19]. The constable standing outside is wearing the 'coxcomb helmet', which was phased out in 1875 - in favour of a Home Office 6 panel helmet and star pattern plate[20].

The station was lit with oil lamps and candles. Gradually, as the local population increased the small local police

34

station was no longer sufficient for policing, and arrangements were made to purchase land and build a new station nearby. By 1898 the station strength was increased to two inspectors, six station sergeants, twelve sergeants and eighty-seven constables[21].

In 1906 the freehold title on land to build a new police station was purchased from Mr. J.W. Glenny at a cost of £825. This land was situated in Ripple Road. Negotiations to purchase the land appeared to be difficult as the threat of compulsory purchase was made against the owner under Legislation, however these powers were never invoked because the sale of the land was concluded in favour of the Receiver. This may have been due to the fact that Mr. Glenny also owned adjacent property, and did not favour a busy police station next door. An agreement was made for a seven feet brick wall (later revised to five feet) to be built between the two properties within 3 months of purchase.

Barking Police Station
4, Ripple Road, Barking, Essex.
1910 – present day

Barking was a station located on 'K' or Bow Division although the headquarters was not in Bow but at 27, West India Dock Road, Limehouse[22].

Building work commenced in 1908 on the new police station site at 4, Ripple Road, Barking. By September 1910 the station had opened for business. Interestingly, the Receiver was also responsible for paying tithe rent charge on the site, which was "part of a field of 3 acre wood and 27 perches" to the Vicars of Barking and a lay impropriator (a person with a claim on the land), amounting to a total of £1. 3s. The old station in North Street was sold in 1911 for £400.

In 1924 two sets of married quarters were built together with section house accommodation for twenty-one unmarried men, paying one shilling a week rent. The cost of the married quarters amounted to 8/6d and 5/6d a week rent respectively[23]. There was extensive re-furbishment in 1926 when the section house accommodation was re-built. The new section house was opened later in the same year. The station was refurbished in 1936[24].

Barking became synonymous with the event of race walking as every police officer in the Metropolitan Police will testify. Barking sub-division hosted the annual Barking to Southend road walk later organised by the Metropolitan Police Athletic Association. The competition and prestige of winning the Barking to Southend race meant that all stations entered

Deputy Commander Walter Batson
1919 - 1964

teams of young officers in the hope of success. This event was originally the idea of a famous police sportsman, Walter C. Batson. The first road walk took place in 1921, and it was an annual event until the 1980's when it was considered too dangerous to stage because of the increase in traffic.

Mr Batson was not only an exceptional sportsman but also a successful police officer rising to the old rank of Deputy Commander in 1953. Mr Batson was born on 16th May 1899, and joined the police in September 1919. He was promoted to Sergeant in August 1928

The ten **Batson Medals** starting at left with the MBE and The Order of St. John of Jerusalem. The medal second from the right is the Police Long Service medal instituted in 1951. The medals are arranged in order.

and to Station Sergeant in November 1930. Promotions quickly followed and he became an Inspector in 1935, a Chief Inspector 1937 and a Superintendent in 1944. He became the "J" Divisional Superintendent and Deputy Commander in 1953. He was a founder member of the Metropolitan Police Athletic Association (M.P.A.A.) and first Hon. Secretary. He won the 10-mile police championships in 1925, 1926, 1927 and the Barking to Southend race also in 1927. He received the King's

Police Medal in 1950, the OBE in 1957 and the Swedish Gold medal in 1963. This was presented by King Olaf of Sweden himself for Mr Batson`s, outstanding contribution to sport. Mr Batson retired in 1964 after 44 years service, and died in 1984.

The enamelled medal at right was awarded by the Metropolitan Police Athletic Association (M.P.A.A) to all participants of the event. The medal was made of gold at first but later, because of cost, participants were honoured with silver medals instead.

Metropolitan Police Athletic Association Medal awarded to participants of the Barking to Southend road walk. This medal is dated 1938.

Records show that in 2002 that the address of the station has changed. The address is shown as 6 (not 4) Ripple Road, Barking , Essex IG11 7NF and is open 24 hours a day 7 days a week[25].

Dagenham Police Station.

Dagenham was first policed in 1840 by the Metropolitan Police, from a shop in Bull Lane. Dagenham was shown on the outer District of 'K' Division and had a station strength of one sergeant and five constables[26]. All the officers at the station were housed privately[27] and lodged near the station. This became the first police station in the area. It was not for another 10 years that arrangements were made for the building of a proper police station in Dagenham.

Dagenham Police Station
High Road, Dagenham, Essex.
1851 – 1961

Prisoners who were charged and detained without bail would be transported often handcuffed and on foot to Ilford Police Station where they would travel by horse drawn police van to prison. Charges were taken at Dagenham and persons would appear before the Petty Sessions at Ilford on the 1st and 3rd Saturday of each month[28].

Surveyors for the Metropolitan Police found a plot of land, which appeared suitable for a police station, which had a freehold title that could be purchased. Arrangements and contracts were made, and the building of the police station commenced in 1850 in Rainham Road South at the junction of Shafter Road, Dagenham, at a cost of £949. The land had been purchased from Mr. John Jarrow for an additional £100.

There was accommodation on the first floor for one married sergeant (later an Inspector) and four unmarried constables. The station was not equipped with a gas supply (this was not fitted until January 1906), and the occupants had to rely on oil lamps and coal for its lighting and heating. Furthermore there was no sewage system and effluent was emptied from the cesspool once a year[29]. There was a charge room and cells in which to house prisoners. There was also a parade room for constables to report for duty[30].

In 1846 Constable George Clark was found murdered at Dagenham. This 20-year-old had recently been posted to Dagenham from Arbour Square Police Station, and was settling into the routine of police work. His sergeant, named William Parsons, was a man who liked a drink, as did most of the men under his command. Constable Clark was a man of strict morals, and was keen to save his fellow officers from the evils of the demon drink. This must have caused irritation among the men.

The lower class inhabitants in the area did not like the new police system. They much preferred the unsuspicious and lazy constables of the old Parish system. Barking, an adjacent village, had long been the centre for smuggling activities, which meant that active policemen were not welcome.

On 1st July 1846 Constable Clark started his night duty shift at 9pm, and was paraded as usual by Sergeant Parsons. At 1am, he was met again by Sergeant Parsons, who arranged to meet him again at 3am. This was the last time he was seen alive. He never turned up at 3am or returned to Dagenham station house at 6am. Later that day he was not found sleeping in the station house where he should have been. A search was ordered but it was not until two days later that his body was found, a quarter of a mile off his beat, on land belonging to Mr. Page a farmer. Constable Clark had a fatal stab wound to the throat, the back of his head had been beaten in and his head had been scalped.

Inspector Richardson and Sergeant Parsons worked on the enquiry, but as there was no quick conclusion the Commissioners became concerned and ordered the newly formed Detective Department to take the case over. In a very short time Dagenham, in the words of one resident, was crawling with the detective force. Two of the department's Inspectors, three of the six sergeants and the celebrated detective of the day, Nicholas Pearce recently promoted to Superintendent "F" Division, appeared on the scene.

Later three arrests were made at Woolwich. However there was no evidence other than that they were in possession of white gloves usually worn by a policeman, and that a woman had overheard a conversation suggesting that two of the men had murdered a constable.

Meanwhile a sensation had been caused at the Coroner's hearing where the farmer's wife, Mrs. Page, suggested that Sergeant Parsons had not been on duty on the night of the murder, because he was ill. She had been told this by one of the constables on the day the body was found, yet no less than six people, including Sergeant Parsons, denied this allegation on oath. In fact it transpired that Parsons and some of the other constables had been drinking whilst Clark was out on his beat.

One of the constables namely, Abia Butfoy, was saying Parsons was well, went to London to see the Commissioners. He told them that he and others had lied on oath. He also told them that Sergeant Parsons had not been on duty that night. When the body was discovered Sergeant Parsons took him to one side and told him that if asked, that both of them had rendezvoused on his (Butfoy's) beat at between midnight and 1am. The murder was re-investigated and the Coroner returned a verdict of murder by person's unknown, and made comments about perjured evidence by police officers in his court. The Commissioners considered their next move. They suspended Sergeant Parsons, Butfoy and four constables, pending inquiry.

The police were unpopular but the case attracted little attention outside Dagenham. The three lesser culprits, including Butfoy, were dismissed from the Force, whilst Sergeant Parsons and two constables remained suspended. During further enquiries the three were kept as virtual prisoners within the station house. The guarding became lax and Sergeant Parsons and one of the constables escaped and went on the run[31]. A poster was put up offering a £50 reward (or by today's value £2,716.)[32] for the apprehension of the two escapees and three weeks later the constable was arrested in Lincolnshire.

A year after the murder the two constables stood trial for perjury, were found guilty and sentenced to seven years transportation. Sergeant Parsons was never found, rather like the murderer of Constable Clark. There was a final twist when some twelve years after the murder, a woman came forward and implicated, her own late husband and another man. At the hearing, after the arrest of a man named Blewett, her evidence was discredited and the man was aquitted[33].

In 1864 there was one Sergeant and eight constables posted to the station[34]. In 1874 the sergeant in charge was Frederick Stratford. These men were supervised by an Inspector who patrolled and supervised police stations at Ilford, Barking, Dagenham, Loughton, Woodford, Wanstead, Chadwell Heath, Barkingside, Chigwell and East Ham[35].

Concern had been raised regarding the activities of constables and sergeants whilst off duty away from the station. In many cases as the drinking water could be contaminated, people drank beer because it was fermented. This led to off duty hours being spent in local public houses. The concerns of senior officers were further heightened when constables and some sergeants became indebted to the Landlord of a public house who provided free drink. Whilst drinking on duty was forbidden by police rules, off duty hours were a different matter. The recruiting policy was to select non-Londoners as it was felt that they were more honest and that Londoners were, in many cases, naturally inclined to crime. The Commissioner was pressed to introduce billiard tables and games rooms into police stations and section houses in order that recreation could be spent under the watchful eye of supervising officers, a method which ensured against drunkenness and contributed towards good behaviour.

In July 1896 instructions were issued to 'K' Division that a recreation room should be created in each station and section house[36]. Barking and Dagenham stations were issued with draughts, dominoes, backgammon, and single sticks (or pick up sticks), whilst the principle section house on the division received a set of boxing gloves[37]. This perhaps explains the fact that even today snooker and boxing is still taken very seriously by many police officers. The principle station on the division, Arbour Square received a miniature billiards table[38].

The officers playing billiards in the picture below are in training at Peel House Pimlico circa 1910.

The Billiard Room, Peel House, Pimlico, London

The billiards tables soon found favour amongst the Superintendents who reported to the Commisioner that;

"The various articles supplied by the Commissioner for the amusement of the Police continue to be highly appreciated by them; no irregularity of any description has arisen in consequence of their use; and I venture respectfully but strongly to recommend and increase of billiard tables for the happiness of the single men. I would suggest that all stations where 30 single men (or upwards) reside, or to which 100 men are attached, that a billiard table should be supplied" (Superintendent W. F. Green 'N' Division[39])

In 1881 John Durley, aged 38 years, was the Inspector in charge of the station. Durley was from Whitechurch in Buckingham, and he resided at the station with his wife Maria and their three sons. Also there were four single constables and a nurse. The nurse was called Hester Purkiss and she was probably there to look after their eight month old son Joseph Durley. It was also likely that Maria Durley and the nurse would cook and clean for the station, which also meant providing meals for the prisoners.[40]

The old Dagenham Police Station was used until 1937 when it was refurbished[41]. Once re-opened for business it remained in continuous use until 1961 when a new station was built on the other side of the Railway Bridge at 561, Rainham Road South. It took eighteen months to build.

The main entrance has a natural Portland stone floor and marble walls. It was one of the first Metropolitan Police stations to have a reading/rest room with armchairs and reading material. When the police vacated the old police station it was sold and became a betting office.

The picture at right is that of Wilfred John Adams who was born on 16th May 1889 at Morse in Gloucestershire. Prior to joining the Metropolitan Police was a collier. He became a Constable, warrant number 99949, on 20th March 1911, aged 21 years. He served on "K" Division as Constable 711 K until 3rd April 1929 when he transferred and became Constable 751 "T" Division. He had a son who was born in 1926. He left the service in March 1936 and lived until 1952. Constable Adams was given a Commissioner's Commendation in July 1919 'for promptitude with another officer at the scene of a fire'. On leaving the service he was awarded an exemplary 'certificate of service',

Police Constable 711'K'/99948 Wilfred John Adams

indicating that his disciplinary record was outstanding.

In 1957 Dagenham Police Station (KG) was a sectional station of East Ham (KD) sub-Divison which was also the Headquarters of 'K' Division. The Officer in charge of the Division in 1960 was Superintendent W. J. Merchant, whilst the Divisional head was Chief Superintendent A. Lockwood[42] who had been promoted from Leman Street sub-Division[43].

Prior to the 1960's information and intelligence about local criminals was usually passed to other officers by word of mouth. The flow of information was inefficient and there was a need for recording and greater accuracy. In 1967 Constable Nevil 'Spike' Hughes (BEM) thought up a new system to collate this information. He progressed the idea without funding or equipment. Originally nicknamed 'SPYKANEDY' (Spike and Eddy) after Constable Hughes and his colleague Constable Eddy Gurney (BEM), who helped refine the process, the collator system was born[44]. Introduced first at Carter Street Police Station it was soon developed across the whole of the Metropolitan Police Service. At Dagenham a collator was appointed and a room was found to house the information in filing cabinets. Only police officers and members of the civil staff were allowed in this room, and visitors were excluded. The system brought together data, including maps, criminal records, vehicle registrations and other information likely to be of assistance in the investigation of beat crimes. The place where the information was held was called the Collators Office, however it has been renamed the Local Intelligence Office manned by the Local Intelligence Officer. Constables Hughes and Gurney were both deservedly awarded British Empire Medals for their innovation[45].

Metropolitan Police Tunic Buttons from 1863 to the present day

Above are shown the large tunic buttons worn by London's police since 1863. The chromed nickel button on the left shows the Victoria crown at its centre and was used from 1863 until 1901. The centre button shows the King's crown and was used from 1902 until 1953 when the button on the left with the Elizabethan crown was introduced.

Dagenham Police Station
561, Rainham Road South, Dagenham Essex.
1961 – present day

In 2002 Dagenham Police Station was shown at 561, Rainham Road South, Dagenham, Essex, and was the Barking and Dagenham Borough Police Headquarters. The station was open to the public 24 hours a day 7 days a week[46].

Marks Gate Police Station
78, Rose Lane, Romford, Essex
1996 to Present day

As a result of Electoral boundary changes in the mid 1990's the policing of Marks Gate changed. Revisions meant that Barkingside Police gave up this remote site located on the north side of the A12, mid way between Barley lane and Whalebone Lane. Because of the remote nature of the station to Marks Gate it was decided to locate a detached police office on the Estate called Marks Gate Police Station. The station is near the border with the London Borough's of Redbridge and Havering at 78, Rose Lane, Romford, Essex. The opening time was Monday to Thursday 12pm until 2pm[47].

[1] Municipal Year book 2000 and Public Services Directory Vol. 2 Newman Books(1999), and publicity literature for the London Borough of Barking and Dagenham
[2] Ibid
[3] Metropolitan Police "K" District Handbook
[4] J.Frogley (1894) History of Barking
[5] MEPO 2/26
[6] Metropolitan Police Orders dated 11th January 1864
[7] John Back collection (1975) Archives Dept, Metropolitan Police
[8] Metropolitan Police Orders 11th January 1864
[9] Ibid
[10] Census records 1881
[11] Leeson, B (1934) Lost London. Stanley Paul, London.
[12] Fido, M and Skinner, K (1999) The Official Encyclopaedia of Scotland Yard. Virgin Press, London
[13] Op. cit.
[14] Metropolitan Police Divisional Records
[15] Kelly's directory 1890
[16] www.ch.net/hmit. Accessed 13.5.2002
[17] Metropolitan Police General Orders 1893
[18] R. L. Pearson, A. McHardy, and T. Bond - Report on the conditions of Metropolitan Police Stations (1981)
[19] Fido, M and Skinner, K (1999) The Official Encyclopaedia of Scotland Yard. Virgin Press, London.

[20] Taylor , M. and Wilkinson V. (1989) Badges of Office Hazell and Co, Henley on Thames
[21] Op cit
[22] The Police and Constabulary Almanac 1907
[23] Metropolitan Police Surveyors Records (1924)
[24] Metropolitan Police Surveyors Records (undated)
[25] http://www.met.police.uk/contact/phone/htm accessed 03.02.02
[26] PRO 'Distribution of men on 'K' Division 1840'
[27] Ibid
[28] Ibid
[29] Metropolitan Police Surveyors records (undated)
[30] Metropolitan Police Orders 11th January 1864
[31] Cobb, B. (1961) Murdered on Duty, W. H. Allen, London
[32] www.eh.net/hmit accessed 13.05.2002
[33] Cobb, B. (1961) Murdered on Duty, W. H. Allen, London
[34] Metropolitan Police Orders 11th January 1864 and Metropolitan Police Surveyors Records (undated) Police Museum, Charlton.
[35] Metropolitan Police Orders 11th January 1864
[36] Metropolitan Police Orders dated 15th July 1896
[37] Ibid
[38] Ibid
[39] Commissioners Annual Report 1871
[40] PRO Census records 1881
[41] Metropolitan Police Surveyors Records
[42] The Police and Constabulary Almanac 1960
[43] The Police and Constabulary Almanac 1957
[44] Fido, M and Skinner, K (1999) The Official Encyclopaedia of Scotland Yard. Virgin Press, London. p252
[45] Ibid
[46] http://www.met.police.uk/contact/phone/htm accessed 03.02.02
[47] http://www.met.police.uk/contact/phone/htm accessed 03.02.02

Chapter Three

The London Borough of Camden

The Borough lies in the centre of London. The southern part of the borough borders the City of Westminster to the west and the City of London to the east. The eastern borough boundary adjoins Islington whilst to the west is Brent. The boroughs of Barnet and Haringey run along the northern edge of the Borough. It is an area of immense contrasts. It includes the exclusive residential districts of Hampstead and Highgate, the youthful energy of Camden Town, the graceful squares of Bloomsbury and inner city areas of Kings Cross and Somers Town. About 200,000 people either work in or travel through this Borough each day[1].

In terms of policing, today's London Borough of Camden and its parishes have, over the years, been located variously within the police boundaries of "E", "Y" and "S" Divisions. However, Camden is perhaps best recognised as being on "E" Division. This division was formed on 29th September 1829 using the men of the 5th and 6th Companies. In those early days the division was responsible for the parishes of St. Andrew and St. George the Martyr, St. Giles and St. George and Bloomsbury, (which it shared with neighbouring "F" Division), part of St. Marylebone and St. Pancras south of the Euston Road[2].

In 1829 there were two police stations located on 'E' Division. These were at George Street, St. Giles and King's Cross, Battlesbridge[3]. The first Superintendent in charge of the division was William Skene. He died of cholera on 26th August 1832 while still serving[4]. Superintendent William E. Grimwood was appointed 29th September 1829 (stationed at George Street)[5], succeeded him from 27th August 1832 until 12th April 1849 when he also died in service[6]. The division suffered from the cholera epidemic, which swept through the Thames side Divisions in August 1832. It claimed the lives of many police officers[7]. Grimwood was assisted by four Inspectors, John Rawley promoted in 1835, Edward Bell promoted in 1835, Gregory Dudley promoted in 1840 and Henry Maude. Rawley had joined the division in 1841[8].

In 1840 "S", or Hampstead Divisional headquarters was at 52, Albany Street, Regents Park with Superintendent John Carter in charge. The division was responsible for Somers Town Police Station, (from 1845), which was located at 10, Phoenix Street, Kentish Town, situated in Junction Place, and St. Johns Wood Police station located at 52, Salisbury Street, Portman Market. By 1845 there had been a number of alterations and additions to station strengths. There were two police stations on 'E' Division located at Clarks Buildings, High Street, St. Giles and Hunter Street, Brunswick Square.

In 1850 the officer in charge of "E", or Holborn Division, was Superintendent Fredrick George Foxall who was appointed on 13th April 1849 and remained until 26th January 1856 when he resigned on pension[9]. Four inspectors namely Roger Harvard, William Clement, Edward Durgan and Richard Checkley assisted him[10]. By 1855 Gregory Dudley had replaced Roger Harvard as inspector[11]. Superintendent Foxall was succeeded by Superintendent S. Hannant who was in charge from 9th February 1856 until 20th February 1857 when he transferred to take charge of 'C' Division. N. S. O'Brian took over from 20th February 1857 until 31st August 1863 when he also transferred to 'C' Division[12].

By 1888 the total strength of the Division had risen to 515. This consisted of Richard W. Steggles, Divisional Superintendent, who was located at Bow Street, 17 Inspectors, 50 Sergeants and 447 Constables[13].

"E", Division was considered small for a Division, and consisted of Bow Street, Tottenham Court Road and Hunter Street. In 1877 "E", or Holborn, Division had one Superintendent, (James J. Thomson), nine Inspectors John Clifford (Chief Inspector), James Dutchess, John Cook, George Cruise, Henry Wood (Chief Inspector), William De. Maid, William Mee, Edmund Arnold, and Henry Aunger, 46 Sergeants and 437 constables. The Detective Branch consisted of one sergeant and eight constables. Commenting on the state of the Detective force within his division the Divisional Superintendent stated in his Annual report of 1871 that he would "gladly double the strength if he could"[14]. The strength of 'E' or Holborn division in 1879 was one Superintendent, 34 Inspectors and 558 Sergeants and Constables[15]. Bow Street Police Station was the Divisional Headquarters. There were a further twelve Divisional Superintendents until 1953[16].

Albany Street Police Station

A police station existed as far back as 1832 and was situated at Albany Street, Regents Park, London. Albany Street was the headquarters station for 'S' or Hampstead Division. By 1836 the Divisional Superintendent was John Carter, and he was assisted by five inspectors who were in charge of the five divisional stations. Details of the old station are sketchy except that the address was shown as Albany Street, Regents Park and was leased from Mr. C. Gore, Her Majesties Commissioner of Woods. The lease was for 80 years although details of costs are unknown.

Albany Street Police Station
104, Albany Street, Regents Park, NW1
1866 -1960

By 1864 the Police force at Albany Street was located on "S" Division[17].

In the same year Superintendent Loxton stated, in a special report, that the station was no longer suitable for police purposes. It was once the watch house to the Crown estate and therefore had insufficient space for an increase in police numbers. In an emergency, he suggested, the Duty Officer had to send to Somers Town and Portland Town, (later re-named St. Johns Wood), for re-enforcements. In the report he judged the site as suitable for the construction of a new station together with residential accommodation for up to thirty single officers[18].

A preliminary report, on the estimated costs for a new building, was in the region of £3,400, although the actual cost when completed was £4,134. The second police station for the area was opened August 1866 at Albany Street, Regents Park[19]. In 1871 Albany Street Police station was shown as being connected to the direct telegraph network located at

Scotland Yard. In 1881 there were 43 single constables resident at the station[20].

In 1882 Albany Street was recorded as being a sub-divisional station on "S" Division. Records show that Albany Street Police Station was Divisional Headquarters for "S" Division and was located at 104, Albany Street, Regents Park, NW1. The site had been leased from the Commissioners of Her Majesty's Woods and Forests from 1896–1995, with a ground rent of £150 paid annually. This was a large station with a Superintendent's office and dressing room, Chief Inspector's office, harness room, Divisional Clerk's office, Superintendent's store, Inspectors' office, lobby, charge room, matron's room, six cells, CID office, recreation room, library and mess room. In the basement there were a variety of rooms including a canteen, lamp store and drying room[21]. The stables and Section House accommodation for eighteen single constables were located not far away at 62, Little Albany Street. The horses were housed in a three stall stable block with two coaching sheds attached[22].

The station telegraphic code was Sierra Delta (SD)[23]. A house at 27, Clarence Gardens was also leased for police use, from the same vendors, and granted in 1896 [24]. New married quarters and a section house opened in November 1897[25] with accommodation for one married Inspector and 33 single men. Albany Street Sub-division was enhanced in 1898 when Portland Town was integrated to form one division called Albany Street Sub-Division.

The cost of the new section house was £6,002, and the station was altered substantially by W. H. Lascelles and Co. Builders of 121, Bunhill Row E.C. in 1900 at a cost of £4,968.The station address was shown as 104, Albany Street, Regents Park, London[26].Re-organisation of the Divisions north of the River Thames meant that Albany Street was transferred from "S" or Hampstead to "D"or Marylebone Division[27] In 1934 the station was significantly enlarged and assigned the status of Divisional Headquarters for "D" Division. The section house was converted into married quarters in 1949.

In the 1950's the question of building a new station was considered, and permission was granted by St. Pancras Borough Council who purchased the old police station site for £45,000. Land was purchased at 60, Albany Street where a modern Divisional Headquarters for "D", Division, including the sub-divisional station, was built. It opened for police business at 6am on Monday 20th August 1960. Force orders reported that the telephone numbers would remain the same -, as would the telegraphic code (which had been changed in the 1930's to correspond with the divisional boundaries we know today) to Delta Delta (DD).

Albany Street was designed with ample space in mind; it was much larger than the station it replaced. It was built with two floors above ground perhaps with a view to place the Divisional Headquarters, their staff and administration there in the future.

A revision of police boundaries occurred in 1963, when the Local

Albany Street Police Station
60, Albany Street, NW1
1960 – Present day

Government re-organisation also took place. Albany Street changed from "D" to "E" Divisional Headquarters in April 1965, and was located within the London Borough of Camden.

In April 1999 Albany Street became the Borough Police Headquarters. Records show that the station was open 24 hours a day, 7 days a week and is still at 60, Albany Street, Camden, London, NW1 4EE[28].

Gray's Inn Road Police Station

In December 1897 the Police Review commented on the opening of a new station in Grays Inn Road in the following terms;

"Another new Station, which is nearly ready for business, is the handsome building in Gray's Inn Road. A noticeable feature in connection with these latest additions to our public offices is the acceptable innovation in the style of architecture. The outward appearance of the majority of the Metropolitan Stations is by no means pleasing even to an uncritical eye." [29]

Grays Inn Road Police Station
27, Grays Inn Road, WC1
1898 – 1965 + (1999 –2002)

The freehold to this site was purchased in 1895, and plans were drawn up to build a new police station at the location shown as 27, Grays Inn Road. It was soon erected and opened in January 1898[30] in Gray's Inn Road just opposite Holborn Town Hall. The three-storey red brick building eventually provided accommodation for nearly 100 Constables on the newly created Holborn Section.

On the ground floor there was a spacious charge room on one side and the Inspectors' office at the other. On the first floor was the police officers' mess room and on the upper floor the dormitories, with sleeping accommodation for the single men. Inspector Miller, of Hunter Street Police Station was in charge. The address of the station was shown as 27, and 29, Grays Inn Road, London WC1. The station closed in 1965 when operational policing was transferred to the new Holborn Police Station, and the old police station became a traffic warden centre.

In 1999 the old station was opened for operational purposes during the refurbishment of Holborn Police station, which had temporarily closed.

Hampstead Police Station

An imposing entrance-porch to a private house in Cannon Lane was once an eighteenth century cell holding horse-thieves and highwaymen. The local magistrate residing in Cannon Hall would detain offenders in this temporary prison – a room built in about 1730, in the thickness of the back wall. The system worked well until the first Hampstead police station was built in the 1830's, and the old "lock up" fell into neglect and became a garden shed. In 1981 the Hampstead Plaque Fund erected a plaque on this Grade One listed garden wall[31].

From about 1730 there was also a lock up in Flask Walk which was used as temporary accommodation for suspected criminals until the magistrate was ready to deal with them[32]. This was also the site of the village stocks and Watchman's Hut. The first police station, known as the Old Watch House, was built in Holly Walk, and used from 1829 until 1834 although

Metropolitan Police records show that in 1832 the address was Holly Place, Hampstead[33]. This is now a private residence – and the old cells serve the present owners as a dining room. Buildings behind the Watch House in Hollyberry Lane are thought to have been the Sergeant's house and stable[34].

Hampstead Police Station
Holly Place, Hampstead.
1829 – 1834

In 1834 the police leased larger premises at the bottom of Holly Hill, at the junction with Heath Street, where the clock tower building now stands[35]. The station was not occupied until 1839, and was shown as a brick built house with small yard with 3 cells, a 3-stall stable and a charge room. It was leased from Mr. Cunnington of High Street, Hampstead for a period of 21 years. The cost of redeveloping the new police station was shown as £62.17s.6d.[36] By 1868, this building had been demolished and rebuilt as a police fire station in the High Road.

In April 1865, permission was given for the police to look for and purchase a suitable site on which to build a station[37].

Additional land had been purchased at a cost of £1500 and £26 ground rent per annum. The cost of the new station was £5363. The owners of the leased land were the Dean and Chapter of West Hampstead who had permitted a 99-year lease. The building was of brick and slate and had 17 rooms, 5 cells and a 4-stall stable. The new police station had been built on the same site opposite the Chapel, and opened for business in May 1868[38]. The station was located on "S" or Hampstead Division. The freehold to this site was purchased later, in 1909. In August 1868 Hampstead and West Hampstead sections were amalgamated to form Hampstead Sub-division.

The new site was sufficiently large enough for a portion of the building to

Hampstead Police Station
26, Rosslyn Hill, Hampstead
1868 – 1913

be used as a court, which the Receiver of the Metropolitan Police leased to the London County Council for twenty-one years with an annual ground rent payable of £150. The police purchased the freehold to land located at 24/26 Rosslyn Hill in 1909 for the sum of £6,250. Approval from the Home Office was sought in 1910, to build a new station. Finally, the present police station and Magistrates Court, at the corner of Downshire Hill, was opened in December 1913[39]. There were two sets of Married Quarters and accommodation for 30 unmarried men. Around the time of the First World War alterations were made to the premises with two sets of quarters being converted into a Special Constabulary office and a canteen. Curiously enough, today its correct postal address is 26½, Rosslyn Hill, Hampstead, NW3.

Furthermore in 1913 there were boundary revisions between Golders Green, Finchley and Hampstead sub-divisions.

The old police station was eventually demolished and the site is now marked by a drinking fountain

Hampstead Police Station
26½, Rosslyn Hill, Hampstead
1913 – Present day

and a new development, Mulberry Close[40].

On 21st July 1915 Detective Constable Alfred Young KPM was fatally shot by Captain Richard Georges whilst the officer was attempting to execute a warrant. The official police funeral took place in Hampstead near the station to which he was attached, and was attended by the Metropolitan Police Commissioner Sir Edward Henry and detachments of officers from every division of the force. Special Constables from Hampstead Division collected twelve guineas (£12. 12 shillings) for the officer's young son[41].

In July 1933 there were further boundary revisions which affected "S" Division, with changes between the surrounding divisions of "J", "Y" and "N" followed by further revisions four months later[42].

Hampstead Police station attracted fame momentarily when, in 1955, Ruth Ellis was charged there with the murder of her lover, David Blakely - a crime, which saw her, convicted and sentenced to death. She then became the last woman to be hanged in Britain.

In 1965 Hampstead left "S" Division and became part of "E", Division when it was amalgamated with West Hampstead with the latter being its sectional station.

In 2002 Hampstead Police Station was shown as an operational station, being open to the public 24 hours a day, 7 days a week. The full address was recorded as 26½, Rosslyn Hill, Hampstead, London, NW3 1PD[43].

Holborn Police Station

One of the first stations in "E" or Holborn Division was located at George Street, St. Giles and was an old Parish Watch house. There was only one other station on the division, a strange looking building in an area known as Battlesbridge, located in the centre of the carriageway at the junctions with New Road (later Pentonville Road), Grays Inn Road and Caledonian Road. In 1837, these premises were vacated in favour of a substantial brick building located in Hunter Street. Another watch house was situated in Giltspur Street, Holborn. It had been built in 1791 and was attached to the church of St. Sepulchre probably to prevent grave robbing[44].

The old building was not demolished immediately, but was converted into a public house, called the "Omnibus Arms". The building was demolished in 1845 however some police officers still visited the old building whilst on duty for refreshment. PC John Robinson was dismissed from the Force for being drunk in the Eagle Street watch house (off Red Lion Square) after a drinking session at the old police station

A unit of "E" or Holborn Division with their Sergeant (circa 1910).

premises[45].

In the early 1960`s local policing arrangements were reviewed, and plans were put in place for a large new police station to be built in Holborn. A suitable building plot was purchased which would not only accommodate the police station, but also several other departments transferred from New Scotland Yard.

Holborn Police Station
70, Theobalds Road, Holborn
1965- Present day

In November 1965 a thirteen-storey building, with a total floor area of more than 110,000 square feet, was opened in Theobalds Road, Holborn. It was 155 feet tall and was topped by a 75 feet wireless mast. This building as well as being the new Holborn Police Station, also housed the Forensic Science Laboratory, relocated from New Scotland Yard, and the Aliens Registration Office, which transferred from Vine Street. The planned cost of construction was £80,000, and the builders were to be, Laing Construction[46]. The station code was shown as Echo Oscar (EO), and located at 70, Theobalds Road, WC1.When this building opened the nearby Grays Inn Road Police Station closed as an operational unit. Outside the new building hangs the 'hundred year old' blue lamp from the original Vine Street Police Station, which was situated off Piccadilly[47].

The Metropolitan Police Architects Department designed the building, whilst the Surveyors Department invited tenders from reputable building companies to construct the station. Thirty-six years later it is now in the process of receiving a £8 million refurbishment and was due to re-open in 2002[48].

Hunter Street Police Station

An old building, known to the public for many years as "Hunter Street" Police Station, came into use in 1837 when the police officers transferred from George Street watch house in St. Giles. This move came about when premises situated in Hunter Street and Compton Street were found and leased. The lease period was seventy-one years in accordance with the owner's wishes. The owners, the Governors of the Foundling Hospital, were paid an annual ground rent of £15.

The station was regarded as a quaint station and had a basement, ground and first floor. It was fitted with a reserve room, charge room, 4 cells, mess room, recreation room, library, boot room and scullery. Entry to the station was by a long dark narrow passage. Upstairs there was section house accommodation for 26 single constables. These single officers paid some £67 per year for their rent to the Receiver. Hunter Street police station was originally shown as being located on "E" Division. The freehold to the site was eventually purchased in 1888 at a cost of £3221.

The picture shows a Victorian Police Sergeant 11 'E' Division, complete with whiskers, attached to Hunter Street Police Station. The

Police Sergeant 11 "E" Division
Taken between 1871 and 1883

photographers Timms, who took the picture were situated close by. The sergeant is still on duty as he is wearing his duty armlet on his left arm. The photograph was taken between 1871 and 1883 as he is wearing the new styled uniform introduced in 1870, and also he does not have a whistle which was not issued until 1883. Additionally the sergeant is holding white gloves issued for ceremonial events like Trooping the Colour or a Royal Jubilee so the likelihood is, that the photograph was taken prior to or after such an event. Only specially selected police officers were permitted to attend ceremonial, processions and other events, like strikes or demonstrations, which required a large numbers of police officers. They were called Reserve Officers and were introduced by the Metropolitan Police in 1870. They made up 10% of the police establishment. They ranged from Inspectors who were paid four shillings per week extra, sergeants who paid three shillings and constables one shilling and sixpence extra. Reserve Officers of Sergeant and Constable rank were required to wear the letter "R" beside their divisional letter. They were supplied with a better grade of uniform for these events. The Sergeant was probably a Reserve Officer but his whiskers hide the rest of the letter "R". Reserve Officers posts were abolished in December 1913[49].

The photograph, below, shows a unit of mixed Reserve and ordinary officers from "E" Division performing duty at an industrial dispute on

"E" or Holborn Division on attachment to the Police at the Hull Dock Strike of 1911

Humberside in 1911. The Hull dock strike was policed by many different Police Forces including the Metropolitan Police who were sent to the docks to deal with the national strike of stevedores, railwaymen, carters and other transport workers who brought much of the country to a standstill. Military detachments prepared to assist the police. Riots broke out in response to fears of widespread famine, and at least two men were shot dead. [50]

The dispute started in early September when about 10,000 Welsh miners came out on strike in sympathy with the dockers who were also on strike. Throughout the autumn of 1910 serious rioting broke out in the Rhondda and Aberdare Valleys of South Wales where the coal strike began in earnest. Units of the Metropolitan police were sent by train to quell the disorder and rioting.

The photograph below shows a contingent of "E" Division officers, in their great coats at Clydach Vale.

Meanwhile, the general health of the police officers and their families

A Unit of "E" Division wearing their Great Coats
- photographed at Clydach Vale.

residing in police accommodation at Hunter Street was of serious concern. Senior officers considered that many of the buildings were substandard and very damp. To improve the general health of those residing at the station, and to relieve the cramped conditions, four beds were removed in 1882 and a further five more in 1883, allowing for a greater living area per officer.

Hunter Street was demolished in 1895 to make way for a modern police station. The freehold to the site was purchased in 1888 at a cost of £3221[51]. In 1890 the Receiver had also purchased 53, 55 and 57 Judd Street, which possibly explains the fact that Hunter Street Police Station was shown with an address in Judd Street. The new station was built of red brick and Portland stone and had five floors[52].

There was accommodation for a married Inspector and fifteen married and fifteen single Constables. The police station had ten cells, which were fitted with the latest sanitary improvements. At the back of the Station there was a yard with sufficient space for a prison van to visit. There was also a covered parade and drill shed, which was 45 feet long and 16 feet wide. The buildings were constructed from the designs and drawings of

Mr. John Butler FRIBA, Metropolitan Police Surveyor, by the builder, Mr. J.O.Richardson, of Peckham, South London. In 1898 and 1902 land was purchased in Hunter Street and Compton Street in order to build a new section house to accommodate single police officers[53].

In 1908 59, Judd Street was purchased in order to extend the station's site, (Hunter Street stands at the junction with Judd Street WC1). In October 1911[54] new section house accommodation was made available for one married inspector at three shillings a week and 80 unmarried men at one shilling a week[55].

The address of the police station was no longer in Hunter Street even

Hunter Street Police Station
53 –57, Judd Street, WC1
1890 - 1940

though it carried on with its name. Hunter Street Police Station was actually shown as 53-57, Judd Street, Brunswick Square, WC1[56]. In 1934 the station was closed for extensive refurbishment together with the Section house, and later reopened, between August 1939 and August 1940, as a temporary police station whilst Gray's Inn Road Police Station was being reconstructed.

After this the building became, Macnaghten Section House, a purpose built residence for single police officers. In recent years the police ceased to use the building, and sold it to the local authority who has converted it to sheltered accommodation for the homeless.

Macnaghten Section House in 1948

The picture above shows Macnaghten Section House taken around 1948. Accommodation for police officers in London had always been a problem. Even in Victorian times accommodation was constructed or bought by the Receiver and rented out to single officers and their families although in recent years accommodation was provided free of charge. Macnaghten Section House, which remained in service until the 1980's, stands as a fine example of a residence for single officers.

Kentish Town Police Station

Kentish Town Station Lamp

Most police stations have a standard lamp at the front of the building. A number of differing designs have been used and shown at right is Kentish Town's lamp, which is still in use today. Commissioner Sir Peter Imbert revamped many station lamps some years ago.

Records show that in 1844 the Inspector in charge of Kentish Town Police Station was Inspector Aggs. He had been an Inspector for fourteen years, having joined the division at its start in 1830[57]. The station was in fact the Old Watch House, which was designated as a station located on "S" or Hampstead Division. The building was located in Junction Place and was a brick and slate built house consisting of a charge room and two cells. It belonged to the

61

Receiver of the Metropolitan Police and remained in service until 1853, and given up in 1860.

In 1853 a police station was erected at the cost of £2,081. The land was leased from General Sir D. Leighton K.C.B. of Charlton Kings, Gloucester for 90 years, with a ground rent of £30 which was payable annually. The officer in charge of the Division, at the time, was Superintendent Edward Worels, whilst Chief Inspector William Odell was responsible for the station and deputy to the Superintendent in the event that he went on leave. The division also had a further 13 inspectors, with George Gilby being favoured as the Reserve Inspector. It is interesting to note that there was accommodation on the premises for twenty-one unmarried men who paid over £54 per year for their quarters. This more than covered the annual ground rent the Receiver paid for the building.

Under the divisional re-organisations of 1865 a new division was formed called "Y" or Highgate Division. Kentish Town Police Station became the Divisional Headquarters for this new division. The new Division stretched from Highgate in the south to Enfield in the north, and even in those early days each station was connected by telegraph[58].

In 1881 Edward Worells the divisional superintendent resided at 1, Lawford Road, Kentish Town which was a short distance from the station. He lived there with his wife and three children[59]. Worells transferred from 'K' to 'Y' Division as a Superintendent in June 1876. He had joined the service in May 1847 (warrant number 24450) after leaving his job as a watchmaker. He became a sergeant within three years, an Inspector within a further five years and superintendent ten years later. The Inspector in charge of the station in 1881 was John Golder aged 33, who resided there with his family[60]. In 1888 the Divisional strength numbered 727 officers with William J. Huntley being the Superintendent in charge, assisted by 46 Inspectors, 73 Sergeants and 607 constables[61]. Huntley remained Superintendent until 2nd November 1891 when he retired on pension[62].

In December 1889 the Receiver purchased the freehold of the station at a cost of £1,200, although a yearly sum of one shilling per annum was payable to the Midland Railway, because station windows overlooked some of the tracks.

In 1892 more land was acquired to accommodate prison vans. A new station at 12 Holmes Road, Kentish Town, was occupied in April 1896 [63].

Architect Richard Norman Shaw who designed the old New Scotland Yard on the Embankment designed the building. The building is now listed as of architectural and historical interest.

Re-organisation in 1933, north of the River Thames saw Kentish Town transferred from "Y" to "N" Division. From 1958 until 1962 the London Probation Service was allowed offices on police premises at 12, Holmes

Kentish Town Police Station.
12, Holmes Road, Kentish Town.
1896 – Present day

Road. The Metropolitan Police District (MPD) was split into four Districts each with a District Headquarters. Kentish Town was located on 3 District, with Stoke Newington being the Headquarters. Each station on the district was linked via a private telephone line, (replacing the old telegraph system), through the headquarters to CO or Scotland Yard. This was a secure non-public line. Kentish Town was also linked to other stations through this network. These were Albany Street (D), Caledonian Road, Hampstead (S), Holloway and Hornsey on "Y" Division.

A section house at 10, Holmes Road was opened in December 1964 to accommodate 108 men. In 1965 the Local Authority re-organisation saw

Kentish Town become a sub-divisional station on 'E' Division. After the re-organisation "E" Division moved to 2 District[64].

In 2002 Kentish Town is shown within the London Borough of Camden at 12A Holmes Road, Kentish Town, London, NW5 3EA. The station is open to the public 24 hours a day 7 days a week[65].

St. John's Wood Police Station (formerly Portland Town Police Station)

St. John's Wood Police Station formerly Portland Town.
New Street, St. John's Wood, NW8
1896 – 1972

In 1849 the Commissioner leased land on which a police station was built at a cost of £2,655[66]. In 1864 Portland Town Police Station was located on 'S' or Hampstead Division. It was a station supervised by an Inspector[67] although there were two Inspectors posted there[68]. The supervising Inspector was supplied with a horse to perform his duty. Instructions were given for the duty inspector to patrol Willesden as well their own station area[69]. There were five sergeants and 62 constables attached to the station[70]. Portland Town was a charging station and cells for the detention of prisoners were attached[71]. The station had been connected to the private wire network so contact could be maintained with Scotland Yard[72]. The station call sign was Papa Tango (PT)[73].

In 1877 Inspector Richard Pope was the Inspector in charge of the station[74]. St. John's Wood Sub-Division had been previously called Portland Town, but had been renamed because of difficulties and confusion with mail deliveries between Portland in Dorset and Portland Town in London. The name change took place in August 1918. In 1896 there were severe problems with the drainage and extensive works to rectify the problems cost a staggering £2, 049[75].

Freehold to the property in New Street, St. John's Wood was purchased in 1893 for £910[76]. The vendors were the Trustees of the will of the noblest William Henry Cavendish Scott, 4th Duke of Portland[77]. The station was built and ready for occupation in 1896[78]. The building included an Inspector's office, a charge room and four cells. There was also a parade shed in the yard and two stables for horses. Accommodation above the station included a section house for single officers[79]. Reconstruction work in the section house took place in 1905 and saw the construction of 33 cubicles for single officers at a cost of £203[80]. Gas was laid on in 1906[81].

At the beginning of the First World War, Portland Town (St. John's

Portland Town Special Constabulary 1916

Wood) Police Station was the home to a Company of the "S" Division Metropolitan Police Special Constabulary (MPSC). They were a dedicated band of men who helped to fill the void left by departing police officers who had joined the colours to fight. Although not fitted with uniforms until 1916, many of the Special Constabulary wore a duty armlet on their own plain clothes until that time[82]. The picture above, taken in the yard at Portland Town, shows the supervising officers of the station's Special Constabulary. In the centre (third right at front) is Chief Inspector Dr. E. Climson Greenwood flanked to the left by Inspector (later Chief Inspector) F. S. Bristowe who compiled a fascinating account of life as a member of the Special Constabulary at Portland Town from 1914 until 1919. The inspectors are seated whilst the sergeants are standing behind.

Following rioting in Camden Town after the sinking of the Lusitania by a German U-boat, the officers of 'S' Division Special Constabulary considered it important for their men to wear uniforms as it was impossible to distinguish them from ordinary civilians. Uniforms were issued after May 18th 1916[83].

The division was particularly well organised and the picture below shows its leadership. The two men seated with canes are (from left to right) Commander R.A. Simson OBE and Assistant Commander C. Wharton Collard who were stationed at Divisional Headquarters at Albany Street.

Top left of the picture and in charge of Portland Town SC was the Police Divisional Surgeon Dr. E. Climson Greenwood. He was sworn into the MPSC on 17th August 1914 as an Inspector. He became a Chief Inspector

Senior Officers of the "S" Division Special Constabulary during World War One.

in November 1915 and an Acting/Assistant Commander in February 1919. Working from left to right along the back row is Chief Inspector J. T. Ash of West Hampstead MPSC, next is Chief Inspector Cross of Finchley followed by Chief Inspector Levick of Golders Green.

The Special Constabulary on "S" Division formed a rifle club, and individual stations competed against each other on a number of occasions. Portland Town Rifle Club was formed in December 1914 with Sub-Inspector Scott nominated as President. Soon there was a working membership of some 113 officers[84]. In January 1915 a weekly Silver Spoon competition was instituted, but later on the competitions were held monthly. Some 44 spoons were competed for and four members each succeeded in winning a set of six spoons, which were engraved with the dates they were won[85].

On the 7th March 1918 a bomb dropped by a German aeroplane destroyed 11,12, and 13 New Street killing six people. This was forty yards from the Police Station at Portland Town. The King and Queen, accompanied by the Commissioner Sir Edward Henry, visited the scene and station where they were presented to Chief Inspector Climson Greenwood. The records show the awarding of a merit certificate to Special Constable J. R. Hodge, stationed at Portland Town, who performed 305 duties and attended 44 emergency calls[86]. In August 1918 Portland Town police station was re-named St. Johns Wood Police Station[87].

In 1931 St. Johns Wood was still on 'S or Hampstead Division[88]. During the Metropolitan Police re-organisation in 1964, St. John's Wood was transferred to 'D' Division where its call sign was changed to Delta Sierra (DS). In 1932 the London County Council informed the Commissioner about a change of road name. New Street was changed to New Court Street[89].

St. John's Wood Police Station is still in use today. It is located within the London Borough of Westminster and is situated at 20½, Newcourt Street, St. John's Wood, London NW8 7AA. The station does not have charging facilities and is open to the public every day from 6.30am until 10pm, although times may vary[90].

Somers Town Police Station

Somers Town is located north of the Euston Road between the railway stations of Euston and St. Pancras. The northern end borders Camden Town. There has been a police presence in Somers Town for some considerable time with a watch house located in Phoenix Street, Somers Town before 1829. Records show that in 1840 Inspector-in-charge George Billers was promoted and transferred there. The watch house, which had belonged to the 'Old Parochial Watch', consisted of a small room and two small cells[91].

Somers Town has a significant place in police history as this area saw the first police officer to be killed on duty. On the 29th June 1830, some nine months after the first police parade had taken place, Police Constable Grantham, attached to Somers Town, was patrolling his beat when he came across two drunken Irishmen quarrelling over a woman. After stepping between the two men to prevent a continued breach of the peace, both men and the woman turned on him. This resulted in Constable Grantham being knocked to the ground where he received a blow to the temple and died a few minutes later. Enquiries in the area, after the event, reported that Constable Grantham got very much what he deserved and was not liked in the small neighbourhood[92].

The original Somers Town Police Station was described as 'an old straight built house in a dilapidated state'[93]. In 1849 Metropolitan Police Commissioner, Sir Richard Mayne wrote a 'requisition report' to the Divisional Superintendent regarding the poor conditions and state of Somers Town Police Station. He instructed that a new site should be found on which to build a new station. The old watch house was closed in 1850[94]. The station was re-located to Blenheim cottages in Park village, with a rent of £20 per annum. However, this was soon unfit for habitation and notice was served on Sergeant Gatesby, the officer in charge of the station at the time, to quit on 22nd June 1860. The house contained 2 cells and a charge room.

Much of the neighbouring land had been taken up with building large railway stations and goods yards, so the small watch house was no longer deemed suitable for policing the expanding area. In those days Somers Town Police Station was shown as a station on "S" or Hampstead Division. The "S" or Hampstead Division radiated from Somers Town to the south, with Kentish Town as the Divisional Headquarters, to Barnet in the northwest.

The Receiver of the Metropolitan Police decided that a purpose built police station should be built in Somers Town, and so enquiries were made to find a suitable site for this purpose. A site located at 23, Platt Street, not far from Brill Row (later the Pancras Road), seemed appropriate, and contracts were drawn up to lease the site from December 1849. This was on a 99-year lease from the Company of Brewers of Addle Street, East Central. Once the contracts had been signed the annual ground rent payment was fixed at £20 per year. Somers Town Police station was transferred from "S" Division and re-designated as a station on "Y" Division[95].

The police station was erected in 1851 at a cost of £3,488. The accommodation comprised of a traditional Victorian style station house. It had a basement, ground, first and second floors. The ground and first floor were used for police business whilst rooms on the second floor housed single officers. There were three public rooms, which are shown as an Inspector's office, Reserve room and public waiting room. The station also had a library, parade room and eight cells on the ground floor, with a kitchen, mess room and a coal store in the basement. The terms of the lease stipulated that the station was to be insured for £2,800 at the Law Office[96].

In 1873 Inspector Gould from Enfield Police Station conducted the novelist Charles Dickens on a fact-finding journey around Somers Town - which at the time had the reputation of being a very unsavoury place indeed. Somers Town Police Station was designated a station under the command of an Inspector and was connected by wire to the Commissioners Office[97].

In 1881 the station was still shown as a station on "Y" or Highgate Division. Records show that there was accommodation for a maximum of 33 single constables, who paid between them a total of £104 annual rent to the Commissioner. They lived in the section house above the station. Records show that 32 single constables were in residence when the census was taken. Five prisoners occupied the eight available cells[98]. Conditions at the station were less than satisfactory when police surveyors inspected the premises in the same year. They found some of the cells and parts of the basement were very dark. In 1904 alterations reduced the numbers accommodated at the station from 33 to 22 single constables. Cubicles for privacy were built into the residential rooms at a cost of £129 [99].

In 1881 Police Constable Francis Carlin, a 47-year-old man from Co. Tyrone, Ireland lived at 37, Middlesex Street with his wife Jane, their three daughters and two sons[100]. One of their sons was to become one of the most celebrated detectives of modern times. Francis Carlin was born in 1871 in Kentish Town, St. Pancras and followed his father's footsteps into the police, although his father had higher aspirations for him[101]. At 15 years old Carlin worked in a coal factors office but after four years he left that job to join the police. After three weeks of foot drill Carlin became a constable on 'K' Division, and was posted to Plaistow Police Station on 15th December 1890[102]. Carlin patrolled Plaistow, Canning Town and Poplar. Later he became one of the so-called 'Big Four' Detective Superintendents responsible for high profile murder enquiries –

the cases of Thompson/Bywaters, the Crumbles, the Norman Thorne murders and the Fahmy affair[103].

Arthur Henry Bishop (second from left) under arrest for the murder of Frank Edward Rix – a butler of Mayfair

Another one of Detective Superintendent Carlin's cases involved Arthur Henry Bishop who is shown seated between two detectives in the picture at left. Here he is under arrest for the murder of Frank Edward Rix – a butler for whom Bishop worked as a pantry boy. Bishop attacked and killed Rix with an axe late one night at a Mayfair residence. Detective Superintendent Carlin is shown at extreme right. Bishop was later convicted of murder and was hanged at Pentonville Prison on 14th August 1925.

Posting the notice of execution of Arthur Henry Bishop –14th August 1925

To the left is the main gate outside Pentonville Prison when the notice of execution of Bishop was posted on the door. Bishop was hanged by Robert Orridge Baxter[104] of Balfour Street, Hertford, the favoured and principal hangman at the time.

He was assisted by Henry Pollard, Edward Taylor and Robert Wilson who were all experts at their trade[105].

The photograph of the constable below right was taken before the First World War, probably in 1912, at a commercial photographer, near to Somers Town Police station. It shows the constable with white gloves, which usually denotes that he was attending a ceremonial event. He is wearing three medals, which are the 1897 Jubilee Medal and the Coronation medals of 1902 and 1911. All Metropolitan and City of London Police who were either on normal duty or at the Coronation in 1911 were entitled to the Coronation Medal. Many other police forces were also represented and they were awarded medals as well. As these medals were personalized with the officer's name, and it took time to collate all the information, they were not issued until 1912.

In 1919 Constable William Rawlings (later Deputy Commander) joined the Metropolitan Police and after training was posted to Somers Town Police Station. Constable 541 'Y' Rawlings was met by Sub-divisional Inspector Pacey who did not

Police Constable – "E" Division 1912

use their names but called the officers by their collar numbers. This practice continues even today. Rawlings was allocated a cubicle in an upstairs dormitory. He describes the accommodation as 'dark and not too clean' and that he was often bitten at night. A policeman's widow used to come in and cook a meal every day for the single men who slept in the upstairs dormitory. They all sat on long benches at a wooden table in the basement for their meals[106].

The police station was very badly damaged by a parachute mine on 17th April 1941[107]. There were no casualties. In 1945 a decision was taken not to re-build the station, but to return the site to the owners as it was, although the lease had several more years to run. Somers Town Police station closed in June 1946, and all police business was transferred to Caledonian Road Police Station. [108]

Somers Town Police Station
23, Platt Street, Somers Town
1851 – (1946).

However this was only a temporary closure as this 1970's picture of Somers Town Police Station shows. It was clearly rebuilt after the war and the owners rented the building out for other purposes. It appears the front of the station was undamaged from German bombing and the rear of the station was re-constructed. This sad picture of this once gracious Victorian police station is the only known surviving example.

West Hampstead Police Station

In 1880 a portion of land, situated in the Parish of St. John Hampstead, was identified as suitable for a police station. The land was located in West End Lane close to West Hampstead Railway station, and was leased from Mr. Thomas Bale to the Metropolitan Police for £40 per annum. However, in March 1882 the Receiver of the Metropolitan Police purchased the title, from G. H. Essington and others at a cost £715. Plans were soon made to build a large station on the site. This was built in

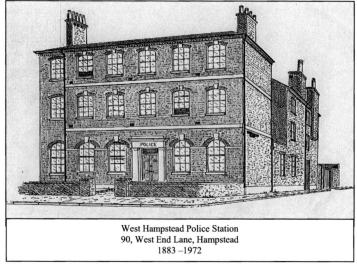

West Hampstead Police Station
90, West End Lane, Hampstead
1883 –1972

1882 at a cost of £3971. When the station was occupied a new sub-Division of "S" Division was established and named "West Hampstead".

The station was built with a charge room, Inspector's office, waiting room and three cells on the ground floor. One of the cells was an association cell, meaning that it could hold a larger number of prisoners than the single cells. It was often referred to as the "drunk tank". The station also had a basement, and a first floor.

There appears to have been a clause in the title deeds stating that the building could only be used for a police station or residence, and for no other purpose. Furthermore, any alterations, which affected the near neighbours, could only be made with the permission of the Cotton family who resided next door. The address of this station was shown as 90, West End Lane, West Hampstead, London, and it was a station located on "S" or Hampstead Division. The station was opened on 1st January 1883. A married Constable, Inspector and six single constables occupied married quarters at the station.

Police orders in March 1893 amalgamated several sub-divisions in further re-organisations. Both Portland Town and West Hampstead were combined to form Portland Town sub-division. Further re-organisation caused the sub-division to be amalgamated with Hampstead sub-division in 1893. West Hampstead Police Station was closed down in 1972.

By 1935 there were plans laid to construct a new station in the area, and in October 1939 recommendations by Estates Branch to purchase 92, West End Lane, next door to the existing station, and to build a station on the enlarged site were considered. However, due to the war and economies, this proposal was turned down. It was felt that if reconstruction was to take place this could be done on the old station site, and that extra space provided by the section house would be sufficient for the purpose.

In the 1965 Local Government boundary changes West Hampstead along with Hampstead Sub-Division was transferred from "S" to "E" Division into the newly formed London Borough of Camden.

In 1972 a new station and stables were opened at 21 Fortune Green Road, West Hampstead, NW6 1DX and the old station was closed. The station is open 24 hours a day, 7 days a week[109].

[1] Municipal Year Book 2000 and Public Services Directory Vol. 2 Newman Books (1999) and Publicity literature for the London Borough of Camden
[2] The John Back Archive (1975) Metropolitan Police Museum, Charlton
[3] Directory for the Return of Mops, 1st July 1832 – Metropolitan Police Museum, Charlton.
[4] Curators List of Divisional Superintendents, Metropolitan Police Museum, Charlton.
[5] The John Back Archive (1975) – Metropolitan Police Museum , Charlton
[6] Ibid
[7] Public Record Office MEPO 4/2
[8] The Police and Constabulary List of 1844 (1990), Monograph No. 3 The Police History Society.
[9] Ibid
[10] Kelly's Directory 1850
[11] Kelly's Directory 1855
[12] Curators List of Divisional Superintendents, Metropolitan Police Museum, Charlton.
[13] Commissioners Annual Report 1888
[14] The Commissioner for the Metropolis Annual Report of 1871
[15] Dickens Dictionary of London, 1879
[16] Curators List of Divisional Superintendents, Metropolitan Police Museum, Charlton
[17] Metropolitan Police Orders dated 11th January 1864
[18] The John Back Archive (1975) – Metropolitan Police Museum , Charlton
[19] Metropolitan Police Orders dated 21st August 1866
[20] PRO Census Records 1881
[21] Metropolitan Police Surveyors Manifest (1882)
[22] ibid
[23] Metropolitan Police General Orders 1893
[24] Ibid
[25] Metropolitan Police Orders dated 5th November 1897
[26] Op. cit.
[27] Metropolitan Police Orders dated 28th November 1933
[28] http://www.met.police.uk/contact/phone.htm dated 13.03.02
[29] Police Review – December 1897
[30] Metropolitan Police Orders dated 22nd January 1898
[31] The Job. 11th September 1981
[32] Wade, Christopher (unknown) "Streets of Hampstead" published by the Camden History Society.

33 Directory for the Return of Mops, 1st July 1832 – Metropolitan Police Museum, Charlton.
34 Wade, Christopher (unknown) "Streets of Hampstead" published by the Camden History Society.
35 Ibid
36 Metropolitan Police Surveyors Manifest (1882)
37 Op. Cit.
38 Metropolitan Police Orders dated8th May 1868
39 Metropolitan Police Orders dated 28th November 1913
40 Wade, Christopher (unknown) "Streets of Hampstead" published by the Camden History Society.
41 The Dailey Graphic 21st July 1915
42 Metropolitan Police Orders dated July 1933
43 http://www.met.police.uk/contact/phone.htm dated 13.03.02
44 Kent, W. (1937) An Encyclopedia of London. J. M. Dent. London
45 The John Back Archive (1975) – Metropolitan Police Museum , Charlton.
46 Police Review, 23rd August 1963 p710
47 Police Review, 12th November 1965
48 The Job, 19th May 2000
49 Metropolitan Police Orders dated 12th December 1913
50 Mercer, 1988 Encyclopaedia of the 20th Century p155
51 The Police Review and Parade Gossip dated 18th January 1895
52 Ibid
53 Ibid
54 Metropolitan Police Orders dated 28th October 1911
55 Metropolitan Police Property Schedule 1924
56 Kirchner's Police Index 1931
57 The Police and Constabulary List of 1844 (1990) , Monograph No. 3 The Police History Society.
58 The John Back Archive (1975) – Metropolitan Police Museum , Charlton.
59 PRO Census records 1881
60 Ibid
61 Dickens Dictionary of London (1888) Moretonhampstead, Devon. Pp 197- 199
62 Curators List of Divisional Superintendents, Metropolitan Police Museum, Charlton.
63 Metropolitan Police Orders dated 25th April 1896
64 The John Back Archive (1975) – Metropolitan Police Museum , Charlton
65 http://www.met.police.uk/contact/phone.htm dated 13.03.02
66 Metropolitan Police Property Register pp 159/60
67 Police and Constabulary Almanac 1864
68 Metropolitan Police Orders dated 11th January 1864
69 Ibid
70 Ibid
71 Ibid
72 Metropolitan Police General Orders 1873
73 Metropolitan Police General Orders 1893
74 Police Office London Directory 1877
75 Metropolitan Police Property Register pp 159/60
76 Metropolitan Police Property Schedule 1924
77 Metropolitan Police Property Register pp 159/60
78 Metropolitan Police Orders dated 5th September 1896
79 Op Cit.
80 Ibid.
81 Ibid.
82 Bristowe, F. S. (1919) Souvenir of St. Johns Wood Special Constabulary
83 Ibid
84 Ibid.
85 Ibid.
86 Ibid
87 Metropolitan Police Orders August 1918
88 Kirchner's Police Index 1931
89 Metropolitan Police Property Schedule 1924
90 http://www.met.police.uk/contact/phone.htm dated 13.03.02
91 PRO MEPO 45/2632

[92] Cobb, Belton (1961) Murdered on Duty. W. H. Allen, London
[93] Metropolitan Police Surveyors Manifest (1882)
[94] PRO MEPO 45/2632
[95] The John Back Archive (1975) – Metropolitan Police Museum , Charlton
[96] Metropolitan Police Surveyors records (undated)
[97] Metropolitan Police General Orders 1873
[98] PRO Census records 1881
[99] Metropolitan Police surveyors records 1924
[100] PRO Census records 1881
[101] Carlin, F. (1925) Reminiscences of an Ex-Detective. Hutchinson and Co. London.
[102] ibid.
[103] ibid.
[104] Fielding, S. (1990) The Hangmans Record. Vol. two 1900- 1929.
[105] Ibid
[106] Rawlings Deputy Commander William Benjamin OBE., MC. (1961) 'A Case for the Yard' John Long, London. pp331-33.
[107] Howgrave-Graham, H. M. CBE (1947) 'The Metropolitan Police at War' HMSO
[108] Metropolitan Police Orders dated 21st June 1946.
[109] http://www.met.police.uk/contact/phone.htm dated 13.03.02

Chapter Four

The London Borough of Enfield & Broxbourne District Council

The London Borough of Enfield is situated twelve miles to the north of the centre of London. Prior to 1850 vestries governed both Enfield and Edmonton. The Vestry originated as an annual meeting of Parishioners, usually held at Easter, to elect the Churchwardens for the coming year. Enfield was an area where royal visitors came to enjoy hunting and riding in the woods of Enfield Chase. Enfield has been a market town since 1303[1].

The area also has a rich industrial heritage, and for more than 200 years the eastern perimeter of the borough was the hub of the capital's manufacturing industry. The area was dominated by the bulk of the Royal Small arms factory, which produced the Lee Enfield Rifle. During World War 1 Enfield saw a lot of bombardment from Zeppelins and Gotha bombers in their attempt to destroy the Enfield factory together with the Gunpowder works not far away. The defence of these establishments was paramount and, as a result, two German Zeppelin airships were destroyed at Potters Bar and Cuffley.

In 1965, as a result of the London Government Act of 1963[2], Enfield, Edmonton and Southgate merged into the London Borough of Enfield. The Borough of Enfield includes Cheshunt, Edmonton, Enfield Town, New Southgate, Ponders End (Enfield Highway), Southgate and Winchmore Hill[3]. A former Metropolitan police station at Goffs Oak, located within Broxbourne District Council Area, has been included in this section.

Cheshunt Police Station

In September 1861 the Home Office allocated £250 for the building of a police station in Cheshunt. It would appear that the police used the old watch house in Turners Hill, Cheshunt until suitable land could be found to build a new station. Therefore the first station to take the name 'Cheshunt Police Station' appears to have been the old watch house because records show in 1864 [4] Cheshunt Police Station as being part of "N" or Islington Division, prior to the building of any new station. With the formation of the new "Y" or Highgate Division in October 1865

Cheshunt, along with a number of other stations, was transferred to "Y" Division.

It was reported that the old watch house was most unsuitable for policing

Cheshunt Police Station
Turners Hill, Cheshunt
1872-1968

purposes and that effort should be made to find an alternative site and premises for a new station. In May 1869 the Metropolitan Police Surveyor reported that a suitable piece of land had been found in Turners Hill opposite the old watch house. The freehold to the land was purchased from the owner, Mr. Cox for £600 in 1870. The building on the site cost £900, and consisted of a two-storey building with a 50ft frontage. This was in need of conversion for police purposes. Messrs. Hill and Son completed this work at a cost of £738. Once completed the ground floor had a charge room, a reserve room, a washing room, 2 cells, a 2-stall stable, 2 water closets and 2 coal sheds. The section house above provided accommodation for 4 constables, a married sergeant and a married Inspector.

Superintendent Walker the Divisional Superintendent for "Y" or Highgate Division reported on 4th June 1872 that the new station at Cheshunt "was now complete and ready for occupation this day".

A revision of Divisional and station boundaries took place in August 1886. Cheshunt reverted back to "N" or Islington Division, only to be transferred back some years later as a sectional station of Enfield Sub-Division in July 1933.

The next boundary revisions occurred as a result of the Local Government re-organisation in 1964, and saw Cheshunt designated as "YC" and remaining as a sectional station of Enfield Sub-Division. The station was located within the Cheshunt area of Hertfordshire. At about the same period negotiations were in hand to purchase and build a new station in Cheshunt, the old site being unsuitable, awkward in shape and not situated centrally. A site was found 200 yards away on the opposite side of the road, from the old station, at 101-117, Turners Hill, and was purchased by the Metropolitan Police for £50,000 in February 1964. The site was cleared ready for building.

Tenders were invited for a two storey modern police station with access from the front, and to include car-parking places at the rear. The station would be faced in brick, contain proper load bearing walls and wood framed windows, with the boundary walls to have blue flint brickwork.

Cheshunt Police Station
101, Turners Hill, Cheshunt, Middlesex
1968 – present day

Builders Messrs. David Chaston Ltd. won the contract, and building work commenced in July 1966 and continued until March 1968. Police Orders recorded. the opening as such:-

"A new sectional station for Cheshunt (YC) at 101, Turners Road, Cheshunt, will be taken into operational use at 6am 1st April 1968, when the existing station will be closed" [5].

In the entrance lobby of Cheshunt Police station, is a small cabinet, which contains the original watch house stone and reproductions of some of the old Watch Committee activities. The old blue police station lamp, which stood outside the old station, was refitted outside the new building. The station contains a front office reception area, 3 cells, and 2 detention rooms. There is a garage at the rear for 2 cars and motor cycles together with parking space for a further twelve vehicles. The police station was transferred to Hertfordshire Constabulary in April 2000[6].

Edmonton Police Station

The old Edmonton watch house was situated in Church Street, opposite Old Saints Church and where Winchester Road is now. In the early 1800's Edmonton had a population of 9,627 and was still a very rural place. The village itself was located around Fore Street, Silver Street, and Water lane (Angel Road), whilst lower Edmonton was centred around the village green (Edmonton Green) and situated at the junctions with Fore Street, Church Street and Hertford Road [7].

Edmonton Fire Brigade outside the Police Station in Church Street in 1870

The Metropolitan boundary extended its limit in 1840 to take in the village of Edmonton[8].

The local parish authorities surrendered the old watch house to the police in October 1840 at a cost of £100, paid over a four-year period at a cost of £25 per year [9]. The watch house, sometimes referred to as the station house, was designated as part of "N" or Islington Division. This was the Area Headquarters responsible for supervision of those divisions within its area. The station house was handed over to the Receiver of the

Metropolitan Police in September 1852. The building was described, in 1845, as being substantial and built of brick and tile, containing four cells and a charge room[10]. The station had the use of two stables, one in Lower Edmonton the other in Upper Edmonton[11]. They were rented from Mr. George Sanderson on a yearly rental. In September 1853 both stables were used by the Metropolitan Police who were then responsible for the rent.

The very first officer in charge was Sergeant John Harrison who also resided as tenant at the station house. Harrison had been promoted to the rank from 1st class constable in January 1840, and posted to Edmonton watch house. Records show that Sergeant Harrison resided at the station with his wife Betty and their three children. Sergeant Harrison was born in Cothill, Berkshire on 18th March 1811 and was recruited into the Metropolitan Police on 12th May 1835[12]. His warrant number was 10640

and, after joining, was posted to "N" or Islington Division. It appears that the family lived in Islington as he married his wife Betty there in 1837.Gradually as the Divisional boundaries were extended more police officers were required to police them. In June 1854 he was further promoted to Inspector, and appears to have transferred from the station. No further information is available, but it is possible that with the growth of the new police extending into the Constabularies he took the opportunity to move to the country[13].

The Station Lamp at Edmonton 1978

The population of Edmonton started to grow with the development of public transport, especially with the Great Eastern Railway Company building two stations at Angel Road and Edmonton Green.

Three new divisions were formed and Edmonton was included as part of the new "Y" Division[14].

The station strength was two sergeants and ten constables with supervision by the Inspector coming from Enfield Highway (Ponders End) Police Station[15]. The Commissioner approved the following to be employed on Station Duties – PS 47 Parsons at Edmonton as from 27th April 1864[16].

A freehold site, on which to build a new station, was purchased in May 1865 from Mr. J.H.Grimley for the sum of £400. The site was purchased at 320, Fore Street, Edmonton, and not only was a station to be built but also stables and a section house for single men were to be included. The building costs were £1,907, and the ground floor contained a charge room, three cells, two stalls (stables), and Inspectors Room, day room and two coal sheds. The first floor provided accommodation for an Inspector, a married sergeant and 8 constables[17]. The old watch house was retained until May 1867 when it was handed back to the parish authorities[18]. In 1881 the station was called Lower Fore Street Police Station with Inspector Henry Hopkins in charge. He resided there with his wife and daughter. The single constables section house was full at the time of the census[19].

In August 1886 a new Division of "J" or Bethnal Green was formed, and

Edmonton Police Station
320, Fore Street, Edmonton
1867 - 1916

Edmonton transferred from "Y" and became a sub-Division of "N" Division once more[20].

In July 1897, during a storm, Edmonton Police Station was struck by lightning[21].

A new parade shed was built in 1903 together with improved drainage at a cost of £436. In 1905 a new section house was built at a cost of £3.093, and in 1907 five more cells were added together with a waiting room at a cost of £2,000.

In March 1916 a new station was completed for occupation on the site of the old 1867 building[22]. As previously mentioned Mr. John Dixon-Butler, Architect and Surveyor for the Metropolitan Police from-1895–1920, designed and built the station to a formula, that he included in over 200 police stations which were built. Dixon-Butler built in the Queen Anne style showing impressive structure including red brick and white stone facings. The design of these magnificent buildings was influenced by two factors; his father who was a Metropolitan Police architect before him and Richard Norman Shaw the architect who designed the New Scotland Yard.

The Section House at the rear of the station was retained, and two sets of married quarters were built within the new station. Officers from Edmonton helped swell the ranks of the Metropolitan Police Centenary Parade in Central London on May 25th 1929. They joined the Divisional Superintendent C. Pearce (from Stoke Newington) together totalling 240 constables[23].

In 1933 a further re-organisation of the divisional boundaries resulted in Edmonton being transferred from "N" to "Y" Division.

During the Second World War a bomb exploded on the parade shed causing severe damage to the shed and accompanying section house kitchen. Constable W.H. Richards, who was on duty on 2nd October 1940, took the force of the blast as he was walking across the yard, and later died of his injuries in hospital. The section house was closed until after the war and re-opened, after re-furbishment, in 1951.

Tanker accident in Fore Street, Edmonton, just north of Edmonton Police Station 1966

With the advent of Local Authority boundary changes in 1965 Edmonton, Southgate and Enfield were joined together within the London Borough of Enfield. The population of Edmonton steadily increased to over 100,00 in 1951 then gradually declined.

The day to day routine of police officers in the 1960's often involved dealing with major accidents of various kinds. Sometimes these involved dangerous substances. The picture at left shows a new Seddon Tanker belonging to Glycerine Ltd. involved in a damage only accident. The tanker has jackknifed on a slippery road surface, and appears to be the only vehicle involved. A constable from Edmonton is reporting the accident watched by an eager crowd of onlookers.

From 1890 until the early 1920's Station Sergeant's would have been identified wearing four strips on each arm. In the early 1920's one stripe was replaced with a Tudor crown which was worn above the remaining three stripes. The rank as such was phased out in 1972, however Edmonton's last Station Sergeant was Station Sergeant 129790 Eric Varney who retired from the Police service on 5th September 1976.

Edmonton Police Station
320, Fore Street, Edmonton N9
1916 - 1989

In 1979 a new system of message handling was introduced on "Y" Division, and together with other pilot sites, Edmonton Police station took part in trials relating to the new computer aided dispatch system. Gradually the success of this system ensured that it spread over the whole of the Metropolitan Police District. Edmonton's call sign was YE, with its sectional stations Winchmore Hill being YW and Southgate YS.

The station at Edmonton was considered far too small to cope with the building of a Computer complex within its walls, so a Portakabin was constructed in the station yard, and stayed there for 10 years. The Portakabin coped well and proved just how robust it was until the high winds of the 1980's caused damage to the cabin when a tree fell on it.

Four more Portakabins were placed beside it as the pressure for office space built up.

It had been recognised in 1972 that the station was far too small for modern policing requirements, so plans were made to build a new station. By 1986 it was also recognised that the police service was changing, and that re-structuring was required with New Scotland Yard losing some of its autonomy. With these moves came the creation of eight Areas with Edmonton being the flagship of the new 1 Area and the devolvement of responsibilities to Deputy Assistant Commissioners. 1 Area North became the sixth largest police area in Britain[24].

A large plot of land was purchased at 462 Fore Street Edmonton N9, just south of Edmonton Green on which to build a station and Area Headquarters.

The modern new station with 6 floors was completed at a cost of £6.5 million, and was taken into service in 1989. The first two floors and the basement belong to the station, whilst the top four floors are given over to Area Headquarters staff. The old station could not be demolished because of a preservation order, but was sold to a developer who converted it into private flats.

Edmonton Police Station
462, Fore Street, Edmonton N9
1989 – present day

Princess Diana formally opened the station for business in July 1990. There were a number of other guests including the Commissioner Sir Peter Imbert, ACTO Geoffrey McLean, ACMS Peter Winship, Director of Property Services Department Mr. Trevor Lawrence and members of the local community including the Mayor and Mayoress of Enfield[25].

The station was open to the public for two days after the Royal visit. Edmonton Police Station was the only station the Princess ever opened.

The new station assumed the call sign of the old Edmonton station Yankee Echo (YE).

The following officers were Chief Superintendents in charge of the Edmonton Division from dates shown during the period 1965 to 1998 [26].

Ch. Supt. Mackinnon	1st April 1965
Ch. Supt. Hunt	1st April 1968
Ch. Supt. Brokenshire	17th November 1969
Ch. Supt. Morris	31st August 1971
Ch. Supt. Thornton	1st September 1976
Ch. Supt. Martin	3rd September 1979
Ch. Supt. Dickinson	24th March 1980
Ch. Supt. Markham	28th April 1980
Ch. Supt. Williams	10th September 1984
Ch. Supt. O'Connor	26th January 1987
Ch. Supt. Pearce	23rd October 1989
Supt. Waring/Supt. Vincent	1st April 1992
Ch. Supt. Searle	1st July 1992
Supt. Watson (later Ch. Supt)	1998 [27]

The advent of Borough based policing and a re-alignment of policing boundaries on 1st April 1999 meant that certain sections of the Area Headquarters would cease to exist or would be transferred. The officer in charge, now has responsibility for the whole of Enfield Borough. Enfield Division lost some of its ground to Hertfordshire under the revision of boundaries. The Borough Commanders, as they are now called, hold the substantive rank of Superintendent 1st class, although they wear the rank of Chief Superintendents (a Tudor Crown and Star) which was phased out in 1995. The purpose of this is to show seniority[28].

Enfield Police Station

The first reference to a police station at Enfield was shown in Police Orders of 1857, and Enfield Town Police Station, as it was then called was part of 'N' or Islington Division. Later, with the formation of 'Y' or Highgate Division[29], Enfield Town was transferred to become a station of the new division.

The first station in Enfield was situated at 22, The Town, Enfield, Middlesex right next to the market place. It was originally the Beadles

House and was called the Vestry Office. The police occupied it until 1873 when it was considered too small for police purposes and was handed back to the vestry. Within its confines stood a central house with two cages either side. These were quite substantial and secure rooms. At the rear was an enclosed yard with 'privy' at the end. The picture at left shows the plan whilst the picture below shows the officers of Enfield outside the old station in 1873 shortly before vacating the building. The old station is still in use today and is now occupied by the Enfield Parochial Charity[30].

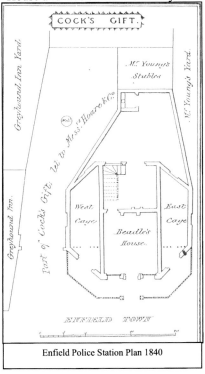

Enfield Police Station Plan 1840

In 1867 land was purchased at the junction of London Road and Cecil Road for the building of a new police station. The Police Surveyor estimated the cost of building a new station at £3,500, and tenders were invited from a number of builders for this task. The contract was awarded to Messrs. Lathey Brothers of Battersea Park, London, SW at £2,690. The new police station was built and ready for occupation in December 1873.

The new station was built with a charge room, an office, a store, a drying room, a mess, a brushing room, a lavatory, three cells, four stalls (stables) and two water closets on the ground floor. The first floor provided the residential accommodation. A married sergeant and his family occupied one room,

Enfield Police Station
22, The Town, Enfield, Middlesex.
(1840-1873)

whilst the remainder were occupied by 6 constables.

Police Orders indicated that the stables for mounted officers were ready for occupation before completion of the police station in July 1873 and

Enfield Police Station
33, London Road, Enfield, Middlesex.
1873- 1965

was supervised by a sergeant[31].

Enfield Division Special
Constable 1920

In 1881 George Head was the Inspector in charge of Enfield Police Station. He resided at the station with his wife, Annie, and seven children. There were six constables at the station and a 'live-in' domestic servant aged thirteen years[32].

Records show that in 1889 the boundaries of Kentish Town, Upper Holloway, Holloway, Hornsey and Enfield Sub-divisions were to be revised, and that this would create a new sub-division called Wood Green Sub Division[33].

The picture at left shows a smartly dressed member of the Metropolitan Police Special

Constabulary with duty armlet and merit stripe during the 1st World War. The photograph was taken in Enfield so it is probable that he was attached to "Y" Division at Enfield Police Station. Special constables wore flat hats with their own bronze cap badge. A Special Constabulary officer's cap badge was silver and more ornate.

The photograph at right is of special interest because it is of Constable 26YR, Henry John Halford who spent 20 years of his service at Enfield. Born in St. Pancras in the County of Middlesex in 1867 he joined the Metropolitan Police, warrant number 74235, on 18th February 1889 as Constable 392 'Y' Division. His previous trade was that of a Cab Driver. Later in his service, and whilst at Enfield, he was granted Reserve status with extra pay. Constable Halford has 4 medals, which are the 1887 Jubilee medal and 1897 bar, the 1901 Coronation medal and the 1911 Coronation medal, which means that he saw duty at these events. In 1913 when the Metropolitan Police abolished Reserve status Constable Halford was issued with the number 1031 'Y' instead. He retired on pension with £69. 11s. 6d per annum in February 1915.

Constable 74235 26YR Henry John Halford

Enfield Police Station Lamp

On the 5th October 1917 the Urban District Council of Enfield wrote to the Metropolitan Police informing them that the address of Enfield Town Police Station was 33 London Road, Enfield. In 1931 records show that Enfield Police Station was a sub-Divisional station of "Y" or Highgate Division with sectional stations of East Barnet, Potters Bar, Southgate and Winchmore Hill.

The re-organisation, in 1933 changed this picture and Enfield was shown as a sub-divisional station of Wood Green Division, and Southgate, Enfield Highway and Cheshunt were now included as its sectional stations[34].

Improvements in 1936 cost £462, but by 1939 the old Victorian Police Station was considered inadequate for present day policing needs. The Receiver of the Metropolitan Police purchased about an acre of land located on a site known as Oak House, Baker Street, Enfield for £5,850 on 21st June 1939.

The land remained empty for the next 6 years at least because of the outbreak of the Second World War in 1939, and not until 1963 did the building of the new station finally get underway. The builders of the station were Messrs. F.R.Hipperson and Son of Dagenham who tendered

Enfield Police Station
41, Baker Street, Enfield, Middlesex.
1965 – Present day

for the work at a cost of £124,244 and completed the work in March 1965 [35].

Enfield was designated a sub-divisional station when the new Local Authority boundary changes occurred in 1965. The station code became YF with Enfield Highway (later called Ponders End) being YI and Cheshunt becoming YC. Force Orders showed the new station located at 41, Baker Street, Enfield.

New Southgate Police Station

In June 1886, land was purchased freehold for the building of a Police station at New Southgate at a cost of £1000. Records reported that the

New Southgate Police Station
Garfield Road, New Southgate
1889 – 1990

new station was located on "Y" Division and police business commenced in May 1889 [36].

New Southgate was part of "Y" Divisions re-organisation involving boundary changes[37] within the Division. Furthermore such re-organisation involved re-allocating personnel therefore Dr. Hugh Scott of Colney Hatch was appointed as Divisional Surgeon to the station of New Southgate. The station was shown according to old surveyors maps to have been built at the junction with Betsyle Road and Garfield Road N11.

Considerable road and house building appears to have shortened Betsyle Road because it now lies some distance from the station which is shown at the junction with the High Road and Garfield Road, New Southgate N11.

New Southgate
Police Station Lamp

In May 1889 a request was made by Southgate Local Board to erect a hut on wheels, which would stand in the yard of the station and contain a fire hose. For this an annual rent of 1/- was paid. This was followed in 1905 by a fire escape ladder, which attracted a fee of 5/- per year until it was removed in 1907. The hut was extended in 1909, but by 1929 it was no longer required for the fire hose when it was removed. The Special Constabulary occupied the hut from January 1930[38].

In 1930 New Southgate was shown as a Sectional Station of Wood Green, but when local Government boundaries were re-organised in April 1965 it was shown as a Sectional Station of Edmonton Sub Division. It was designated as "YN".

New Southgate was one of the police stations, which were closed for night duty 10pm-6am purposes[39]. A telephone for public and police use was installed in a pillar near the front door of the station. The temporary closure later became permanent[40].

New Southgate Police Station was given the status of police office and re-opened to the public for limited periods[41]. The area of New Southgate was then policed as a neighbourhood unit from Southgate Police Station. By 1990 the station was still owned by the police, but was closed for operational purposes although various area squads used its offices.

Ponders End/Enfield Highway Police Station

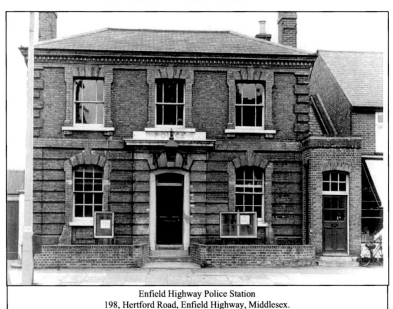

Enfield Highway Police Station
198, Hertford Road, Enfield Highway, Middlesex.
1868-1968

The area of Ponders End before 1969 was known as Enfield Highway. In January 1864 details showed Enfield Highway Police Station, as it was then known, as a station located on "N" or Islington Division. When the new Division of "Y" or Highgate Division was formed, Enfield Highway Police Station was transferred from "N" to "Y" Division[42].

The expansion of the police areas and revision of boundaries in June 1886 meant that Enfield Highway was transferred back to "N" or Islington Division. The freehold title to a parcel of land was purchased in 1866 for £520 in order to build a new police station. The land was located at 198, Hertford Road, Enfield Highway, and plans were completed by the Surveyor who instructed a building company to complete the work. The new police station was opened in March 1868[43] at a cost of £2,525. The station was built with a loft to the first floor whilst on the ground floor there was a charge room, 3 cells and an office. In the yard was a two stall stable. An Inspector supervised the station[44].

The boundaries between Chingford and Enfield Highway were again revised when Chingford Police station was built on Kings Head Hill in March 1888. This revision meant that Enfield Highway was transferred to "Y" Division.

The 'N' Division group responsible for the Royal Small Arms Factory
at Enfield Lock in 1915

The photograph above shows a unit of "Y" Division Officers performing special duty at the Royal Small Arms Factory, Enfield Lock in 1915. The special duty included factory security in times of war under the Emergency powers legislation. The reason for taking this picture is unclear – as it appears to be some special occasion, particularly as some are wearing their medals and decorations. The Inspector (seated with the flat cap in the centre front), two sergeants and eleven constables were posted to a small station within the small arms factory. Later in the war women special constables took over the security of policing the small arms factory. This enabled the male officers to supplement the war effort either by joining the ranks or returning to normal station duties. The women shown located there in December 1916 were;

> Sub Inspector Buckpitt
> Sergeants R. Green, M. Johnson, A. Moore and G. West
> Corporal K. Canter
> Constables, M. Beaney, E. Boyes, E. Buckingham, E. Daniels,
> A. Everfield, A. Ayre, D. Gardiner, C. Gosling, K. Kaye,
> C Knight, N. Little, A. Mackay, E. Mouland, S. Pernull,
> E. Pickard, M. Read, E. Tolfield, A. Wheeler and A. White[45].

The Metropolitan Police Surveyor R.G. Strachan included in his records that Enfield Highway Police station was situated at 198, Hertford Road, Enfield Highway. In 1926 there were alterations made to the station and one set of the married quarters was converted for operational purposes. Alterations and additions were completed in September 1926[46].

The station remained on "N" Division until the boundary revision was completed north of the River Thames in July 1933. Enfield Highway (now located on "N" or Stoke Newington Division) was transferred back to "Y" or Wood Green Division. It would appear that a rationalisation of stations and Divisional boundaries, especially Divisional Headquarters stations, was also completed at the same time.

In 1962 there had been concern expressed that the old station had come to the end of its operational life and efforts should be made to build a new modern station. The Metropolitan Police Surveyor suggested that suitable freehold land, on which to build a police station in Ponders End, had become available and should be purchased at a cost of £41,000. In fact efforts had been made since 1956 to obtain a suitable parcel of land to no avail. Home Office consent preceded the purchase in November 1962. Tenders were invited to build the new Police station, and the contract was awarded to Messrs. Robert Hart and Sons Ltd. for £130, 685. The Local Authority boundary review of April 1965 placed Enfield Highway within the London Borough of Enfield. The station at 204-214, High Street, Ponders End, Enfield was completed for use in July 1969.

The opening of the new station in July replaced the old station in Enfield Highway[47]. There was no opening ceremony to mark the occasion,

Ponders End Police Station
204-214, High Street, Ponders End, Enfield, Middlesex
1969 – Present day.

however in June 1970 there was a station open day where invited local dignitaries and members of the public were shown around the new station. The station housed Traffic Wardens, and the Regional Crime Squad office, in addition to members of the CID and uniform branch. The Police Station now operates within a reduced number of hours.

Southgate Police Station

In 1859 the Metropolitan Police for £285 purchased land in Chase Side, Old Southgate. The site was considered suitable for the building of a new police station and section house. Tenders were invited to build the new station, which was finally completed in 1861[48] at a cost of £1528. The building comprised ground and 1st floors with charge room, office, mess, 4 cells and 2 water closets located on the ground floor. In the yard was a 3 stall stable for horses. Land was also purchased at the rear of the station to allow access into Crown Land[49].

Southgate Police Station
Chase Side, Southgate
1861 - 1970

The Commissioner approved the following to be employed on Station Duties – Constable 214 Kirby (Acting Sergeant) at Southgate as from April 1864 [50]. In 1873 Southgate was a station situated on 'Y' or Highgate Division[51].

The picture at left shows the old Victorian Southgate Police Station in Chase Side. It was built from traditional brick. In 1881 records show that Inspector Thomas E. Maher[52] was the officer in charge of the station, although in 1873 it had been a sergeant designated station[53]. Inspector Maher resided there with his wife Jael and five children. There were six single police officers also resident at the station[54].

Local people and dignitaries who arranged parties and events for their entertainment often treated the police and their families. One such event took place in Southgate where Sub-Inspector Lambert from Southgate, whilst competing in an obstacle race at the Annual Police Party of Mr Cory Wright, J.P., on the 20th July, 1897, collided violently with one of the obstacles, breaking his leg. He was taken to the Great Northern Hospital, where he was detained[55].

By 1909 the area within the Southgate Parish had become well populated with a number of new houses being built. In fact the population trebled between 1899 and 1909[56].

Consideration was given in 1965 to replacing the police station, which was no longer suitable for modern policing requirements. The contract to build a police station, women police hostel and two sets of married quarters was awarded to Messrs. Chas. S. Foster and Sons for the sum of £152,000[57]. The new station was opened in 1970 together with the hostel at 59, Crown Lane, Southgate N14[58]. The station was built with a charge room and cell accommodation; although today they are rarely used as all prisoners are transported to the new Divisional Headquarters at Edmonton. The station code is YS. The new station was located about 100 yards away from the Victoria line at Southgate.

Once built New Southgate Police Station was given the status of police office, and only open to the public for limited periods[59].

The area of New Southgate was then policed as a neighbourhood unit from Southgate Police Station. Since 1970 Southgate Police Station has been the home of the "Y" Division Youth and Community Section who occupy the hostel accommodation. This was not an ideal building for the administration of youth justice in the boroughs of Enfield, and Haringey (within the old Y Divisional boundary), as each room had a sink and wardrobe as standard.

Southgate Police Station
Chase Side, Southgate,
1970- present day

Winchmore Hill Police Station

The Winchmore Hill area grew in size in the early 1900's with the development of a number of housing projects, and with the influx of large numbers of people came the justification for the building of a police station. The Metropolitan Police looked around for a site, which it obtained from the London Brick Company in the vicinity of Compton Road. This land originally formed

Winchmore Hill Police Station
687, Green Lanes, Winchmore Hill, N21
1915 – 1998

part of the Highfield House Estate. The freehold land was purchased for the sum of £1,215 on 8th January 1907.

Winchmore Hill Police Station Lamp

The new station was built and came into use in December 1915[60] and included two sets of married quarters (rent at 10s per week), cells and a charge room. The code signal for the station was WV. In 1912 Winchmore Hill was also shown as an ambulance shelter, which housed the hand ambulance for conveyance of sick and injured people. To the left is illustrated the station's particularly ornate blue lamp. It is lit during the night, this often attracted members of the public like taxi drivers who, passing along the busy road of Green Lanes, stopped and deposited property found in their cabs before continuing their journey home. Often a night duty shift at Winchmore Hill could be a busy one for the station officer.

This photograph below shows a line up of the Metropolitan Police Special Constabulary "Y" Division dated 1916. In 1931 Winchmore Hill was a sectional station on "Y" or Highgate Division although the Divisional

A section of 'Y' Division Special Constabulary 1916

Headquarters was located at Kentish Town Police station. The sub-Divisional station appears to have been Enfield.

During the re-organisation in 1933, Winchmore Hill Police Station was shown as a sectional station of Wood Green Sub-Division at 687, Green Lanes N21. Further reorganisation in 1964 showed the station as re-assigned to Edmonton sub-division as a sectional station situated in the Borough of Enfield. The Station closed in 1998.

Broxbourne District Council

The district lies on the northern boundary of the Greater London Area. The towns in this area are located along the western side of the Lea Valley. It is mainly residential although it does include some areas of industrial and commercial development[61].

Goffs Oak Police Station

In 1895 the police erected two adjoining cottages in Goffs Lane at the junction of Newgate Street Road. They were built as a result of pressure from Lady Meux of Theobalds who was suffering from poachers on her land.

In November 1896[62] two police officers and their families occupied the buildings. One was a sergeant who paid four shillings a week, and one was a constable who paid three shillings a week, for their accommodation. In addition, one side of the building also contained a police office entered through a lobby. There was also one cell.

Goffs Oak Police Station circa 1920

During the 1930's it was decided to convert the police office into a living room for the police house, whilst the lobby was made into a police box for use by the public. Police continued to patrol the area, and then on 1st April 1965, due to an increase in population and work, a police office was opened in the building. This time the front ground floor room on the opposite end of the building was used as an office. The officers used the kitchen at the rear and upstairs was left empty[63].

Finally the police station closed on 31st October 1972 and the property reverted back to two separate police houses.

---

[1] Municipal Year book 2000 and Public Services Directory Vol. 2 Newman books (1999), and publicity literature for the London Borough of Enfield
[2] Metropolitan Police Orders dated 6th August 1964
[3] Op cit
[4] Metropolitan Police Orders dated 11th January 1864
[5] Metropolitan Police Orders dated 29th March 1968
[6] http://www.met.police.uk/enfield/history.htm 15.05.02
[7] Elmes, E. Constable (1990) Pamphlet on 'Edmonton Police' produced to commemorate the opening of the new Edmonton Police Station
[8] Ibid p1
[9] Metropolitan Police Surveyors Manifests and John Back Archive (1975) Metropolitan Police Museum, Charlton.
[10] Ibid
[11] Census Records 1841
[12] Census Records 1851
[13] Elmes, E. Constable (1990) Pamphlet on 'Edmonton Police'
[14] Metropolitan Police Orders dated 28th October 1863
[15] Metropolitan Police Orders dated 28th January 1864
[16] Metropolitan Police Orders dated 27th April 1864
[17] John Back stated there was no record of occupation in respect of Edmonton Police Station given in police orders.
[18] John Back Archive (1975) Metropolitan Police Museum, Charlton.
[19] Census records 1881
[20] Metropolitan Police Orders dated 22nd July 1886
[21] Police Review 30th July 1897
[22] Metropolitan Police Orders dated 3rd March 1916
[23] Metropolitan Police Centenary Celebration Programme 1929
[24] http://www.met.police.uk/enfield/history.htm 13.03.02
[25] Metropolitan Police News Release 3rd July 1990
[26] Elmes, E. Constable (1990) Pamphlet on 'Edmonton Police'
[27] The Police and Constabulary Almanac 1998
[28] Fido, M. and Skinner, K. (1999) The Encyclopaedia of Scotland Yard. Virgin Press. London
[29] Metropolitan Police Orders dated 28th October 1865
[30] Sykes, R. (1988) History of the Enfield Parochial Charity
[31] Metropolitan Police General Orders 1873
[32] Census records 1881
[33] Metropolitan Police Orders dated 4th May 1889
[34] J. Back (1977) Archive "Enfield Station History"
[35] Ibid
[36] Metropolitan Police Orders dated 22nd November 1888
[37] Metropolitan police Orders dated 4th May 1889
[38] Metropolitan Police Surveyors Records
[39] Metropolitan Police Orders dated 25th November 1960.
[40] Metropolitan Police Orders dated 4th August 1961.
[41] Metropolitan Police Orders dated 3rd May 1968
[42] Metropolitan Police Orders dated 28th October 1865
[43] Metropolitan Police Orders dated 11th March 1868
[44] Metropolitan Police General Orders 1873
[45] Heyneman, J. (1925) The Pioneer Policewoman. Chatto and Windus London.
[46] Metropolitan Police Property manifest 1924
[47] Metropolitan Police Orders dated 19th September 1969
[48] Opened 20th September 1861 (Metropolitan Police Order 19th September 1861)
[49] John Back Archive (1975) Metropolitan Police Museum, Charlton.
[50] Metropolitan Police Orders dated 27th April 1864
[51] Metropolitan Police General Orders 1873

[52] Census records 1881
[53] Metropolitan Police General Orders 1873
[54] Census records 1881
[55] Police Review July 1897
[56] John Back Archive (1975) Metropolitan Police Museum, Charlton.
[57] Ibid
[58] Metropolitan Police Orders dated 12th June 1970
[59] Metropolitan Police Orders dated 3rd May 1968
[60] Metropolitan Police Orders dated 11th December 1915
[61] Publicity literature for Broxborne District Council
[62] Metropolitan Police Orders dated 8th December 1896
[63] Histed Graham, Constable 531 (YF) Unpublished report on Goffs Oak Police (undated)

Chapter Five

Epping Forest District Council

The Epping Forest District Council area of 131 square miles extends out in a fan shape from the edge of the Greater London area, north along the Lea Valley and the length of Epping Forest[1]. It stretches as far as the River Stort and the town of Harlow. Then north east along the Roding Valley.

In April 2000 the Metropolitan Police handed over the policing of Chigwell, Loughton and Waltham Abbey to the Essex Constabulary. However, the policing of these areas by the Metropolitan Police reaches back some 160 years and their past are worth recording.

The Metropolitan Police retained the old Claybury Police Station, now known as Claygate House, at Woodford Bridge in April 2000. It is located in the London Borough of Redbridge but the strong links with Chigwell Police station, and the fact that it is only a few yards outside of Epping District Council Area has dictated its position in this book.

The stations shown within Epping Forest District Council Area are Chigwell/Claybury, Debden, Limes Farm, Loughton and Waltham Abbey.

Chigwell and Claybury Police Stations

Claybury Police Station Lamp

In 1840 Chigwell Police station strength was shown as one sergeant and four constables. The sergeant was shown as a mounted officer and all five officers were shown as being lodged privately. In rural areas it was normal for the sergeant to live at the station house, which was usually a private house whilst the constables lived nearby also in private rented accommodation.

Supervision was undertaken from Ilford Police station where the officer in charge was an Inspector and it was the place to take prisoners for safe-keeping and charging. The petty sessions were also shown at Ilford so it was a simple task to escort them to court from the station. Some three constables were also shown stationed at Lamborne (End) and lodged privately[2].

In January 1864 Chigwell Police station was described as a station with no cells and a place where no charges were taken[3]. By this time the authorised strength had increased to 1 sergeant and 8 constables however it appears that a constable was also used as an acting sergeant allowing for supervision of both the day and night shifts. Two constables paraded for day duty and four constables for the night shift[4]. There was no further increase in strength to replace the acting sergeant.

Further supervision of Chigwell continued from Ilford Police Station, which was on a neighbouring division. Chigwell was a station on 'N' division whilst Ilford was on 'K' division[5]. The Inspector had considerable responsibility, which necessitated him covering the stations at Ilford, Barking, Dagenham, Loughton, Woodford, Wanstead, Chadwell Heath, Barkingside, and East Ham. This was a huge area in those days to supervise, which was probably completed by horse. The instruction concluded that one horse was to be ridden by two sergeants alternately at Ilford Police Station[6].

The Commissioner had issued instructions in December 1864 for the building of a number of Police station houses. Within this instruction Superintendents were required to make an effort and obtain sites for these new stations and Chigwell was one station specifically mentioned[7].

In 1865 three new Divisions were formed "W" for Clapham, "X" for Paddington and "Y" for Highgate. Chigwell is shown on "N" or Islington exterior Division and also on "K" or Stepney Green exterior Division as being sergeant's houses only.

In 1871 the newly acquired Woodford Police Station became the Sub-divisional station for the others located at Wanstead, Chigwell, Loughton and Waltham Abbey. It appears that the sergeant was removed to Waltham Abbey because records in 1873 indicate that Chigwell as it was called was a constable station[8].

A cottage at Woodford Bridge, owned by Mrs. P. McAvoy, was found and later leased by the Metropolitan Police for use as Chigwell Police Station. Accordingly when the adjoining cottage became available with stable and loft in 1875[9] Mrs. E. McAvoy offered this to the police. It appears that the offer was accepted with an annual rental of £20 for each cottage. The exact location of this station was unknown, but it appears to be on the same site as the current building.

Both cottages were known as Chigwell Cottage. In 1875 it was reported that the new Police station at Chigwell should be occupied forthwith and 'that rent in the sum of 3s per week should be paid by the occupying married constable' for 4 rooms[10]. Over the years the cottages deteriorated and conditions were unhealthy. During an inspection by the Metropolitan Police Chief Surgeon he described the station as 'two small ordinary cottages with a poor stable rented in neighbours outhouse'. The cottages were shown as being occupied by 1 married sergeant and 1 married constable. He recommended the cottages should be pulled down and a purpose built station erected in its place[11].

The address was shown in 1884 as Woodford Bridge, Chigwell. Records show that it was called Chigwell Cottage and the lease was renewed yearly with an option of a 3-month notice to quit on either side. The Receiver paid for all repairs and taxes. The ground floor space included a charge room, a reserve room, one water closet and a coal shed. Use of a stable was also provided however this was given up in 1884[12].

In 1886, Chigwell was transferred from "N" or Islington Division with the formation of the new "J" or Bethnal Green Division. On 23rd March 1900 a new Police station at Claybury was opened and replaced Chigwell, which started a 70-year gap when Chigwell Police station ceased to exist although officers covered the Chigwell Area.[13]

Claybury Police Station
Manor Road, Woodford Bridge, Chigwell, Essex.
1900- Present day

The Metropolitan Police purchased the freehold site in 1892 and work soon began, to build a new station at the location. Claybury Police station was completed in 1900 and was the first purpose built station for the area. It was built at the fork in the road where Chigwell Road and Manor Road meet and contained stables for horses and cells to hold prisoners in addition to 2 sets of married quarters.

In 1898 Sergeant Hankerville was the sergeant in charge of Woodford Bridge Police station as it was referred to then[14]. In 1907 Claybury was a sectional station of Woodford on 'J' or Hackney [15]Division, and in addition to the station itself it had two sets of quarters probably for the sergeant-in-charge and his family[16]. Later the address was shown as High Road, Claybury,[17] however this was later changed to Manor Road, Woodford Bridge, Essex. After 1900 telegraphic codes were issued to stations to help with communication. Claybury had (CL) as its telegraphic code.

Chigwell Police Station
24, Brook Parade, High Road, Chigwell, Essex
1976-2000

In 1937 all stations received standardised station codes to assist operators of telegraphic equipment in order to facilitate the identification of not only individual stations but also of their Division as well. Claybury being a station on "J" Division was allocated the code (JY). In the same year Claybury was re-furbished and a number of improvements were made to modernise the station

A review of police areas as result of the Local Authority boundary revisions in 1965 found that Claybury Police station was wrongly situated so instructions were given for the purchase and building of a new station at Chigwell.

Chigwell was shown to have an Ambulance shelter some distance from the station, located at the Rectors House in Chigwell Row with the agreement that for this service 2/6d per year was paid[18].

Instructions were issued that the new station at 24 Brook Parade, High Road, Chigwell will be taken into use and on 12th January 1976 and that the present Claybury Sectional station should close[19].

Claybury is still in use by the police but not as an operational police station. It has been for some time now the Area dogs section headquarters it is known as Claygate House. Force re-organisations caused Chigwell to become the Headquarters station for 'J' Division when the Divisional suite and staff transferred from Leyton Police Station on 30th December 1975[20].

The new station at Chigwell was built to a high specification and considerable cost since senior officers and area headquarters staff were to be housed there. In 1989 the Area Headquarters and their staff moved once more, to Edmonton Police station where purpose built accommodation was prepared for them.

Further reorganisation and border realignment in April 2000 meant that Chigwell Police station was transferred to the Essex Police. The station was surplus to requirements and has been shut down and sold off.

Debden Police Office.

In 1970 the first of three new police offices was opened on Barkingside Division on the Debden Estate in Essex. Others were planned for Hainault and Limes Farm[21]. This was in line with the policy of building police offices where larger communities were located.

This photograph shows a purpose built police office designed to be opened at particular times to deal with enquiries from the public. The station was built without cells or other facilities for prisoners. Until 2000 any arrests were taken to Barkingside Police Station. Today they are taken to an Essex Police Station at Loughton or Epping.

Debden Police Office
Barrington Green, Debden, Essex
1970 – present day

The Debden Estate was a Greater London Council estate which had developed following the 1939-1945 War, and was designed to re-house families from London[22]. The station call sign was JE.

Hainault Police Office

The picture at right shows Hainault Police Office situated at 182 Manford Way, Hainault, Essex. It was built was opened in November 1970 on a new housing estate to deal with local enquiries by the new residents moving into the local area[23].

Limes Farm Police Office

In 1972 another new estate was being built on the

Hainault Police Office
182 Manford Way, Hainault, Essex
1970- Present day

borders of Chigwell and Barkingside. This was called Limes Farm and contained 1000 houses. It was felt that due to the large numbers of people living there a police office should be opened to the public at limited times. A Police house called Limes Farm Police Office was opened in May 1972[24]. The station call sign was JT.

Loughton Police Station

The police arrived in Loughton in 1840. A 'police residence' was established at Cage Green Cottage. It was situated on the cricket field nearly opposite the War Memorial where the village cage was placed.

The Old Police Station,
Cage Green Cottage, Loughton, Essex.
1840 - 1872

In a special report dated 24th November 1859 Superintendent Howie, the chief officer of "K" or Stepney Division reported on the suitability of the current station house located at Loughton in Essex. He felt that the station was badly situated and inadequate for police purposes being some distance from the new railway. The Commissioner had informed his Divisional Superintendents to be vigilant in locating suitable sites for the building of police stations. Superintendent Howie reported that a suitable parcel of land had become available at the corner of Forest Road and the High Street Loughton. The freehold owner Mr. Doyle was leasing the land for 99 years with an annual ground rent of £11.

In November 1860 Home Office approval was granted to build a station on the site. The land was sold to the Metropolitan Police in 1872 for the sum of £330[25].

Accordingly a police station was built on the land and included a ground and first floor. The living space was cramped as records show that on the first floor there were six rooms and four single constables who resided in just one communal room. A married constable occupied the another three rooms and a married sergeant and his family, occupied a further two rooms[26]. Records also indicated that the station which was located on "K" or Stepney Division had a strength of two sergeants and seven constables[27].

In October 1884 there was a revision of the station boundaries together with the formation of three new Divisions namely 'W', 'X' and 'Y'. During these changes Loughton transferred to 'N' or Islington Division. In 1886 formation of the new 'J' Division took place and saw Loughton transfer from 'N'[28]. In 1898 the location of the police station was shown in the High Road. Station Sergeant Harry Clarke was in charge and there

Loughton Police Station
158, High Road, Loughton Essex.
1872-1964

were three other sergeants and fourteen constables[29].

The station address of Loughton Police station has changed over time even though the station itself never moved. For example in 1864 it was shown as High Road, Loughton, however police records show [30] the address as Forest Road but in July 1931 the Urban District Council of Loughton notified the Officer in charge of Loughton Police station that as of the 29th the location and address would be changed to 158 High Street[31]. The station house was shown to have been originally built with one set of married quarters[32].

The picture below shows the local police escorting a parade through the town in about 1910. Behind is the old station house. On no less than two occasions Loughton Police station was nearly consumed by fire. On

January 16th 1906 when the station was not 50 years old, a fire broke out in adjacent premises however the police alerted the fire brigade who put out the fire in good enough time. The same thing occurred on 9th June 1937 with the same result. No damage was caused to the station[33].

In the 1930's the Commissioner for the Metropolis reported twice that

Police from Loughton escorting a band through the High Street circa 1910

Loughton Police Station was inadequate for current policing needs however it was not until 1957 that something was done about it[34].

In the mid 1930's the Metropolitan Police introduced wireless equipped radio cars which were used to patrol the division on increasingly busier trunk roads, although they were not delivered immediately to each police station[35].

The Kings Police Medal

An amazing incident occurred in Loughton in 1930 that demonstrates the dedication and commitment to duty, police officers have. Early on the morning of 11th July, Constable 273 'J' Alfred Charles James saw a man with a motor car which had been reported stolen to police. He approached the vehicle and spoke to the man who offered an explanation as to the ownership of the vehicle which the officer was not satisfied with. Constable James then told the man that he was under arrest however the man produced a gun placed the muzzle against the officers body and threatened to shot him.

There was a struggle in the street however some members of the public nearby who were attracted to the commotion came to the officer's assistance and together they managed to over power the man who was arrested. Such brave meritorious actions were recognised that year when the King bestowed on Constable James the award of Kings Police Medal [36]. The picture on the last page shows the medal awarded.

Loughton Police Station
158, High Road, Loughton, Essex.
1964 – present day

Additionally both Police and public, to improve communications also installed a system of Police Boxes at major road junctions throughout the Metropolitan Police District, for use. There were four shown located on Loughton section (JO) and three for Claybury (JY). These were Box by Woodford Railway station (JY), Box at Roding Lane near railway bridge, Buckhurst Hill (JO), Box at Epping New Road junction with Rangers Road (JO) Box 7 at Roding Road junction with Valley Hill (JO), Box 9 at Goldings Hill opposite England lane (JO), Box at Hainault Road near the Bald Hind Public House (JY) and lastly Box in the village, Chigwell Road, by Vicarage lane (JY)[37].

It was common practice to post a constable on station security usually for the purposes of diverting casual members of the public from troubling the Station Officer (the sergeant). During time of war this principle did not change and the constable positioned himself behind the wall of sandbags which ringed the front door to the station. On 12th May 1941 War Reserve Albert Hinds PC 1084J and recalled police pensioner Constable Samuel Jordan 133JR who had originally retired in 1933 after 25 years loyal service, were standing near the front door to Loughton Police Station. At roughly the same time 3 men was passing long the High Road to take up Air Raid Precautionary duties further along the road when a huge explosion occurred. An anti- aircraft shell exploded right outside the station making a 3 foot diameter hole in the road and killing two of the passing men and War Reserve Police Albert Hinds. The shell probably came from one of the anti aircraft guns protecting the small arms factory at Enfield. Constable Jordan lost an arm in the explosion and in consequence was retired medically unfit with an enhanced pension. He died in 1987 in his mid-80's[38].

Loughton was a sectional station of Woodford sub-division and shown as a station on 3 District (the District HQ was located at Macnaghten Section House), whilst the Divisional Headquarters was shown at Hackney Police Station[39].

Needless to say the war intervened making the building of a new station at Loughton unimportant. However in September 1957 Estates Branch recommended the purchase of 2, 4, and 6 Forest Road should be purchased and demolished to make way for a larger station. In February 1958 the freehold to these properties were acquired for £11,500 however both 2 and 4 Forest Road were occupied by Messrs. Ingle (Furnishing) who still had leasehold status on the addresses. Negotiations for the leasehold commenced resulting in Ingles vacating the premises in October 19 when the leasehold was purchased for £7, 500[40].

Local Government boundary changes and police re-organisation designated Loughton (JO) as a sectional station to Barkingside Sub-Division situated in Chigwell Urban District Council area. The new three-storey police station was built and came into operational use at 6am on 2nd November 1964[41].

In April 2000 Loughton Police station was handed over to the Essex Police as part of the boundary changes that co-incided with the introduction of Borough based police in the Metropolitan Police.

Waltham Abbey Police Station

In 1840 Waltham Abbey was incorporated into the Metropolitan Police Area and the old time watchmen and the new police replaced Town Constables. The three town constables still remained in the town but mainly in an honorary role. The station strength consisted of 4 sergeants, one mounted constable and 9 other constables. All lived in private accommodation locally. Several outlying local hamlets had their own constable[42]. White pained cast iron posts mark the northern boundary of the Metropolitan Police, which are said to have been present since 1666[43]. The pay for a constable from 1829 until 1869 was £1. 1s for which they worked every day of the week for 12 hours each day[44]. Such was the demand from the police that a number of officers were retired as being worn out. Police Sergeant 15"N" Henry Sturgeon was retired from Waltham Abbey in 1872 under precisely these circumstances.

The station was located at Highbridge Street, opposite the Abbey Church and was small badly constructed and lacked rear windows. Furthermore the earth closets in the cells together with bad ventilation provided an almost constant stench which was aggravated in summer. This station remained in use until 1876. The station shown below lasted from 1840 to 1876.

Waltham Abbey Police Station
Highbridge Street, Waltham Abbey, Essex.
1840 - 1876

In 1864 the Commissioners gave instructions for Superintendents to take steps to erect a police station at Waltham Abbey, which almost certainly came about as a result of complaints from prominent local citizens who wrote to the Commissioners about the small station already in use which was no longer suitable for use as a police station.

Superintendent Green proposed two suitable sites to the Commissioners with one located in Sun Street a one-acre orchard, which eventually became the favoured location. This was purchased from Mr. Richard Clayton Brown Clayton for the sum of £400. Almost immediately a section of the site was sold to Mr. Chetwood for the sum of £25 in September 1872. A new building was constructed on the site for the sum of £3,570[45].

One room downstairs provided the operation accommodation whilst the remainder provided living space for one sergeant and his family, 1 constable and his family and four single constables. The constables shared 1 room upstairs. Privacy was at a premium. To the right of the entrance was the operational room, which contained three cells, a meal room or canteen which was communal. The premises had been opened in 1876 and charges for accommodation were levied on the occupants as 4s a week for the sergeant, 3s for the constable and 1s a week for the single officers[46]. It was common to hire a servant to look after the single constables but often the married constable's wife took on this obligation[47].

Annual leave was allowed for officers at a rate of 14 days for Inspectors, 10 days for sergeants and 7 days for constables, although leave of absence was sometimes allowed without pay on Form 139 for the

Waltham Abbey Police Station
Sun Street, Waltham Abbey, Essex
1876 – Present day

Assistant Commissioners approval together with any other applications for leave for more than 3 days at a time.

One of the main responsibilities of the Divisional Superintendent was to ensure the safe policing of the Royal Small arms factory at Enfield Lock and the Royal Gunpowder factory at Waltham Abbey. Responsibility for security of the Gunpowder Factory commenced in April 1860[48]. In 1869 there was a police station on both sites[49]. The Gunpowder factory required an Inspector to be in charge whilst down the road at the other site a sergeant was in command. The duties of the Inspector were that he should visit the small arms factory daily. The rules for running these factories were strict and it was the responsibility of police to ensure their security [50]. In 1869 the strength for such duties was one Inspector, four sergeants and twenty constables. There were two sergeants stationed at each factory with the Gunpowder Factory having thirteen constables whilst the Small Arms factory had seven[51]. By 1874 the Gunpowder Factory strength was reduced by two constables[52].

In 1886 "J" Division was formed which included Waltham Abbey. An electric telegraph was installed at the lock in 1883, which connected it to Waltham Abbey station. In 1893 records show that one Chief Inspector, three sergeants and nine constables were the established strength of the Small Arms factory although the Chief Inspector was based at the Gunpowder Factory.

Deaths in harness were common and often the men died young. One such case occurred in 1876 when Acting Sergeant Jepthah Farrow who was stationed at the Royal Gun Powder Factory at Waltham Abbey. He had spent ten of his fifteen years service there but had also seen duty at Sun Street station. He died at the age of 39 years having succumbed to a lingering illness where he was on sick leave for four months. He left a widow and two children both under eight years old[53]. Being ten years short on his pension his family may have received a gratuity but an application would have been made to the Secretary for the Home Department. They would have had to vacate any police residence they occupied.

Records show that in 1888 a police station was located at Mott Street, High Beech[54].

In January 1908 some ten or so constables from Waltham Abbey Police station were involved in the pursuit of two Russian anarchists who had killed two innocent people (one a constable) and wounded 25 others. The chase stared in Tottenham, ended six miles away, some two hours later. Both anarchists committed suicide rather than be captured. This became known as the Tottenham outrage[55].

In 1911 the police horse patrol was removed from Waltham Abbey Police station. The reason for their withdrawal was unknown although the introduction of the telegraph in 1907 and the increased use of bicycles would have rendered them inefficient. The stables were converted into a parade room - a role it performed for the next forty years. The section house for four constables was withdrawn in 1913[56].

The Great War saw the introduction of the Metropolitan Police Special Constabulary and Waltham Abbey Police station was given strength of some 50 Specials far out numbering the number of regular officers. At the beginning of the war specials wore arm bands denoting they were on duty with differing colours signifying what rank they were, e.g. blue, yellow and red. Uniforms didn't arrive until three years after the war started. Their duties included air raid warnings and war hospital postings at the Town Hall where the local Red Cross had set up a 32-bed ward. The dangers to Waltham Abbey by German bombers and Zeppelins were apparent. Not only was the Royal Small Arms factory a target but so was the Royal Gun Powder Factory nearby. So too were the barges of Gun powder which were en route along the River Lea supervised by Police Officers from the Gun Powder factory, destined for the Woolwich Arsenal - to be made into bombs and munitions[57].

After the war had finished people were commemorating the Great War dead at the Cenotaph a year after on the eleventh hour of the eleventh day. Waltham Abbey joined in observing the firing of a maroon into the morning sky thirty seconds before the hour, and again two minutes beyond a tradition which continued until the 1970's[58].

In 1923 the Metropolitan Police ceased to police the Royal Gun Powder Factory and the twenty or so officers were dispersed throughout London. In 1929 a fire brigade siren was erected on the roof of Waltham Abbey police station after a member of the Town Council sent a request. A charge of five shillings per year was charged for the sirens use on police premises by the Receiver of the Metropolis[59].

The Great Depression of the 1930's hit police officers very badly when a mandatory deduction of 5/- a week was withdrawn from constables and 6/3d from sergeants regardless of rate of pay in 1931. Police constables earned at least 78s were particularly hard hit. The following year saw a further deduction of 3/6d and 11s respectively[60].

On 1st August 1933 along with Walthamstow, and Chingford, Waltham Abbey left "N" Division and joined "J" Division, the headquarters station being located at Bethnal Green in the East End of London. The Divisional boundary changes were reported in 1933. The order shows the most senior officer Inspector 105743 Alexander Robertson as earning 129s per week at that time whilst the most junior constable 120488 Leslie Welham as earning 74s per week[61]. In 1937 a commemorative medal was struck to mark the coronation of King George VI, however traditionally all Metropolitan Police officers received a coronation medal to date however this precedent was to change and only limited numbers were produced two of which were awarded to Sergeant James Styles and Constable Albert Clare at Waltham Abbey Police station. Also in 1937 the 999 emergency telephone system was introduced which meant the change of the stations telegraphic code from "WY" to "JA"[62].

By 1939 there were 25 officers working at Waltham Abbey Police station serving a population of some 7000 people. The onset of trouble in the wake of the Munich crisis saw the return to duty of many retired officers as War reserve, a precaution in the event of war. Special constables were also recruited as war reserve officers and supplied with special badges of office[63]. Up until the war the Metropolitan Police had been responsible for security at the Gunpowder factory which had been taken over by the War Department Police[64]. In January 1940 a huge explosion rocked the little town of Waltham Abbey. This was due to the levels of unskilled operators who had been recruited to work at the factory. Another major explosion took place three months later. This occurred in the mixing house killing five people and injuring fifteen more. This explosion was said, to have been heard as far away as Brighton, and caused severe damage to the centre of Waltham Abbey – even damaging the Police Station [65].

Noddy bikes or Velocettes were introduced to Waltham Abbey from late 1959 and remained until the 1970`s[66].

In 1960 Constable Robert Kents efforts to improve the garden at the station won him the first ever police station garden competition something which the station won a further 3 times. Later that year as part of an experiment the station was shut for night duty to visitors although a cabinet was installed in the front of the station for enquirers to contact Walthamstow Police station by telephone. Boundary changes in April 1965 ceded Chingford E4 to Waltham Holy Cross Urban District Council and under the authority of Waltham Abbey Police sub division.

Manpower was shown as one Inspector, five sergeants, thirty-five constables and 2 officers from the Criminal Intelligence Department[67].

In January 1984 a new police lamp was fitted to the wall outside the station to replace the lamp that had been removed in 1954. A site for a new police station had been ear marked in Highbridge Street, previously the Superintendents residence of the Royal Gun Powder factory had been purchased by the Metropolitan Police in 1975 for £75,000. Vandalism and theft had made the building dangerous and refusals to demolish the existing building were given by the Local Authority. Demolition was finally agreed in January 1977. Part of the site was sold off causing problems of access to the remaining site. The station at Sun Street is still in use today with Local Authority plans shelved for High Street development reasons for relocation to a new site has receded[68].

In 1987 Waltham Abbey was re-located onto the new Epping Forest Sub Division together with Loughton and Chigwell as part of Barkingside Division. The aim was to re-locate borders so that the division fell within the boundaries of the new local authority[69].

Furthermore on 1st April 2000 Waltham Abbey Police station was handed over to the Essex Police as part of a rationalisation process in making Borough and Council boundaries co-terminus with police borders. It is hoped that this will ensure a more Borough based policing system.

[1] Epping Forest District Council publicity material
[2] Metropolitan Police Surveyors records (undated)
[3] Metropolitan Police Orders dated 11th January 1864
[4] Ibid
[5] Ibid
[6] Ibid
[7] Metropolitan Police Orders dated December 1864
[8] Metropolitan Police General Orders 1873
[9] John Back Archive (1975) The Metropolitan Police Museum, Charlton
[10] Metropolitan Police Orders dated 9th August 1875
[11] Report on the conditions of the Metropolitan Police Stations. 1881
[12] Metropolitan Police Surveyors records (undated)
[13] Metropolitan Police Orders dated February 1900
[14] Kelly's directory of Essex 1898
[15] Kirchners Almanac 1907
[16] Metropolitan Police Property records 1924
[17] Metropolitan Police Property records 1912
[18] Metropolitan Police Property records 1924
[19] Metropolitan Police Orders dated 30th December 1975
[20] Ibid
[21] The Job 20th November 1970
[22] Ibid
[23] Elliott, B. (1993) A History of the Police Stations of 'J' Division 1886 – 1986

[24] Metropolitan Police Orders dated 1st May 1972
[25] Metropolitan Police Surveyors records (undated)
[26] ibid
[27] Metropolitan Police Orders dated 11th January 1864
[28] Metropolitan Police Orders dated 22nd July 1886
[29] Kelly's Directory of Essex 1898
[30] Metropolitan Police Property records 1924
[31] John Back Archive (1975) The Metropolitan Police Museum, Charlton
[32] Metropolitan Police Property Records 1872
[33] John Back Archive (1975) The Metropolitan Police Museum, Charlton
[34] Ibid
[35] Elliott, B. (1991) History of Loughton and Chigwell Police. Chigwell and Waltham Abbey History Society.
[36] The Police Review and Parade Gossip January 9th 1931
[37] Elliott, B. (1991) History of Loughton and Chigwell Police. Chigwell and Waltham Abbey History Society.
[38] Ibid.
[39] The Police and Constabulary Almanac 1957
[40] John Back Archive (1975) The Metropolitan Police Museum, Charlton
[41] Ibid
[42] Elliott, B. (1987) The Abbey
[43] Ibid
[44] Ibid
[45] Ibid
[46] Metropolitan Police Orders dated 10th January 1876
[47] Elliott, B. (1987) The Abbey
[48] Elliott, B. (1987) The Abbey
[49] Metropolitan Police Commissioners Annual Report 1869
[50] Metropolitan Police General Orders 1873
[51] Metropolitan Police Commissioners Annual Report 1869
[52] Metropolitan Police Commissioners Annual Report 1874
[53] Elliott, B. (1987) The Abbey
[54] Elliott, B. (1993) A History of the Police Stations of 'J' Division 1886 – 1986
[55] London's Armed Police (1986) Gould, R and Waldren, M- Arms and Armour Press, London
[56] Elliott, B. (1987) The Abbey
[57] Ibid
[58] Ibid
[59] Ibid
[60] Ibid
[61] Metropolitan Police Orders dated 27th July 1933.
[62] Elliott, B. (1987) The Abbey
[63] Ibid
[64] Ingleton, R. (1994) The Gentlemen at War. Policing Britain 1939 – 45. Cranborne, Maidstone, Kent.
[65] Ibid.
[66] Elliott, B. (1987) The Abbey
[67] Metropolitan Police Orders dated April 1965
[68] Elliott, B. (1987) The Abbey
[69] Ibid

Chapter Six

The London Borough of Hackney

There had always been a proud tradition of policing in the Borough even before the introduction of the "new police" in 1830. Old Hackney Town had had an efficient system of Parochial police which consisted of horse patrols and Parish constables who took their duties seriously. The Lighting and Watch Trustees of the Parish who had a responsibility for ensuring the Parish constables performed efficiently also ensured that gas lamps were adequately maintained. The Trustees, who had been responsible for the police since 1763, took pride in reporting the fact that in 1828, night time robberies had been completely eradicated from the borough[1].

A team of four Inspectors assisted by 26 constables of the evening patrol and 30 constables of the night patrol kept order. Additionally eight Parish constables were responsible for inns, shops and the serving of warrants. This force was so efficient that Hackney was one of only two petitioners who voted against the new Police Bill, when it was proposed [2]. Prior to the formation of the uniformed police, the charge made to Hackney ratepayers, to pay for constables and watchmen, was £3,380 in the last year of operation. When the new Metropolitan Police rate was announced the rate fell to £3,164 [3]. This was a substantial saving and was probably made to appease the parishioners.

By the 1830's Hackney was fast developing into a fashionable residential area for the professional and clerical classes. Hackney's population doubled between 1841 and 1861 to 81,000, however by 1881 it had risen again to 163,000[4]. By the 1880's development in Hackney had reached Seven Sisters Road, and some parts of the borough around Hackney Fields, Hackney Wick and along the flooded stretches of the River Lea were attracting the lower classes [5].

The largest parish was Hackney, which contained the hamlets of Homerton, Clapton, Dalston and Shacklewell. In this time the only development was the construction of Stoke Newington High Street, which was the main route to Cambridge. Road development also took place in the quiet hamlets of Clapton, Homerton, Hackney and Dalston [6]. Between these hamlets were fields, market gardens, pastures, watercress beds and brick fields [7]. This meant that the small hamlets were growing into small towns connected by main roads that ran through farmland.

With the coming of the railway in 1850, the area became very populated and the rich businessmen moved out of their large houses and moved further into the countryside.

The London Borough of Hackney was formed in 1965, and stretches from Bishopsgate in the south to Stamford Hill in the north, and from the River Lea in the east to Islington in the west. Hackney Borough contains the former boroughs of Shoreditch, Stoke Newington and Hackney. Each of these names has their origins in Anglo-Saxon times[8]. Now the area is vibrant and culturally diverse, with people from Africa, the West Indies, Turkey, Cyprus and the Indian subcontinent[9]. At the southern end of Hackney Borough the boundary borders the City of London which is policed by a separate police force [10].

The policing of Hackney Borough has, since the late 1960's, often attracted significant attention from academics, politicians and the press, as a result of insensitive policing. Attention has also focused on the care and custody of prisoners especially those drawn from minority ethnic groups. Hackney and Stoke Newington share an important place in police history where from the very early days police sought to become accepted by the population[11].

The police stations on the Division consist of City Road, Dalston, Hackney, Hoxton, Old Street and Stoke Newington.

City Road Police Station

In 1899 a sizeable portion of land became available in Shepherdess Walk on the old site of the Grecian Theatre[12], which was bounded by Nile Street and City Road. The site was purchased from the Bishopsgate Foundation[13].

The Metropolitan Police

City Road Police Station
4-6, Shepherdess Walk, London N1
1901 - 1961

Surveyor considered the site suitable for a police station, and negotiations commenced for the freehold purchase of the land from the owners.

The sale was finally agreed in November 1899 when ownership of the land passed to the Metropolitan Police. The site was made ready and a new station was soon built.

Police Orders of 1901 reported that;

"....the new Police Station in City Road is to be taken into occupation by Police, and business commenced therein by 19th instant. The lodging assessment will be:- 1 Married Inspector at 5s 6d per week, 30 single constables at 1s per week. The Police Station at Old Street will be vacated on the 13th instant."[14]

City Road
Station Lamp

A substantial station was built at the front of the plot in Shepherdess Walk, not in City Road itself, although the station took the name of the nearest main road. At the rear of the station a section house was built in Shepherdess Place N1, which accommodated 30 single officers.

Problems occurred with access to the section house, because the Metropolitan Police did not own the right of way, so access was negotiated with the Governors of the Bishopsgate Foundation for the annual sum of 10s. The police also leased two buildings, one at 16, Nile Street to Mr. David Hazel for the annual sum of £155 rent for 84 years, and the other at 7, Shepherdess Place for the rent of £170 to the Turret Button company (later the Autostop Safety Razor Company and then Gillette Industries).

Arrangements for the transfer and re-negotiation in respect of the lease with Autostop Razor in December 1926 for the sum of £18,500. The leasehold title passed to Gillette Industries Ltd in June 1931. The address of the station was recorded at the time as being 4 and 6, Shepherdess Walk, Shoreditch.

A larger and better equipped section house was built at City Road in 1911 with space for 102 single officers. One single Inspector and a married officer and his family also resided there[15]. The Section house was re-named Shepherdess Walk Section House[16]. In line with policy to provide affordable housing for its officers the police purchased a freehold site in 1920. Located in Ironmonger Row, between Lever Street and Old Street, the site included some 30 sets of married quarters which were called Warren Buildings[17].

In 1931 "G" or Finsbury Division consisted of three police stations. These were Kings Cross, Old Street and City Road. The division had a strength of 672 police officers[18]. Kings Cross Road Police Station was the Divisional Headquarters, although on a revision of boundaries City Road Police Station took over when the former station was transferred to "E" or Holborn Division during the 1930s.

Records show that a police ambulance shelter for the hand ambulance was located at Rosemary Branch Bridge over the Regents Canal in the London Borough of Shoreditch[19]. Experience had shown that having the ambulance site near the canal helped to save people's lives if they fell into the water, because they could be taken quickly to hospital.

In 1932/3 extensive reconstruction work began at the old station. This included the permanent closing of the old section house and conversion of the ground floor into stables. Reconstruction work on the old station began immediately. It was completed by August 1933, and designed to accommodate the increased administrative functions on becoming the Divisional Headquarters. The stables were taken into service at the same time. In the interim the Borough of Shoreditch had purchased the land in Shepherdess Place from the Governors of the Bishopsgate Foundation, which included the right of access. The land was turned over for general public use, and the annual cost of 10 shillings for access to the rear of the station lapsed.

In 1939 it was decided to rebuild the Police Station on the original site. Police business carried on using temporary accommodation in the Section House. The station reopened for business in August 1940[20]. However on 15th October 1940 a large bomb which caused half of the building to be demolished hit the Shepherdess Walk Section House[21].

The start of World War II meant plans for a new station were shelved, and the old station was re-occupied in August 1940. It took another twenty years before a new station was finally built on the site.

In 1960 the old station was demolished[22] to make way for a new modern police station, which was also to include sufficient space for the Divisional Headquarters and their staff. A new station was built at City Road, on the same site and whose call sign was Golf Delta (GD). It was taken into service in January 1961[23].

The boundary changes of 1965, due to the Local Authority revisions showed City Road as the "G" Divisional Headquarters and sub-Divisional station, with Old Street (GS) having sectional status. Old Street station was closed in 1973 [24] when the court took over responsibility for the building.

In 1968 there was further restructuring which replaced the existing 23 Divisions and their sub divisions, and divided them between 8 Districts, each sub-divided into 8 Divisions. This left City Road Police Station on 'G' Division, still with the status of Divisional Headquarters[25]. In 1986 Sir Kenneth Newman, the Metropolitan Police Commissioner,

City Road Police Station
4 -6, Shepherdess Walk, London N1
1961 – present day

restructured the police by creating 8 Areas rather than 4 Districts, and removing Commanders from having direct responsibility for a Division. This meant that a Commander had Operational responsibility for a number of Divisions within the Area. Divisions became the basic unit for policing[26]. City Road Police Station lost its Divisional HQ status, and this was transferred to a station of 2 Area based at Chigwell Police Station.

In 1990 27 year old Constable Lawrence Brown was shot dead in Pownall Road. A tribute to his devotion and courage is marked in stone at the place where he fell, a gesture instigated by the film producer Michael Winner[27].

In 1995 the Service went through another restructuring exercise which reduced the Areas to 5 from 8, and this meant that Leman Street ceased as Area HQ, when City Road Police Station became attached to 3 Area (North East) Headquarters located at Edmonton Police Station. A further change occurred in 1998 when the 5 Areas were reduced to 3, although this meant no change for City Road, which by now had changed its name to Shoreditch Division[28]. The Borough of Hackney Police Headquarters is open to the public 24 hours a day 7 days a week[29].

Dalston Police Station

Records show that the parish watchouse was originally situated on the east side of Stoke Newington High Street, just south of Shacklewell Lane and opposite Robinson's Place[30]. This building backed onto Alvington Crescent next to Kingsland Independent Chapel. The watch house remained there until 1880's although it was no longer used for police purposes. It was probably given up in 1845 when the new Dalston Police Station was occupied.

Dalston Police
Station Lamp

The new station at Dalston was taken into service at 6, Caroline Terrace, Dalston in 1845 and it was rented from Samuel Culff of Median House, Median Road, Clapton[31] for £40 per annum. It consisted of a brick and slate building which included a station and section house and was located on "N" or Islington Division.

Dalston Police Station (circa 1906)
41, Dalston Lane, Dalston, E.9.
1871-1914

The picture shown at left is Dalston Police Station circa 1906. This is situated to the right of the larger building, which had also been leased and was used as a section house[32]. A constable is standing in the foyer of the police station.

In 1882 Constable George Cole was patrolling in Dalston when he disturbed a man attempting to illegally enter a dwelling. In the process of being arrested the burglar produced a gun and shot the officer in the head. Constable Cole died of his injuries[33].

The new station at Dalston was taken into service in September 1871[34]. In 1873 records show that this was designated as a station with a sergeant in charge[35]. New leases had been negotiated in 1870 for three years at £40 rent per year, and again in 1880 for 31 years[36] at £100 rent per annum. The building was very small and appears not to have had any cells, although there was a charge room. There were first and second floors which housed a married sergeant and his family, and six single constables. During this time the address of the station changed to 39 instead of 41 Dalston Lane.

Instructions were given that a new sub-division should be formed. Dalston Police Station was created with a strength of 2 Inspectors, 8 sergeants and 91 constables[37]. Both Kingsland and Hackney Sub-divisions were split to become Stoke Newington, Dalston and Hackney.

Dalston Police Station
39 and 41, Dalston Lane, E9
1914 - 1991

Records also show that two Inspectors were shown stationed at Dalston

Police Station at this time. They were Inspector Overy and Inspector Jenkins[38].

The Home Office approved the acceptance of tenders in order to build a new police station[39] in Dalston Lane. In 1883 the land was leased for a period of 99 years. The cost of the building was borne by the Metropolitan Police and not the owner of the land. Restrictions were placed on the Receiver of the Police, which determined the relative disruption to the neighbouring area and conditions under which the station could operate. For example he was required to paint the outside of the building every three years and the inside every seventh year. He was also required to build a police station within eighteen months of the removal of any building on the site, and to clear the ground within three months of the 14th September 1883. Any premises built must be either a police station or a private dwelling house. The station was built in 1884 on the original site and cost £5004[40] Once built, the large house next door was incorporated into the premises.

In August 1886 the Metropolitan Police formed 'J' Division or Bethnal Green Division, which meant a revision of boundaries with Dalston transferring from 'N' to 'J' Division[41].

The Metropolitan Police Surveyors decided in the early 1900's that a new station should be built on the existing site together with a much larger section house. To build the section house required the purchase of further land adjoining the old station. Accordingly, in 1910 the Receiver acquired a site in Ramsgate Street, at the rear of the station, on which a section

house for 50 single men was built. This opened in June 1913[42]. Land in the area was scarce so it was decided to demolish the old Station and rebuild it on the same site at the cost of £4,283. The new station opened in June 1914, and included two sets of married quarters[43].

The freehold for the station was purchased from the owners in 1923. In 1933 there was another re-organisation with Dalston transferring from 'N' to 'G' Division. This meant that Dalston was a sectional station of Islington Sub-Division, with City Road becoming the Headquarters station for 'G' Division.

Police Constable 737 'N'
Richardson

The picture on previous page shows a young police officer - Constable 117297/737 'N' Joseph Ernest Richardson. A Dalston photographer took it in 1928. Constable Richardson probably lived at the back of Dalston Police Station in the section house. It is also likely that he was attached to the station. Born in 1904, in Sheffield, and on leaving school became a turner. He joined the army from 7th August 1923 until 9th January 1928 and later joined the Metropolitan Police on 13th February 1928[44].

In the 1930's London saw the rise of Fascism. The British Fascist Movement led by Sir Oswald Moseley had a significant effect on the Metropolitan and City of London Police particularly in the policing of political demonstrations. Moseley was allowed to be protected by his own uniformed, black shirted and booted guards. Demonstrations were commonplace in the East End often leading to violence and disorder[45]. High numbers of police officers regularly paraded for duty to keep the peace and provide a 'thin blue line' between the demonstrators and their attackers. The picture below shows police officers parading at the back of Dalston Police Station ready to travel to police the latest Black Shirt march in the East End. You will notice that the officers are smartly dressed, and have been instructed to parade with rolled capes which can be seen. The police cape provided protection in the event of rain or inclement weather.

Several serials of police at Dalston Police Station in 1936 preparing to travel to police the Black Shirt demonstrations.

The 1965 local government re-organisation caused police boundaries to be revised, and with effect from April 1965 Dalston became a sectional station of Hackney Sub-Division. In 1962 a substantial section of land was purchased by the police at 175-189 Balls Pond Road and 202, Southgate Road, N1, on which to build a new modern purpose built station[46]. However a combination of events, together with a lack of finance, caused the police to shelve any ideas of building the station. The site was used for parking vehicles and as a vehicle test site[47]. This has now been sold to a developer who has built luxury flats on the site.

By the late 1970`s Dalston became a sectional station to Stoke Newington Sub-division, and it ceased to take prisoners. All prisoners were dealt with at Stoke Newington Police Station. The station was closed in 1991, when all police work was transferred to Stoke Newington Police Station, where a far larger, more modern station had been built.

By 2002 the situation had changed and Dalston was provided with an operational police station. It was called Dalston Cross as it is located at the rear of The Kingsland Shopping Centre in Kingsland High Street, London E8 2LX. It is open every other Monday, then Tuesday – Saturday from 10.30am to 5.30pm, although these times might vary occasionally[48].

Hackney Police Station

There have been a number of stations in the Borough of Hackney over the years. The original station house was situated in Jerusalem Square, Hackney Church Street, Hackney Old Town[49]. The property in this area was demolished in 1906, and the road passing through it was named Vallette Street[50].

Site of the original Hackney Police Station in Jerusalem Square in 1831

The local census records of 1831 show that twelve police officers were resident there, together, with Robert Messinger - the blacksmith. A number of police officers lived nearby in Jerusalem Passage. One such officer was Constable William Gillett who joined the Metropolitan Police as the 999th applicant on 21st September

1829, and was posted to 'N' Division on 30th June 1830[51]. Promotion was fast in those times as he resigned as a Superintendent in July 1835[52]. Also living nearby was Constable William Underwood who was the 2694th applicant to be accepted on the 4th February 1830, He also became a Superintendent in May 1831, resigning in April 1838[53]. The officer in charge of Hackney Police Station in 1844 was shown as Inspector William D. Cooper who was promoted in 1837[54]. Hackney was shown as a station on 'N' or Islington Division.

In 1845 a substantial brick and slate building was occupied at 1, Churchyard[55], Hackney Old Town, on the south side of St. John's Church Yard at the corner of what is now Mare Street[56]. This was the second Hackney Police station and was designated with an Inspector in charge. The address of the building then was shown as Hackney Church Street however it was later re-named and numbered as 422 Mare Street[57]. Records also indicate that the Receiver leased the land in 1848 from J. R. D. Lesson of Hackney for 99 years, and paid £20 per year ground rent for the property. The Receiver paid all the taxes and insured the building with the Law Office for £1700. In 1852, at a cost of £1,832. (including the leasehold for £850) substantial alterations were made to the existing

Hackney Police Station
1, ChurchYard (later Mare Street),
Hackney Old Town
1845 - 1904

building. These included a brick dressed surround to the front of the ground floor, showing prominent arched windows either side of an arched front entrance. It had twenty rooms with four cells, a four stall stable and five coal vaults. Some further alterations to the building were made in 1851. In 1891 the freehold lease was purchased[58].

The station was large and had a basement, ground, first and second floors. In the basement there was space for locker rooms, a scullery, a cooking room, a clothes room and four coal sheds. On the ground floor were a charge room, four cells, an Inspectors Office, a store, a drying room, a library, a parade room and three water closets. Outside there was a four stall stable for horses. The first and second floors provided cramped accommodation for 36 constables. There was also space for one married Inspector who rented three rooms. The freehold to these premises was obtained on 11th December 1891.

Records show that in 1864 Hackney Police Station had a total strength of two Inspectors, eight Sergeants, 83 Constables and two Horse Patrols[59]. The Police Authorities ensured that duties were split into two shifts – day and night duty. Each day there were four sergeants and sixteen constables for day duty and four sergeants and sixty seven constables for night duty[60]. There were fourteen walking beats by day and sixty three night duty beats[61]. The importance of Hackney Old Town Station was recognised early, and instructions were given that an Inspector should supervise the station[62].

Later, in 1878, during restructuring a new sub division was formed. The Kingsland and Hackney division was split into three sub-divisions namely, Stoke Newington, Hackney and Dalston. Hackney sub-division's strength increased by a further three sergeants and 24 constables.

Thirty six constables were shown as residing in the section house at the station in 1881[63]. Senior officers were reassured to know that such large numbers of officers could be drawn on at a moment's notice to deal with any incident. In fact since early times off duty men were informed that they could be called on at all times and that they should prepare themselves to be available at the shortest notice[64]. Records show that an Inspector resided next to the police station in Mare Street. William J. Sherlock his wife and four children resided at 9, Churchyard, Hackney. He appears to have been the Inspector in charge of Mare Street Police Station in 1881. In 1883 he was promoted and transferred, becoming the Divisional Superintendent for 'G' or Finsbury Division based at Kings Cross Road (Bagnigge Wells) Police Station[65]. He stayed there until April

1885, when he was sixty years of age and then he was transferred back to 'N' Division[66].

Hackney sub-division was transferred to 'J' Division in 1886 as part of further re-organisation[67].

On occasions in the past there have been glimpses of heroism and bravery. There has always been a long tradition of this in the British Police and the police officers of Hackney were no exception. In July 1897, Constable Green (J) of Hackney Police Station, whilst on duty near Lea Bridge, was awarded the Royal Humane Society's Bronze Medal for rescuing a woman from the River Lea.

In 1890, in conjunction with a number of further boundary changes, there was the creation of another sub-division called Victoria Park[68]. These changes saw a revision of the supervisory staff of Inspectors; to three Inspectors and two Sub-Inspectors. New police quarters for single men came into operation in April 1891 at the police station[69].

Instructions were also published merging Hackney and Victoria Park sub-divisions into one called Hackney sub-division. Victoria Park station still remained open[70].

One of the last Inspectors in charge of the old Hackney station was Sub Divisional Inspector Austin Askew. Born at Banbury in 1850 he joined the Metropolitan Police in 1871 having left the Life Guards as Corporal of Horse. He quickly rose through the ranks to take command of this very important station. He retired in September 1902. At this time the sub Division could boast having the most number of recipients of the Royal Humane Society's medals for saving life from fire and drowning. At his retirement celebration held at Hackney

Sub Divisional Inspector Austin Askew of Hackney Police Station 1902

Town Hall the Mayor Dr. F. Montague Miller JP presented Inspector Askew with a gold watch and a cheque for £100 in recognition for his integrity, courtesy and efficiency[71].

In early 1900 arrangements were made for a new police station to be built to replace the old Victorian station. Accordingly a large piece of land was acquired in March 1900 at 38, St. John's Church Road, Hackney – on the opposite side of the entrance (north side) to St. Johns Church yard. Originally an agreement had been reached with another buyer for the sale of the land, however on the 27th April 1900 the owner, Miss Emily Isabella Clark, changed her mind and decided to sell the freehold to the Metropolitan Police instead. The cost of the purchase was not disclosed. Additionally, negotiations commenced with the owners for the acquisition of both 2 and 4, Lower Clapton Road. This was a site used by the Young Women's Christian Association. They demanded compensation as sitting tenants, and received an out of court settlement of £1,400 in 1902.

The Freehold of 34, St. Johns Church Road and the leasehold of No. 36 were acquired on 9th May 1900.

Hackney Police Station
2, Lower Clapton Road, London, E5
1904 – present day

A considerable amount of money was spent obtaining a good site with plenty of space as re-organisation stipulated that Hackney was to become the Headquarters Station for `J` Division. The new station was built at the junction with Lower Clapton Road and St. John's Church Road, and was completed for occupation in October 1904[72]. The call sign for the station was Hotel Kilo (HK)[73].

The station provided accommodation for one married inspector and 30 unmarried constables. Records also showed that its designation was altered from that of a sub-division of Bethnal Green to Hackney or "J" Division. Hackney Police Station was not only where normal police work was carried out, but it was also became the Divisional Headquarters where the Divisional Superintendent would be stationed[74].

Henry Lovatt Ltd. built the station, at a cost of £13,216. It was well fitted out and of considerable size. It was shown to have accommodation which included an Inspector's office, a charge room, two single cells for females, one large association cell or drunk tank, four single cells for males, a parade room and an ambulance shed. On the 1st floor the Divisional Headquarters staff were located. After the station was completed a stable block was built by Messrs. Jathey Brothers, at a cost of £1,075, and was occupied in 1905. The stable block consisted of a four stall stable, horsebox and situated on the floor above were married quarters occupied by a married sergeant and his family. New gates to the station were purchased because the old ones had been badly damaged during the building work. The Receiver purchased 34 and 36 St. Johns Church Road and occupied by two married Inspectors.

The old Hackney Police Station located on the other side of the churchyard remained in service as a section house to accommodate single and married police officers until at least 1910[75]. The senior officer in charge of the station was a Sub Divisional Inspector

A number of stations were designated to receive deceased persons and at the back of the old station was a mortuary which still remains in use today. When the old station site was sold, the police retained the mortuary and Coroners office.

Superintendent Fitt "J" Division
1918

In 1912 the Division was headed by Superintendent William E. Fitt who supervised the stations of 'J' until November 1916 when he was transferred to southwest London.

The accompanying photograph shows Superintendent Fitt in ceremonial uniform with the sword of office. William E. Fitt joined the Metropolitan Police on 18th April 1887. His warrant number was 72486. The picture postcard clearly shows that he was awarded four medals. These were the 1887 Silver Jubilee medal, the 1897 Jubilee bar, 1901 Coronation medal and the silver 1911 Coronation medals. This meant that he was present at all these celebrations. The records also show that Superintendent Fitt retired on pension after 32 years of exemplary service[76]. It is likely that the card was produced privately by friends or relatives of the superintendent as a mark of respect, after a long and distinguished career. He was a very powerful man responsible for a sizeable section of East London that included the sub divisions of Hackney, Bethnal Green, Barkingside, Claybury, Dalston, Leyton, Leytonstone, Loughton, Victoria Park and Wanstead. The total number of officers of the Division was also considerable, and by 1925 there were some 956 officers and men[77].

In May 1913 Metropolitan Police Surveyors purchased land and a building at 146, Mare Street near Hackney Triangle from the London County Council for £2,100. The purpose for this acquisition was to build a section house to accommodate single and married police officers. This was called Mare Street Section House and was later re-named Ede House[78] after the Home Secretary J. Chuter Ede.

The picture below shows the entire strength of Hackney Special Constabulary just after they were formed in August 1914. It was taken at

Hackney Special Constabulary circa 1914

the end of the station yard.

Hackney was 'J' Division headquarters and was shown as being on No.4 District. The division covered an area of 39 square miles and spread as far north as Loughton and Epping Forest, as far west as Stoke Newington or 'N' Division, and as far east as 'H' Division or Whitechapel. Enrolment for the Special Constabulary commenced on 14th August 1914, and attestations before Magistrates were taking place in court houses and police stations for some duration. Each Special Constable (SC) was required to take an oath, and was presented with a warrant card which showed his number and the signature of the magistrate[79].

There were eleven Special Constabulary stations on 'J' Division, apart from Hackney. These were Barkingside, Bethnal Green, Buckhurst Hill, Claybury, Dalston, Hackney, Leytonstone, Leyton, Loughton, Wanstead and Woodford [80].

One of the major influences on the organisation and running of 'J' Division Special Constabulary was Mr. H. Jerburgh-Bonsey who is shown in the picture on previous page, second row from the front, kneeling at the extreme left, and wearing a bowler hat. He was a sergeant during 1914, but rose up the ranks to become a Commander and was later awarded the MBE. The picture below shows Commander Jerburgh-Bonsey in 1919 displaying his MBE.

Commander H. Jerburgh-Bonsey M.B.E.
(Captain)

A number of members of the special constabulary were honoured in 1919 for valuable service to the Force.

In 1918 Detective Sergeant Charles Richard Lee, who had been pensioned from the Force, died of injuries he had received in the execution of his duty whilst attempting to arrest suspects in the street. Stationed at Hackney, Lee was retired and removed to an asylum (hospital) for treatment. However, he never recovered from the injuries which, hastened his death[81].

After the First World War discontent rose within the Police Force over pay and conditions of service. Times were harsh, pay was low and discipline was strict. Many police officers voiced their concerns by demonstrating in Central London. The Police Protest Demonstrations, as they were called, took place on 4th May 1919, and officers from Hackney were involved. In the centre of the demonstration standing above and holding the banner is a contingent of Hackney Police officers in Hyde Park. In those days police officers could be paid up union members and Hackney 'J' Branch were members of the National Union of Police and Prison Officers. The

A contingent of Hackney Police voice their discontent in Hyde Park in 1919

demonstration was peaceful and was well attended. Estimates of the numbers suggest that some 20,000 took part in the day of protest.

Further boundary changes between `J` Hackney and `K` Bow took place in 1926. In 1933 a complete re-organisation north of the River Thames saw Hackney or `J` Division boundaries revised again, with the removal of both Dalston and Bethnal Green from `J` Division. The creation of new Local Authority Boundaries in 1965 saw a further revision of Police boundaries to ensure they were coterminous, with Hackney being transferred to `G` Division (GH) and becoming a sub-division of Dalston Police Station which had Sectional station status.

The picture below shows Constable 761 102972 'J' Division Cope

Constable 761 'J' Cope

attached to Hackney Police Station. He joined the Metropolitan Police in 1918, at the end of the World War 1. This photograph was taken in 1938 probably to show his two medals, the 1919 British War Medal and the 1937 Coronation Medal. It appears that Constable Cope took part in the 1937 Coronation, and was rewarded with the medal in recognition of this fact. Constable Cope retired in 1938 and received pension of £153. 13s. 5d [82].

Mare Street Section House (Ede House) which was situated on Hackney Division just south of Wells Street, was hit by a High Explosive bomb on 25th September 1940. The section house, which was in the course of construction, received considerable damage, but only one person was injured[83]. It was intended that a new police station would be incorporated into the section house building to enable the old station in Lower Clapton Road to be replaced. Additional land had been purchased in Tudor Road in 1936 to enlarge the site[84]. These plans were put back by Hitler's bombing, and the section house was rebuilt, after the war finished. Rebuilding work commenced in 1950[85] although it was decided, probably for economic reasons, not to include the station in the revised plans. When finished Ede House provided accommodation for 135 single officers[86]. Also in 1940 a bomb during an air raid in Hackney killed War Reserve Constable Thomas Robert Pickett[87].

Surveyors for the police then decided that Hackney Police Station should be completely rebuilt on its present site at Lower Clapton Road and create a police station in Mare Street. This re-building did not happen, for some time but substantial alterations to the front office, custody room and reserve room eventually took place in 1978. Ede House now belongs to a Housing Association for homeless single men.

Police officers at Hackney have had to deal with many difficult situations sometimes resulting in tragic circumstances for the officer. For example, in 1952 Sergeant Frederick Henry Keil was injured in the course, of his duty, whilst stationed at Hackney. The injuries were to the officer's head, and it was found that he had developed a brain tumour. Sadly within a short time the officer died from the effects of his injury and the tumour[88].

In 1957 another tragic incident occurred. This time it involved a very senior officer from Hackney Police Station. Superintendent Cornelius Carson collapsed and died going to the assistance of a child who had become trapped in a fire at the police station[89]. He is remembered, like so many others, in the Roll of Honour the citation reads;

'In the afternoon of 26th October 1957, a fire broke out in the basement of Hackney Police Station. Superintendent Carson assisted to extinguish the flames and was exposed to much smoke and fumes. On returning upstairs, he heard a child scream in the second floor married quarters above and he hurried immediately up the fire escape to her assistance. Before Superintendent Carson could take the child down, however, he collapsed on the fire escape, and he died on the way to the hospital'[90].

Other officers who gave their lives during WW2 are mentioned in the Roll of Honour including Police Constable Ernest George Emsley who joined the RAF as a Sergeant Air Gunner. He was killed on active service off Grimsby on 24th April 1944[91].

Any person who had worked at the station would have been aware that there was a ghost. By the mid 1970's when the co-author was a sergeant there, the ghost was said to frequent the top floor administration section, and the rumours circulated that a superintendent had shot himself in his office with a service pistol drawn from the station safe. In fact, the Divisional Detective Superintendent committed suicide in this way in February 1960, leaving a wife and daughter[92]. It is assumed that the ghost is attributed to him.

In 1970, whilst on his way to work at Hackney Police Station, Sergeant David James Hems was killed whilst riding his motor cycle[93].

The station is still in use today and in 2001 the Borough Commander was Chief Superintendent Peter Robbins QPM[94].

Hoxton (Kingsland Road) Police Station

In 1830, a year after the start of the Metropolitan Police, 'G' or Finsbury Division, was formed and consisted of two stations located at Clerkenwell and Old Street[95]. The eastern limit of the Metropolitan Police was 'N' or Islington Division, which extended up to the banks of the River Lea at Hackney Marshes. Records show that the original Hoxton Police station was located in Robert Street, (now called Fanshaw Street N1), in the Parish of St. Leonards, Shoreditch[96].

Each station kept a Lamp Report book which was a thick hardbound register into which reports of unlit, broken or defective gas lamps would be written. The parish authorities were responsible for lighting, repairing and maintaining these lamps, and whilst the officers were patrolling their beats they would note the various unlit lamps. The Lamp Report book for Hoxton Police Station began on 13th January 1836, when Constable 56 'G' Edwin Ayland reported a defective lamp. The workmen responsible for the repairs would visit the station, inspect the Lamp Reports and repair the lamps. Between the 13th January and 16th February 1837 there were 22 reports[97]. In those days police officers were responsible for lighting the lamps, calling the time and watching for fires, because they had taken on many of the functions of the old Parish Watch officers[98]. The Officer in charge of the station in 1844 was Inspector John Tonge [99].

Records also show that in 1844 another station existed on 'G' Division. It was situated at 36, Featherstone Street, between Bunhill Row and City Road south of Old Street[100]. This station was an original police watchhouse situated in the Parish of St. Lukes. Henry Jervis and Joseph Shackell were both Inspectors stationed at Featherstone Street[101]. The other station on 'G' Division at the time was Bagnigge Wells, or Kings Cross Road as we know it today[102]. The station was closed in favour of the new station which was built at 55, Old Street, not far from the old watch house[103].

The strength of 'G' was 346 officers including a reserve force, which was kept to deal with any civil disturbances[104].

The Receiver of the Metropolitan Police sought permission from the Home Office to purchase land to the east of the existing Old Street station, in Kingsland Road, Hoxton in 1860. A parcel of freehold land became available at the bottom end of Kingsland Road at a cost of £3,600. The Receiver bought this land and a police station was erected on the site. The station was attached to 'N' Division and an Inspector was in charge. This was a large division covering some sixty square miles[105].

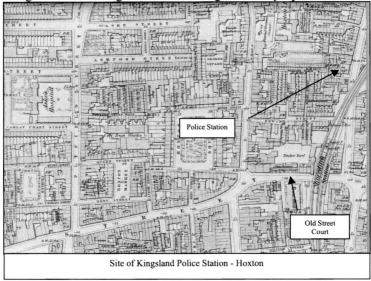

Site of Kingsland Police Station - Hoxton

Hoxton Police Station contained a Charge room, an Inspectors Office, a parade room, six cells, two water closets and a two stall stable which were all located on the ground floor. There were also nine rooms located in the basement, including four coal sheds. The Commissioner's made a conscious decision to help with lodgings in an effort to maintain standards of health and hygiene. They duly built accommodation for both single and married police officers. Hoxton had two further floors above the ground floor, which housed one married Inspector and his family, and 37 single constables in very cramped conditions. The cost of building the station was £3609, and it became operational in 1861[106]. In effect this made the Commissioners of Police one of the largest landlords in London, as it did seem sensible that if a station was built then accommodation should be included. Furthermore the cost of accommodation could be deducted from pay, therefore defraying the daily costs of policing. There were two inspectors, eight sergeants and 84 constables attached to the station in 1864[107]. A reserve constable was posted each day for 12 hours to man the Robert Street watch house[108].

In 1872 Hoxton Police Station was directly connected to Scotland Yard by the telegraphic network. The station call sign was HX (hotel x-ray). In 1873 Hoxton was designated a station with an Inspector in charge[109]. On 1st July 1880 Hoxton Police Station was transferred to 'G' Division from 'N' Division. The address was shown as 17, Kingsland Road, Shoreditch[110].

In 1881 records show that Inspector Henry Parker was in charge of the station. He resided there with his wife Caroline and their only son. Also on the premises were thirty two single constables who lived in the section house[111]. Also living at the section house, and stationed at Kingsland Road Police Station, was Constable David Garner, aged 22 years from Whittlesea in Cambridgeshire. He found fame when he was involved in an armed incident and was shot at by a burglar William Wheatley early on the morning of the 18th July 1884. Wheatley and another man had attempted to break into a furrier at 46, New North Road - when they were discovered by police. The suspects could not be found straight away. However after several hours Wheatley was discovered by Constable Garner who went to arrest him. It was at his point that Wheatley produced a gun and fired three shots. Two of the shots missed but the third went straight through the constable's thigh. Garner, bleeding heavily, managed to hold on to Wheatley, and help was close at hand as Inspector Maynard and a local fireman came to his assistance.

A short distance away Constable 462 'G' William Snell tackled the other burglar whom also pulled a gun and shot the officer in the stomach. Snell was not thought to be seriously injured at the time, and managed to capture the suspect with the aid of passers-by. While they were being taken to Kingsland Road Police Station a crowd of about twenty people demanded that the officers give up the prisoners to them. The police resisted the demand, but not before several of the crowd had successfully managed to land a number of blows on the prisoners [112]. Constable Snell was later taken to hospital where the bullet was removed, but he was unwell for sometime. In 1894 Snell, by then a sergeant, was pensioned off and died soon afterwards, the shooting having hastened his death[113].

In 1888 records also show that certain designated stations were used as 'places appointed for receiving persons drowned or dead, and at which drags and other apparatus was kept'. Hoxton Police Station was a designated mortuary[114].

Much has been written about the police culture, and comradeship of police officers and their families. Their social life very often focused on the police station which usually had its own social club, athletics section, police band, billiards table, library and recreation room. To engender team spirit and comradeship, competitions were organised amongst the work force. For example The 'G' Divisional Billiards championship took place at Hoxton Police station on 15th July 1898. There were 48 entrants. This handicapped event was won by Police Sergeant Wiltshire who received a monetary prize. Such events helped to re-enforce the culture and notion of the police family [115].

In 1898 there was another fatal injury to a police officer. Police Constable James Baldwin was on patrol in Hoxton when he attempted to arrest a drunken man. During this process the drunk produced a knife and a violent struggle ensued. Constable Baldwin was stabbed and died from his injuries[116]. In 1908 the station was no longer required for police purposes and was leased to Mr. Davis for 21 years at an annual rental of £110 for the first seven years and £120 for the remainder[117]. The old station at Hoxton was vacated once City Road Police Station was opened. It was considered unsuitable for further use as a police station and the interest was purchased by the London County Council[118].

Old Street Police Station

There have been three police stations located in the Old Street area. Two were located in Old Street itself, whilst another was situated at 58, Featherstone Street, Finsbury in the Parish of St. Lukes, just north of Bunhill Fields.

This station was originally named Old Street, St. Lukes Police Station and was not only an operational police station but also a section house. It was leased in December 1833 for 21 years from Mr. William Mouls of Newington Butts, Lambeth. The building consisted of an old brick and tile house with a small yard, four cells, two water closets and a dirt hole. This station was vacated in 1852 in favour of Old Street Police Station situated not far away, where all police business was transferred.

The Metropolitan Police Surveyor was interested in some land, which became available for lease in 1850 in Old Street, St. Lukes on the north side of the road just east of Goswell Road in Finsbury. The site was considered suitable for the building of a police station. The arrangements for the lease ensured that the owners Messrs., H. B. Ray and R.J. Olives (Trustees) would receive £52. 10s per year ground rent, and that the lease would run for 70 years expiring in 1920. The Receiver was required to pay the rates and deal with any repairs, although no insurance was required to be paid by the police.

In 1852 a station was built at 55, Old Street, Finsbury, in the parish of St. Lukes, on the north side opposite the junction with Norway Street some distance from Goswell Road. This was the first station to be located in Old Street. The station cost a total of £2,400 and included a basement, ground, first and second floors. On the 1st and 2nd floors 32 constables resided in cubicles under cramped conditions. A married sergeant occupied 2 rooms on the first floor. This meant that the Receiver made a profit out of renting premises at the police station. The net income of £92. 6s 0d meant a profit of just under £40 for the Receiver of the police. In 1862 the station was shown as located on "G" or Finsbury Division. In 1873 "G" Division comprised of only two stations, Old Street and Kings Cross Road, both were stations with Inspectors in charge covering an

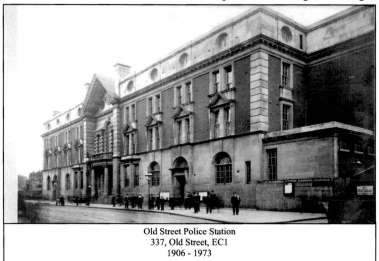

Old Street Police Station
337, Old Street, EC1
1906 - 1973

area of just over one square mile[119].

In 1881 a married constable, Charles Denlow from Yarmouth in Norfolk, and his wife and son lived at the station with 31 single constables[120]. Records also show that the freehold title to the site was obtained in December 1900. These included buildings located at 335, 337 and 339, Old Street, together with 1a, 2a, 4,6,8, and 10, Hoxton Street. Furthermore, land on which the Weavers and Porters Alms houses stood was also purchased. A builders yard and adjacent almshouses cost the Receiver £16,500 and £11,300 to buy. Old Street Police station was built at a cost of £11,120, whilst the court building was more expensive to construct at £16,680. The builders were Grover and Son, Wilton Works, New North Road, Islington. The whole Old Street Court complex including the land purchases and buildings, had cost the Receiver £82,209 which was a large amount of money in those days. The facilities at the station and courthouse were considerable. For example there was one large association cell which could take anything up to twenty prisoners, whilst there were five single cells for men and four cells for women. There was also an Inspectors' room and a charge room on the ground floor. Records indicate that an Inspector (married) paid rent of 9/6 per week for a medium sized room on the 1st floor whilst thirty seven single constables paid 1/- per week rent.

The new police station and court were completed in January 1906[121]. In 1924 a telephone line was installed as part of air raid precautions in the event of war, and the station remained open until 1973[122]. It was considered no longer useful as a police station, and the building was taken over by the court[123].

Stoke Newington (Kingsland) Police Station

Stoke Newington was included in the Metropolitan Police District in 1829/30. The Vestry[124] declared satisfaction with the new police declaring that;

> "...they were better than the watch, although Cut Throat Lane, Lordship Lane, Woodberry Down and the north parts of Green Lanes were insufficiently policed[125].

The numbers of watchmen were gradually reduced from twenty-five in 1828 to twelve in 1834. In 1829 their swords were removed and by 1830 their pistols were declared unnecessary[126]. Prior to the building of a police station at Stoke Newington there was an old Watch House and Parish

Pound situated in Stoke Newington Church Street just behind the Red Lion Public House[127]. The station was the Divisional Headquarters and housed the officer in charge of the division.

In 1845 Superintendent James Johnston was responsible for the vast "N" or Islington Division. At the Divisional Headquarters a Divisional Clerk Sergeant assisted the Superintendent. The Superintendent was issued with a horse and accordingly a Constable was appointed as groom to ensure that the senior officer could supervise the division[128]. The officer in charge at Kingsland Station was Inspector Daniel Howie[129]. Apart from Kingsland Johnston supervised, Church Street Hackney, Robert Street, Hoxton, Islington Green, Islington (the previous Divisional Headquarters), Green Street, Enfield Highway, Lordship Road, Stoke Newington, Hornsey, Tottenham near Scotland Green, Edmonton near the Old Church, Enfield, Cheshunt, Walthamstow and Waltham Abbey[130]. In 1850 Johnston was still the officer in charge, and five Inspectors namely Joseph Mellish, George Thatcher, Edward Tarlton, John Pascoe and James Coward assisted him[131].

Stoke Newington Police Station
33, High Street, Stoke Newington, N16
1866 - 1990

Land was purchased at 33, High Street, Stoke Newington in 1864 on which to build a police station[132]. The new station was built at a cost of £5678, and was opened in 1866[133]. The station was built next to one public house called 'The Victoria' and seven doors away from another[134]. This new station was called Kingsland Police Station, and must not be confused with Kingsland Road Station, which was built in 1866 and situated at the junction with Robert Street, Hoxton.

The station had four floors containing 36 rooms. Originally the Superintendent of the Division occupied a room on the ground floor, but later he moved to the first floor together with his headquarters staff.

In 1873 records show that communication by wire had been established with Scotland Yard and that the operational management of the station was in the hands of an Inspector[135]. In 1881 there were forty single constables residing at the station together with the Station Inspector George Dudman, and his large family. Inspector Dudman was born in Lugershall in Wiltshire in 1832 and lived at the station with his wife, Louisa and their seven children. They had five daughters and two sons. Records show that there were four prisoners in the cells (two males and two females) at the time details was taken[136].

In 1888 the officer in charge of the Division was Superintendent William J. Sherlock, (who had been an Inspector at Hackney in 1881) and his headquarters were re-located to Stoke Newington Police Station. He had a divisional strength of 37 Inspectors, 66 Sergeants and 536 Constables[137]. A new coach house and stables were erected in February 1889 with eight stalls. The station had a charge room, six cells and in the yard was a parade shed. At one stage there were 41 single constables living in cramped conditions on the second floor of the station. In 1886, however, there were only 38 constables living there.

Stations were often the focus of sporting and social activities and also for annual events for the officers and their families who lived or worked at or near police stations. For example, on 16th August 1894 the second 'N' Division Annual sports day took place at the "To te tum" sports ground in Stamford Hill. It well attended although it rained all day. The sports day was attended by Superintendent McFadden accompanied by his wife, who supplied and later presented all the prizes. Also in attendance were Chief Inspector Parsons and Sub-Divisional Inspector Nean. Additionally the "N" Division Police band played tunes all afternoon[138].

Often sad or tragic events happened and the death of any police officer even of natural causes was of great distress to those who knew the officer. It was reported that a single officer Constable Patrick McGowan aged 44 years, was found dead in his section house bed at Stoke Newington on 6th January 1898. The cause of death was later established as consumption (pulmonary tuberculosis), which was a fairly common cause of death at the turn of the 20th century. Constable McGowan a popular member of the station, received a traditional police funeral. His remains were buried at Abney Park cemetery on 9th January 1898, and 200 members of the force attended in uniform to pay their last respects. The police station band played the Funeral March en route to the cemetery. His supervisory officers, Inspectors Ford and Osgood and Sub-Divisional Inspector Thorpe headed the procession[139].

Other events took place at the station involving recreation or sport. The photograph below shows Stoke Newington football team in 1914. The police have always enjoyed playing competitive sports, encouraged by senior officers who were not only keen to maintain an active and fit police force, but also to re-enforce the bond of comradeship and loyalty, often referred to today as meaning the 'Police Culture'. Playing sport for the Force, rather than the station, ensured time off from active duty. Many individual clubs were being run in the Metropolitan Police including football, boxing, rugby, cricket etc; however

Stoke Newington Police 2nd football team in 1914 with trainers

"It was not until after the war that the Home Office made a grant which enabled the different games clubs throughout the Metropolitan Police to join together into one general association and shoulder the burden of the upkeep of the ground that was bought"[140].

At the rear of Stoke Newington Police Station a new section house for 72 officers was built. It opened in December 1913[141]. Some additional married quarters were also built and these opened in August 1914[142].

In 1929 the Metropolitan Police celebrated their centenary with a parade in Hyde Park, an inspection by HRH The Prince of Wales, and a march past Buckingham Palace. Superintendent Pearce, (the Divisional Superintendent) stationed at Stoke Newington, was in attendance together with the No. 3 District Chief Constable Major M. Tomlin O.B.E. With them were eight Inspectors, 32 Sergeants and 240 constables taken from the whole division. Over 12,000 officers, members of the Criminal Intelligence Department and Special Constabulary attended the ceremony[143].

In the 1970's and 80's policing in Stoke Newington and Dalston became the scene of black confrontation with the police. Black people regarded the police with suspicion and distrust, and when highly publicised cases of deaths in police custody occurred, then the closed and secretive nature of policing provoked public annoyance and anger. Over a period of time Stoke Newington Police Station and its police officers developed a reputation of apparent racist conduct. Asseti Sims died in 1970, Michael Fereira in 1978, Colin Roach in 1983, Tunay Hassan (at Dalston) in 1987 and Trevor Monerville in 1987[144]. In the meantime in 1981 there were major riots and unrest in the Stoke Newington area, near JJ's Café in Sandringham Road[145].

Under re-organisations in 1999 basic command units (BCU) were introduced and placed in the charge of a Chief Superintendent[146]. Stoke Newington became a station of Two Area.

A new station in Stoke Newington was planned as far back as 1938, and efforts to start rebuilding on the old site also came to nothing in 1976[147]. A new £5.25 million police station, in a very modern style, was built on the old site whilst normal operational policing continued at the same time.

Stoke Newington Police Station
33, High Street, Stoke Newington, N16 8DS
1990 - Present

The station opened in April 1990[148]. The three storey building took two and half years to complete, using 134,000 bricks, 560 tons of steel and 4000 cubic metres of concrete. New police stations are designed in such a way as to be modern and pleasing to the eye, but also resilient enough to withstand a siege or a bomb blast. In fact entrances can be sealed off and there are certain protections and shutters behind windows which afford better security[149].

In 1995 a Service restructuring exercise reduced the Areas to five from eight. This meant that Leman Street ceased to be Area HQ, when Stoke Newington Police Station became attached to 3 Area (North East) Headquarters located at Edmonton Police Station. The further changes in 1998 meant no change for Stoke Newington Police Station[150].

In 2002 the station is shown as being open to the public 24 hours a day 7 days a week[151].

Victoria Park Police Station

The freehold site within the Parish of St. John, Hackney and situated at 184, Wick Road, Hackney Wick, Homerton, E9 was purchased by the Metropolitan Police in 1888 from the executors of the late Mr. J. Fenton for a freehold price of £850.Plans were made to build a station on the site and these were passed in 1889. Victoria Park Police Station was built at a cost of £3739, and was completed for occupation in September 1890. On this site a station house was built together with a section house to accommodate ten single officers.

The station was built with a charge room, Inspector's Office, waiting lobby, parade room and four cells on the ground floor. In the yard at the rear was a two stall stable together with a loft for the storage of hay and feed. Also in the yard was a hand ambulance shed, which housed the wooden hand cart on which drunken or ill people would be conveyed to a Police Station or doctor. There were two further floors to the station with the first floor housing single constables quarters and the second floor in the roof having a day room and library.

Victoria Park Police Station
184, Wick Road, Homerton, London, E9
1890 - 1936

There were extensive refurbishments made in 1912 which cost the sum of £1326[152].

Her Majesty owns much of this area in Hackney and the Crown Estate administers the land on her behalf. This not only includes Victoria Park but also many of the properties surrounding it. The Crown Estates lease out land and properties to tenants and ensure their general maintenance and upkeep.

Police Sergeant taken near Victoria Park 1870

During the Victorian Era it became a custom for people to take walks, push prams or take the children to play in the local parks. On a Sunday for example, people would congregate at the bandstand and listen to bands playing.

The picture at left was taken between 1864 and 1870, and shows an off duty Sergeant of 'H' division. He was probably attached to Church Street Police Station located at the bottom end of Bethnal Green Road. Sergeants were accommodated as close as possible to the stations where they were attached. Often accommodation was found for them or they organised rented housing nearby[153]. He is dressed in the new style of uniform which replaced the swallow tailcoat and top hat introduced in 1829.

This blue serge uniform had an eight button tunic, and a cox comb helmet which displayed the number of the officer in the centre of the helmet plate. At the southern edge of Victoria Park lies the boundary between Hackney and Bethnal Green Police sub-divisions. This boundary ran through the centre of the Regents Canal. Regularly people fell or jumped into the canal.

On 8th July 1898 at 5am Constable George Lees, stationed at nearby Victoria Park Police Station, was on patrol in London Fields, when he saw a man by the name of George Johnson from Clapton jump into the canal from the Cat and Mutton Bridge. The constable ran to the bridge discarding his bulls eye lamp, and helmet, and according to witnesses, jumped into the canal to rescue the man. In those days it was a criminal offence to try to commit suicide, and this was the intent of Johnson who was desperate, unemployed, and starving. A fearful struggle took place and the men disappeared twice under the water. The constable eventually got the man to the bank. A witness had heard Johnson say he would drown the constable if he did not let go.

Johnson was charged and appeared at North London Magistrates Court where, after hearing the evidence, the magistrate recorded that a commendation should be awarded to Constable Lees and that his superiors should hear of his brave conduct. Johnson's plight was made worse because having failed to commit suicide then prison was the likely punishment[154].

During duty one evening in 1900 Constable George Stephen Funnell and other officers came across a fire raging out of control in a public house. He quickly found out that there were three women trapped in the premises and went to their aid. It was in the process of rescuing them that he was severely injured. Once the women had been rescued he was taken to hospital where he died from his injuries[155].

In 1924 Victoria Park Police Station was shown as a station on "J" Division, where it was a sectional station to Hackney Sub-Division.

In January 1936 the station strength was shown as one Inspector 109701 White, one Station Sergeant 108279 Hitchcock, three sergeants and 6 constables. In August 1936 Victoria Park Police Station was shut and all the staff were transferred to Hackney Police Station[156]. In 1937 the building and land were sold to The Hackney Wick Agency and Garages of 10, Riseholme Street, Hackney Wick for £1850[157].

---

[1]. The Victorian County of Middlesex (1995) p112
[2] F.H.W. Shepherd, London 1808 – 70: The Inferno Men (1971), p35; 10 Geo. IV, c.44
[3] Ascoli, D. (1979) The Queens Peace. Hamish Hamilton, London
[4] Hunter, M (1981) The Victorian Villas of Hackney. (in The Hackney Society).
[5] Inwood, Stephen (1998) A History of London p584
[6] Ibid, p583
[7] Ibid p583
[8] The Municipal Year Book 2000 and Public Services Directory Vol 2. Newman Books 1999
[9] http://www.hackney.gov.uk/history/data/potted.htm dated 07.02.00
[10] The London Borough of Hackney Material
[11] Ibid
[12] John Back Archive (1975) The Metropolitan Police Museum, Charlton.
[13] Ibid.
[14] Metropolitan Police Orders 17th August 1901
[15] Metropolitan Police Orders 2nd December 1911
[16] Metropolitan Police Orders 17th August 1912
[17] Metropolitan Police Surveyors Records 1924
[18] Bacons Atlas 1926
[19] Metropolitan Police Surveyors Records 1924
[20] Metropolitan Police Orders 16th August 1940
[21] John Back Archives (1975) also The Metropolitan Police at War (1947) HMSO.

[22] Ibid
[23] Metropolitan Police Orders 27th January 1961
[24] Metropolitan Police Orders 6th July 1973
[25] Fido, M. and Skinner, K. (1999) The Encyclopedia of New Scotland Yard, Virgin Press. P78
[26] Ibid p 71
[27] B. Brown. (1996) 'Policing old Hackney', in Peeler magazine Friends of the Metropolitan Police Museum
[28] Op cit p 71
[29] http://www.met.police.uk/contact/phone.htm dated 12.03.02
[30] Stanfords London Suburbs February 1862 – Margate, Kent
[31] Metropolitan Police Surveyors Records
[32] John Back Archive (1975) Metropolitan Police Museum, Charlton.
[33] http://www.policememorial.org.uk/Forces/Metropolitan/metroll.htm dated 12.03.02
[34] Metropolitan Police Orders dated 7th September 1871
[35] Metropolitan Police General Orders 1873
[36] John Back Archive (1975) Metropolitan Police Museum, Charlton.
[37] Metropolitan Police Police Orders dated 3rd March 1878
[38] John Back Archive (1975) Metropolitan Police Museum, Charlton
[39] Ibid.
[40] Metropolitan Police Surveyors records (undated)
[41] Metropolitan Police Orders 22nd July 1886
[42] Metropolitan Police Orders 28th June 1913
[43] Metropolitan Police Orders 27th June 1914
[44] Metropolitan Police Service Records
[45] Fido, M. and Skinner, K. (1999) The Encyclopedia of New Scotland Yard, Virgin Press.
[46] John Back Archive (1975) Metropolitan Police Museum, Charlton.
[47] Ibid.
[48] http://www.met.police.uk/contact/phone.htm dated 12.03.02
[49] Census Records 1831
[50] Bacons Atlas of London and Suburbs 1926 by G. W. Bacon of London
[51] Metropolitan Police Recruiting ledgers for the first 3000 Metropolitan police officers
[52] Metropolitan Police Orders 17th July 1835
[53] Metropolitan Police Recruiting ledgers for the first 3000 Metropolitan Police officers
[54] The Police and Constabulary List 1844. Parker, Furnivall and Parker, London.
[55] The Police Station address at a later date changed from 1 Churchyard to Hackney Church Street.
[56] Bacons Atlas 1888
[57] Metropolitan Police General Orders 1873
[58] John Back Archive (1975) Metropolitan Police Museum, Charlton.
[59] Metropolitan Police Orders 11th January 1864
[60] Ibid
[61] ibid
[62] Police and Constabulary Almanac 1864
[63] Census records 1881
[64] Metropolitan Police General Instructions 1829 and 1871
[65] Census records 1881
[66] John Back Archive (1975) Metropolitan Police Museum, Charlton.
[67] Metropolitan Police Orders dated 3rd April 1878
[68] Metropolitan Police Order s dated 30th August 1890
[69] Police Review July 1897
[70] Metropolitan Police Orders 19th November 1894
[71] The Police Review and Parade Gossip dated 20th February 1903
[72] Metropolitan Police Orders 10th October 1904
[73] Metropolitan Police General Orders 1893
[74] Metropolitan Police Surveyors Records
[75] John Back Archive (1975) Metropolitan Police Museum, Charlton.
[76] Metropolitan Police Service Records
[77] Bacons Atlas 1926 published by G. W. Bacon Fetter Lane EC4
[78] Metropolitan Police Surveyors Estate Register (undated)
[79] Reay, Col. W. T. (1920) The Specials. Billing and Son, Guildford, Surrey.

[80] Ibid p 61
[81] http://www.policememorial.org.uk/Forces/Metropolitan/metroll.htm dated 12.03.02
[82] Metropolitan Police Service Records
[83] Howgrave-Graham, H. M. (1947) The Metropolitan Police at War. HMSO
[84] Metropolitan Police Surveyors Estate Register (undated)
[85] John Back Archive (1975) Metropolitan Police Museum, Charlton.
[86] Metropolitan Police Surveyors Estate Register (undated)
[87] http://www.policememorial.org.uk/Forces/Metropolitan/metroll.htm dated 12.03.02
[88] ibid
[89] ibid
[90] Metropolitan Police Roll of Honour dated 29th November 1957.
[91] Metropolitan Police Orders dated 12th May 1944
[92] Metropolitan Police Death in Service Register 1960
[93] http://www.policememorial.org.uk/Forces/Metropolitan/metroll.htm dated 12.03.02
[94] Police and Constabulary Almanac 2001
[95] John Back Archive (1975) The Metropolitan Police Museum, Charlton
[96] B. Brown. (1996) 'Policing old Hackney', in Peeler magazine Friends of the Metropolitan Police Museum
[97] Metropolitan Police Lamp Reports 1837 – Hoxton Police. Guildhall Library
[98] http://65.107.211.206/victorian/history/police.html dated 12.03.02
[99] The Police and Constabulary List 1844 p3
[100] Ibid
[101] ibid
[102] ibid
[103] See Old Street Police Station
[104] Metropolitan Police Orders 12th January 1864
[105] Metropolitan Police General Orders 1873
[106] John Back Archive (1975) The Metropolitan Police Museum, Charlton.
[107] Metropolitan Police Orders dated 11th January 1864
[108] Ibid
[109] Metropolitan Police General Orders 1873
[110] Metropolitan Police Orders 1st July 1880
[111] Census records 1881
[112] Gould, R. Waldron, M. (1986) London's Armed Police. Arms and Armour Press.
[113] http://www.policememorial.org.uk/Forces/Metropolitan/metroll.htm dated 12.03.02
[114] Dickens Dictionary of London, 1888. Old House Books, Moretonhampstead, Devon pp132-3
[115] Police Review July 1898
[116] http://www.policememorial.org.uk/Forces/Metropolitan/metroll.htm dated 12.03.02
[117] Metropolitan Police Surveyors Records 1924
[118] Ibid
[119] Metropolitan Police General Orders 1873
[120] Census records 1881
[121] Metropolitan Police Orders 6th January 1906
[122] Metropolitan Police Orders 6th July 1973
[123] John Back Archive (1975) Metropolitan Police Museum, Charlton.
[124] The Church Vestry often concerned themselves with the relative safety of their parishioners and expressed their opinions to the Watch Committee when necessary. Sometimes members of the Vestry were also representatives of the Watch Committee.
[125] The Victorian County of Middlesex (1995) p 201
[126] Ibid 201
[127] John Back Archive (1975) Metropolitan Police Museum, Charlton.
[128] Metropolitan Police Orders 11th January 1864
[129] The Police and Constabulary List 1844 p3
[130] Ibid
[131] Kelly's Directory 1850
[132] Metropolitan Police Orders 21st December 1866
[133] Metropolitan Police Orders 21st December 1866 and The Jack Back Archive(1975) Metropolitan Police Museum, Charlton.
[134] Ordnance Survey Map (Stoke Newington) 1868

[135] Metropolitan Police General orders 1873
[136] Census records 1881
[137] Dickens Dictionary of London, 1888. Old House Books, Moretonhampstead, Devon pp132-3
[138] Police Review August 1894
[139] Police Review January 1898
[140] Tomlin, M. (1936) The Police and the Public. p45
[141] Metropolitan Police Orders 20th December 1913
[142] Metropolitan Police Orders 3rd August 1914
[143] The Metropolitan Police Centenary Programme 1929
[144] Keith, M (1993) Race, Riots and Policing. UCL Press, London.
[145] Ibid p37
[146] Fido, M. and Skinner, K. (1999) The Encyclopedia of New Scotland Yard, Virgin Press.
[147] John Back Archive (1975) Metropolitan Police Museum, Charlton.
[148] The Job 13th April 1990
[149] Fleming, R. and Miller, H. (1994) Scotland Yard. Penguin Books, Harmondsworth.
[150] Fido, M. and Skinner, K. (1999) The Encyclopedia of New Scotland Yard, Virgin Press.
[151] http://www.met.police.uk/contact/phone.htm dated 12.03.02
[152] John Back Archive (1975) Metropolitan Police Museum, Charlton.
[153] Metropolitan Police General Orders 1829 and 1871
[154] Police Review July 1898
[155] http://www.policememorial.org.uk/Forces/Metropolitan/metroll.htm dated 12.03.02
[156] Metropolitan Police Orders 8th January 1936
[157] Metropolitan Police Surveyors Records (undated)

Chapter Seven

The London Borough of Haringey

The Borough is situated in the centre of north London and is surrounded by six other boroughs. To the south lie Camden, Islington and Hackney; to the east lies Waltham Forest and to the west lies Barnet. Enfield runs along the northern boundary.

The London Borough of Haringey was formed in 1965 when the former councils of Tottenham, Wood Green and Hornsey merged. Tottenham and Hornsey were ancient parishes dating from before the Norman Conquest. Wood Green, which was formally part of Tottenham, emerged as a separate district in 1885.The place name Haringey is the medieval form of the modern name Hornsey[1].

The stations within the Borough of Haringey include Highgate, Hornsey, Muswell Hill, St. Ann's Road, Tottenham and Wood Green.

Highgate Police Station

In 1849 a new police station was erected at 51, South Grove, Highgate for the sum of £1,475[2]. A letter dated 14th February 1850 from the Home Office to the Receiver authorised him to re-surrender the old watch house to the Parish authorities at Highgate, as it was no longer required for Police Service as the new station was now open[3].

In 1863 an Inspector and his horse were transferred from Kentish Town Police Station to Highgate[4]. The station was shown located on 'S' Division and was referred to as Highgate Grove. It misleadingly showed that a sergeant supervised the station; however instructions corrected this error and confirmed that there were two Inspectors in charge[5]. This was further confirmed with records showing that the station strength was two Inspectors, six sergeants and 41 constables[6]. There were twelve beats to patrol split between two shifts, night duty and day duty. Two sergeants and 14 constables covered the day duty whilst two sergeants and 27 constables were responsible for the night duty shift[7]. The two remaining sergeants covered the station duties between them. The station had cells, took charges and paraded police officers for duty[8]. Supervision was carried out between the two Inspectors who took it in turns to ride the horse to ensure the men were carrying out their duties. The horse was stabled at the rear of the station[9].

By 1878 there were problems in the cell area of the station. Sewer gas was apparently leaking into the building. It is not certain whether this

prompted the Home Office to look for a new site on which to build another police station.

There was a high turnover of police officers, who joined the force only to find the arduous conditions of service and the meagre pay caused them to resign.

The picture of Constable 96 'Y' Division is that of William Rivers Sawyer (warrant number 57621) aged 19 years, a gardener from Crayford in Kent. Sawyer stayed in the police for only a short while. He joined the Metropolitan Police on 23rd January 1874 and resigned on 11th June 1877. Sawyer would

Constable 96 'Y William Rivers Sawyer

have left the police without any pension or other gratuity. Those who resigned before serving for 25 years left without a promise of financial support, even if any injuries received on duty precluded them from further employment. They usually presented their case to the

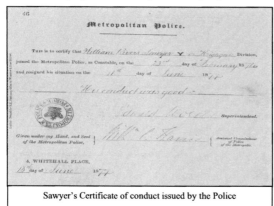

Sawyer's Certificate of conduct issued by the Police

Commissioners. It was at their discretion as to whether recommendations were made to the Home Secretary for the grant of a gratuity. The officer was awarded a certificate of conduct in lieu of any references, which would enable an ex-police officer to obtain further employment. Sawyer's certificate stated that his conduct was 'Good'. This was signed by Superintendent Edward Worells, the Divisional Superintendent. Sawyer returned to market gardening in Kent.

In 1886 the Divisional Headquarters for 'Y' Division was established as Kentish Town Police Station even though the name of the division was Highgate[10]. Facilities were introduced at Highgate Police Station in 1888 that allowed for the receiving dead bodies and bodies found in rivers, canals and waterways[11]. The 1891 census shows twelve constables being in residence at the station[12].

On 21st February 1894 the officers and men of Highgate and Upper Holloway Police stations met in the Archway Tavern for their annual dinner. The dinner was attended by the guest of honour Mr. Frank Beal, Clerk to the Justices at Highgate Court who listened to the vocal and instrumental music and then ended the evening with a speech and compliments to the Highgate Division[13].

Highgate Police Station
Archway Road, Highgate, London
1902 -1960

The August Bank Holiday of 1897 was celebrated with the laying of a foundation stone for the new police court by Mr. R.D.M. Littler, Q.C., at

Highgate. This was erected by the London County Council, near Highgate Police Station, at a cost of some £8000 and was designed by the Metropolitan Police Surveyor John Dixon Butler.

On 15th October 1897 reports showed that a divisional Inspector had met with an accident. On 9th October Sub-Divisional Inspector Mountifield (Y), of the Highgate and Upper Holloway Districts, met with a serious accident, the result of which would incapacitate him for duty for sometime. On returning from superintending the policing arrangements at an important football match at Caledonian Park, he crossed the Police Station yard at Upper Holloway, and, treading on some decayed leaves fell heavily to the ground. His right side struck some iron railings, and he had to be assisted into the Station. Dr. Rattray, the Divisional Police Surgeon, was called, and found that the Inspector was suffering from fractured ribs[14].

In 1898 the police paid £1300 for a new site in Archway Road, Highgate[15]. The new station opened in January 1902[16]. The building was modernised in 1936[17]. The station telegraph code signal was HI[18].

In the early 1930's station telegraphic codes were revised and issued to stations based on the Division and station name rather than the previous random format. Highgate changed to YH the code that it still has today.

Highgate Police Station
407 – 409, Archway Road, Highgate N6 1 NW
1960 until present day

In August 1944, during World War II, Highgate Police Station was seriously damaged by a V1 flying bomb. This was one of ten Metropolitan Police Stations that were badly damaged. The adjoining Court House was demolished and a set of married quarters had to be vacated. There were four people injured in the attack[19]. Until the station was fully repaired in January 1945[20] all business was transferred to Muswell Hill Police Station, Fortis Green, N.2[21].

In 1957 Highgate was a sub division of Hornsey under the supervision of Superintendent J.L Sims-Kirby[22].

A new police station at 407-409, Archway Road, Highgate, N6 1NW was erected on the same site and was opened in March 1960 at a cost of £49,088[23].

In 2001 the station was still in use, but charges were no longer taken there. Whilst having cell space available, prisoners were no longer detained at the station[24].

Hornsey Police Station

According to records there has been a police station in Hornsey since 1864 when the station was shown as part of "N" Division[25]. The station had a compliment of two sergeants and fifteen constables. There was also one mounted constable and his horse located at the station[26]. Further supervision was supplied from Tottenham where the Inspector resided. He was also in charge of Walthamstow and Tottenham. This was achieved on horseback, so supervisory officers in Victorian times had to be good horsemen[27]. Charges could be taken at Hornsey and there were cells for the detention of prisoners for court[28].

Hornsey Police Station Lamp

This 1890 photograph of Hornsey Police Station shows it situated at the bottom end of Crouch End Hill near the Broadway at the junction with Coleridge Road. It shows a substantial three-storey building with what appears to be accommodation on the third floor. In the distance is Christ Church. The station lamp situated outside the front of the station clearly shows a Victorian crown on the top. The current station lamp is shown above.

Hornsey Police Station,
Crouch End Hill, Crouch End, London, N8.
1883 – 1915
Photograph taken in about 1890

With the formation of the new "Y" Division in 1865 the interior divisions were shown as including Tottenham, Hornsey, Southgate, Enfield Town, Enfield Highway, Edmonton and Cheshunt. Inspector Webb was shown as the Acting Superintendent in charge of the division[29]. A rather strange but tragic incident occurred in 1867 when Constable John Kennedy collapsed and died from the effects of sun stroke whilst patrolling his beat in Hornsey[30].

In 1881 a suitable parcel of land became available in Tottenham Lane, about a mile away from the original station. It was on a 100-year lease from the owner the Revd. J. Jeakes, Rector of Hornsey[31]. Ground rent of £30 per year was payable by the Receiver who also had to insure the land and station with the Law Fire Office[32].

In 1883 a new station at Hornsey was completed at a cost of £5,852. The station was supervised by an Inspector. It had a charge room on the ground floor with two cells, a waiting room, Inspector's Office, a store, a day room, a mess room, a kitchen, a scullery, a clothes room, a drying room, a boot room and five water closets. On the first floor were a lavatory and a bathroom. Married quarters were also located on the first and second floors, and housed one married Inspector who occupied for five rooms and a pantry, whilst the married constable occupied four rooms and pantry. Inspector George Carr was shown as the officer in charge of the sub-division although he lived at Tottenham Police station[33]. Apart from Hornsey and Tottenham the Inspector was also responsible for Walthamstow. A horse was provided at Tottenham to enable the Inspector to perform his supervisory duties[34].

In 1886 there was a revision of police boundaries and Police Orders attributed "Y" or Kentish Town Division with Somers Town, Caledonian Road, Holloway, Highgate, Hornsey and Enfield. The stated strength of the division amounted to 49 inspectors, 67 sergeants and 768 constables. There were 22 horses also attached to the division. These figures were revised downwards after the boundary changes to 37 inspectors, 55 sergeants, 605 constables and 18 horses[35].

In 1889 the introduction of Wood Green Division meant boundary changes to Hornsey division.

Hornsey Police Station
94, Tottenham Lane, Hornsey
1915 - 1936

On 2nd October 1894 Police Sergeant Mortlock of Hornsey Police Station retired from the service after 26 years. A gathering of friends and relatives took place to commemorate the officers retirement usually at the station although they are also held in a hall or public house. Inspector King, in the absence of the Superintendent made the retirement speech and the presentation of a marble time piece to the officer[36].

This photograph is dated around 1906 and shows the ceremonial retirement photograph of three police officers from "Y" Division, they are in plain clothes in the centre - with their retirement presents. This photograph is un-identified yet this is exactly what would have happened to Sergeant Mortlock who would have been left with a similar photographic memento of his service with the Metropolitan Police.

A retirement picture for three police pensioners together with their comrades and gifts

The social club would arrange for presents to be given to the officers, which in this case is a carved mantle clock for the man in the centre and carved figures for the other two officers. The official photograph was followed by a retirement party, which would have been attended by family, friends, and members of the community and work colleagues.

On 4th June 1897 the Royal Society presented Protection of life from Fire Certificates and money grants to Constable 205 'Y' Ernest Newman and Constable 384 'Y' Patrick Connell who rescued four people from a fire in a grocer's shop in Hornsey[37]. The station telegraph signal was HE[38] and changed in the 1930's to YR.

Records show that in 1909 Hornsey sub-division was re-named Highgate sub-division under the supervision of Inspector Thomas who will transfer to Highgate Police Station[39].

In September 1912 the Receiver was able to purchase the freehold title to the land and station from the Rev`d Bernard Spinks of Hornsey. Records show that there was a police fixed point box located on land belonging to Messrs. Huggins and Co. Ltd. at Green Lanes Hornsey[40]. An ambulance shelter, containing the two wheeled hand ambulance was located in Hornsey Road on property belonging to Great Northern Railway Co. Ltd[41]. The address was shown as 94, Tottenham Lane, Hornsey[42].

In February 1916 a new station was built in Tottenham Lane together with a section house. The section house contained accommodation for twenty-two unmarried constables and one set of married quarters[43].

Gradually as the roads in the area improved, following the Great War, new methods of transport for police were tried. The introduction of pedal and motor cycles meant that large distances could be covered in a very

Hornsey Police Station
98, Tottenham Lane, Hornsey, N8 7EJ
1916 – present day

short time. The Metropolitan Police needed to move with the times. Areas like Hornsey were still policed on horseback; however instructions were soon given for the authorisation of cyclists. Permission was given for a certain number of police officers at each station to use their own cycles on duty, for which they were entitled to an allowance. The use of cycles was particularly encouraged especially for constables whose beats were some distance away from the station. At Hornsey, the authorised cyclists included Inspector William James Clarke. In 1922 Clarke was a station Inspector living and working at Hornsey Police Station. Before he joined the police service in 1904 he was a cycle mechanic[44]. This was particularly relevant under the circumstances. Cycle racks were usually supplied in the station yard.

In 1933 boundary revisions north of the River Thames made Hornsey a sub-divisional station with both Highgate and Muswell Hill being sectional stations. The station was re-constructed in 1936. The London Government Act of 1965 re-drew Local Authority boundaries causing the police to revise their own borders along the same lines.

The introduction of the police telephone boxes was extended to Hornsey sub-division on 1st April 1934. A number of police boxes were installed to allow for direct communication to adjoining stations and the divisional boundary. At the same time a police van especially equipped with first aid apparatus (including a stretcher) was also issued to Hornsey sub division[45]. The telegraphic call sign for Hornsey was Yankee Romeo (YR) and the address shown as 98, (not 94) Tottenham Lane, N8 7EJ[46].

In 1999 Hornsey Police Station became part of a Borough based policing initiative under the supervision of a senior Superintendent referred to as a Borough Police Commander. The station was shown as having full charging facilities[47]. In 2002 Hornsey police division formed part of Haringey Borough Policing Area and the police station is open to the public 24 hours a day seven days a week.[48].

Muswell Hill Police Station

In 1899 the Metropolitan Police searched for a site for a new police station in the east Finchley area. The Surveyor reported that a suitable site had been found midway between Finchley and Muswell Hill railway stations, at Fortis Green. Authority was given by the Home Office for the purchase of this land which was situated at the junction with Fortis Green Road and Fortis Green Crescent in the parish of Hornsey, at a cost of £2,500. The sale was completed on 25th June 1900[49]. A further application for capital to build a new station was authorised by the Home Office on 7th March 1900 with a stipulation that the new station was to cost no more than £2,700[50].

Tenders were invited and the successful builder completed the new station for occupation in September 1904[51].

The records show that an annual rental of 1/- was paid to Messrs. Mann, Crossman and Paulin "in respect of light and air easement". Apart from the station, two sets of married quarters and section house accommodation were provided. There were quarters for the Inspector and his family together with room for ten single constables in the section house[52].

Muswell Hill Police Station
115, Fortis Green, Finchley, London N2 9HW
1904 – present day

The station has on occasions been known as Fortis Green Police Station. The above photograph was taken in 1907, and there is no visible police station lamp, as it was installed later.

A brief insight into the personal arrangements can be seen when inspecting the 'Y' Divisional Seniority Records. On arrival at the station from the Training School, the officer's details were entered into a variety of police ledgers. These were created to ensure that all officers were paid correctly and received appropriate courses and training. It was important to ensure that all constables were trained in first aid so that they could help save lives on the street. Station Inspector 88268 Axten became an authorised cyclist having arrived at the station on promotion at the end of October 1922. It had long been recognised that there were not enough Inspectors at Sub-Divisional stations and even the men began to recognise Station Sergeants[53]. Axten was responsible for inside duties, however on occasions he would leave the station on his cycle and supervise the sub-division. He had joined the police on 24th February 1902, giving up his job as a fitter. After training he was posted to a police station he was supplied with uniform and other items of equipment. This would have included a police whistle. Each whistle was numbered and the number, in this case 8162, recorded on his records. He had been promoted in August 1908 to sergeant and in December 1912 to Station Sergeant. In 1922 he was made up to Inspector[54]. The increased administrative obligations of Superintendents and Sub-Divisional Inspectors who ran stations meant that the rank of Inspector was to be split into classes. These were Chief Inspectors, 1st and 2nd Class Inspectors. Axten was a 2nd Class Inspector.

Prior to the revision of station signal codes, Muswell Hill Police Station had been shown as MU[55] however in the 1930's this was altered to YM.

During the early 1960`s economies required the station to be shut for the night shift from 10pm-6am commencing on Sunday 11th September 1960. Initially this closure was for an experimental six months and required outside duties to be performed by those on the night shift[56]. A telephone was installed in a container in the window of the station for use by members of the public and police officers as part of what was called the "Telephone box system". This telephone was connected to the sub-Divisional police station whilst telephone calls from the public were diverted by the GPO to Hornsey Police Station. Records also show that night closures for certain police stations were ordered although from 16th April 1968 Muswell Hill Police station was removed from the list and would cease to close at night[57].

Re-organisation in 1965 designated Muswell Hill (YM) as a sectional station to Hornsey (YR) Sub-Division within the newly formed Borough of Haringey.

In 1998 Muswell Hill was an operational station without designated charging facilities[58], but by 1999 it was no longer an operational station open to the public[59]. The station is still retained by the police, and is used for offices. It is also a place where police officers parade for duty[60].

St.Ann's Road Police Station

The growth of population in this area of Tottenham (previously called the waste of the Manor of Tottenham) caused police to consider building a new police station there. They searched for suitable land and found an available plot owned by Mr. R Bushfield. The Receiver negotiated to purchase the freehold title of the land in St.Ann's Road, Woodbury Down, and Tottenham for £1,088.

Once purchased the police surveyors designed a new large brick and tile police station on the land. It was an impressive two storey building and included a section house for twelve single constables. Just a year later in 1885 the new St Ann's Road Police Station was opened[61]. The cost of building the station had been £3,222[62].

St. Ann's Road Police Station,
289, St. Ann's Road, N15
1885 – Present day.

The building was designed with an Inspector's office, a charge room, a store, a waiting room, two cells, an association cell (often called the drunk tank as it could hold a number of drunken men), a kitchen, a scullery, a drying room, a boot room and a brushing room located on the ground floor. The first floor had a mess room, a food locker room, a clothes room and a day room. The second floor contained three large rooms for the single constables and also contained a bathroom and lavatory. In the loft a room was built to accommodate three constables. In the station yard was a parade shed, an ambulance shed, seven water closets, a urinal, two coal cellars and a coke cellar[63]. The land acquired enabled a large station yard to be laid to the side of the station. This would later be used as a District Traffic Garage.

There seemed to be a problem for the previous owner of the site Mr. Bushfield, because the building of the station prevented access or further development of other land owned by him. In 1886 the Metropolitan Police gave permission for a right of way to be given to the public for access to land in Hermitage Road. Additionally certain monies had to be paid by the police for the right of way over the land, which was jointly owned by the Tottenham Vestry and the Lord of the Manor. In the case of the Lord of the Manor this was done via the Trustees of the settled Estate of Sir William M. Curtis (Bart), the previous Lord of the Manor of Tottenham, and was not properly settled until 1888.

The address of the station was shown as 289, St. Ann's Road London N15[64]. In 1904 the Metropolitan Police paid Tottenham Urban District Council £197 which was a proportion of the cost to make up Hermitage

St. Ann's Road police pictured in the yard in 1912

Road. In June 1895 a telephone line was installed in the station and paid for by Tottenham Council at 5 shillings per annum[65].

Permission was granted for a fire engine kept on standby to be located in the yard of the station[66]. In 1907 the station was designated a sectional station of Wood Green[67].

In 1924 the single officers were moved out and extensive structural alterations converted the accommodation into two sets of married quarters, which were quickly occupied[68]. A district Traffic garage was built at St. Anns Road in 1936 beside the North Eastern Fever Hospital occupying a substantial site next door. A garage unit was built to house traffic police and their vehicles. It also became a workshop for repair and maintenance of police vehicles[69].

This photograph shown above was taken in the yard of St. Ann's Road Police Station and shows the station compliment with their medals. The picture above shows those on duty and who were present at the

Coronation of King George V. This occasion was marked by the award of a medal, which took time to prepare for presentation - officers received the award later. The picture appears to have been taken in 1912 when those who had performed duty at the coronation in 1911 received their medals. The names of those who took part were collected and presented to the Home Department in order that that the name, rank and division could be inscribed around the rim of the award.

King George V's Police Coronation medal was only struck in silver and had a red ribbon with three vertical blue lines. They were awarded to the City of London Police, Metropolitan Police, County and Borough Police, the police ambulance service, London Fire Brigade, Royal Irish Constabulary, Scottish Police, St. Johns Ambulance Brigade, St. Andrews Ambulance Corps and 109 were awarded to Park Keepers of the Royal Parks[70]. There were 19,783 medals awarded to the Metropolitan Police and 1400 to the City of London Police[71].

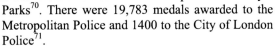
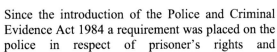

Coronation medal
1912

The call sign for St. Ann's Road was Sierra India (SI)[72], and this was changed in the 1930's to November Alpha when it was the sectional station to Stoke Newington[73]. Later it was changed again to Yankee Alpha (YA) when it was transferred to 'Y' Division.

Since the introduction of the Police and Criminal Evidence Act 1984 a requirement was placed on the police in respect of prisoner's rights and identification evidence. To this end in the early 1990's there were some structural alterations made to the station, mainly to the rear which included a purpose built Identification Suite (ID) which could deal with identification parades in a more effective and professional manner. The new ID suites serve the whole area.

In 1998 the station was still open to the public[74], but was shut a year later for operational purposes[75]. Records show that it is still in use in 2001 although charges are no longer taken there[76].

Tottenham Police Station

In January 1859 the Home Office authorised the purchase of a freehold site for £550 for a new police station in Tottenham. The station cost £1,966 to build and had four cells on the ground floor. On the first and second floors there was accommodation for twelve constables and one married inspector[77]. In 1864 the address of the station was shown as 'near Scotland Green, Tottenham and was a station on 'N' or Islington Division[78]. In 1864 the Commissioner gave approval for Acting Sergeant, Constable 337 'N' Bacon to be posted to Station Duties at Tottenham Police station[79]. Records also show that there was an Inspector in charge of the station, with four sergeants to assist him[80].

In 1873 Tottenham was a station under the supervision of an Inspector and shown as part of "Y" or Highgate Division[81].

Tottenham Police Station
Scotland Green, High Road, Tottenham
1864 - 1914

By 1881 Tottenham Police Station was shown with the address of High Road, Tottenham and had accommodation for one married Inspector, including family and 13 single constables[82]. However there were only eleven single constables in residence when the census was taken. The officer in charge of the station was Inspector George Carr who resided there with his wife and four children[83]. The records show that in 1893 the call sign for the station was Tango Mike (TM)[84].

In 1904 Constable Leonard Russell collapsed and died whilst arresting a man in Tottenham for drunkenness[85].

It is not often that events in other parts of Europe have repercussions in London, and especially not in Tottenham, but this was the case in 1909. In 1907 there was a failed attempt to blow up the President of France –

instead the bomber blew himself to pieces. His two companions (one of whom was his brother) fled France and found refuge in England. On 23rd January 1909 they decided to rob the Schnurmann Rubber Factory in Chestnut Road, Tottenham. This became known as the Tottenham outrage[86].

One conspirator had left the factory after finding the work too hard, but suggested they would be a soft target when the wages were delivered on a Saturday. The robbery was a farce except that a number of shots were fired and the thieves managed to escape with the money. The shots alerted two police officers at Tottenham Police Station – Constable 510 Newman and Constable 403 Tyler jumped into a passing car to give chase. The section house above the station also turned out to help even though they were off duty[87].

There was a hue and cry because a number of police officers and members of the public followed the robbers. Several times the robbers turned and on one occasion shot and killed a young lad, Ralph Joscelyn, who was running towards the car to evade being hit by the multitude of bullets. The two constables in the car attempted to head off the conspirators, but when confronted one took careful aim and shot Constable Tyler straight through the head. He died instantly. The chase lasted more than two hours, covered a distance of six miles and saw 400 rounds of ammunition fired by the conspirators. Perhaps 400 rounds was an exaggeration because this is a considerable amount of ammunition to carry let alone to fire. Whilst trying to scale a fence and being pursued by a multitude of police, one of the conspirators shot himself in the head. The conspirator was not killed outright, but stayed alive for an agonising three weeks before he died in hospital. The other made off and eventually took refuge in the bedroom of a nearby house where he shot himself when the room was stormed by police[88].

This hand drawn 'In Memorium' card was published to commemorate this tragic event

The 'In Loving Memory' card shown left was produced to mark the deaths of Constable Tyler, aged 30 years and Ralph Joscelyne, aged 10 years. The conspirators also managed to wound twenty-one other people during their attempt to escape.

This picture at right shows the funeral procession of Constable Tyler and Master Ralph Joscelyne through the streets of Tottenham on their way to Abney Park cemetery. Both were buried in the same place on 29th January 1909.

The funeral procession of Pc Tyler and Ralph Joscelyn preceded by the police band

A collection for the widow of Constable Tyler was raised by the public who collected a total £1,055. Constable Tyler's widow invested the money and lived off the interest, which she added to the £15 per year police-granted pension. The wages bag with £80 was never found, but it was said that the owners of the cottage, where one conspirator was cornered, found it in the chimney flue and lived for some time on the proceeds[89]. Constable Tyler received the posthumous award of the newly instituted King's Police Medal[90]. In time the station became

Constable Tyler's carriage flanked by police officers

too small for policing requirements and a larger building was required. It was in 1910 that the Commissioner of Police, Sir Edward Henry, visited the station and wrote, " The accommodation here – residential and administrative is inadequate and unsatisfactory". Accordingly, a year later in 1911 steps were taken to acquire the adjacent freehold sites of 394 and 396 High Road, Tottenham, which included several cottages located at the rear. The building of a new police station then became a priority. The adjoining buildings at 394-396 High Road, Tottenham were purchased for the sum of £1500[91].

The illustration on the previous page shows the coffin of PC Tyler borne by a carriage and horses flanked by his comrades and a multitude of people who attended the official police funeral as a mark of respect for the murdered persons [92].

The new building provided accommodation for 31 single men, and was erected and opened in May 1914[93]. Surveyor's records indicate that the station was re-furbished in 1936[94].

Mr Gilbert Bowles (second left) Commandant of 'Y' Division Special Constabulary pictured in 1937 at Tottenham with other officers

The picture above shows a line up of four officers taken in 1937 - one a regular officer and three members of the Metropolitan Police Special Constabulary. The taller man in the centre without medals is the Sub Divisional Inspector for Tottenham Police Station who was almost certainly responsible for the "Y" Division Special Constabulary. To the left of him is the Special Commandant for "Y" Division Mr. Gilbert Humphrey Bowles MBE. The commandant is proudly showing his MBE, which was the likely reason for the picture. The two remaining special officers are Mr Coucher (Special Chief Inspector) attached to Tottenham

Police Station and Mr Woodhouse (Special Inspector) attached to Edmonton Police Station.

In 1960 Superintendent S. A. Palin was the officer in charge of the station, and the call sign was Yankee Tango (YT)[95].

The station was then refurbished in 1975[96] and again in 1990[97].

In 1985 a tragic incident occurred on the Broadwater Farm Estate in Tottenham. On 5th October police searched the address of Mrs Cynthia Jarrett in Thorpe Road, Tottenham as a result of the arrest of her son

Tottenham Police Station
398, High Road, Tottenham, N17 9JA
1914 to present day

Floyd. During the search Mrs Jarrett collapsed and died. Community leaders at Tottenham Police Station made complaints the following day, and perceiving a lack of action a breakaway group of people began to congregate and demonstrate outside the police station. This resulted in a disturbance where the windows of the station were broken. A Police Inspector driving past the Broadwater Farm Estate was set upon by two youths on a motorcycle causing injury to the officer and damage to the car. Police responding to an emergency call to the estate were surrounded. Officers with riot equipment attended but were ill prepared for what happened next. Under sustained attack some time later,

Constable Keith Blakelock, attached to Tottenham Police Station, was stabbed to death by the angry crowd. Later in the evening the crowd dispersed and a murder enquiry commenced[98].

In 1998 the station was shown as a designated charging station[99], however by 2002 it had become the Borough Police Headquarters for Haringey and was open to the public 24 hours a day seven days a week[100].

Wood Green Police Station

A new police station opened in August 1866[101]. Freehold land was purchased in 1865 for the building of Wood Green Police Station at 347, High Road, Wood Green, N22. The original station was built with a section house, and two sets of quarters. The new station shown on "Y" Division was ready for occupation on 10th September 1866[102].

Wood Green
Station Lamp

This picture shows the front view to Wood Green Police Station and was designated a sergeant supervised station in 1873[103].

According to records a new division was formed which was known as "J" or Bethnal Green division, and this meant boundary changes for the surrounding divisions. This order stated that "Y" Division was composed of Kentish Town, Somers Town, Caledonian Road, Holloway, Highgate, Hornsey, and Enfield with stations also at Wood Green, Southgate and Potters Bar[104].

Wood Green became a sub-division on 4th May 1889. By the turn of the century it was felt that the present station was not large enough for current requirements so land adjacent was purchased in 1903 from Mr. C.L. Finch. The address of the purchased property was shown as 343 and 345, High Road, Wood Green. The new station was completed and occupied in April 1908[105]. Two sets of married quarters and accommodation for 11 constables were included above the station[106].

Religion played a part in the culture of policing. The International Christian Police Association (ICPA)[107] was formed by Miss Catherine Gurney OBE[108] who had also formed the Police Institute, located at 1a, Adelphi Terrace, Adam Street, Strand, WC2. The Police Institute, which was affiliated to the ICPA was like an exclusive club for police officers and their families. It had a reading room, writing room with library, restaurant and bed and breakfast cost 3/6 in 1924[109]. Miss Gurney was a very influential person with respect to the police because she was not only Hon. Sec. of the Institute but on the boards of the Seaside Home at

Wood Green Police Station
347, High Road, Wood Green
1866 - 1908

Brighton, Hove, the Northern Convalescent Home, Harrogate, Provincial Police Orphanage, Redhill, and the Northern Police Orphanage Harrogate[110]. Most police divisions had ICPA representatives which were usually ladies who volunteered for the post. Officers from 'Y' Division (which included Wood Green) had Miss Bridger located at 48, Mercers Road, Tufnel Park, N as their delegate. Funds were collected from charitable donations and publications. For 6d (six pence) one could purchase a small pocket size almanac and diary.

Inspector 87670 Horace Elphick was attached to "E" Division but seconded to the Law Courts in the Strand. He had joined the Metropolitan Police in August 1901 and was a devout Christian and keen member of the ICPA. When he retired from the police in 1927[111] he continued to raise funds for the charity and published a pamphlet entitled 'The Experiences of a London Police Officer', priced at one shilling. Inside were Elphick's experiences with other police officers or members of the public together with words of wisdom and extracts from the Bible[112]. The

Catholic Guild was formed in 1913 by a group of officers who found

Special Chief Inspector William Yalden

themselves meeting after mass at Westminster Cathedral[113].

It was realised in 1919 that members of the Special Constabulary could have a role in peacetime. Between 1919 and 1934 a Special Constabulary Reserve was maintained numbering 10,000 men. In 1926 the General Strike caused the Government to ask for further volunteers. Some 61,000 responded to the call and recruitment to the Special Constabulary was suspended for some time[114].

The application on the next page relates to William Yalden of 82, Victoria Road, Alexandra Park N22 who applied to join the reserve on 16th May 1926. It appears that Yalden had already been a member of the MPSC before re-applying as a reserve. The medal he is wearing is the Special Constabulary Long Service Medal with two bars. This medal was instituted on 30th August 1919, and was awarded to members of the Special Constabulary for 9 years unpaid service with a minimum of 50 hours duty per year. War Service counted as triple

Special Constabulary Long Service Medal with bar.

time. At the time of taking this picture Yalden is a Chief Inspector, and has completed either 27 years continuous service or more probably earned at least one clasp during World War Two. There are two special awards shown above. The medal on the right is a Long Service award showing a clasp whilst the other is awarded in recognition for service during the First World War.

Metropolitan Police Special Constabulary medal issued, during WW1

Special Constables were often not trusted by their regular colleagues because they were seen as strike breakers. This occurred in both 1918 and 1919 because during the police strike and demonstrations they carried on performing beat and station duties against the express wishes of those who were attempting to get a better deal for police officers[115].

In 1929 the Sub Divisional Inspector in charge of the station was William Abbey. He had joined the police on 28th November 1898 and was given the warrant number 84628. He had been promoted to Sergeant in September 1912, Station Sergeant in January 1921 and Inspector in February 1924. He was further promoted to Sub- Divisional Inspector in January 1929. Registers at the station show that he was also an authorised cyclist – and had been so since March 1922[116].

During the boundary revisions of 1933 the status of Wood Green was enhanced and it became Divisional Headquarters for "Y" Division.

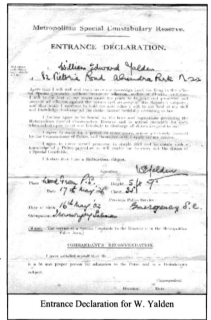

Entrance Declaration for W. Yalden

On 1st April 1934 the Police telephone box system was extended to include Wood Green sub-division, which involved the delivery to the station of a fully equipped police van with first aid apparatus to deal with serious accidents[117].

Wood Green has suffered with a number of fatalities since the beginning of the Second World War. In 1941 Special Constable Bertie Mazetti died when he collided with a lorry whilst cycling to duty at Wood Green during the blackout. Also in 1944 Constable Fredrick Ernest Clarke was killed by enemy action when a long range V2 rocket exploded in Wood Green[118].

Tragically in 1950 Constable Samuel Lock was cleaning a police issue pistol at the station when it accidentally discharged itself killing him instantly[119]. In 1967 Constable James Brian May was directing traffic at a busy road junction in Wood Green when he was struck by a vehicle and died of his injuries[120].

In 1998 Wood Green was part of 2 Area (North West) and was a designated charging station, however by 2002 it had become a Borough based station operational 24 hours a day, seven days a week[121].

Wood Green Police Station
347, High Road, Wood Green, N22 4HZ
1908 to present day

[1] The Municipal Year Book 2000 and Public Service Directory.Vol.2. Newman Books (1999) and publicity literature for the London Borough of Haringey.
[2] John Back Archive (1975) The Metropolitan Police Museum, Charlton.
[3] Ibid.
[4] Metropolitan Police Orders dated 30th January 1863
[5] Police and Constabulary Almanac 1864 and Metropolitan Police Orders dated 11th January 1864
[6] Metropolitan Police Orders dated 11th January 1864
[7] Ibid
[8] Ibid
[9] Ibid
[10] John Back Archive (1975) The Metropolitan Police Museum, Charlton.
[11] Dickens's Dictionary of London (1888) Moretonhampstead, Devon. p 132-3
[12] PRO Census Records 1891
[13] Police Review February 1894
[14] Police Review October 1897
[15] John Back Archive (1975) The Metropolitan Police Museum, Charlton.
[16] Metropolitan Police Orders dated 31st January 1902
[17] Op cit.. (J. Back)

[18] Metropolitan Police General Orders 1898
[19] Howgrave-Graham, H. M. (1947) The Metropolitan Police at War. HMSO
[20] Metropolitan Police Orders dated 2nd January 1945
[21] John Back Archive (1975) The Metropolitan Police Museum, Charlton.
[22] Police and Constabulary Almanac 1957
[23] John Back Archive (1975) The Metropolitan Police Museum, Charlton.
[24] Police and Constabulary Almanac 2001
[25] Metropolitan Police Orders dated 11th January 1864
[26] Ibid
[27] John Back Archive (1975) The Metropolitan Police Museum, Charlton.
[28] Metropolitan Police Orders dated 11th January 1864
[29] The Post Office Index 1864
[30] http://www.police memorial.org.uk/Forces/Metropolitan/metroll.htm dated 12.03.02
[31] In 1881 the census records show James Jeakes was the widowed Rector of Hornsey aged 51 years residing in the High Street, Hornsey together with William and Jane Turner his coachman and servant.
[32] Metropolitan Police Surveyors records
[33] Kelly's directory of London 1883
[34] Metropolitan Police Orders dated 11th January 1864
[35] Metropolitan Police Commissioners Annual Report 1886
[36] Police Review October 1894
[37] Police Review June 1897
[38] Metropolitan Police General Orders 1898
[39] Metropolitan Police Orders dated 9th December 1909
[40] John Back Archive (1975) The Metropolitan Police Museum, Charlton.
[41] Metropolitan Police Surveyors records 1924
[42] Kitcheners Police Index 1931
[43] Metropolitan Police Orders dated 4th February 1916
[44] Metropolitan Police 'Y' Divisional Seniority Register
[45] Metropolitan Police Orders dated 1st April 1934
[46] Metropolitan Police Records 1978
[47] Police and Constabulary Almanac 1998
[48] http://www.met.police.uk/contact/phone.htm dated 12.03.02
[49] John Back Archive (1975) The Metropolitan Police Museum, Charlton.
[50] Ibid.
[51] Metropolitan Police Orders dated 10th September 1904
[52] Metropolitan Police Surveyors Records 1924
[53] Fido, M. and Skinner, K. (1999) The Official Encyclopaedia of Scotland Yard.
[54] Metropolitan Police 'Y' Divisional Seniority Register (revised 1922)
[55] Metropolitan Police General Orders 1898
[56] Metropolitan Police Orders dated 10th September 1960
[57] Metropolitan Police Orders dated 7th May 1968
[58] Police and Constabulary Almanac 1998
[59] http://www.met.police.uk/contact/phone.htm dated 12.03.02
[60] The Police and Constabulary Almanac 2001
[61] John Back Archive (1975) The Metropolitan Police Museum, Charlton and Metropolitan Police Orders 25th November 1885.
[62] Metropolitan Police Surveyors Records 1884
[63] Ibid
[64] Kitcheners Almanac 1931
[65] Metropolitan Police Surveyors Records 1924
[66] Ibid
[67] Kirchner's Almanac 1907
[68] Metropolitan Police Surveyors records 1924
[69] John Back Archive (1975) The Metropolitan Police Museum, Charlton.
[70] Cole, H. N. (1977) Coronation and Royal Commemorative Medals 1887 – 1977 p31-32
[71] Mackay, J. (eds) Medal News Yearbook 1995. Token Publishing Honiton, Devon.
[72] Metropolitan Police General Orders 1893
[73] Police and Constabulary Almanac 1957 and 1960
[74] Police and Constabulary Almanac 1998

[75] http://www.met.police.uk/contact/phone.htm dated 12.03.02
[76] Police and Constabulary Almanac 2001
[77] John Back Archive (1975) The Metropolitan Police Museum, Charlton.
[78] Police and Constabulary Almanac 1864
[79] Metropolitan Police Orders 27th April 1864 and John Back Archive (1975) The Metropolitan Police Museum, Charlton.
[80] Metropolitan Police Orders 11th January 1864
[81] Metropolitan Police General Orders 1873
[82] Metropolitan Police Surveyors Records (1881 entry)
[83] Census records 1881
[84] Metropolitan Police General Orders 1893
[85] http://www.police memorial.org.uk/Forces/Metropolitan/metroll.htm dated 12.03.02
[86] Gould, R. W. and Waldron, M. J. (1986) London's Armed police. Arms and Armour Press, Hampstead, London
[87] Ibid
[88] Ibid
[89] Ibid
[90] Ibid
[91] John Back Archive (1975) The Metropolitan Police Museum, Charlton.
[92] It is not possible to cover the whole story regarding the Tottenham Outrage but a mere outline. A more comprehensive version can be found in Gould, R. W. and Waldron, M. J. (1986) London's Armed Police. Arms and Armour Press, Hampstead, London
[93] Metropolitan Police Orders 16th May 1914 and Metropolitan Police Surveyors records 1924
[94] Metropolitan Police Surveyors records 1924
[95] Police and Constabulary Almanac 1960
[96] Metropolitan Police Records 28th November 1975
[97] Metropolitan Police Surveyors records (undated)
[98] Fido, M and Skinner, K. (1999) The Encyclopaedia of Scotland Yard. Virgin Press.
[99] Police and Constabulary Almanac 1998
[100] http://www.met.police.uk/contact/phone.htm dated 12.03.02
[101] Metropolitan Police Orders 9th August 1866
[102] Metropolitan Police Orders 10th September 1866
[103] General Orders 1873
[104] Metropolitan Police Orders 22nd July 1886
[105] Metropolitan Police Orders 18th April 1908
[106] John Back Archive (1975) The Metropolitan Police Museum, Charlton.
[107] The International Christian Police Association was formed in 1883 by Ms Gurney who encouraged the formation of associations from all over the Empire. She was awarded the OBE in recognition for her devotion and organisational skills in establishing the ICPA.
[108] Fido, M and Skinner, K. (1999) The Encyclopaedia of Scotland Yard. Virgin Press p40
[109] The Policeman's Pocket Almanac and Diary 1924
[110] Ibid
[111] Metropolitan Police Service Records
[112] Elphick, H. (1927) The Experiences of a London Police Officer. International Christian Police Association, 29, Dennison House, London, WC1.
[113] Fido, M and Skinner, K. (1999) The Encyclopaedia of Scotland Yard. Virgin Press. p35
[114] Ibid.
[115] Ibid
[116] Metropolitan Police 'Y' Divisional Seniority Register (revised 1922)
[117] Metropolitan Police Orders 1st April 1934
[118] http://www.police memorial.org.uk/Forces/Metropolitan/metroll.htm dated 12.03.02
[119] ibid
[120] ibid
[121] http://www.met.police.uk/contact/phone.htm dated 12.03.02

Chapter Eight

The London Borough of Havering.

This Borough is situated at the most easterly point of all the London Boroughs. To the north and east the Borough is bordered by the Essex countryside. To the south there is a three-mile frontage on the River Thames, and to the west are the boroughs of Redbridge and Barking & Dagenham. It is one of the largest London Boroughs, and fifty per cent of it is Green Belt Land. The name 'Havering' originates from the picturesque village of Havering-atte-Bower, where at one time there had been a royal palace[1].

However, the London Borough of Havering was created in 1965 with the merger of the Borough of Romford and Hornchurch Urban District Council. In the same year the Metropolitan Police took over the responsibility for the Essex police buildings, and for the 139 police officers attached to them, from Romford, Collier Row, Harold Hill, Plough Corner, Hornchurch, Rainham and Upminster[2]. The Borough Police division now has over 200 police officers and nearly 90 civilian support staff. In addition there are some 20 police vehicles patrolling the Borough[3].

Collier Row Police Station

In 1841 there were two constables posted to Collier Row and Havering (Atte Bower as we know it today). This situation remained the same certainly until 1851[4]. At Collier Row there were Constable 31 James Parslow who had joined on 26th August 1841 and who had been a painter born in Kingston, Surrey,[5] and Constable 30 Jonathon Birdseye who had joined a month later than his colleague[6]. Constable Parslow remained at Collier Row for some time[7] eventually transferring to Romford Town Centre.

Collier Row Police Lamp

It was decided to establish new beats in this area to cope with the growth of the population in the village. Supervision of the area was undertaken by the Inspector who was stationed at Romford[8].

In 1900, due to divisional boundary changes, Collier Row became a station within Brentwood division[9]. Records show that in 1931 this area was policed from Romford (South Street) Police Station[10], although cottages in the area had police officers and their families in residence. In 1930 the population of Collier Row was estimated at 3,000 people and it was a rapidly growing residential area[11]. The station strength remained at two constables. There was a proposal by the surveyor to purchase four further houses in the area[12].

When the Metropolitan Police arrived in 1965 they found that the station was one of the few which had a beer cellar, as the building was originally an off-licence. A spring flowing under the building frequently caused flooding of the basement[13]. It was suspected that beer was brewed on the premises because of the abundant supply of fresh spring water. The police lamps in Havering are all of a similar design, like the one illustrated. The station was shut in 1968 together with Plough Corner, however a petition

Collier Row Police Station,
22, Collier Row Lane, Romford, Essex. RM5 3BP
1936 – present day

of 1000 signatures from the local residents meant that it reopened, albeit under limited opening times. The station has no cells or charging facilities.

Collier Row has been taken out of service under Borough Based policing implemented in April 2000 and is no longer open to the public[14]. Today, although still retained by the Metropolitan Police, it functions as administrative offices for Romford Division where the Accident Inquiry Section is based.

Harold Hill Police Station

In 1930 Harold Wood was expanding rapidly and was estimated to have a population of 3000 people. A house was rented by a constable (exact location unknown) and this also acted as the police station. There were no facilities for housing prisoners, so they were taken to the nearest Divisional station at Romford. Two constables were attached to the area but it was envisaged that further officers would be needed. The surveyor recommended the purchase of four further houses nearby[15].

The Area around Harold Hill was developed in 1949. This major council housing development was also designed to accommodate overspill

Harold Wood Police Station
Gooshays Drive, Romford, Essex.RM3 8AE
1955 – Present day

families from London. During the planning it was decided to build a modern police station. The station was built in Gooshayes Drive, Harold Hill, Romford, Essex[16] and opened in 1955[17].

A new bus route was introduced to serve the large estate being built and to provide direct transport to the Ford Motor Works at Dagenham. Harold Hill became a part of Romford sub-Division which also included Plough Corner, Collier Row and Rydal Mount, Havering. The other sub-division was Hornchurch.

The station is only open to the public between 10am and 6pm daily[18].

Hornchurch Police Station

In 1841 there were two constables posted to Hornchurch. The Constabulary Act 1840 allowed distribution lists showing the location of the police force in Essex to be produced for the benefit and information of the Clerk for the Peace. They showed that in 1843 Constable 24 James Fowler (joined 23rd November 1840) and Constable 104 Uriah Fuller (joined 29th January 1841) were stationed at Hornchurch. Both constables had been transferred by May 1843[19]. The distribution lists also showed that in early 1861 Constable 47 William Harrington (Joined 4th May 1859) and Constable 145 Albert Ridley (joined 3rd March 1860) were

Hornchurch Police Station
74, Station Lane, Hornchurch, Essex. RM12 6NA
1955 – Present Day

stationed at Hornchurch[20].

In 1881 Constable George Wapling, his wife Eliza and their two children lived in Hornchurch village where he was the village constable[21].

In 1900, because of a revision of divisional boundaries, Hornchurch became a station within the division of Brentwood[22]. Although there was a station in Hornchurch in 1931, located in a small terraced house in the High Street[23], the main policing of the area took place from Romford (South Street)[24]. One sergeant and two constables were stationed there. In essence the house purchased for the sergeant and constable to live in, also acted as the police station[25]. The population was estimated at 7000 and recommendations were made to purchase four houses in the area as the neighbourhood was expanding rapidly[26].

The area around Hornchurch steadily grew. To the south the Royal Flying Corps Aerodrome had been built on Suttons Farm, Hornchurch, to combat the threat of German Bomber and Zeppelin raids. In fact the first three Zeppelins to be shot down in 1916 were all downed by pilots from Hornchurch. During the Second World War the RAF pilots and crew from Hornchurch Aerodrome, saw action against the German invaders during the Battle of Britain. The aerodrome was finally shut in 1962[27].

In 1930 two constables operated from their houses in Emerson Park and one constable who was responsible for Gidea Park at Plough Corner[28].

In 1955 the Essex Constabulary built the station at 74, Station Lane, Hornchurch. The station was part of Hornchurch Sub-division which included Emerson Park section and Harold Wood.

This station (and Sub-division) was transferred to the Metropolitan Police in 1965 with Romford, Upminster, Harold Wood, Plough Corner and Rainham during boundary changes. The station at Hornchurch is still operational and located at 74, Station Lane, Hornchurch, Essex. It is open 24 hours a day 7 days a week[29].

Plough Corner Police Station

This was a small detached police station which was originally a pair of houses used for accommodating two police officers and their families. This station is situated just north of Gallows Corner flyover in Straight Road, Romford. The station was built near a public house in 1924 called, The Plough, hence its name. These are shown to the left of the direction sign in the picture below.

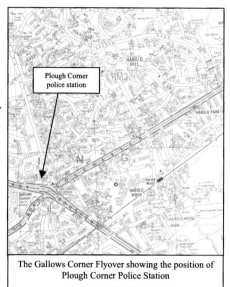

The Gallows Corner Flyover showing the position of Plough Corner Police Station

In the early 1930's the station strength was shown as one sergeant and four constables.

Gallows Corner junction in the 1930's showing the police station on the left

The station was located near a most important traffic point at the junction with the A12 at Gallows Corner. Aid was frequently called from other parts of the division to man the post during the summer months. It was estimated that the local population was about 1000 persons[30].

Plough Corner Police Station
Plough Corner, Romford, Essex.
1924 -2000

The photograph above of the station was taken in 1925. In addition to the station the houses provided accommodation for police officers and their families. One famous occupant was Sergeant Woodgate who is the Essex Police Historian. During his early service in Essex he lived in one of the houses and later published an extensive account of policing in the County of Essex.

The station was closed in December 1968, and then used as a police office until March 1970.[31] Prior to closing it for good in 2000[32] it housed officers from the Juvenile Bureau (or Youth and Communities Section) for 'K' Division for some time. Today the junction is extremely busy being on the main routes to Colchester (A12) and Southend (A127). The nearest police station is Harold Hill in Goosheys Drive.

Rainham Police Station

In 1850 there was one constable posted to Rainham and was long overdue an addition of four constables. The constable would have either been supplied with a cottage/house or had to find accommodation in the area for himself and his family. Constable 38 George Johnson, who had joined in January 1859, was the local village constable in 1861[33]. In 1891 there were extensive boundary changes with the Essex Constabulary, which resulted in Rainham becoming a station within the Orsett Division[34]. This station at 3, New Road, Rainham was built in 1935 by the Essex Constabulary, and transferred to the Metropolitan Police during boundary changes in 1965.

Essex Police Star Pattern Helmet Plate Badge circa 1901 -1936

The picture above shows a star pattern helmet plate badge of the Essex Constabulary worn between 1901 and 1936. It identifies the officers number which was shown in the centre of the star pattern plate. The plates were made of japanned black metal and consisted of a seven pointed star with a garter surround. They were worn by sergeants and constables. Helmet plate badges were introduced into the Metropolitan Police in 1864 and consisted of a japanned black laurel wreath type plate, bearing the Victoria Crown and garter ribbon. The name of the force was contained in the garter ribbon in raised letters. The plates were worn with a coxcomb helmet, but in 1870-71 a new six panelled helmet was introduced without the comb. Inspectors were permitted to wear kepis in 1870 whilst performing ordinary duties, retaining their helmets for special occasions[35].

Some observers suggest that the plate was black so that during night duty there was less chance of being seen by villains and poachers, however the numbers were silver chromium plated. This led to many officers having two helmets, one for day wear as shown and the other with the numbers blacked out. The Essex Police followed the example of the Metropolitan Police who introduced their star pattern helmet plates in 1863.

The station does not have charging facilities and therefore all prisoners are transferred to Hornchurch Police Station. It has a properly fitted station counter and office. It opens periodically.

Rainham Police Station
3, New Road, Rainham, Essex
1935 until the present day

Romford Police Station

The Bow Street Horse patrols were formed in 1777 and patrolled the 'Turnpike Roads' out of London. They were under the jurisdiction of the Bow Street Magistrates. These horse patrols were stationed at various places on the outskirts of London. Romford formed part of the 4th Division with further patrols situated at Enfield, Lea Bridge Road, Woodford, Loughton, Epping, Stratford and Ilford[36].In 1805 a single horse patrol was stationed in Romford Town. There were patrols at Romford Road (Maryland Point) and two in Ilford[37]. In 1830 the nearest Metropolitan Police Boundary was the Bow Bridge which marked the boundary between Middlesex and Essex, although by 1840 when the boundary moved it stopped short of Romford[38]. The horse patrols were incorporated into the Metropolitan Police in 1837 so Romford was policed by them until 1840 when the Essex Police were formed.

In 1839 the Parish of Romford sent a testimonial to the Metropolitan Police Commissioner asking to be included into the MPD, however this was ignored. Romford became a station included within Brentwood Division of the Essex Police under the newly appointed Captain McHardy[39].

Romford Town has always been a busy location and certainly in policing terms it was one of the busiest stations in Essex. Questions have been asked whether Romford should have become the divisional headquarters but for reasons that have been unexplained, it was located at Brentwood instead. In 1841 the town had a population of over 5000, half the size of Romford. Superintendent Marsingale was the first officer in charge of the Division having joined the force on 31st March 1841 as an Inspector. Marsingale had been a schoolmaster and came from Norton in Somerset.[40]

The station strength was one Superintendent and four constables. These were Constable 45 James Barnard (who had joined in November 1840 and resigned in April 1841), Constable 17 Joseph Copsey, Constable 63 Cracknell and Constable 96 F. Lambert. Constable Lambert, who had also seen service at Romford, was previously a cornfactor from Dunmow in Essex,[41] and had joined the Essex Constabulary in September 1841. He could have had a problem, perhaps with discipline or even drinking, as by May 1843 he had been transferred to four different stations eg. Orsett, Rainham, Averley and Stifford[42].

In 1844 the Superintendent (First Class) in charge of the Division was Thomas Coulson who had previously been attached to Chelmsford Headquarters[43], was appointed on 22nd April 1840[44]. It was a thriving town heralded for its leather works, brewery and busy cattle market. Added to this was a workhouse designed to cater for 500 people. Romford was regarded as a 'detached' police station and records show that Inspector John Haydon, who had been appointed in November 1840, was the officer in charge[45].

The Essex Constabulary was formed in 1840 and had been responsible for this area since that time. Its headquarters were shown at Brentwood, under the supervision of Superintendent Edward Davis. In the same year one inspector and three constables were posted to Romford where a building was acquired as a police station in the High Street[46]. The parishes of Havering, Hornchurch and Romford were policed by eight constables an area of over 12,000 acres[47]. In early 1861 Romford had a station strength of one Inspector and seven constables. The officer in charge was Inspector William Gilpin who joined July 1854. The other officers were Constable 1 William Dennis, Constable 54 William Cousins, Constable 126 James Manning, Constable 31 James Parslow (who was posted to Romford in May 1859 and now had 20 years service - see also Collier Row), Constable 63 James Danes and Constable 45 William King (there was a vacancy for one more constable at this time). James seemed to be a popular first name for the constables at this station.

In 1881 James Farrow was the Sergeant of police at Romford, and he was assisted by Constables Charles Archer, George Emmery, Benjamin Free, William Spalding, John Mount, Alfred Lazell, and Charles Harrington[48]. The police operated from the Liberty Hall, Market Place, Romford[49].

Romford Police Station
South Street, Romford
1892 – 1965

Romford Police received notoriety in 1885 when a tragic incident occurred. Inspector Simmons, his wife Mary and their two children, resided near the station at a house in the South Street Gas works. He had been posted to the station in 1881 and was then aged 34 years having been born in Holloway, London[50]. He was on patrol together with another officer, when they spotted a well-known burglar called David Dredge on the road between Romford and Hornchurch. After a failed attempt by the officer to gather re-inforcements, the Inspector returned to the vicinity and confronted Dredge who was with two other men. The taller man of the group pulled a gun and shot the Inspector, who died four days later.

The funeral of Inspector Simmons took place on Tuesday 27th January and was watched by an enormous crowd. Simmons was buried at Oldchurch cemetery. In attendance were The Chief Constable Major Poyntz, and Assistant Chief Constable Raglan Somerset, and every county and divisional superintendent and 140 inspectors, sergeants and constables also attended the funeral. The Metropolitan Police also sent 100 officers to the ceremony as a token of respect [51].

A nationwide hunt took place and, with the incentive of a reward, eventually Dredge and another man called James Lee (who had tried to pawn a gun in Euston) were tried, convicted and hanged in April 1885. It was widely believed at the time that Lee was in fact innocent and wrongly convicted[52]. This was one of the high profile cases, which resulted in police officers on the outer fringes of the Metropolitan Area being allowed to carry revolvers. Inspector Simmons was succeeded by Inspector Thomas J. Cooper, aged 42 years, and born at Alresford, Essex. He was promoted from sergeant to fill the vacancy, and transferred from Rayne Road Station near Bocking with his wife and two children[53].

One of Inspector Cooper's main problems in Romford was the policing of the Salvation Army. Organised along military lines, their headquarters were at Holm Lodge Romford. Cooper had to report disturbances to the local magistrates who were concerned that the banging of drums and singing caused a nuisance. In any event the police often protected the Salvationists who would be followed by ever increasing groups of the lower classes bent on violence if they got the opportunity[54]. Romford was described as the busiest town in Essex, and its station as hardly adequate for policing the town. Romford had strength of one inspector, one sergeant and eleven constables[55].

The original Romford Police Station in the High Street, remained in use until it was no longer suitable for police purposes. In 1891 it was agreed to build a new police station and Court House at South Street, Romford[56].

The new police station was finished and occupied in 1892, although the Court House was not built onto the rear of the Station until the 1930's[57]. Rather than walk the prisoners through the streets of Romford the magistrates moved to buildings in South Street which now house the County Court[58]. In 1894 the introduction of the new telephone system meant that Chelmsford, Romford, Brentwood and Chadwell Heath were all connected to the telephone

Superintendent W.T.J. Howlett later Deputy Chief Constable (1866 –1926)

network, and they could then directly communicate with each other[59].

Romford Police Station became the Divisional Headquarters in 1916. In

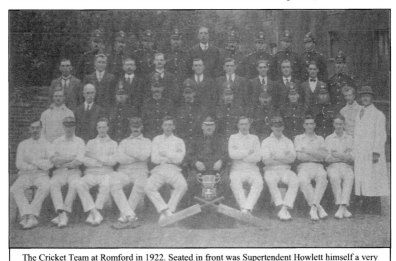

The Cricket Team at Romford in 1922. Seated in front was Supertendent Howlett himself a very keen cricketer

the same year the newly promoted Superintendent W.T.J. Howlett took charge at Romford Police Station, where he was a well-respected, keen and conscientious senior officer. William Howlett lived with his parents in a tied cottage at Little Maplestead before becoming a Corn factors assistant[60]. He joined the Essex Constabulary in 1886 and was promoted acting Sergeant in January 1894[61].

Obviously other senior officers had recognised his skills and by 1922 he was promoted to Deputy Chief Constable of Essex, and transferred to Essex Police Headquarters at Springfield, Chelmsford. The town of Romford was expanding as people moved out from London because of the growth of the railways.

When the First World War started in August 1914 many policemen

Woman Special Constable 2478
Dora Jordan

voluntarily joined the colours and fought for their country. Superintendents had to decide on minimum numbers of officers required to police each area, and to send remaining officers for war service. The county of Essex was indeed vulnerable to aerial attack by German bombers and Zeppelins, and resources were stretched to the limit.

During the war Romford Division of Essex Constabulary was one of the first stations in the county, if not the country, to receive women Special Constables. Manning levels had been reduced and special constables were used extensively to supplement the numbers of regular police. In 1917 Romford Justices asked for female Special Constables to patrol the town. Authority was given in June 1918 to pay two women 5 shillings a day with 3s 8d per month boot allowance and deductions of 1/3d for insurance. The picture above, taken in 1918, shows Women Special Constable 2478 Dora Jordan who is also shown at right in the next photograph showing a group of officers. They were well accepted by the regular officers even though they were not permanent nor did they have any police powers. Their appointment was terminated in October 1919.

When recruiting for the force commenced in 1919 Fred Joslin, a war veteran and farm worker, together with 21 other ex-soldiers signed up and joined the Essex Constabulary. Joslin was posted to Romford Police Station where he lived in single officers quarters. A resident housekeeper there cooked all single officers' meals.

In 1922 a demonstration involving 2,000 unemployed men marched to Romford to persuade the Poor Law Guardians to increase the poor rate to 9 shillings a week[62]. Inspector Hyde and his Constables from Romford were overwhelmed, but the personal intervention of the Chief Constable, who drove to Romford, prevented a serious disturbance when he managed to influence the guardians to agree the change and bring rates into line with Metropolitan workhouse unions[63]. In the same year Romford Division were successful at cricket, and celebrated the fact with a photograph of the whole Division, with the Divisional Cricket Team proudly displaying their trophy. (See page 194)

Romford Division 1918 with Superintendent Howlett at centre

In the picture above is Constable Havers located at the extreme right of the 2nd row from the top. He had joined the service in October 1913 and, after initial training, had been posted to Brightlingsea. However he was soon called-up during the First World War and joined as a Royal Military Police Officer. He was injured in September 1917 eventually returning to Romford Division in April 1918 where he served with Superintendent Howlett for the next 10 years[64].

In front of Havers (in plainclothes) is Detective George. H. Totterdell. By the 1950's he had become one of the most respected and celebrated detectives of the Essex Police. Totterdell was born on 2nd July 1892, the son of a village constable at Eastwood near Southend. Totterdell's father had entered the police service when his ex employer Lord Rookwood of Down Hall Harlow, who was recognised as the father of the Essex Police, recommended him[65].Detective Totterdell was involved in many famous cases during his service. He assisted in the murder inquiry of

Detective Superintendent Totterdell

Constable George Gutteridge who was gunned down at Howe Green on the Romford to Ongar Road on 27th September 1927. G. H. Totterdell became the first Detective Superintendent of the Essex Police, and followed in the footsteps of Detective Inspector Hyde (later responsible for the Criminal Investigation Department for the whole force)[66] who is in the same picture seated to the right of Superintendent Howlett who later became Deputy Chief Constable of the Essex Constabulary.

It is perhaps a less common facet of life today than in previous years, that

The Funeral procession of Superintendent Howlett in 1926

police officers died 'in service' or shortly after commencing retirement. However that is exactly what happened to ex Deputy Chief Constable Howlett. He died suddenly on 12th June 1926 some six weeks after he retired. He received a full police funeral where the whole of Romford Division and Senior Officers of the Constabulary turned out to escort the horse drawn hearse. His passing was a sad loss to the Service and to the community of Romford.

The picture below represents the view a prisoner would receive when taken from the custody office to the cellblock after having been booked in or charged with a criminal offence. It shows the cell passage to the cells. The cell passage was of painted brickwork whilst inside each cell glazed tiles were used from floor to ceiling to enable quick cleaning. In the case of drunken or dirty prisoners it was necessary to mop up debris quickly from the

A typical cell at Romford Police Station in the 1920's

stone floors or walls. There were few comforts for prisoners who were allowed blankets and a mattress usually of horse hair which was hard and robust to cope with the constant usage. There was also little for the

The cell passage at Romford in 1920

prisoners to damage or harm themselves with. Often people arrested for serious matters decide to end it all rather than suffer or face the consequences, therefore the police practice of taking possession of articles like matches, belts and knives has been sensible since the first prisoners were detained at stations.

It was usual for constables to walk up to twenty miles a day in rural areas. Patrolling could be more effective by using a cycle. The picture on the next page shows Sergeant Havers in the rear yard of Romford Police Station with his police issue pedal cycle. Often police officers could be issued with cycles which were hired, or they could purchase their own and claim cycle mileage allowance in order for them to patrol their beats. The cycle allowance was 1d per mile. The cycle proved a cheaper and more effective option than hiring a horse and cart especially when dealing with the problem of 'scorchers' as they were called at the time, who rode furiously along the county's roads[67].

Supervising sergeants were often issued with pedal cycles in order to perform their duty yet they were required to keep them clean at all times. The cycle below certainly looks very new and clean. It would have been housed in the cycle rack in the rear yard. Inspectors had traditionally been allocated a horse and trap for supervisory purposes.

Sergeant Havers at Romford 1920

In 1930 the strength of Romford Police Station consisted of one Superintendent, two Inspectors, five Sergeants and 45 constables. There were also 13 sets of married quarters, however all the 21 single men lived nearby in rented lodgings[68]. The station was described as somewhat old -fashioned but on a restricted site in an excellent position. There were four cells which the surveyor reported were in some ways inadequate for the purpose with the heating and lighting in need of replacement as they were obsolete[69]. The surveyor suggested that a new site should be sought but this not followed up[70].

The Superintendent resided in accommodation at the station. The population total was estimated at 27,000, and covered an area of 29 square miles[71].

By 1949 the Romford Division was divided into sub-divisions. Romford Division also included other stations like Plough Corner and police officers stationed in Collier Row and Rydal Mount, Havering[72].

Essex Police Orders in 1951 gave instructions for the amalgamation of Brentwood and Romford Divisions under the control of the Superintendent at Brentwood. The Essex Police still had a horse located at Romford however instructions were given in the following manner;

'The county horse should be transferred to Brentwood from Romford for the use of the Superintendent'[73].

The Local Government Act 1963 created the Greater London Council, and together with the Police Act 1964 changed policing boundaries. It was unacceptable for a county force to police a metropolitan area. The Essex Constabulary moved out of Romford on 1st April 1965. There had been a ballot of staff and out of 229 officers and men – 139 chose to say behind and transfer to the Metropolitan Police[74]. The cadets were also given the option to transfer. John George Smith who became an Essex Police Cadet on 12th November 1962 transferred to the Metropolitan Police Cadets as 21958 on 1st April 1965. He become a constable, with warrant number 155158, in August 1965 and after training school was posted to Hackney Police Station as 212 'G' Division. Constable Smith gained much experience at many stations during his service, however he remained longest in Traffic Division at TDJ Rigg Approach, Leyton. He took promotion to sergeant and retired from Barkingside Police Station as an Inspector, after thirty years service.

Sergeant (later Inspector) John George Smith

The re-organisation of boundaries meant that the existing stations of Romford (KR), Collier Row(KL), Upminster (KU), Hornchurch (KC), Harold Hill (KA), Rainham (KM) and Plough Corner (KP) were transferred to the Metropolitan Police District[75].

In 1965 Romford Police Station and the Court House were demolished soon after the Metropolitan Police took over the policing of the Division. The Metropolitan Police occupied the newly built Police Station at 19, Main Road, Romford almost as soon as they arrived[76]. The modern police station was built next to the new Magistrates Court and was opened officially in November 1965[77]. Romford was to be the Divisional Headquarters for 'K' Division, however whilst the operational side commenced on the 1st of April the Divisional staff did not move from East Ham until 28th November 1965[78].

The new divisional station was opened and the existing station in South Street (KR) was closed.

The new station at Romford was given the code Kilo-Delta (KD) to mark its headquarters status. Simultaneously East Ham changed its telegraphic code to (KE)[79]

In 1990 Romford Police Station was shut to allow for modernisation which cost £3million. The re-fit was estimated to take some time therefore the headquarters staff and Criminal Investigation Department were re-located to rented buildings at Blackburn House, Eastern Road, Romford, Essex RM1 3BJ[80]. After 18 months building work, which took place besides operational police duties The Commissioner Sir John Stevens re-opened the new station. The Borough of Havering Police Headquarters then returned to Main Road and the rented accommodation was vacated. The re-fit was designed to bring new improved technology

Romford Police Station
19, Main Road , Romford , Essex.
1965 – Present day

to the station with state of the art computers with on-screen mapping etc. Recent CCTV coverage of the town means that officers can now target areas and video crimes and arrests for later use as evidence[81].

Upminster Police Station

There was a system of parochial police in Upminster which the residents were happy with. From 1829 the new system of police, introduced by Sir Robert Peel, began to spread out from London into the surrounding areas and shires.

In 1834 Upminster increased the number of parish constables to three, however by 1842 this was increased to eight[82]. By the following year the numbers were reduced to five (two blacksmiths, a butcher, a farmer and a carpenter). This was due in part to what was referred to at the time as the 'hungry forties', which drove people elsewhere to seek better conditions.

By 1840 the Essex County Police was formed and by 1851 there was an increase in the force by four constables of which one was posted to Upminster[83]. No station was built, as the area was still very rural. Often the police house where the village constable lived acted as the focal point for enquiries. By 1861 the strength had risen to two constables namely Constable 72 Alexander McFadden (joined April 1852 and had probably been at Upminster since then), and Constable 171 George Digby (joined April 1859)[84].

In 1881 Constable Isaac Boreham lived in a cottage in this village with his wife Mary Jane[85]. The Essex Police, like the Metropolitan Police, sought to employ efficient constables. In early 1886 Constable Drew was the local officer in Upminster, however he was brought before the Chief Constable in a somewhat embarrassing situation. The constable could not account for his uniform greatcoat, belt and gloves which he had been wearing on night duty. These items had been found in a field in the early morning. The constable, apart from being the butt of jokes throughout the county, was ordered to resign his position[86].

In 1886 Constable J. Webb became the village policeman and stayed for ten years. On his transfer a grateful public presented him with a marble clock[87]. In 1891 (and again in 1900) the Chief Constable set about reducing the size of the two largest County Divisions, Colchester and Brentwood[88].

At the turn of the century in 1900, because of boundary revisions, Upminster became a station within Brentwood division[89]. A new officer Constable Beasley arrived in 1901 and quickly established himself as a hard working and vigilant officer. In 1912 he was promoted to sergeant and remained until 1917 when he was transferred to Harwich to assist the war effort[90].

In 1910 the Essex Standing Committee recommended the purchase of a semi-detached house with adjoining piece of land on the Cranham Road, for not more than £640. However later that year a double fronted house was purchased for £750. There was plenty of room on which to build a lock up for the purpose of detaining drunks and disorderly persons.

Later Upminster Police Station was an end of terrace house built in 1928. The 1930's review of the Essex Police building stock showed that one sergeant and four constables were stationed there. Five police houses were built there in 1929, and there was a recommendation to build four more. The population was shown as 7,000 persons[91].

In 1965 the station was extended by including 225, St.Mary's Lane and 62-64, St.Lawrence Road. The address of the present station is shown as 233, St. Marys Lane, Upminster, Essex. RM14 3BX. In 2002 Upminster police station was open from 12 noon until 8pm Mondays to Fridays for enquiries from the public. The Community Constables who police the local area are stationed there, however emergency calls are dealt with

Upminster Police Station
233, St. Marys Lane, Upminster, Romford, RM14 3 BX
1929 to present day

from Hornchurch. The station is used for training from time to time and is fitted out with a classroom for these purposes[92].

[1] Municipal Year Book 2000 and Public Services Directory vol.2 Newman Books (1999), and publicity literature for the London borough of Havering

[2] Brown.B. 3Area Magazine - date unknown

[3] www.met.police.uk/police/mps/3hq/3kd/havering 03.02.02

[4] Brown, B. (1990) Romford Police : The Anniversary of a Change in the Romford Record, Romford and District Historical Society.

[5] Woodgate, J. (1985) The Essex Police, Lavenham, Suffolk.p138

[6] Essex Record Office Q/Apr. 1 – Distribution List

[7] Ibid

[8] Woodgate, J. (1985) The Essex Police, Lavenham, Suffolk.p179

[9] Ibid.

[10] Kitchners Police Index (1931)

[11] Essex County Constabulary – Police Stations and Police Houses Booklet (c1930) Essex Police Museum, Police Headquarters, Springfield, Chelmsford, Essex

[12] Ibid

[13] The Job dated 10th May 1968

[14] http://www.met.police.uk/contact/phone.htm 03.02.02

[15] Essex County Constabulary – Police Stations and Police Houses Booklet (c1930) Essex Police Museum, Police Headquarters, Springfield, Chelmsford, Essex

[16] The Job 10th May 1968

[17] Scollan, M. (1993) Sworn to Serve. Phillimore, Chichester, Sussex. P 134

[18] http://www.met.police.uk/contact/phone.htm dated 03.02.02

[19] Essex Record Office Q/Apr. 1 – Distribution List

[20] Essex Record Office Q/Apr. 12 – Distribution List

[21] Census records 1881

[22] Woodgate, J. (1985) The Essex Police, Lavenham, Suffolk.

[23] Brown, B. (1990) Romford Police : The Anniversary of a Change in the Romford Record, Romford and District Historical Society.

[24] Ibid

[25] Essex County Constabulary – Police Stations and Police Houses Booklet (c1930) Essex Police Museum, Police Headquarters, Springfield, Chelmsford, Essex

[26] Ibid.

[27] Brown, B. (1990) Romford Police : The Anniversary of a Change in the Romford Record, Romford and District Historical Society.

[28] Op cit

[29] http://www.met.police.uk/contact/phone.htm 03.02.02

[30] Essex County Constabulary – Police Stations and Police Houses Register (circa 1930)

[31] PRO. MEPO 11

[32] verified by a telephone call to Romford Police Station 21st February 2002

[33] Essex Record Office Q/Apr. 12 – Distribution List

[34] Woodgate, J. (1985) The Essex Police, Lavenham, Suffolk.

[35] Metropolitan Police Museum documentation, Charlton.

[36] PRO. MEPO 14/40

[37] Brown, B. (1990) Romford Police : 'The Anniversary of a Change' in the Romford Record, Romford and District Historical Society.

[38] Ibid

[39] Ibid

[40] Woodgate, J. (1985) The Essex Police, Lavenham, Suffolk. P 138

[41] Ibid P 138

[42] Essex Record Office Q/Apr. 12 – Distribution List Essex

[43] Essex Record Office Q/Apr. 1 – Distribution List

[44] The Police and Constabulary List 1844. Parker, Furnival and Parker, London.

[45] Ibid.

[46] Scollan, M. (1993) Sworn to Serve. Phillimore, Chichester, Sussex.

[47] Woodgate, J. (1985) The Essex Police. Lavenham Suffolk.

[48] Census records 1881

[49] Ibid.

[50] Census records 1881

[51] Woodgate, J. (1985) The Essex Police. Lavenham Suffolk.

[52] Scollen, M. (1993) Sworn to Serve. Phillimore, Chichester. Sussex
[53] Census records 1881
[54] Ibid
[55] Woodgate, J. (1985) The Essex Police, Lavenham, Suffolk.
[56] 3 Area Magazine 1975
[57] Woodgate, John (1985) The Essex Police. Terence Dalton Ltd., Lavenham, Suffolk
[58] Ibid p67
[59] Scollan, M. (1993) Sworn to Serve. Phillimore, Chichester, Sussex.
[60] Census records 1881
[61] The Police Review and Parade Gossip 12th January 1894
[62] Scollen, M. (1993) Sworn to Serve. Phillimore, Chichester. Sussex
[63] Ibid
[64] Havers Family History records
[65] Totterdell, G. H. (1956) Country Copper. Harrap, London
[66] Ibid
[67] Scollan, M. (1993) Sworn to Serve. Phillimore, Chichester, Sussex.
[68] Essex County Constabulary – Police Stations and Police Houses Booklet (c1930) Essex Police Museum, Police Headquarters, Springfield, Chelmsford, Essex
[69] Ibid
[70] Ibid
[71] Ibid
[72] 3 Area Magazine 1975
[73] Essex Police News and Views 1965
[74] Brown, B. (1990) Romford Police – Anniversary of change. In the Police History Society Journal No. 7
[75] Scollen, M. (1993)Sworn to Serve. Phillimore, Chichester. Susses
[76] 3 Area Magazine 1975
[77] Ibid.
[78] PRO. MEPO 14/40
[79] Ibid
[80] http://www.met.police.uk/contact/phone.htm 03.02.02
[81] The Job 4th January 2002
[82] The story of Upminster by the Upminster Local History group, Book 11 1960. p22.
[83] Brown, B. (1990) Romford Police : 'The Anniversary of a Change' in the Romford Record, Romford and District Historical Society.
[84] Essex Record Office Q/Apr. 12 – Distribution List
[85] Census records 1881
[86] Woodgate, John (1985) The Essex Police. Terence Dalton Ltd., Lavenham, Suffolk
[87] The story of Upminster by the Upminster Local History group, Book 11 1960 p23
[88] Woodgate, J. (1985) The Essex Police. Terence Dalton Ltd., Lavenham, Suffolk
[89] Ibid.
[90] ibid p25
[91] Essex County Constabulary – Police Stations and Police Houses Register (circa 1930)
[92] Local enquiry of the station officer on 26.7.02

Chapter Nine

The London Borough of Islington

This inner London Borough lies with the Boroughs of Haringey to the north, Camden and Hackney to the west and east and the City of London to the South. The Borough consists of a number of what were once separate villages. The best known are Clerkenwell, Highbury, Barnsbury. Holloway and the Angel. In 1965 the Metropolitan Boroughs of Finsbury and Islington were merged to form the London Borough of Islington[1].

Nowadays Islington is described as a melting pot of race, religion and social classes. It is home to numerous personalities, from actors, artists and crafts people to journalists and politicians[2].

There are six principle police stations within the London Borough of Islington. These are Caledonian Road, Highbury, Holloway, Islington, Kings Cross and Upper Holloway.

Caledonian Road Police Station

The original station in Caledonian Road was built on a plot of land purchased from a local landowner, Mr. Pocock, a dairyman. It cost £2,526 in 1855. The police purchased the freehold for the sum of £1,040 in 1866. There have been two stations named Caledonian Road Police Station, both of which have been located on the same piece of land. The land was situated near the corner of Georges Road and Caledonian Road.

In 1864 the strength of the station was shown as two inspectors, six sergeants and fifty Constables[3]. There was also a mounted constable and horse located at the station. It was a station where charges were taken and police officers paraded for duty. The cost of building the station was £2515. The ground floor consisted of the Inspectors' office, Charge Room, Library, three cells, five stalls for horses and three toilets. In the basement there was a mess kitchen with cooking facilities, a lavatory and six coal vaults. On the ground floor there were three cells for detaining prisoners[4].

The station also contained accommodation for police officers and their families. One married Inspector lived on the first floor in a set of rooms, whilst twenty unmarried constables lived together in dormitories on the second floor. The main reason for the location of the station was to be close to the new Metropolitan Cattle Market.

Due to its proximity to the market it became a very important station. Its markets and also its public houses, required strict supervision by the police. It is interesting to note that since July 1865 there had been 159 police officers removed from street duties in the Metropolitan Police District who were solely employed in connection with the Cattle Plague Act. The effect of the Act meant that no cattle could be moved for a distance of more than 500 yards except with a Licence from the Commissioner of Police[5].

During the three years, since the introduction of legislation in 1866, 20,720 licences were granted by Police in order that 301,526 head of cattle could be moved out of London[6]. As from the 24th March 1866

Caledonian Road Police Station
470, Caledonian Road, Islington, N7
1917 -1992

Police had been posted day and night at every road around the Metropolis, forming a complete cordon to prevent cattle being moved. Police officers were also posted to railway stations and wharves. They were required to watch infected Districts especially the transportation of manure, which was possibly infected. The Commissioner reported that after three and a half years of this responsibility had been not only a drain on the Metropolitan Police Fund but also on the available strength of his men. In 1873 Caledonian Road was designated a station on 'Y' Division under the command of an Inspector[7].

In 1881 the Station Inspector was Edward Wilkes a 39 year old man from Rousham near Oxford. He resided there with his wife Fanny. There were twenty two single police officers resident at the station. The address was published as 470, Caledonian Road, Islington London [8].

The policing of the Metropolitan Cattle market at Caledonion Road was the cause of a great injustice. The market was always the subject of letters to the Commissioner regarding its regulation and control possibly because of the disruption and chaos, which descended on the area[9].

Policing market areas could be a demanding and testing duty for police officers. Sub-divisional Inspector Robert Ruff [10] was responsible for markets at Caledonian Road, and also the taverns, inns and other licensed premises in the vicinity. These premises could remain open during market hours, normally when other public houses were shut. This was to allow market workers, herdsmen and drovers the chance for refreshment. It created difficulties because locals purporting to be cattle drovers tried to drink in these establishments[11].

When two Caledonian Road constables arrested two local men for drinking at one of the establishments the Inspector released them without making an official entry in the Occurrence Book[12]. The Commissioner, Sir Edward Bradford, had received a number of letters of complaint from outraged members of the public regarding the drinking of local people. One anonymous letter pointed out the Inspector's decision to release local suspects for drinking during market hours. An investigation concluded that the Inspector, who was highly thought of and had nearly twenty-five years exemplary police service, should face a discipline hearing. At the hearing he was found guilty, reduced in rank to Constable and transferred (as was usual) half way across London. He was so shocked that he was too ill to commence work and he appealed to the Home Secretary to be re-instated. The irony was that he needed to complete just six months more service before he could retire on full Inspector's pension. His appeal failed[13]. This underscores the fact that discipline in the police is harsh and often unjust.

In 1894 a cottage at the rear of the station was purchased for the purpose of housing an Inspector and his family. He paid five shillings and sixpence a week. A new police station was built in 1917 on the same site at 470, Caledonian Road, N.7[14].

The station was scheduled for a re-fit and was up-dated in 1937[15].

Up until the 1965 Local Government re-organisation Caledonian Road had been a station located on "Y" Division, but after this date it became a station on "N" Division. The communication code for Caledonian Road was NC (November Charlie). In the early 1970's Caledonian Road was a sub-divisional station of Islington and the Area Car November 2 was stationed there. The size of the yard and facilities at the station also allowed for the Special Patrol Group (SPG) to be stationed there until they were disbanded in 1985.

The police station was finally closed in 1992. Police officers had served the community for over 145 years from this station. Today it is known as Anguilla House and has been sold and converted into apartments.

Highbury Vale Police Station

In 1888 Mr. Frederick Baker who owned a parcel of land which he wished to sell made an approach to the Commissioner of the Metropolis. The Commissioner was at the time seeking to buy a suitable plot on which to build a station. The land was located in Blackstock Road opposite Myrtle Street (now known as Hurlock Street). The offer was considered but the plot of land was considered not only too expensive but not large enough for police requirements. Discussions between the Receiver and Commissioner concluded that there was no urgent need for a station at this moment, so the matter was postponed[16].

In 1902 the residents of Highbury petitioned the Secretary of State requesting that a police station be built on land owned by the London County Council. This was the same parcel of land considered in 1888 but with a change of ownership. The Metropolitan Police were not keen, as the land was considered small. However suggestions were made that with the compulsory purchase of several houses in Canning Road backing onto the land their requirements would be satisfied. When approached the London County Council did not want to sell the land but suggested an 80-year lease instead. A considerable amount of correspondence exchanged hands and the London County Council finally decided to sell the freehold after all, as the land was going to be used for a public purpose[17].

Accordingly the site was bought for £2,250 in 1903, and compulsory purchase orders were served on the owners (British Equitable Insurance

Company) of the houses located at 29, 31, 33, 37 and 39, Canning Road. One of the leaseholders was unhappy about the purchase and claimed compensation of £4,100. A court case followed with a jury assessing the compensation as £2,379, which was more than the cost of the original parcel of land. The site remained empty for over three years presumably because of the court action for compensation. Finally the Town Clerk of the Metropolitan Borough of Islington wrote to the Commissioner for the Metropolis following a resolution passed at a council session stating;

"That having regard to the distress prevalent in the borough owing to the unemployment the council respectfully urge His Majesty's Government to proceed with the erection of the proposed police station and officers quarters in Blackstock Road, at a cost of £80,000 (the site cleared nearly 3 years ago) at the earliest moment"[18].

Highbury Vale Police Station
211, Blackstock Road, Islington, N4
1910 – 2000

The police station was built shortly after the letter to the Commissioner and was ready for occupation in July 1910[19]. The station was built with a section house for thirty unmarried men and two sets of married quarters (A former Metropolitan Police Commissioner, Sir Kenneth Newman, once lived at these premises). One set of married quarters cost 10/6d per week, whilst the other quarters were 9/- The address was shown as 211, Blackstock Road, Islington, N4[20].

Highbury Vale section house was re-opened after refurbishment on 7th September 1925. The building of the new station caused a revision of the boundaries and the status of the surrounding stations. Police Orders showed that Highbury Vale was a sectional station of Stoke Newington Police Station. Further re-organisation of local authority boundaries introduced on 1st April 1965 removed Highbury Vale as a sectional station of Islington Police Station, however after a month a re-think transferred Highbury Vale to Holloway Police Station instead.

A decision was taken to shut Highbury Police Station to the public and this took place in January 2000[21]. Two surveys had been completed which showed that on average the station was used by fourteen callers a day and most of these were signing on bail or producing their motor vehicle documents[22]. The station is still in use today and officers parade in the basement for duty at Arsenal Football Club, which is situated only about 400 yards away. The station still provides a valuable resource to the police as a place for briefings, planning and administrative work[23].

Holloway Police Station

The station at Holloway has often been referred to as Hornsey Road Police Station confusing some observers that it was located in Hornsey, not on the road to it. Records show that the first police station in Holloway was set up in a house in Hornsey Road. The building was acquired in 1835 for an annual rent of £20 from a Samuel White who had used the building as an audit office[24].

In 1845 a brick and slate station house existed called Bellefield House, in Seven Sisters Road. It was rented from Mrs. Hannah Enkell of 4, Holloway Terrace for £60 per year. It appears to have remained in service until 1872 when temporary accommodation was found nearby. A new temporary police station was also opened on 8th May 1871[25] in Seven Sisters Road, staffed by one Inspector, seven sergeants and sixty Constables[26].

In 1874 a new police station was built at 256, Hornsey Road, some one hundred yards south of the present police station. The land for the station was purchased in 1873 at a cost of £1,700 and the building then erected for £3,592. It opened for business in January 1875[27]. The ground floor was occupied by an Inspector's Office and two store rooms, four cells, a recreation room, a reserve room, a drying room and three W.C's. In the basement there was a mess kitchen and cooking area, washing room, brushing room, boot room, lamp room and four coal vaults. The first floor housed the married inspector and his family, and sixteen single constables occupied the second floor. In 1893 the telegraphic code for the station was published as Hotel Yankee (HY),[28] however by 1960 this had become November Hotel (NH)[29].

Holloway Police Station
256, Hornsey Road, Holloway.
1875 – 1941

Discipline was very strict in the police and to fail to turn up for duty without proper reason required severe action on the part of police supervisors. Absence without leave or absconding from the police force was a grave offence punishable before a court of law. In August 1897 Constable George Aubyn, attached to Holloway Police Station, failed to turn up for duty and was posted missing. He had hired a pony and trap, which he had failed to return, and had ridden it to Woking in Surrey. He had been arrested on a warrant several days later when he gave himself up at the station. Inspector Joseph Davies, prosecuting, told the magistrate that Constable Aubyn had 18 months police service and had been dismissed from the service in consequence of his absence. Mr Bros the magistrate fined the officer £1 and stated that discipline must be maintained [30].

Only six stations out of fifteen on 'Y' or Highgate Division were important enough to have Sub Divisional Inspectors in charge of them. These were Kentish Town, Somers Town, Hornsey, Enfield, Caledonian

Road and Holloway. The officer in charge of the police station at Holloway from 1897 until 1902 was Sub Divisional Inspector Mountifield[31]. William Steggles Mountifield was born at Walton on Naze, Essex, in 1856 and joined the Metropolitan Police in 1877. In London he met and married Emily Oade who was a year younger and was born at Gosport, Hampshire. In 1881 he was a constable living with his family (son Charles aged 4 years and Emily aged 3 years) at 31, Union Street, Clapham, Surrey[32]. Gradually over the years he rose through the ranks after coming to the attention of senior officers. Inspector Mountifield was indeed a character. Not only was he a strict disciplinarian, but he also understood the importance of sport and recreation in the police service. He was a competitive billiards player and a keen swimmer. The Hornsey Road swimming baths were situated next to the station so swimming galas were a regular event. Mountifield was also 'Y' Divisions football representative for the Lady Bradford Challenge Cup and was often seen supporting the Divisional Football Team. He commanded loyalty and respect. In September 1899 he found Constable 566 'Y' M'Kelvie drunk in full night duty uniform in Seven Sisters Road at 8.45am. The officer was off duty and Mountifield walked back with him to his lodgings. Just outside the lodgings the constable became upset with Mountifield and assaulted him. The constable appeared at North London Court charged with assaulting the Inspector. The case was heard by Mr. Fordham who also listened to four witnesses supporting Mountifield[33]. M'Kelvie was sentenced to one month imprisonment.

The 1907 Retirement photograph of a Holloway police officer after 25 years service .

The Inspector was an active figure so on a number of occasions he either won or came second in the station Billiards competitions and veterans swimming races[34].

In 1907 Holloway was shown as a station of 'Y' or Highgate Division with its Divisional Headquarters being located at Kentish Town[35]. All prisoners charged with offences appeared at North London Court, Stoke Newington. This meant frequent visits by officers from Holloway to a court, which was open daily.

The station was refurbished in 1911 when the section house accommodation was added[36] and was opened in February 1912[37].

Day trips in charabancs were often organised by the social clubs that grew up in police stations throughout the Metropolitan Police District during this time. Subscriptions paid weekly by the contributors towards the social club often meant that a trip to Brighton or Goodwood races (both very popular places of recreation in Edwardian England) required no further payment. The picture above shows a happy group of Holloway police officers outside the station prior to departure in 1921. These open topped buses were susceptible to the elements so suitable rain-ware was also carried.

In 1941 a High Explosive bomb pierced the roof of the police station and exploded in the basement. Half of the building was

Holloway Police Outing 1921

demolished. Those killed in the incident were Sub-Divisional Inspector MacAlan Gibson (and wife and married daughter, Joyce Unwin), Inspector Leonard Clark, Station Sergeant 19N John (Jack) Curry, Detective Sergeant Alick Stanley, Constable 377N James Rosen and Constable (War Reserve) Tom Killen. There were also five others injured. On 9th April 1941, Their Majesties King George VI and Queen Elizabeth visited the damaged Holloway Police Station and three other London police stations. At the station Their Majesties were able to talk to a number of representatives from other stations in the area and all different ranks were assembled[38].

During the 1939-45 War there were almost 1,900 reported cases of damage to police buildings in the Metropolitan Police area. Of these some 124 received serious damage. Ten police stations were so badly damaged that they were either totally or partially abandoned. Some were reoccupied after extensive repairs[39].

After the war one of the problems police faced were street gangs who would resort to fighting each other often with offensive weapons. Police Constable Raymond Henry Summers was on patrol in Holloway at night in 1958 when he came across a street gang fight and went to intervene. In the days before personal radios to raise the alarm were issued to individual police officers, officers walking their beats were on their own unless they were near a police box or telephone. During the fracas Summers was stabbed in the back with a thin

The destroyed police station at Holloway in 1941

bladed knife and died of his injuries[40]. There was insufficient evidence to prosecute anyone in this matter resulting in no one standing trial for the murder of a police officer.

Holloway Police Station
256, Hornsey Road, Holloway, N7
1965 – present day

In 1960 Holloway (telegraphic code NH) was shown as a station of 'N' Division under the supervision of Superintendent G. Reay[41].

The complete Holloway Police Station building was later demolished and the section house at the rear of the station yard was converted from living accommodation for single officers into a temporary police station. This building remained a police station until 1965.

The original site of the demolished police station, when cleared, had a frontage of 48 feet and was 160 feet deep. This was considered too small for redevelopment and so a new location nearby had to be found. Land was found and the present police station was built at 284, Hornsey Road, N.7., a short distance away. Arrangements were made to design and build a new purpose built modern station on the site, which opened on 19th July 1965. The new stations were built without separate single officers accommodation and married quarters. Separate buildings were constructed nearby to house the vast numbers of single officers who were joining the police. The nearest section house to Holloway was built in Canonbury, Islington and was called Olive House.

In 2002 the station was still open to the public 24 hours a day 7 days a week[42].

Islington Police Station

A watch house at Islington Green was re-built in 1797 after the old one had fallen into decay[43]. It was located at the corner of the green where Hugh Middleton's statue now stands. Previously there had been a place of detention near St.Mary's Church Street, Upper Street. It had a cage and a whipping post attached[44]. In 1828 the Parish employed fourteen officers to prevent nuisances during the night and for other duties during the day. These included six constables and six headborough[45].

In 1829 the policing of Islington came within the Metropolitan Police[46] The 12th Company of the new police marched into the Parish of St. Mary's Middlesex, from their Headquarters in Whitehall Place, on 1st February 1830[47] and took over the watch house with its front room, charge room and two cells. It was still in operation in 1840[48]. It belonged to the Receiver of the Metropolitan Police and was shown located within the "N" or Islington Division, although the Headquarters were situated at Kingsland, or Stoke Newington as it is now known. Divisional Superintendent James Johnson was in charge and his supervisory responsibilities included travelling by horse to the surrounding stations of Hackney Old Town, Robert Street, Hoxton and Islington[49].

By 1852 the station on the green was no longer suitable for police purposes, so they were to be relocated to 277, Upper Street next to the Town Hall, where a new site was leased for a period of 21 years[50]. The building on the site was unsuitable until it was rebuilt so a temporary station was established in the Section House at Birds Buildings. The freehold became available and was purchased by the police in 1857, although work was not completed on the new station until 1858 at a cost of £3256 plus an additional £2000 for the freehold[51].

Islington Police Station
277, Upper Street, Islington, N1.
1858 – 1992

Once complete it had eight cells, a charge room and Inspector's office on the ground floor. The basement was used for the constables' uniform storage, and the usual drying room and cooking facilities for the officers. The station strength was reported as two Inspectors, nine Sergeants, and 89 Constables[52].

By 1864 there were two Inspectors, nine Sergeants and eighty-nine Constables at the station [53]. There was also one horse, which was ridden alternately by the Inspectors on duty. In 1871 the address of the Police Station was shown as 277, Upper Street.

At this time the Constables from this station were only a short walk from the fields surrounding Canonbury Manor. There was open farmland after crossing Highbury Cross (Highbury Corner). Therefore much of the officer's work at that time related to the licensing of animals and their associated diseases.

The Islington Vestry occupied premises next door to the police station. The relationship between the two parties was not always harmonious. On one occasion the Vestry asked the Superintendent of Police to remove the airbricks in the police station wall to prevent the foul air from the cells polluting the vestry hall. The Superintendent later retaliated by asking the

Vestry to brick up windows in their property which overlooked the parade area in the station yard where Constables were drilled every morning, so as to prevent undesirable persons looking at his officers.

Officers who worked at the local station often lived nearby and the Receiver of the Metropolitan Police had purchased or rented houses for this purpose. They were located at 14, Chapel Street, 28, Colebrook Row and 20, Camden Street now Camden Walk. These three premises were given up in 1837 in favour of a much larger property at Birds Buildings in Lower Road[54] now called Essex Road.

Telegraph communications using the code IN were established in 1872 although from 1965 onwards it became November India (NI)[55].

Records show that Islington (Upper Street) was supervised by an Inspector[56]. In 1881 the officer in charge of the station was Inspector Bateman who resided at the station with his wife and two children. There were thirty nine single police officers and women who appear to have been servants/cleaners[57]. In 1888 St. Mary's Islington ceased to be located in Middlesex and instead became part of London County Council (LCC). There were now four Inspectors, twelve Sergeants and 120 Constables on Islington sub-division[58].

The newspapers often reported details of crimes and unusual incidents, particularly acts of heroism, which had taken place in various parts of London. In 1894 The Daily News reported that a new and very young Constable 325 "J" Pipes had fame thrust upon him. On his first day of service he was alone, just before dawn, when he saw a man trying to leave a house through a window in Grosvenor Road, Canonbury. The officer stopped the man who put up a vicious fight, cutting the officer with a knife, causing serious injuries to his hands and beating him with his fists.

At North London Magistrates Court the Stipendary Magistrate, Mr. R. O. B. Lane commended the officer, for his great courage and resolution. The facts were reported to the Commissioner of the Metropolis. As a result of the publicity several members of the public sent rewards to the Court which totalled £25 10s. 6d. The officer was allowed to retain this particular reward for his heroic act of courage. Constable Pipes was further rewarded for his heroism with £10 from the Bow Street Reward Fund. An Edward Purdoe was later sentenced to three years imprisonment for assault and house breaking[59].

The picture shown below is that of Inspector Pocock who served on "N" Division for a short period of time. He joined in 1882 but was medically discharged from the police with fourteen years service in April 1896. The

Inspector was retired medically because he had received an injury on duty in 1884 during an arrest of a drunken man who was assaulting his wife.

This incident caused a degenerative spinal injury resulting in the officer's inability to walk. This situation was unlikely to improve. However a gratuity was offered to the Inspector by the Commissioner, which was not accepted because the injury was sustained in the line of duty entitling the officer to his pension. The Commissioner persisted and paid the officer the gratuity even though he knew the circumstances that caused the injury. Pocock made an appeal to the Home Secretary but this was unsuccessful and the gratuity of £138. 1s 5d was paid nonetheless.

Inspector James Pocock

James H. Pocock was promoted to Sergeant in October 1887 and transferred to 'N' Division. He served two months at Walthamstow and then was selected for special duty at the Royal Gunpowder Factory, Waltham Abbey, where he remained for two years. He was then moved to Islington, at his own request. In April 1892 he arrested John Roxe, a notorious thief, for highway robbery with violence on an aged cabman in Liverpool Road. In October the same year he arrested William Holmes for attempting to murder his wife at Islington Green. Both men were later convicted. At his retirement he was presented with a handsome marble clock and a pair of bronzes as a mark of respect[60].

Police officers could retire on pension once they had completed 25 years service. This was thought of as a waste of experienced officers. Retirement celebrations were a good chance for officers to meet back at the station to say farewell to a colleague. Divisional Superintendent McFadden made the presentations to two retiring officers at Upper Street Police Station (Islington) in October 1896. They were Constable Brewer of the 'N' Division Mounted Branch and Constable Hutchings. Both received timepieces. Brewer had spent 19 years of his service at Islington Police Station[61].

Shortly before Christmas 1900 Constable 42 'N' (Reserve) Stanton was on mounted duty in Upper Street, Islington when he was set upon by a gang of men who surrounded him, knocked him to the ground and started to kick him. The officer was then stabbed in the neck. A member of the public Mr. Ambrose Harnett came to the officers assistance and the men ran off. As a token of their appreciation for the assistance rendered, Sub Divisional Inspector Mason the officer in charge of Islington Police made a presentation of a silver snuff box to Mr Harnett, in front of invited guests at the station[62].

The picture at right is that of Constable 351H/95975 Charles Victor Efford, who was later stationed at Islington Police Station. He had joined the Metropolitan Police in August 1908 and he was posted to "H" Division. However in April 1920 he was transferred, on promotion, to Islington "N" Division. He left the police through ill health in April 1932 (24 years service). He died in March 1975. In this photograph he is still a constable of 'H' Division[63]. Even in ill health Sergeant Efford 'made old bones' living to the age of nearly 90 years and drawing 43 years police pension.

Constable Charles Efford

In 1904 there was extensive refurbishment to the station. A new building was constructed at the rear of the premises on the site of the old stables and parade shed. It become a new section house and opened in October 1906[64]. The parade room was relocated to the basement. There was now accommodation for forty-two single men. Further work included the front door and steps being relocated right in the next window recess. This enabled an entrance hall to be built and also for a waiting room to be constructed to the right of the hall. There was now new accommodation in the police station for a married Inspector to occupy four rooms and accommodation for thirty-eight single men[65].

In June 1933 as part of extensive re-organisation the station area was transferred from "N" or Islington to "G" or Finsbury Division instead. Additionally in 1965 the boroughs of Islington and Finsbury combined under local Government re-organisation causing a change of police boundary, and Islington became part of "G" Division.

During the Second World War Islington took a pounding throughout the bombing campaign. The police worked tirelessly throughout the action and sometimes paid the ultimate price. In 1940 War Reserve Constable Charles Henry Huck was killed by a bomb during an air raid when he left the shelter to go and investigate a fire[66].

Photograph of the class passing out from Hendon Police Training School in January 1973

In 1973 the co-author, Constable Peter Kennison (later Inspector), was transfered from the Training School to his first posting at Islington Police Station. He remained there until 1977 when he transferred on promotion to Hackney Police Station. Above is the Training School photograph where the co-author is shown middle row extreme right.

Superintendent David Swinden (co-author) finally closed this station in April 1992 when the new police station in Tolpuddle Street at the junction with Penton Street, Islington was opened.

This new station was officially opened in October 1992 by the then Commissioner of Police, Sir (now Lord) Peter Imbert, accompanied by Lady Imbert, The Receiver of the Metropolitan Police District, Mr. Graham Angel and the Mayor of the London Borough of Islington, Councillor Edna Griffiths.

The new police station was built on the site of an old country mansion named White Conduit House and gardens known as 'The Cockney

Retreat'. This was a park where people could eat a 'hearty meal' or have

Islington Police Station
Tolpuddle Street j/w Penton Street, Pentonville, London N1
1992 until the present day

a good pint of ale, or just wander through the various displays and exhibitions set up for the entertainment of all. The park was also used for political meetings, and in 1836 the Dorchester Labourers, known as the 'Tolpuddle Martyrs' were entertained to a dinner to celebrate their release.

Kings Cross Road Police Station

There were two watch houses in the Kings Cross area. The first was at Rosoman Street, Sparfields and was set up in 1813. On the formation of the Metropolitan Police in 1829 the building was improved, with a large lofty room on the first floor and two strong cells, one for males and one for females.

Kings Cross Police Station
Euston Road, Kings Cross, London.
1829 – 1845

The picture on the previous page shows the old station at Kings Cross Police Station being demolished in 1845. The old station became a beer house, but the building became an obstruction to traffic because happy and drunken customers overflowed into the road outside and it was soon closed[67].

The watch house closed in 1842 and they moved to premises in Bagnigge Wells Road (King's Cross Road). There was a second watch house at Clerk's Well, in Ray Street[68].

In 1829 when Sir Robert Peel introduced his new police force a 'new' police station was set up in an exhibition hall under the column erected to George IV that stood at the junction of the present Euston Road (formerly New Road), York Way (formerly Maiden Lane), and Grays Inn Road (formerly Grays Inn Lane). It was opposite the smallpox hospital, which is now the site of Kings Cross Railway Station, on the corner of Maiden Lane[69].

In 1860 the Metropolitan Railway Company purchased the land, on which the Bagnigge Wells Road Police Station now stands, from the New River Company. The first underground railway in London was then built from Paddington to Farringdon. The work was completed by 1863 and the police station located on the site, with the railway running beneath it, became known as the 'Clerkenwell' Police Station and was later renamed

Kings Cross Road Police Station
76, Kings Cross Road, London, N.
1870 – 1992

'Kings Cross Road' Police Station[70]. In 1864 the station compliment consisted of two inspectors, fourteen sergeants and 169 constables. As this was the divisional headquarters there was also a Superintendent. There were a further two Inspectors located at the station, one attached to the reserve detachment and another who was responsible for the van service which transported prisoners to court and prison. There were three further sergeants and thirty constables attached to the reserve. The van service detachment consisted of two sergeants and five constables. There were six horses housed in the large stable, five for the van service and one for the Superintendent[71].

By 1868, the building had become somewhat overcrowded and a new police station was built on the same site. The address was shown as 76, Kings Cross Road. It was opened in January 1870[72] although they had used the new cells since the previous October[73].

In 1888 twenty three Inspectors, forty six sergeants and 480 constables assisted Superintendent Charles Hunt, who was in charge of the Division[74]. The station telegraphic code in 1893 was Golf Delta (GD)[75].

Police officers are very often rewarded for their bravery, and in April 1894 a ceremony was held to honour Constable 47GR Joyce who was given a cheque for £5 from the Metropolitan Police Commissioner, Sir John Bridge, for saving the lives of two men in a serious fire in Northampton Street, Clerkenwell. The officer in charge of the station, Superintendent Hammond, attended the ceremony and thanked the Commissioner for the reward on the constable's behalf[76].

In July 1897 'a cowardly outrage' was committed upon a police officer in Clerkenwell when Constable 329G John Moore was patrolling Warner Street, and a gang of 'roughs' suddenly attacked him. The Constable drew his truncheon to defend himself, but was quickly overwhelmed and knocked to the ground. One of the gang grabbed the officer's truncheon from him, and hit him on the head until the Constable became insensible. He was taken to the Royal Free Hospital, where he was detained and treated for his serious injuries. Later that year a James Daley was sentenced to nine months' imprisonment with hard labour, and John Saunders was fined 40 shillings, or in default, one month's imprisonment for the attack on the officer[77].

The police station is situated next door to Clerkenwell Magistrates Court where Charles Dickens, at one time was a Court reporter. One of his books, Oliver Twist, was written against the background of the 'Rookeries' (places of low morals and deprivation) in the vicinity of the Court[78].

In 1913 the Station was enlarged to accommodate extra staff. The building was re-built to include two sets of married quarters and accommodation for 53 unmarried men[79].

Plans were prepared in 1939 to erect a new police station on the existing site but with the outbreak of the Second World War the plans were abandoned. Land at the rear of the station, known as Percy Yard, was used during those war years for growing vegetables. The freehold was purchased in 1955, for £2,500, to provide extra car parking space[80].

In 1960 Kings Cross was EK or Echo Kilo as it was a station on 'E' or Holborn Division under the supervision of Superintendent Wharton[81].

It remained an operational police station until 1992 when a new police station was opened at Tolpuddle Street, Islington. The old police station is still used for non-operational police purposes.

Upper Holloway Police Station (Also known as Archway Police Station)

In 1869 it was proposed that a new sub-division be formed at Upper Holloway and a new police station erected. A site was purchased in 1870 where a temporary station operated until 1873.

Upper Holloway Police Station was situated at Scholefield Road at the corner of Zephany Street (now Zoffany Street, N.7) within the Parish of St. Mary, Islington. In 1886 the Receiver purchased the freehold title to the land at a cost of £750 from Mr. R.D.Lown, a master builder residing at Bartholomew Road, Islington. The station was built at a cost of £2,992 and was taken into service in November 1887. Upper Holloway was shown as a station on "Y" Division[82].

The station was a typical three-storey Victorian police station house. On the ground floor of the building there were a Charge Room, an Inspectors' Office, a waiting room, a store, an association cell (often called the drunk tank) and three other cells. On the ground floor there was also a kitchen, a scullery, a brushing room, a clothes room, a drying room, a boot room, eight W.Cs and a urinal. In the yard there was also a parade shed and hand ambulance shed. The first floor had a Day room, a mess room, a food locker room and a lavatory. Eight single men lived on the first floor and twelve on the second floor. In the yard were a parade shed and a hand ambulance hut.

Being a London police officer very often had its dangers, especially the risk of assault or even death. On 4th October 1896 a constable stationed at Upper Holloway Police Station was severely wounded by a violent assailant. It was reported that a George Chamberlain in Upper Holloway assaulted Police Constable 302 "Y" William Haynes. He stabbed the officer in the head with a knife. This action left the officer unconscious and allowed the prisoner to escape. He was captured later and taken before the magistrates at North London Magistrates Court in Stoke Newington, and dealt with later at a higher court[83].

In 1905 permission was granted for Islington Borough Council to leave a mobile fire escape between 7am until 9pm each day in the station yard positioned opposite the yard gates for ease of access. This ladder was placed there by the Fire Brigade in case of fire in buildings with a number of storeys. This service attracted a rental of 5-shillings per annum. The escape was removed in April 1907[84].

A retirement at Upper Holloway Police Station in 1910

The picture above shows the retirement of a constable in 1910 from Upper Holloway Police Station. The officers and men include two Inspectors (one Station and one Sub-divisional) two Station sergeants (identified with four bars on each upper arm) four sergeants and 37 constables. The officer retiring has been awarded a handsome marble clock for his mantle-piece and probably a purse of money. Retirement presents came from collecting subscriptions from the officers and men at the station. The Metropolitan Police did not contribute except perhaps in the provision of a pension after 25 years loyal service and also the provision of a certificate of service, which was provided in lieu of a reference.

During World War One the police station at Upper Holloway was

Special Constabulary Upper Holloway 1914

considered to be a Special Constabulary station. The photograph above shows the entire Special Constabulary of Upper Holloway (46 in number), in about 1914, in the yard at the rear of the station. This is an early photograph as none of the special constables has been issued with uniforms and are wearing their civilian clothes with their duty armlets. They were asked to complete four hours a week duty, which was unpaid. It was generally difficult to distinguish between ranks, but in the front row a number are wearing an additional band on the opposite arm to the duty armlet signifying either a Sergeant or Inspector.

The war volunteers were disbanded in 1918 when the war was over although some would have carried on if needed. Those who had served during the war were rewarded with a medal.

The police station was closed in 1933, but the building still stands although not used for police purposes. In 1936 the Islington Borough Council purchased the title for £1,800 and it is still in use today as offices for the council.

In 2003 a Police Sector Office was shown located at Gill House, Highgate Hill, Upper Holloway, London N19. It is for police use only and has no facilities for the public[85].

The picture below shows the old station as it is today.

Upper Holloway Police Station
Zopheny Street Upper Holloway, London N19
1887 - 1933

[1] The Municipal Year Book 2000 and Public Services Directory Vol.2 Newman Books (1999)
[2] www.discover-islington.co.uk accessed 07.02.00
[3] Metropolitan Police Orders dated 11th January 1864
[4] John Back Archive (1975) Metropolitan Police Museum, Charlton.
[5] Commissioner's Annual Report 1869
[6] Ibid.
[7] Metropolitan Police General Orders 1873
[8] PRO Census Records 1881
[9] John Back Archive (1975) Metropolitan Police Museum, Charlton.
[10] In 1881 Sergeant Robert Ruff, his wife Eleanor and four children resided at 7 Grange St. Shoreditch, London. (PRO Census Records 1881)
[11] The Police Review and Parade Gossip 4th May 1894 p209
[12] Ibid
[13] Ibid
[14] Metropolitan Police Surveyors Records, dated 1924
[15] Metropolitan Police Surveyors Records, undated
[16] John Back Archive (1975) The Metropolitan Police Museum, Charlton.
[17] Ibid
[18] Minutes of Council meeting - December 1908
[19] Metropolitan Police Orders dated 23rd July 1910
[20] Metropolitan Police property schedule 1924
[21] http://www.islingtonfocus.com/articles/art030.htm accessed 27th May 2003

[22] ibid
[23] Op cit.
[24] John Back Archive (1975) The Metropolitan Police Museum, Charlton
[25] Metropolitan Police Orders dated 5th May 1871
[26] John Back Archive (1975) The Metropolitan Police Museum, Charlton.
[27] Metropolitan Police Orders 22nd January 1875
[28] Metropolitan Police General Orders 1893
[29] Police and Constabulary Almanac 1960
[30] Police Review and Parade Gossip Aug. 1897
[31] Police Review and Parade Gossip Sept 1902
[32] PRO Census Records 1881
[33] Police Review and Parade Gossip Sept 1899
[34] Police Review and Parade Gossip Sept. 1902
[35] Kirchener's Almanac 1907
[36] Metropolitan Police Surveyors Records
[37] Metropolitan Police Orders dated 19th February 1912
[38] Howgrave-Graham, H. M. (1947) The Metropolitan Police at War. HMSO
[39] Ibid.
[40] http://www.policememorial.org.uk/Forces/Metropolitan/metroll.htm dated 12.03.02
[41] Police and Constabulary Almanac 1960
[42] http://www.met.pol.uk/contact/phone.htm dated 12.03.02
[43] Vestry Min. Book 1777-1811, 119, inf. from Mr. J. C. Connell
[44] The History of Middlesex (1995) p84
[45] Ibid
[46] 10 Geo. IV c.44
[47] Brown, B. (1992)"The Station on the Green" in Islington History Journal. Marketprompt Ltd.
London N7
[48] Ibid.
[49] Ibid
[50] Ibid
[51] John Back Archive (1975) The Metropolitan Police Museum, Charlton.
[52] Brown, B. (1992) 'The station on the Green' in Islington History Journal. Marketprompt Ltd London
N7.
[53] Kelly's Directory 1864
[54] Brown, B. (1992) 'The station on the green' in Islington History Journal. Marketprompt Ltd London
N7.
[55] Ibid
[56] Metropolitan Police General Orders 1873
[57] PRO Census records 1881
[58] Ibid
[59] Police Review - April 1894
[60] Police Review - April 1896
[61] Police Review and Parade Gossip dated 9th October 1896
[62] Police Review and Parade Gossip dated 15th Feb 1901
[63] Metropolitan Police Service Records
[64] Metropolitan Police Orders dated 22nd October 1906
[65] Metropolitan Police Surveyors Records dated 1924
[66] http://www.policememorial.org.uk/Forces/Metropolitan/metroll.htm dated 12.03.02
[67] Bird, M. (1992) – unpublished research. New Scotland Yard, London
[68] John Back Archive (1975) The Metropolitan Police Museum, Charlton
[69] Ibid.
[70] John Back Archive (1975) The Metropolitan Police Museum, Charlton
[71] Metropolitan Police Orders dated 11th January 1864
[72] Metropolitan Police Orders dated 10th January 1870
[73] Metropolitan Police Orders dated 27th October 1869
[74] Dickens Dictionary of London (1888) Mortonhampstead, Devon. Pp197 - 199
[75] Metropolitan Police General Orders 1893
[76] Police Review April 1894
[77] Police Review July 1897

[78] John Back Archive (1975) The Metropolitan Police Museum, Charlton.
[79] Metropolitan Police Surveyors Records and Metropolitan Police Orders dated 28th April 1913
[80] John Back Archive (1975) The Metropolitan Police Museum, Charlton.
[81] Police and Constabulary Almanac 1960
[82] John Back Archive (1975) The Metropolitan Police Museum, Charlton.
[83] Police Review and Parade Gossip dated Oct 1897
[84] Metropolitan Police Surveyors Records 1924
[85] http://www.islington.gov.uk/community.asp?sectionis?=1190 accessed 4th June 2003

Chapter Ten

The London Borough of Newham.

Prior to the formation of the Greater London Council in 1965, which led to the creation of the London Borough of Newham, the area had been divided into the County Boroughs of East Ham and West Ham. Until then, each borough had its own Fire and Ambulance Service. Policing was separate and the local police enjoyed an excellent working arrangement with the other local emergency services.

The Borough is surrounded by the River Lea and the Borough of Tower Hamlets to the west, the River Roding and the boroughs of Redbridge and Barking & Dagenham to the east, the River Thames to the south and Waltham Forest to the north. The Newham residents form the communities of Beckton, Custom House, Cyprus, East Ham, Plaistow, Canning Town, North Woolwich, Manor Park, Forest Gate, Stratford and West Ham[1].

There were two police Divisions, "H" and "K", which had previously covered the London Borough of Newham. In 1890 for example "K" Division consisted of Barking, Barkingside (so called because it was located on the Barking side of Epping Forest), Bethnal Green, Bow Road, Dagenham, Great Ilford, Isle of Dogs, Limehouse (Pigot Street), North Woolwich, Plaistow, West Ham Lane, Chadwell Heath and Canning Town.

The stations discussed in the chapter, within the London Borough of Newham, are Canning Town, East Ham, Forest Gate, North Woolwich, Plaistow and West Ham.

Canning Town Police Station.

The area of Canning Town is situated on the south side of Barking Road and lies to the north of the Victoria Docks. Today the Barking Road is called the A13, and the first indication the motorist receives that Canning Town is near is when the road rises over what is now known as the Canning Town Flyover.

The first station to be built was situated closer to the Victoria Docks than it was to the centre of Canning Town itself. A police station called 'Barking Road Police Station' was situated not far from Canning Town at the junction with Newham Way and Butchers Road (eastside). Butchers Road was originally called New Barn Street – a section of which still exists today to the north of the Newham Way (A13)[2].

At the beginning of 1886 a freehold site was purchased by the Receiver of the Metropolitan Police at a cost of £800. The land used for the station and nearby housing was taken from re-claimed marshland known as Plaistow Marsh situated south of Becton Road[3]. The new station was called Canning Town and opened in 1888 at 46, Lansdowne Road, Tidal Basin, E16[4].

At the time of purchase Canning Town was shown as a station on "K" Division. This appears to have been a large station, which had four public rooms on the ground floor. These were the Inspector's Office, the charge room, the store and the public waiting room[5]. The station appears to have been a busy one because it was built with five cells which perhaps reflects the levels of crime in the area. The

Canning Town Police Station
46, Lansdowne Road, Tidal Basin, E16
1888 – 1938

constables paraded for duty in the yard where a parade shed had been constructed. Additionally there was a hand ambulance shed located in the yard, which housed the Bishoffen hand ambulance, which was used for the conveyance of drunken prisoners, ill or sick people and dead bodies.

On the first floor there was a mess room, day room, food locker room, bathroom and lavatory. The cooking took place in the kitchen next to the scullery on the ground floor[6].

On the second floor there were two large rooms which housed eleven constables. In 1888 the station was demolished and the impressive station shown pictured above was built[7].

In 1917 during the height of the war, there was a major incident in this area, which attracted a large amount of attention but little publicity and became known as the 'Silvertown Explosion'. A chemical factory site in Crescent Wharf, West Silvertown, between Canning Town and North Woolwich, was used for the production of munitions for the war effort. It was not an ideal site as it was situated next to a wood yard to the west and an oil depot to the east. Also in the vicinity were substantial residential accommodation, Tate and Lyle Ltd. sugar refinery and, a paint works. All this added up to an accident waiting to happen[8].

On the morning of 19th January 1917 a fire, followed by a massive explosion, occurred and seventy-three people lost their lives. This included 13 women and 17 children. Two people were reported missing believed killed in the tragedy, 170 persons were injured and 60-70,000 properties were damaged. One brave police officer, Constable George Greenhoff was seen rescuing people from the fire and warning people to keep away from the vicinity as the chemical factory contained quantities of TNT[9]. Later he was caught by the full force of an explosion and died in hospital of his injuries two days later. His widow and eight-year-old son, Edward, later accepted the King's Gallantry Medal, a posthumous award for his bravery. Edward Greenhoff later joined the Force and served 27 years before he retired in 1955[10].

This incident was entirely the result of an unfortunate set of circumstances rather than good military precision by the German fighting machine. Special constables had been sent from Canning Town and North Woolwich to help with the situation, and were quickly followed by re-enforcements from East Ham and Forest Gate. Regular constables were supplied from Bow, Poplar, Limehouse and East Ham. They helped the firemen deal with the flames, carry out the dead and attend to the injured and homeless. They also helped to secure the huge number of damaged properties. Special constables assisted and supported the regular officers for sixteen days after the event, during some of the coldest days for some time. The homeless slept in partly constructed shelters in the area and were helped by the goodwill of the constables and specials who attended[11].

One of the major problems facing new police officers, who have come from outside London, is accommodation. Senior Police Officers have, since the very earliest times, been conscious of the need for clean and adequate dwellings for police officers and their families not only for health reasons but also in case of corrupt practice. The highly regulated nature of policing ensured that approval to live at certain locations was given by senior officers, to avoid problems like criminal or problem neighbours. The police made a conscious decision to build both married and single officers' quarters thus making them the largest London landlord.

A need was identified at the turn of the 20th Century for more quarters and various premises were selected to cater for this. It was to this end that Canning Town Police Station was planned to have sufficient space and work in April 1911 and provided accommodation for thirty-five unmarried men at the station[12].

Canning Town Police Station remained operational until it closed in June 1938, and all business and other policing functions were transferred to Plaistow Police Station[13]. A new police office for Canning Town was opened in Tarling Road in 1989. By 2002 the office, which was located in a parade of shops which had all ceased trading, was no longer in use and was closed.

East Ham Police Station.

In 1864 a police station existed at East Ham from which two sergeants and eight constables patrolled[14]. The station had no cell accommodation, so prisoners were taken to either Plaistow Police Station or another station if closer. The station, which was probably a pair of cottages, was shown as being located at East Ham Gate, East Ham[15].

East Ham
Station Lamp

In 1881 Inspector Mark Veronne aged 45 years from Newton in Suffolk and his wife Anne resided at the station. Four unmarried constables also lived at the station[16].

In 1901 enquiries were made to purchase land in East Ham on which to build a new station as the older one was considered unsuitable for continued use. In November 1904[17] the existing police station was opened in High Street South, East Ham. The station had accommodation for one married Inspector, one married constable and ten unmarried constables.

The picture shown right shows Constable 101187/166"K" Sidney Charles Clackett who joined the Metropolitan Police in April 1912 at the age of 22 years. His initial posting after Training School was to "K" Division, although it is unclear from records at which station he served. Clackett was born at St. Lawrence in Kent on 8th September 1890 and took up market gardening prior to joining the police. He was 5 feet 9 inches tall. He was a married man and had a son who was born in September 1926. He stayed on "K" Division until 26th July 1915 when he transferred to Woolwich Arsenal where he became Constable 121 Dockyard Police. He stayed there until 22nd July 1923 when he transferred back to "K" Division. He was of

Constable 166 'K' Sidney Charles Clackett

East Ham Police Station
4, High Street South, East Ham, London. E6.
1904 – present day

good character and appears not to have been involved in any disciplinary matters. In 1935 the Commissioner commended him for his diligence in offences involving licensing, betting and gaming in the streets. He retired at the age of 46 years on the 4th April 1937 with just over 25 years exemplary police service. He died on 15th April 1965 aged 75 years[18].

In 1937 East Ham Police Station was reconstructed at the cost of £40,000, although much of the existing frontage was left intact. In addition, at a cost of £30,000, they built a new police section house for ninety single men. It was named after Assistant Commissioner Sir Norman Kendall. It was occupied from 1940 when section houses at Canning Town, Forest Gate, West Ham and North Woolwich were closed. It was also the official home of Superintendent Swinden (co-author), who lived there as a young constable between 1958 until 1963.

From time to time divisions and also stations formed Tug of War teams, which would compete against each other and against outside teams. Successful teams would be entered

Metropolitan Police 'K' Division Tug of War Team circa 1910

for the National Police Championships or the Commonwealth or Olympic Games if they were good enough. Over the years a number of police teams have been very successful at winning medals for their country in these events. The "K" Division team shown was one such team and also shows their trainers and managers. Notice that the qualification for the team seems to be the wearing of a moustache!

Prior to 1937 East Ham became the Divisional Headquarters and the Divisional Superintendent was also responsible for the operational running of East Ham Sub-division. T. W. C. Aylett was the Officer in charge[19], but by 1957 Superintendent H. Timmins had operational control of the sub-Division whilst Chief Superintendent A. H. Thompson was the officer in charge of 'K' Division[20].

In 2001 East Ham was shown as an operational station, and was open 24 hours a day, 7 days a week and where charges were taken and prisoners housed [21]. However by 2002 the station no longer took charges and housed prisoners, as it had limited opening times. It was shown as open Monday to Saturday 6am until 10pm[22]. Prisoners are now taken to nearby Forest Gate Police Station.

Forest Gate Police Station

Forest Gate
Station Lamp

The policing of Forest Gate before 1855 was carried out by means of police patrols from the "Night Watch Houses" in Angel Lane, Stratford. During the 1880's the area of Forest Gate expanded rapidly as a dormitory region like so many other areas of London. With the influx of large numbers of people into the rural outskirts came the need to have greater numbers of police officers and its own police station.

After 1855 the policing of Forest Gate had been carried out from West Ham Police Station. The Divisional Superintendent George Turner had for some time been put under great

Forest Gate Police Station
444, Romford Road, East Ham, London. E7
1888 - 1992

pressure from the local people to have a greater presence in the area. The local Parish Safety Committee reported;

"The roaming about the streets of gangs of louts and vagabonds, the throwing of bricks and brick bats by them at the windows of properties, careless of the safety of tender ladies therein"[23]

Large sums of money were collected from local inhabitants towards the cost of a new station. These local people lived in the more affluent area, situated north of the Romford Road, and centred mainly around Windsor Road[24]. Accordingly arrangements were made to search for available land on which to build a police station. The Home Office authorised the purchase of a site at Forest Gate in 1884 for the building of a police station. After a failed negotiation for this site another was soon found at a place called "Manor Waste". The Lord of the Manor of West Ham was approached, and he was asked to give up the waste in exchange for consideration money of £20 and costs amounting to £11.10s. He agreed to the sale of the land under these circumstances and the land was purchased on a leasehold basis. The freehold was finally purchased on 16th November 1886, at a further cost of £900. The cost of building the station was £3, 341[25].

The first Police Station at Forest Gate was erected at 444 Romford Road, Forest Gate and opened in May 1888. The area to be policed covered the districts of Forest Gate, Manor Park, and part of Plaistow. Records show that not only a station was built but also a section house for ten single constables paying one shilling a week, and one set of married quarters where four shillings a week, rent was paid[26]. With the opening of the new building came a re-organisation of the surrounding station areas. West Ham and Ilford were altered to accommodate the new sub-division.

The authorised strength of the station was two Inspectors, two sub-Inspectors, four sergeants and 69 constables. The first officer in charge of the new sub-division was Inspector Death. Joseph Death was then aged 41 years and was from Barking in Essex. In 1881 he resided in Cable Street, Shadwell with his wife Eliza who was from Colchester in Essex. They did not have any children[27].

In 1910 the strength of the station was two Inspectors, nine sergeants and 94 constables[28]. The new station was shown as a sub-divisional station of Bow Road Police Station, the Divisional Headquarters.

The picture below shows a serial of ten constables from Forest Gate Police Station. They were on duty at the Coronation of King George V in June 1911. They have dressed in ceremonial uniforms plus white gloves and paraded at the photographers to commemorate the issue of the coronation medal. Sometimes the medals were not issued until a year after the event. The medal was designed by Sir Bertram MacKennal M.V.O., A.R.A., and was struck in silver and suspended from the ribbon by a silver ring swivelled on the claw affixed to the top of the medal.

The section house, which was attached to the station, was closed in May 1926 when the additional space was absorbed for offices. In 1962 following the publication of the Deller Report on Re-organisation it was recommended that Forest Gate should be shut, the ground be split in half and that policing should revert back to Ilford and West Ham. Needless to say these recommendations were shelved. By 1965 following local

A group of constables from Forest Gate showing their medals from the Coronation in 1911

Government re-organisation on station areas, Forest Gate became a sectional station of West Ham and had the station code of "KF"[29].

Further Force re-organisation during 1985 saw West Ham and Forest Gate become a Division of the newly established 2 Area (east). Although a small two storey building, it remained an operational police station for longer than really necessary until a new building was opened in 1992.

The site, at 370, Romford Road, E7, had been purchased by the Metropolitan Police from the London Borough of Newham and a suitable police station building was designed by the Property Services Department at Scotland Yard. Construction of the station, by Bernard Sunley and Sons Ltd., commenced at an estimated cost of £7 million. Plaistow became the Divisional headquarters of Newham (north) and Plaistow was headquarters for Newham (south). West Ham Police Station took over the role as office for the Borough Chief Superintendent Ivan L.A. Brown[30].

The new station was built at the corner of Romford Road and Green

Forest Gate Police Station
350-360, Romford Road, Forest Gate, E7
1992 – present day

Street and was opened for police business in June 1992. In September 1992 the Rt. Hon. Kenneth Clarke, Q.C., M.P. Secretary of State for the Home Department conducted the official opening. Also present were the Metropolitan Police Commissioner Sir Peter Imbert, the Mayor of the London Borough of Newham, Bill Chapman, the Receiver Mr. Graham Angel, Assistant Commissioner Robert Hunt and Property Services Department Director Trevor Lawrence. The opening ceremony attracted over 200 people as well as a number of other local dignitaries and school children[31].

The established strength of the station is shown as, Superintendent, three Chief Inspectors, twelve Inspectors, 45 sergeants, 240 constables and 52 members of the civil staff. The officer in charge of the station was

Superintendent (later Chief Superintendent) David Solman[32]. In 2001 the station was shown being open 24 hours a day seven days a week.

In 1998 the officer in charge of the station was Superintendent Barry Vincent and his deputy was Superintendent Dave Almond[33]. Records show that in the same year the Borough Headquarters were located at Stratford Police Station[34] but by 2002 they had been transferred to Forest Gate[35].

By 2002 the old station was still there but it was boarded up and in a sad state of repair.

North Woolwich Police Station.

North Woolwich has had a police station in Albert Road since November 1873 when Police Orders gave instructions for the opening of a new Station on "K" or Stepney Division[36]. The station was built with single accommodation for four constables and married quarters for the sergeant. It was located on the corner of Albert Road and Station Street on the opposite side of the road from its present location, some six roads east[37].

During up-grading of police buildings at the turn of the century Police

North Woolwich Police Station
Albert Road, North Woolwich
1904 – Present day

Surveyors felt that a new station was required in North Woolwich. They looked around for land for sale and found that John and Annie Clare owned a site large enough for a police station. Negotiation with the Home Office commenced for the grant of authority to purchase the freehold site at a cost of £2,050, and this was approved in March 1881. The land was purchased in June 1894[38] and the new station opened in December

1904[39]. It housed one married constable and 10 single men paying 4/6d and 1/- per week respectively[40].

In 1912 there was a dock strike and detachments of police were drafted in to ensure essential supplies were transported from the docks to their

'K' Division on duty at the Dock Strike 1912

destinations. The event was marked by photographers taking pictures of goods being transported, mounted police and foot duty escorts. The picture above shows two Inspectors, three sergeants and 22 constables (two dressed in plain clothes) taken by photographers G.L. Shotter of 340, Barking Road, East Ham. This photographer was prolific in taking pictures of the dispute. This picture appears to have been taken in the Victoria and Albert Docks at North Woolwich.

The second picture shows mounted officers from Woodford on 'J' Division. Duty at such disputes involved long hours at work

Mounted officers in London's Docks during the 1912 strike.

especially for mounted officers who often paraded at their stations, then tended and fed their horses before riding them to the docks. Often these officers worked twelve hour days or longer, but they were compensated with overtime pay. This meant that to be selected for such duty was extremely lucrative.

In 1927 the section house at North Woolwich was closed for renovation and re-furbishment but re-opened in January the following year.

North Woolwich Police Station was badly damaged during the 1939 – 45 World War and there were four casualties. It remained an operational building in spite of the damage[41].

During the re-organisation of Local Authority Boundaries in 1965 North Woolwich was shown as a sectional station to East Ham Sub-Division.

In 2002 North Woolwich is shown open from Monday to Friday between 9am until 5pm[42].

Plaistow Police Station.

The Old Watch House known as the Old Cage, which was situated in the local area, was surrendered to the parochial authorities, as being no longer required for police purposes in April 1851.

Plaistow Station Lamp

The Metropolitan Police decided to build a police station on "K" or Stepney Division in Barking Road, and it was called Barking Road New Station.

This station was built in 1862 and cost £1,729. Ground rent of £21 per annum was paid to the owner Mr. Benjamin Bosher of 12, Duke Street, Manchester Square. The leasehold was purchased for 100 years, and was set to expire in 1962, however it was essential for the freehold to be purchased and this occurred in May 1899 at a cost of £880[43].

The ground floor of the station had five main rooms. They were an Inspector's office, a charge room, a mess room, a library, and a kitchen and drying room. There were also two cells. The basement was for the storage of coal and had one room which was used as a cleaning room. On the first floor there was accommodation for one married sergeant and six constables[44].

Refurbishments prior to 1891 led to an extra cell being built. In the same year the station was inspected and a report stated that the accommodation was badly arranged. It showed that one married Inspector occupied two sets of quarters at the station. This was considered unsuitable and was to be rectified. Five constables were reported as occupying the single men's accommodation.

The cell space was reported as being insufficient for its needs, so the station drying room was converted to take prisoners. The station had ventilation and heating problems, and there was a bad smell from the sewers. Often both men and women prisoners shared the same sanitary arrangements[45].

Barking Road Police Station
386, Barking Road, Plaistow, E13
1864 – 1912

Early reference was made to the new station when details appeared in Police Orders that "The Police of "K" Division are to take charge of and occupy the new Police Station and Section House", with effect from September 1864. Instructions stated that;

"the horse of the mounted constable now stabled at West Ham Station is to be removed to Barking Road Station"[46].

West Ham Sub-Division had to surrender some of its area, during re-alignment of the station boundaries, to Barking Road Police Station together with three constables for reserve duty. These were selected by the Superintendent for transfer. Furthermore the officers who policed this section (both sergeants and constables) were now to parade and take up duty at the new station. Barking Road new station was shown as being a station in the exterior district of "K" or Stepney Division. On 14th August 1869 the name of the station was changed to Plaistow Police Station[47].

In November 1874 instructions were given for two new sub-Divisions to be formed. These were called West Ham Sub-Division and Plaistow Sub-Divisions respectively. This re-organisation saw the separation of Plaistow and North Woolwich into one division leaving West Ham on its own[48]. The instruction noted that the Inspector would now be stationed at Plaistow[49]. In 1881 Eccles Golding aged 36 years from Sligo, Ireland was the Inspector in charge of the station. He resided there with his wife Adelaide aged 33 years from Fressingfield in Suffolk and his daughter Anne aged 11 years, born in Hackney, Middlesex. They lived there with nine single constables[50].

In 1884 Plaistow Police Station was located at 386, Barking Road at the junction with New Barn Street, Plaistow and shown to have one Inspector, nine sergeants, 57 constables and three horses. The freehold of the property was purchased in 1899[51].

The picture below shows the station strength on the date shown, and was taken in the yard of the station. The picture includes officers of the Criminal Investigation Department, who are dressed in plain clothes, and senior officers. Notice they are all wearing their ceremonial dress including their medals.

A picture taken in the yard of Plaistow Police Station on July 15th 1908

At the turn of the century there was a need to update the housing stock of police stations within the Metropolis, and the station at Plaistow was identified as one for re-siting. Accordingly in August 1908 the freehold of the premises a short distance away from the old station was acquired. The site was located at 444, 446 and 448 Barking Road, and was purchased for £2,360. Tenders were accepted for the building and a new station was constructed after all the houses were demolished. There were problems with the building of Plaistow Police Station because a number of restricted covenants stated that the building could only be of a certain height and specification which created difficulties for the planners. These problems were soon overcome and an acceptable plan was agreed and implemented[52].

Plaistow Police Station
444, Barking Road, Plaistow, E13
1912 – present day

The opening of the new station was in September 1912. The station was built with two sets of married quarters for which rent cost 9/- and 6/6d respectively, whilst thirty unmarried men could be housed at 1/- per week each[53].

During World War One London was bombed by German Gotha bombers and Zeppelins. On the night of 19th – 20th May 1918 'K' Division was bombed for the last time during that conflict killing three people and injuring several others[54].

In September 1919 the old station house was leased to a branch of the Westminster Bank for 80 years on an annual rental of £70, however in August 1935 the building came up for public auction and was sold to Ironstone Freeholds for the sum of £2,250[55].

The picture at left features two officers of Plaistow Police Special Constabulary and was taken during the First World War. Notice the Special sub-Inspector is riding a motor cycle and sidecar with the Inspector being chauffeured.

A motor cycle and sidecar used for supervision during the First World War at Plaistow

The section house was re-furbished and re-opened in November 1924.

Local Government re-organisation in 1965 shows that Plaistow (KO) was designated as a sectional station of East Ham (KE) sub-Division situated in the London Borough of Newham.

In 2002 Plaistow still remained open 24 hours a day 7 days a week. The station also takes charges and houses prisoners[56].

West Ham Police Station

The presence of the Metropolitan Police in West Ham dates back to 1829. The Metropolitan Police took over the old watch houses and although one was known to exist at Stratford; its precise location is unknown. There also appears to have been a Metropolitan Police Horse patrol operating from a rented house at Maryland Point, Leytonstone Road owned by Mr. Curtis of the Broadway, Stratford[57]. The National Census in June 1841 shows a number of police officers living in private lodgings in and around the Stratford area[58].

West Ham Station Lamp

The first police station was built at 44a, West Ham Lane at the corner of Langthorne Street in 1850 at a cost of £1297. 10s. 8d. Occupation of the building occurred in March 1851. It contained eleven rooms, three cells, and stables for two horses. Prisoners were detained and charged at West Ham and retained for court the next day. The three cells were of a particular size and specification and often situated near to the charge room or Inspector's Office for ease of supervision. Prior to 1890 the cell space was increased from three to five cells.

The National Census took place in March 1851, just as the police officers moved into the new police station. The census shows the following officers, and family living at West Ham Police Station at 48, West Ham Lane - note the change of

West Ham Police Station
West Ham Lane j/w Langthorne Street, West Ham, London E.
1851 - 1895

street number[59]. Officers from West Ham patrolled a lot further than their current boundary; they often made their way on foot to Canning Town and Forest Gate[60].

Rank	Name	U/Married	Age	Birthplace
Sergeant	John M **Manning**	M	35	Streatham, London
Constable	John **Walch**	M	44	Ireland
	Bridget **Walch**	U	46	Ireland
	Ann **Walch**	U	14	Ireland
Constable	Thomas **Bean**	U	25	East Guildford
Constable	Charles **Lovett**	U	20	Thorndon, Suffolk.
Constable	John **Moore**	U	22	Cornwall
Constable	John **Saunders**	U	28	Dunstable, Beds
Constable	Isaac **Gay**	U	26	Higham, Norfolk
Constable	Ebenezer **Daws**	U	29	Hayley, Oxfordshire

Above the ground floor a section house was built to accommodate twelve single constables[61]. The site had been leased for 71 years from Thomas Henry Golden of 16, Bassett Road, North Kensington, with a ground rent of £16 per annum. The freehold title, according to Police Surveyors, could be purchased, for £390. Authority for purchase of the freehold title was sanctioned by the Home Office in November 1864.

Police Orders in April 1864 reported re-organisation in Divisional boundaries and recorded that portions of Bow and Poplar sub-Divisions would be formed into a new division. This was called West Ham Sub-Division and was located on "K" or Stepney Division. Instructions noted that police duty should be carried on there where police officers paraded

for duty, charges were taken and prisoners housed in the cells. In 1864 records show that two new Inspectors Arthur Mason and William White were posted to the station[62].The strength of the station was shown as two Inspectors, six Sergeants, and 51 constables with one horse, which was to be ridden by the two Inspectors on their alternate tours of duty[63].

West Ham Sergeant 1870 - 1883

This photograph of a West Ham Sergeant was taken between 1870 and 1883 with whiskers. Police orders in March 1869 gave authority for police officer's to wear whiskers or beards. Previously it had been felt that whiskers would obscure the collar numbers on uniforms, which this example nearly does. In the event that members of the public wished to complain or bring to light good police work it was important that each constable or sergeant should be identifiable. The officer is not wearing a whistle and chain, which were introduced in 1883. The photograph taken at a studio in Stratford shows the sergeant with ceremonial white gloves and best No.1 uniform, a sign that he was required to perform duty in central London, possibly in connection with Royalty, at an event such as Trooping the Colour at Buckingham Palace.

Police orders gave instructions for two new sub divisions to be formed. These were West Ham and Plaistow respectively. This saw the breaking up of Plaistow and North Woolwich into one division leaving West Ham on its own. The orders noted that the Inspector would be stationed at Plaistow[64]. The strength of both stations in 1874 was recorded as follows;

Station	Inspector	Sergeants	Constables	Horses
West Ham	1	7	66	1
Plaistow	1	9	57	3

In 1880 the address of the station was shown as West Ham Lane, corner of Langthorne Street. In 1891 an inspection was carried out which reported that the accommodation for two sergeants was now occupied by thirteen single constables. The station had ventilation problems and it was considered too small, so more ground space was required. There were several unhealthy stations where from time to time typhoid would break out often due to unsanitary conditions. There were several outbreaks of this disease at Bow Road Police station between 1883-1891. Furthermore the section house was inspected in 1891 and found to be overcrowded, having at least two more occupants than it should have had. A recommendation was made for larger premises to be built.

In 1881 there were twelve constables living at the station. The Head constable was shown as Benjamin Coleman aged 35 years from Sarre in Kent[65]. In 1888 parts of West Ham and Ilford Sub-Divisions were taken away to form a new Division called Forest Gate. Sub-Divisional Inspector Thompson, assisted by Inspector William Rooks, was in charge in 1890, with eleven sergeants and ninety two constables[66].

In 1890 the Metropolitan Police Surveyor, Mr John Butler recommended the purchase of a freehold site located at 64-66 West Ham Lane on which to build the new police station. The parcel of land was purchased from Mr. S. R. Bastard for the sum of £950. A station and section house was built at a cost of £6,393, and occupation was taken up in July 1895[67]. The old station became a lodging house when police moved out.

In 1891 senior police officers agreed that there was insufficient cell space in the metropolis to cope with the demand. There were 531 cells located in London's police stations and this number was considered woefully insufficient. The standard size for cell space was 6ft x 9ft x 9ft giving 486 cubic feet of space, although there were some slightly larger cells which had a capacity of between 4 – 6 persons in what was described as rather unsanitary conditions. It was recommended that each prisoner should have not less than 600 cubic feet of space. Cells were often without independent lighting, although heating would come from the basement coal boiler, which often over-heated the cells[68].

Sir Edward Bradford, the Metropolitan Police Commissioner, visited the station on 28th May 1895 and expressed himself very satisfied with the new building[69]. The old premises at 48 West Ham Lane were leased in 1897 to the Rev. Augustus Scott-White at a yearly rent of £20. A small two storey cottage was erected in the station yard and housed the sub-Divisional Inspector and his family. It was used as married quarters until 1967 when it was converted to office accommodation[70].

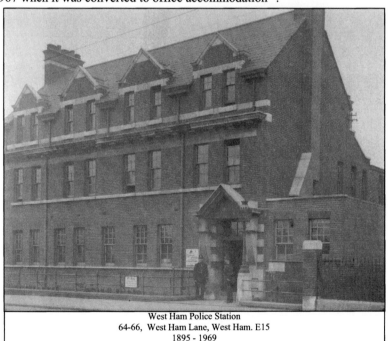

West Ham Police Station
64-66, West Ham Lane, West Ham. E15
1895 - 1969

The first sub-divisional Inspector to take charge of the new station was Inspector K. Quigley who was assisted by Inspector H. Titcombe as his deputy[71]. In 1901 Inspector Murray became Sub-Divisional Inspector followed by Inspector Arthur Ferrett in 1910. By this time West Ham also had Detective Inspector Albert Yeo and three other Inspectors, John Simmonds, John Harding and Frank Bookson. The working strength also included six station sergeants, nine sergeants and 127 constables[72].

The following list includes all the Sub-Divisional Inspector's at West Ham between 1920 and 1949 when the rank was abolished.

29.3.20 C. Brailey	21.2.21 J. Parson	17.7.22 J Bradley	20.8.23 A. Thompson
26.8.29 A. Sawyer	2.10.33 J. Crowley	18.4.38 A Barnes	4.8.43 W. Watts

.

William Watts was appointed Superintendent in charge of the sub-Division on 1st July 1949[73].

On 1st June 1933 all of 'K' Division west of the River Lea, became 'H' Division meaning that Limehouse, Bow, Poplar and the Isle of Dogs were transferred to 'H'.

Every day police officers patrol the streets of Britain and deal with all sorts of situations, events and incidents. The only difference between these was their scale of seriousness. Today police officers have the benefit of radio's and communication so that in the event of trouble help can be called immediately. From the early 1880's until the late 1960's the only communication which would attract the attention of another officer in times of distress would be three blows on his police issue whistle. Police officers often deal with uncertainty and their experience and good humour ensures the minimum of conflict. Police officers often risk their lives in the routine exercise of their duty and this is a factor, which they readily accept as part of the job. The bravery of Britain's civilian police has been well documented yet today past bravery is often forgotten in the mists of time, and when faced with formidable opposition his only protection is recourse to a medium sized wooden truncheon. Whilst danger is always present it is not often that an officer comes near to death, nor is it a common occurrence for firearms to be used, yet both these events happened simultaneously on 2nd January 1898 near West Ham Court, in Stratford not far from the police station.

A builder by the name of John Jolly was involved in shooting Constable George Hill near the court which was witnessed by Constable Bateman, who was standing nearby. Furthermore Constable Bateman turned around and saw the assailant pointing his firearm in his direction. The prisoner was arrested and taken before the court where he was remanded for trial for the felonious shooting of Constable Hill with intent to murder. The officer survived the incident after the removal of a bullet.

Police officers and their families are often involved in social events that take place at the police station. These social events help to bond the police together in what is often described as the police family. Certain events are marked with commemoration and celebration. Events such as receipt of commendations, medals and rewards for good police work often take place as they always have done behind the scenes and out of public view. An important day for any police officer is his retirement on pension where old comrades, friends and relatives join together to mark the event where they celebrate and give their colleague a good send off. This is marked with pictures, gifts and speeches. Police retirements are published in Metropolitan Police Orders informing the force that another officer is leaving the service.

Police history shows that retirement very often occurred after 25 years service, although an officer could work until he had 30 years pensionable service. In the last part of the 19th century there was widespread concern that many good men were taking their pensions early with 98% retiring at 25 years[74].

Even senior police officers like Sub-Divisional Inspector Henry Pipe, attached to West Ham Police Station, took his pension at 26 years service. He had been the officer in charge of the police station, and as a mark of respect all the serving officers turned up at his retirement to bid him farewell[75]. Henry Pipe was from Woodbridge in Suffolk and was married to Eliza, also from Suffolk. They had four sons. In 1881 Henry Pipe was the sergeant at Stoke Newington Police Station residing not far from his place of work at 2 Stoke Newington Common, Hackney[76].

Very often presents to the retiring policemen would be given both from the officers at the station and also from local traders and publicans. The event would be captured with a photograph, which was given to the retiring officer. Many officers left before their time because discipline was very strict and as one error of judgment meant a lost pension, officers retired whilst they were eligible for a pension. Correspondence highlighted the dilemma regarding wastage, but it appears that no early solution was forthcoming[77].

This photograph below taken about 1908, shows a typical retirement scene on a police sub-Division. The two officers retiring are seated to the left with two local dignitaries occupying the seats opposite

The presentation of gifts to retiring officers circa 1908

They are proudly showing the presents that have been bought for them by their colleagues, which in this case consist of two expensive mantle clocks. Usually the whole station was present in the picture which when shift work is considered those off duty are dressed in plain clothes. In the centre is the Divisional Superintendent who is wearing the ornate uniform

Special Constable 'K' Division

came to the event as a mark of respect. Traditionally the officer in charge of the station would give an account of the officer's service to the gathered audience, a custom that still takes place today.

In May 1908 another officer retired from the Force after just over 26 years service. He was Inspector C Lanktree who was at that time the tallest officer in the Metropolitan Police, his height being 6 feet 5½ inches[78].

During World War One Special constables were sworn in to replace many regular officers who had been called to arms. Special constables were required to guard vulnerable points and to assist at the scene of a serious incident. Specials were required to complete twelve four-hour shifts in thirty days. Specials wore a Divisional letter on their collar together with a collar dog featuring the letters "SC" below a small Kings crown, like the one shown above. In essence their uniforms were similar to the regulars except that they wore flat caps instead of helmets, and had no identifying numerals on their collars. In the photograph above the special is wearing his whistle in the wrong pocket and it should be worn hooked from the second button into the left pocket.

Constable David Swinden
attached to
West Ham Police Station
1960

Re-organisation in 1933 made West Ham a sub-divisional station of (K) or East Ham Division, with Forest Gate becoming its sectional station.

With the distribution of station codes which were introduced to improve communication, West Ham was allocated "KW" or Kilo Whiskey[79].

The above picture shows Superintendent Swinden (co-author), as a young constable, in the Mall, London in 1960. The occasion was the visit of the President of France, General Charles de Gaulle. Police officers from the outer Divisions were sent to assist officers on the central divisions.

Notice the black helmet plate badge with white centre, which was worn together with the Number One uniform. The jacket was buttoned all the way to the top and

West Ham Police Station
18, West Ham Lane, Stratford, E15
1969- Present day

the officers' number was worn on both sides of the collar. A snake hook belt was also provided, to be worn outside the jacket. The officer would have been wearing white gloves.

In 1961, a most tragic incident occurred on West Ham Police Station Division, whilst the author was stationed there as a police constable. This incident involved the unfortunate death of two colleagues. Mr John Hall had been arrested and was being interviewed in the C.I.D Office at the Police Station when he produced an automatic weapon and escaped from the Station. Sergeant Frederick Hutchins and Constable Charles Cox, who were both unarmed, together with a number of other police officers gave chase and close to the station the two named officers caught up with Hall who turned and pointed his weapon and shot both officers.

A little further away Hall was confronted by Inspector Philip Pawsey who he calmly shot and killed as the Inspector also tried to stop him from escaping from custody.

Hutchins died later in hospital whilst Cox survived his terrible injuries. Later that day Hall turned the weapon on himself and he too died of his injuries. Both Pawsey and Hutchins received the posthumous Queen's Police Medal for Gallantry and Constable Cox was awarded the George Medal. Constable Leslie England, who was also involved in the chase,

Unveiling the plaque to commemorate the brave officers who lost their lives in 1961.
Charlie Cox (second left) and Les England (left)

received the British Empire Medal[80]. A plaque was unveiled in the foyer of the West Ham Police Station, by Sir David McNee, Metropolitan Police Commisioner in 1981. In the picture shown on previous page, the Commissioner is flanked on the right by the officer in charge of the station Chief Superintendent Redgewell. To the left are Les England (in uniform) and Charlie Cox.

In 1964 Local Authority re-organisation designated West Ham (KW) as a sectional station within the London Borough of Newham. By the 1960's the station was unsuitable for further use and was condemned as it fell below the standards required by the Home Office. Another site was chosen some 200 yards away on which the Stratford Conference Centre had stood until it was destroyed by a German air raid during 1941. The land was owned by the Methodist Church who sold the plot to the Metropolitan Police for £7,000. The new station was ready for occupation by the late summer of 1969. It cost £165,000 and the address is 18 West Ham Lane, London E15.The old police station was no longer required and now occupied by local community groups.

In February 1994 West Ham was re-named Stratford Police Station and was allocated a different station code of 'KS'. When Borough based policing was introduced later in 2000 Stratford Police station became the Borough Headquarters [81] until the new police station was built at Forest Gate.

[1] Municipal Year Book (2000) Newham Book (1999) vol. 2 and The Public Services Directory.
[2] Master Atlas of Greater London (1998)
[3] Bacons London Atlas 1888
[4] John Back Archive (1975) The Metropolitan Police Museum, Charlton.
[5] Ibid
[6] Metropolitan Police Surveyors Records 1924
[7] Ibid
[8] John Back Archive (1975) The Metropolitan Police Museum, Charlton
[9] Fido, M. and Skinner, K. (1999) The Official Encyclopaedia of Scotland Yard. Virgin Press. p109
[10] John Back Archive (1975) The Metropolitan Police Museum, Charlton
[11] Reay, Col. W. T. (1920) The Specials, Billing and Sons Guildford
[12] Metropolitan Police Orders dated 3rd April 1911
[13] Metropolitan Police Orders dated June 1938
[14] Metropolitan Police Orders dated 11th January 1864
[15] Dickens Dictionary of London 1879
[16] PRO Census Records 1881
[17] Metropolitan Police Orders dated 26th November 1904
[18] Metropolitan Police Service Records
[19] Police and Constabulary Almanac 1937
[20] Police and Constabulary Almanac 1957
[21] Police and Constabulary Almanac 2001
[22] http://www.met.police.uk/contact/phone.htm accessed 06.05.02
[23] Parish Safety Committee Reports 1855
[24] West Ham Police Station'(1970) author unknown. The Metropolitan Police Museum, Charlton

[25] John Back Archive (1975) The Metropolitan Police Museum, Charlton
[26] Metropolitan Police Surveyors Records (undated)
[27] PRO Census records 1881
[28] West Ham Police Station'(1970) author unknown. The Metropolitan Police Museum, Charlton
[29] John Back Archive (1975) The Metropolitan Police Museum, Charlton
[30] Open day publicity material June 1992
[31] Ibid
[32] Ibid
[33] Police and Constabulary Almanac 1998
[34] Ibid
[35] http://www.met.police.uk/contact/phone.htm accessed 06.05.02
[36] 'K' Division Handbook 1967
[37] Bacons London Atlas 1888
[38] 'K' Division Handbook 1967
[39] Metropolitan Police Orders dated 10th December 1904
[40] Metropolitan Police Surveyors Records
[41] Police at War (1947) HMSO.
[42] http://www.met.police.uk/contact/phone.htm accessed 06.05.02
[43] Metropolitan Police Surveyors Records (undated)
[44] Ibid
[45] Metropolitan Police Sanitation Inspection Report 1891 – Chief Medical Officer
[46] Metropolitan Police Orders dated September 1864
[47] John Back Archive (1975) The Metropolitan Police Museum, Charlton and Metropolitan Police Orders dated 14th August 1869
[48] Metropolitan Police Orders dated November 1874
[49] Ibid
[50] PRO Census Records 1881
[51] Metropolitan Police Orders dated 20th June 1884
[52] John Back Archive (1975) The Metropolitan Police Museum, Charlton
[53] Metropolitan Police Surveyors Records (undated) and John Back Archive (1975) The Metropolitan Police Museum, Charlton
[54] Reay, Col. W. T. (1920) The Specials, Billing and Sons Guildford, p215
[55] Metropolitan Police Surveyors Records (undated
[56] http://www.met.police.uk/contact/phone.htm accessed 06.05.02
[57] Metropolitan Police Surveyors Records
[58] PRO Census Records 1841
[59] PRO Census Records 1851
[60] West Ham Police Station'(1970) author unknown. The Metropolitan Police Museum, Charlton
[61] Metropolitan Police Surveyors Records
[62] Metropolitan Police Orders dated April 1864
[63] Ibid
[64] Metropolitan Police Orders dated November 1874
[65] PRO Census Records 1881
[66] 'West Ham Police Station'(1970) author unknown. The Metropolitan Police Museum, Charlton
[67] Metropolitan Police Orders dated 6th June 1895
[68] Metropolitan Police Sanitation Inspection of Police Stations 1891 by The Chief Medical Officer
[69] 'West Ham Police Station'(1970) author unknown. The Metropolitan Police Museum, Charlton
[70] Ibid
[71] Ibid
[72] Ibid
[73] Ibid
[74] Police Review, March 11th 1898 p112
[75] Police Review May 1897
[76] PRO Census Records 1881
[77] op cit
[78] Police Review May 1908
[79] John Back Archive (1975) The Metropolitan Police Museum, Charlton
[80] Fido, M. and Skinner, K. (1999) The Official Encyclopaedia of Scotland Yard. Virgin Press.
[81] Police and Constabulary Almanac 2001

Chapter Eleven

The London Borough of Redbridge

Three other London boroughs surround Redbridge. Waltham Forest is to the west, Havering lies to the east, and the borough of Barking and Dagenham covers the south and southeast corner. The County of Essex runs along the northern edge. In 1965 the London Borough of Redbridge was formed when Ilford and Wanstead & Woodford, and small parts of Dagenham and Chigwell joined together. The name of 'Redbridge' was derived from an old red (brick) bridge, which spanned the River Roding, which runs through the Borough[1].

The Borough contains a number of police stations and includes Ilford, Chadwell Heath, Wanstead, Barkingside and Woodford. "J" Division, as it stands today, is a major police division of East London.

Prior to the Local Government re-organisations in 1965 the local authorities were much smaller and were called urban district councils. The complexities of policing and the locations of stations and other facilities meant that very often Local Authority Areas did not match with police boundaries. This caused severe problems over the years as both police and council areas have expanded and contracted, although Borough based policing came into effect in the Metropolitan Police on 1st April 2000. This has now aligned the police boundary to that of the local authority.

The tradition of the police has always been one of reflection especially in terms of organisation. Therefore when stations, senior officers and other resources could be better located this was often done to improve effectiveness and better use of resources. The rapid changes of recent years have meant many movements of senior staff, for example "J" Division, which presently encompasses all of Redbridge, had its Divisional Headquarters at Hackney in 1912, Leyton in 1970, Chigwell in 1985, Edmonton in 1989 and Ilford in 2000.

In 1912 the officer in charge of "J" Division was Superintendent William E. Fitt who supervised there until November 1916 when he was transferred to another part of London. Today, Superintendents head Divisions, although between 1965 and 1985 Commanders were in charge[2].

When a police officer is posted from the Training School he arrives at his new station as a probationer and is soon learning the art of policemanship. This is as true today as it ever was. From the moment the police officer first arrived at the station he became a member of an exclusive family or culture which catered for virtually all his daily requirements. These involved accommodation, recreation and social needs. He entered a culture steeped in tradition, discipline and control.

The stations within Redbridge include Barkingside, Chadwell Heath, Ilford, Wanstead and Woodford.

Barkingside Police Station.

There was a station listed in 1864 at Barkingside as part of 'K' Division[3]. In 1869, after pressure from the local residents for their own police station, the freehold of the Mossford Arms, a beer house with grounds at the junction of High Street and Church Road, was purchased from Mr. L Ingram. The building was formally the vicarage to the nearby Holy Trinity Church. After conversion into a police station the building opened in 1872[4]. The address was shown as Cranbrook Road, Barkingside and was under the supervision of a sergeant[5].

Barkingside Police Lamp

Barkingside Police Station
Cranbrook Road, Barkingside, Essex
1872 – 1964

In 1881 the population of Barkingside was over 2000 people[6], and in 1890 there were two inspectors, James Dickson and Thomas Saunders and eighteen constables at the station[7].

In 1900 two mounted officers were allocated to the station and a stable was erected in the yard[8]. By 1939 there was a need to find additional accommodation to assist with overcrowding in the old police station. A bungalow across the road was rented to house the canteen, Special Constabulary and a lecture room[9].

In 1962 a pre-fabricated timber building was used as a temporary police station until the new one was built[10].This was used until 1964.

Mossford Cottage, the Forge and No.2 Upper Cranbrook Road were purchased and demolished, and the new police station was erected on the same, but enlarged site. Station reception duties at Barkingside were performed from a portakabin near the old front entrance where members of the public were seen[11]. The address of the new police station was now 1, High Street, Barkingside and it opened for business in September 1964[12].

Barkingside Police Station
1, High Street, Barkingside, Essex
1964 – present day

There was then a need to further expand the accommodation and deal with some structural problems within the building. The basement was also subject to flooding. The police purchased and eventually demolished the old cottages in Mossford Green situated between the police station and the recreational ground. This gave the station additional ground space for parking and expansion. Plans were made to add additional office space and a much needed Communications centre to the station. The building work commenced in 1991 when the senior staff and administration moved to nearby (and recently vacated) Chigwell Police Station. Chigwell had been used as the Area Headquarters, however they had moved to the newly built Edmonton Police Station.

Barkingside Police Station
1, High Street, Barkingside, Essex
2003

The new extension to the Barkingside Police Station in effect doubled the size of the station and is shown to the right of the picture above. It was eventually built and officially opened in May 1993.

One of the last officers in charge of the division before Borough Policing was implemented was Chief Superintendent 151198 Sidney Mackay. On promotion he transferred to Barkingside on 2nd June 1989. It was one of the largest police divisions in the Metropolitan Police District (MPD) at the time. Barkingside Division included Woodford, Chigwell, Loughton, Debden, Limes Farm, Hainault and Waltham Abbey. Chief Superintendent Mackay had a long and distinguished career having served at a number of stations which included Bow Street. Together with other senior officers he retired from the police in 1995 at a time when there were financial incentives for them to do so. This co-incided with re-organisation that involved cutting by half the superintending ranks of the force.

To the left is Chief Superintendent Mackay pictured with his daughter Nina who so tragically gave her life in 1997 when she was stabbed whilst attempting to detain a man during a search of a house in Newham. She was attached to the Terrritorial Support Group at the time. Her name appears on the Metropolitan Police Roll of Honour[13].

In April 2000 the re-organisation of the Metropolitan Police into Borough based Operational Command Units (OCU's) reduced the status of this station and saw Chigwell, Loughton and Waltham Abbey removed from its area of responsibility. The Borough

Chief Superintendent Sidney Mackay with his daughter, Constable Nina Mackay

headquarters was established at the newly built Ilford Police Station. Whilst still a charging station it is open to the public 7 days a week 24 hours a day[14].

Chadwell Heath Police Station

In 1840 Chadwell Heath was shown as a station on "K" Division and situated on the outer district. It had a station strength of one sergeant and three constables[15] who all lodged privately. All prisoners were transported to Ilford Police Station[16] for charging, and were remanded to the Petty Sessions at Ilford.

The exact location of Chadwell Heath Police Station was unknown except it was a station without cells and no charges were taken there[17]. It is strongly suspected that the old watch house in the centre of the village was used as a police station before the purchase of a purpose built police station house[18]. The records show that in 1873 Chadwell Heath was designated a station of 'K' Division and had a sergeant in charge. The division was a large one covering

Chadwell Heath Station Lamp

fifty square miles. The Divisional Superintendent needed to travel from his base at Stepney (Arbour Square) for supervision purposes[19].

The station strength was one sergeant and seven constables[20]. There were no senior ranks at Chadwell Heath, so further supervision originated from Ilford Police Station. An Inspector and a Section Sergeant would supervise, (sometimes across divisional boundaries), a large area which included Ilford, Barking, Dagenham, Loughton, Woodford, Wanstead, Chadwell Heath, Barkingside, Chigwell, and East Ham. This would be achieved on horseback, as there were two sergeants at Ilford who would share the station horse for this purpose.

In 1880 arrangements were made for the lease of land in the Romford Road, from the owner Mr. Thomas Hearn of Chadwell Heath, Essex, for an annual rental of £20. The Landlord was required to pay the rates and was also responsible for the insurance in case of fire. The building could only be used for police business and for no other purpose. Records show that Chadwell Heath was a station on "K" or West Ham Division[21]. In 1881 a new station was to be occupied for a short period by police with accommodation for a married sergeant who occupied four rooms at the station[22] and the

Chadwell Heath Police Station
High Road, Chadwell Heath
1892 – 1969

address of the station was published as Romford Road, Chadwell Heath[23].

In 1889 a parcel of land became available, at the corner of the High Road and Station Lane, Chadwell Heath, on which to build a new police station. This site was where old stocks once stood for the public humiliation of offenders. The freehold land was purchased from Mr. Pritlove for £400 and over the next two years a station was built on the site[24]. Meanwhile Chadwell Heath was being policed by Sergeant Gibson and eight constables[25]. The station was completed and ready for occupation in December 1892[26]. In 1931 Chadwell Heath was described as a sectional station of Ilford Sub-Division[27].

The picture on the previous page was taken in 1911.

Inspector Thomas Hill circa 1936

In January 1938 Inspector 112439 Thomas Hill, his wife and two children took up occupancy of the married quarters above Chadwell Heath Police Station. He soon became involved in the community issues at Chadwell Heath and Ilford. Inspector Hill was born in Deptford in South East London. He joined the Metropolitan Police Service in 1923 at the age of 23 years. He served on inner police divisions as a Constable, Sergeant and Station Sergeant. On promotion to Inspector, in 1936, he was posted to "E" Division. He then came to Ilford Sub-Division, on "K" Division, in 1938. Sadly, however, he died in May 1953, just six months before he reached his thirty years service and his pension.[28] He was a well liked and respected officer during his fifteen years on Ilford Sub-Division and his colleagues sorely missed him. His family (although compensated with a death in service award) had to leave the married quarters and find private accommodation.

By the late 1950's there were doubts that the old Chadwell Heath Police Station could continue to perform adequately as a police station, and instructions for the purchase of new land to build a modern police station were issued to the Surveyors Department. A substantial piece of

Chadwell Heath Police Station
14, Wangey Road, Chadwell Heath, Essex
1969 – 2000

land became available a short distance away from the old station in Wangey Road and Cedar Park Gardens, just off the High Road.

In 1961 negotiations to purchase this land were undertaken and by 1962 the land had become the property of the Metropolitan Police[29]. Meanwhile, the Traffic Police used the old station until 1978. It then remained empty until 1981 when the property was sold to a local building company called 'Harts'[30]. It is now licensed premises called the 'Eva Hart' – named after a survivor of 'RSS Titanic' who died recently but had lived locally.

In the meantime there was a re-organisation of boundaries which coincided with a Local Authority revision of boundaries. As a consequence Chadwell Heath and Ilford located on "K" Division were transferred to "J" Division with effect from April 1965. Records show that both Wanstead and Chadwell Heath were section stations to Ilford Sub-Division.

The new station was built at 14, Wangey Road, Chadwell Heath and became operational in December 1969. In April 2000 Chadwell Heath Police Station joined with Ilford, Wanstead, Barkingside and Woodford to become part of the Borough of Redbridge Police Division. Chadwell Heath became a non-operational police station in 1997.

Ilford Police Station

In 1840, some 57 years before William Fitt joined the Metropolitan Police, the boundary of the new professional police moved out into Ilford. Firstly they occupied a small brick-built house on the north side of Ilford Hill near the junction of Mill Place. This was on the opposite side of the road to where the next police station was to be built in 1861. The small brick-built house is often referred to as Little Ilford Police Station[31]. In 1844 William Richardson was the Inspector in charge of the station although the area was called Great Ilford, Barking[32]. Richardson was an experienced man having been recruited into the Thames River Police in 1814 some fifteen years before the start of the Metropolitan Police[33]. Ilford Police Station was then on "K" or Stepney Division[34].

The Home Office gave authority in 1860 to lease a site for a new police station with a ground rent of £13. 13s. 0d. which was paid annually to the owner, the Marquis of Salisbury. Later that same year the police station was erected at a cost of £1,744. On the first floor of the building there was accommodation for one married inspector and four constables[35]. In 1864 records show that Ilford Police Station had one Inspector, four Sergeants and nine Constables working from that building[36]. In 1873 the station name changed from Little Ilford to Great Ilford and was supervised by an Inspector. The station was linked to Scotland Yard (Commissioners Office) by telegraph or wire[37]. By 1888 the

Ilford Police Station
40, High Road, Ilford, Essex
1861-1995

number of officers at the station had risen to one Inspector, seven sub-inspectors, ten Sergeants and seventy-three Constables[38].

One of the many events, which took place annually on "K" Division, was the Ilford Police Station's Fete and athletics day. This was an event for all the family. The thirteenth annual fete of the Ilford Police took place in 1897 on the local sports ground in the presence of a large number of spectators. The profit from the Athletics Day was divided between the Metropolitan Police Orphanage, the Ilford Philanthropic Society, and the Ilford Infectious Hospital Convalescent Fund. The band of the "K" Division Police, by kind permission of Supt. Cresswell Wells, played during the afternoon, and in the evening the Band of the Ilford Volunteers rendered selections. Dancing took place, and the proceedings ended with

Ilford Special Constabulary taken in the yard at the rear of the station about 1916

a grand display of fireworks by Mr S.W.Hayden. (There was also a cricket match between the resident's (148 runs) and Police (82 runs))[39].

In 1900 the freehold of the police station was purchased from the Marquis of Salisbury for £500[40]. Additional land adjoining the site was bought in 1902 and new married quarters and a section house were built for occupation in November 1906[41].

In 1914 the Metropolitan Police Special Constabulary were formed to assist the regular police in its daily task of policing the divisions. Limehouse Police Station was the Headquarters station for "K" division, and the remainder of the division consisted of Poplar, the Isle of Dogs, East Ham, West Ham, Forest Gate, Plaistow, Canning Town, North Woolwich, Ilford, Barking and Chadwell Heath[42]. Special constables were appointed and posted to Ilford Police Station from the headquarters station where the newly appointed Commanders Captain J.R. McLean and his assistant Mr. H. W. Castle (Assistant Commander) were based[43].

Much of Ilford's responsibility during this time of war was to guard vulnerable points on the Division, however "K" Division would often

supply aid to neighbouring divisions. For example "J" Division was particularly large and quite remote in places. It also had a number of reservoirs, pumping stations, and railway bridges which were considered vulnerable and often Special constables from Ilford walked to Hog Hill in Chigwell, which was one of the most elevated spots in Essex, to guard the two reservoirs. The Special constables from Ilford performed this duty from 2am-6am without complaint for two years. Unless they were cyclists theirs was a long walk there and back[44].

Metropolitan Police Special Constable Walters

The above post war photograph shows Special Constable Walters of "K" Division Special Constabulary proudly showing his medals and awards. He rescued a person from a fire in 1877 and won 'the Nine Stone' boxing belt for being champion of England in June 1881.

Additionally he won a special Constabulary Cup and Special Constabulary long service medal with bar for services during the Great War. Walters must have been a dedicated officer to receive the special award of a trophy[45].

Some major reconstruction to the internal part of the building to put right some faults at a cost of £23,000 took place in 1939 but few details are known[46].

In 1939, the Government established a Police War Reserve in order to supplement the reduction in number of the regular police officers and Special Constabulary being called-up for active service in the Armed Forces. One such person was William Dunn, a carpenter living with his wife and daughter in Ilford, Essex, and who, at the age of 31 years, joined the M.P. War Reserve on 28th October 1940[47]. He became Police Constable 729'K'/ 24093 Dunn, and after initial training at Peel House in London, he was posted to Ilford Police Station for street duties. Each

War Reserve officer was given an individual and separate warrant number from the regular police officers.

In March 1944 the Government, after a review of available manpower, decided that Special Constables and War Reserves under the age of 35 years on 1st January 1944 were liable for call-up for service with the Armed Forces or transference to Industry. William Dunn had by this time found himself in that category and resigned from the Police on 31st May 1944[48] and joined the Royal Artillery as a Gunner.

Constable 729'K' William Dunn

Ilford remained a station on "K" Division until the 1965 Local Government re-organisation, which saw a significant change in boundaries and which had last been set in 1933. In the same year both Ilford and Chadwell Heath Police Stations transferred for the first time to "J" Division, Chadwell Heath was no longer the furthest Metropolitan station in the east, because Romford was transferred into the MPD from the Essex Constabulary[49].

By the late 1980s a review of police station stock showed that the old Ilford Police Station was no longer suitable for modern police purposes, so arrangements were made for a new station to be planned. At the other end of the High Road, leading towards Seven Kings, a parcel of land was purchased and arrangements were made for building a new larger police station.

The new £5 million Ilford Police Station opened in June 1995[50] at the opposite end of the main shopping area in Ilford at 270 – 294, High Road. A lounge within the building has been dedicated to Police Constable Phillip Waters who was shot and fatally wounded whilst on duty in April 1995 answering a call to an address at Mayfair Avenue, Ilford. A monument has also been erected at the scene of the shooting.

Ilford Police Station
270 –294, High Road, Ilford, Essex
1995 – Present day

The new station is within yards of the site of two cottages, which served as a 'police station' for the Bow Street Mounted Patrol, which preceded the Metropolitan Police, nearly two hundred years before[51].

Wanstead Police Station

The general area of Walthamstow, Wanstead and Low Leyton were patrolled by the Metropolitan Horse Patrol. A total of one Sergeant and three Constables from the police station at Great Ilford policed Wanstead in 1840. In 1845 a station and section house were occupied in Wanstead Broadway. The premises were leased from Mr. A. J. Cooper of the George Inn, Wanstead on a yearly lease of £20. Records show that it was small, but it had a charge room and a kitchen. Stables were available at the rear at an additional cost of £10 per annum.

Wanstead Police Station Lamp

In 1864 Wanstead was shown as a station where constables paraded for duty, charges were not taken and the building did not have cells. There was one sergeant in charge together with an acting sergeant who split night and day duty between them. Two constables worked the day shift whilst seven constables took over during the hours of darkness[52]. An Inspector supervised Wanstead from nearby (Little) Ilford Police Station[53].

The police were still occupying the house as a temporary police station house in 1867. Records showed that as from that date,

> "The police of 'N' Division are to take charge of and occupy the house at Wanstead Broadway, recently taken as a temporary police station. All prisoners charged at this station are to be conveyed to Walthamstow Police Station, to be kept there in safe custody after charges have been preferred"[54].

In 1877 Wanstead was a minor station of 'N' or Islington Division and was designated a station with a sergeant in charge[55]. The following Police Sergeants and Police Constables are appointed to perform Station Duty at Wanstead temporary Station in periods of 12 hours each, PS 2N Phillips, PS 1N Lucas, PC124N Howe, PC271N Gardener[56].

After the Broadway building had been occupied police found a number of other buildings for use as a temporary police station. For example at 1, George Lane a rather dilapidated two-stall stable in the yard of the George and Dragon public house was used to house police horses for an annual rent of £40.

In 1881 Constable John Creasey lived at the station. He was 41 years old and resided there with his wife Elizabth (aged 36 years) and their four children[57].

Police Orders in June 1884 showed the new address of the station as 1, Tenterden Terrace, Nightingale Lane, Wanstead[58]. These premises were let for £25 per annum[59].

A freehold site was purchased for the sum of £700 in 1885 for the erection of a new police station in Spratt Hall Road, at the junction of Chaucer Road, Wanstead. It was built for the sum of £2,366. The new station opened in September 1886[60].

Wanstead Police Station
Spratt Hall Road, Wanstead.
1886 – present day

The accommodation included space for one married Inspector, who lived in four rooms on the first floor and two rooms on the second floor above the police station. A married Constable lived in three rooms on the ground floor of the stable block and two rooms on the first floor[61]. By 1890 there were four Inspectors, James Ware, Thomas Groves, John Gillies and George Rolfe, one sergeant and sixteen constables posted to the station[62].

On 1st January 1897 a retirement presentation took place – Ex Sub-Divisional Inspector Alexander Wallace, of "J" Division now stationed at Hackney, and formerly stationed at Wanstead, was presented with a handsome saddle, bridle, and riding whip, as a mark of respect, by a number of the residents of Wanstead[63].

Wanstead was a sectional station to Leyton in 1930[64]. Wanstead Police Station was re-furbished in 1935[65].

In 1957 Barkingside, Claybury, Loughton and Wanstead were sectional stations to Woodford Sub-division. Superintendent A. L. Barratt, who was located at Woodford, was in charge of the station. Wanstead was situated on 'J' or Hackney Divison which supervised by Chief Superintendent H. E. Howlett[66]. In 1960 Wanstead's call sign was Juliet November (JN)[67].

In July 2000 Wanstead (with Chadwell Heath Police Station) was a sub divisional station of Ilford Division however because of boundary changes it became part of the Borough of Redbridge Police.

Woodford Police Station

Policing the Woodford area prior to the formation of the Metropolitan Police in 1829 was left very much to the Bow Street Horse Patrol and the locally recruited and not very able Parish constables. The Horse Patrols were formed in 1805 to combat the many highway robberies taking place on the roads around London. Recruits were taken from married ex-Cavalrymen aged between 30-65 years old who were paid 4s per day[68]. It took a further ten years, until 1839 for the Metropolitan Police borders to take in Woodford[69].

In 1836 there were fifteen horse patrol stations numbered from 51-65 in the forth Division. There were three horse patrols responsible at three different places (called stations), in the Woodford area. Station 54 was rented for £15 per year from Mr. P. Mallard. This station was occupied by Constable John Emerson who was a 46-year-old Leicestershire man who had joined the horse patrol in 1823. Station 55, which was also rented from Mr. Mallard, was occupied by Constable John Marlow, aged 32 years, and his family. Marlow came originally from Sussex and had joined the Horse patrol from the Metropolitan Police in 1833. Station 56 was situated at Snakes Lane and was rented from Lady Thynne.

Constable William Fair, aged 35 years and born in Jamaica, was also recruited to the Horse patrol from the Metropolitan Police in September 1833. Constable Fair was responsible for patrolling between Woodford and the thirteen mile post at Abridge, whilst the two patrols covered the New Road as far as Walthamstow[70].

The general description and exact location of the first police station at Woodford is not known, however they were usually the same buildings which were used by the Parish Constables and vacated when the borders of the Metropolitan Police District was extended.

In 1840 the station was known as Woodford Police Station although a Woodford Bridge Police Station is also shown. Records show that Woodford was in the outer district of "K" Division and was one of only three stations, which were able to take charges. The station strength comprised of one sergeant and five constables with supervision by the Inspector coming from Ilford Police Station. The sergeant at Woodford was also responsible for supervising the three constables at Loughton. Records show that the four officers all lived in private lodgings.

A little further away the Receiver of the Metropolitan Police acquired two houses in Abridge and Epping. These were both Horse Patrol stations and the Epping station was called "Holly Wall Station". It consisted of a brick and slate house with a small garden and a stable. It was shown as a station on "K" Division, and was rented from Mr. Payton of Copt Hall, Loughton. The premises were given up in 1853. The house in Abridge had no name but was almost identical to the Epping property, and was rented yearly from Mr. Chinery of Loughton for an undisclosed rent[71].

A likely location for the station was a single storey premises referred to as Woodford Goal situated in what was later the High Road outside the building called "Elmhurst". This structure was positioned close to the excavation cut in modern times to build the North Circular Road, where it joins the start of the M11 Motorway, above and a short distance from, Charlie Brown's Roundabout.

In 1855 Charles Reeves, the Metropolitan Police Surveyor, reported that the Receiver had been given permission by the Home Office to lease land and premises to be used for police purposes at Woodford, in Essex. Temporary accommodation had been found which was reported at the time, to be of indifferent character and lacking in cell and stable facilities.

Mr. Wood, offered the Metropolitan Police a plot of land having a frontage to Woodford Green together with a 60-year lease and ground rent of £10 per annum. The local Superintendent reported that the site was suitable for the police building and permission was given by the Home Office for leasing the land in November 1855. The temporary accommodation cost £39 per year to rent and stable boarding cost 4/- per week[72].

In 1864 Woodford Police Station was shown to have an available strength of two sergeants and ten constables, and was shown as a station on "K" or Stepney Division where charges were taken, although there were still no cells available[73]. Directions were given by the Commissioner to build a new station in December 1864. Records show a suitable site was found in Woodford on land belonging to the Earl of Cowley, which was held in trust from the Estate of the Earl of Mornington. Their agents Messrs. Glaisse and Bristowe negotiated for a 99 year lease from mid-summer 1867 to 1966 costing £52.10d per year, with restrictions. The Receiver of the Metropolitan Police was responsible for the repair of the building, the payment of all taxes, and the provision of insurance of three-quarters the value of £2,500 with The London Assurance Office[74].

In October 1865 re-organisation meant that Woodford was transferred to "N" or Islington Division[75]. Work started on the new station in 1870 and it included a basement, a ground floor and a first floor.

The ground floor was built with a charge room, a reserve room, an Inspector's Office, a day room, stores, three cells, four stalls (stables) and two water closets. The first floor provided residence for four single constables and for a married sergeant who paid 2/3d per week rent. The station opened in March 1871 and was supervised by the sergeant in charge[76]. The address of the station was later described as 1, Mornington Road, Woodford Wells, Essex[77].

Further re-organisation and the creation of a new Sub-Division at Woodford were reported in 1873[78]. This allowed for one mounted Inspector to be stationed at Woodford, together with six Sergeants, two at Woodford (one mounted) two at Loughton (one mounted) and two at Waltham Abbey. Some 53 constables covered the Division including 18 at Woodford with one on detective duties, two mounted constables and five Reserve constables. (Reserve constables were trusted reliable officers who could be sent anywhere to deal with public order problems. They were paid slightly more than ordinary constables.) The remaining distribution was shown as ten constables for Loughton including one mounted constable; 14 constables for Waltham Abbey; one mounted officer and six constables for Chigwell and five constables for Chingford. All the officers were split into ten sections with five sections patrolling during the day and five sections patrolling at night[79].

Woodford Police Station
1, Mornington Road, Woodford Wells, Essex.
1871 - 1968

Soon after this an augmentation of Woodford Sub-Division saw an increase of one Inspector and one horse. Records show that accommodation upstairs at the station was revised to provide rooms for the Inspector who was married. The sergeant was removed and five rooms were allocated to the Station Inspector and his family. In 1884 the address of the station was reported as Woodford Wells. When "J" or Bethnal Green Division was formed on 1st August 1886, Woodford was transferred to the new Division as a Sub-Divisional station[80].

One of the most rewarding social events, which have taken place at all stations since the police, were formed was that of an officer's retirement after exemplary service. In May 1894 over 50 constables and sergeants congregated at Woodford Police Station for the retirement of Inspector William Pearman whose testimonial took the form of a handsome marble clock, which had been inscribed to recognise the twenty-six years service

Woodford Police Station
509, High Road, Woodford Green, Essex
1968 – present day

which he had given to the Force. In his speech Inspector Pearman congratulated the police officers present and stated that the Superintendent would find it hard to find finer officers anywhere else on the division[81].

The Metropolitan Police obtained the freehold to the station in 1898[82].

Records show that in 1924 there was one fixed point box located in the High Road, Woodford on a site owned by Messrs W. and S. Single[83]. This dated from an agreement of 27th April 1907. In 1925 this box was removed to the junction of High Road, South Woodford with Grove Road, and was re-sited on land owned by the Ministry of Transport. Furthermore it was reported that in George Lane, Woodford, on land owned by the Woodford Urban District Council, were premises designated as an ambulance shelter[84]. This was probably for the handcart used to convey ill, injured or drunken people to a place of recovery[85].

Divisional alterations in December 1926 reported Woodford Sub-Division as being responsible for policing Woodford, Loughton, Claybury and Barkingside. In 1931 records show that Woodford Sub-Division was attached to "J" or Hackney Division[86]. In 1933 Wanstead, Barkingside, Claybury and Loughton were shown as sectional stations to Woodford after re-organisation. Chingford and Waltham Abbey were now shown on "N" or Islington Division.

In the mid 1930's Police Boxes were placed at major road junctions to facilitate communications. These boxes were intended to be used by both police officers ringing in and also by members of the public. There were two police boxes on Woodford Division. These were located at the junction of Epping New Road and High Beach Road (Box 38) and Epping Road near the Wake Arms junction (Box 40)[87] both on Woodford Section.

Some of the police boxes were also fitted with air raid warning sirens. They were simply furnished and contained first aid facilities and a single non-dial telephone in a cabinet, which opened from outside or inside as required. There was also a fixed table with a drawer and a hard oval stool to enable the officer to sit and write reports and take refreshments. In wintertime a small electric heater was used to heat the box, which also had an interior light and interconnected telephone bell and flashing light. Some later boxes were made of concrete and situated on new housing estates[88].

In 1965 Local Government boundary changes caused a status change for Woodford (JF) which was reduced to a sectional station to Barkingside (JB) and situated within the new Borough of Redbridge[89].

By 1962 the station, which despite alterations including absorbing the married accommodation within the station, was reported as being inadequate for current policing needs[90]. A new leased site was found at 94-100, High Road, Woodford that was situated on the south west corner of Chestnut Walk. Tenders were invited for the new station however Messrs. Hawkins Bros. (Gosport) Limited won the contract at a cost of £95,856. Work commenced in June 1967 and was ready for occupation by the end of 1968[91]. Renumbering of properties in the High Road meant that Woodford was now located at 509 High Road, Woodford Green, Essex on the main A11 trunk road to Newmarket[92].

The location of the new station was about 400 yards north east of the old station. In October 1974 the Metropolitan Police purchased the freehold to the new station for £30,000[93]. Today Woodford is still the sectional station to Ilford within the Borough of Redbridge.

---

[1] Municipal Yearbook 2000 and Public Services Directory Vol. 2. Newman Books (1999) and London Borough of Redbridge publicity material
[2] Martin Fido and Keith Skinner (1999) The Encyclopedia of Scotland Yard. Virgin Press
[3] Brown, B. (1993) Private correspondence date 22.9.1993
[4] John Back Archive (1975) Metropolitan Police Museum, Charlton
[5] Metropolitan Police General Orders 1873
[6] Census records 1881
[7] Kelly's directory 1890
[8] Metropolitan Police Surveyors records (undated)
[9] ibid
[10] John Back Archive (1975) Metropolitan Police Museum, Charlton
[11] Elliott, B. (1993) A History of the Police Stations of 'J' Division 1886 – 1986
[12] Metropolitan Police Orders 4th September 1964
[13] Martin Fido and Keith Skinner (1999) The Encyclopedia of Scotland Yard. Virgin Press
[14] http://www.met.police.uk/contact/phone.htm accessed on 6th May 2002
[15] John Back Archive (1975) Metropolitan Police Museum, Charlton

[16] In the early days the station was referred to as 'Little Ilford Police Station' by Senior Officers and those responsible of issuing of Police Orders.

[17] Elliott, B. (1993) A History of the Police Stations of 'J' Division 1886 – 1986

[18] John Back Archive (1975) Metropolitan Police Museum, Charlton

[19] Metropolitan Police General Orders 1873

[20] Elliott, B. (1993) A History of the Police Stations of 'J' Division 1886 – 1986

[21] Metropolitan Police Surveyors Records (undated)

[22] Metropolitan Police Orders 24th March 1881

[23] Kelly's directory 1884

[24] Elliott, B. (1993) A History of the Police Stations of 'J' Division 1886 – 1986

[25] Kellys Directory 1890

[26] Metropolitan Police Orders dated 4th December 1892

[27] Kirchner's Police index (1931) Police Review Publishing.

[28] Metropolitan Police Records

[29] Elliott, B. (1993) A History of the Police Stations of 'J' Division 1886 – 1986

[30] Ibid

[31] John Back Archive (1975) Metropolitan Police Museum, Charlton

[32] The Police and Constabulary List 1844. Parker, Furnivall and Parker, London

[33] Ibid

[34] ibid

[35] John Back Archive (1975) Metropolitan Police Museum, Charlton and Elliott, B. (1993) A History of the Police Stations of 'J' Division 1886 – 1986

[36] Elliott, B. (1993) A History of the Police Stations of 'J' Division 1886 – 1986

[37] Metropolitan Police General Orders 1873

[38] Kelly's directory 1888

[39] Police Review August 1897

[40] Elliott, B. (1993) A History of the Police Stations of 'J' Division 1886 – 1986

[41] Metropolitan Police Surveyors records (undated)

[42] Reay, W. T. (1920) The Specials. Billing and Son, Guildford, Surrey.

[43] ibid.

[44] ibid.

[45] Kennison, P. (2001) unpublished correspondence

[46] Metropolitan Police Surveyors records (undated)

[47] Metropolitan Police Orders dated 31st October 1940

[48] Metropolitan Police Orders dated 21st March 1944

[49] John Back Archive (1975) Metropolitan Police Museum, Charlton

[50] Metropolitan Police Orders dated 24th May 1995

[51] Ilford Police Station publicity material

[52] Metropolitan Police Orders dated 11th January 1864

[53] Ibid

[54] Metropolitan Police Orders dated 11th March 1867

[55] Police Office London Directory 1877

[56] John Back Archive (1975) Metropolitan Police Museum, Charlton

[57] Census Records 1881

[58] Elliott, B. (1993) A History of the Police Stations of 'J' Division 1886 – 1986

[59] John Back Archive (1975) Metropolitan Police Museum, Charlton

[60] Metropolitan Police Orders dated 22nd September 1886

[61] Metropolitan Police Surveyors Records (undated)

[62] Kelly's directory 1890

[63] Police Review January 1897

[64] Kirchner's Police Index 1930

[65] Metropolitan Police Surveyors Records, MPS Museum, Charlton.

[66] Police and Constabulary Almanac 1957

[67] Police and Constabulary Almanac 1960

[68] Elliott, B. (1987) The Abbey – Policing since 1840. Unpublished paper

[69] John Back Archive (1975) Metropolitan Police Museum, Charlton

[70] Elliott, B. (1987) The Abbey – Policing since 1840. Unpublished paper

[71] Metropolitan Police Surveyors records (undated)

[72] ibid

[73] Metropolitan Police Orders dated 11th January 1864
[74] Metropolitan Police Surveyors records (undated)
[75] Metropolitan Police Orders dated October 1865
[76] Metropolitan Police General Orders 1873
[77] Metropolitan Police Surveyors records (undated)
[78] Metropolitan Police Orders dated 18th October 1873
[79] Elliott, B. (1987) The Abbey – Policing since 1840. Unpublished paper
[80] Elliott, B. (1993) A History of the Police Stations of 'J' Division 1886 – 1986
[81] Police Review May 1894
[82] Metropolitan Police Surveyors records (undated)
[83] The Metropolitan Police Surveyors Records 1924
[84] Ibid
[85] Elliott, B. (1987) The Abbey – Policing since 1840. Unpublished paper
[86] Kirchner's Almanac 1931
[87] Op cit Elliott, B. (1987)
[88] ibid
[89] Elliott, B. (1993) A History of 'J' Division 1886 – 1986
[90] ibid
[91] ibid
[92] ibid
[93] ibid

Chapter Twelve

Thames Division

The police of the Thames Division were formed before the Metropolitan Police were established. The Thames Police Preventative Force was established in June 1798 because vast wealth was pouring into the Port of London and it was established that;

> "....there were no fewer than 10,000 thieves, footpads, prostitutes and pilferers at work on the jetties, quays that lined the riverside and that the plunder and pillage represented an annual loss of over half a million pounds." [1]

With the formation of the Metropolitan Police in 1829 the River Police became a division of the Metropolitan Police. The first station to open near the Thames was Wapping followed by an office at Greenwich, which had an establishment of one hundred Constables. Police were recruited not only to stem the tide of crime on the river, but also to deal with the frequent robberies on the roads leading into the metropolis and thefts in the dockyards at Deptford and Woolwich.

The division extended practically through the whole navigable area of the River Thames. This stretched from Teddington Lock in the west to Dartford Creek, Kent and Rainham, Essex in the east[2]. The following stations, description and events of the Thames Division relate mainly to the east of Tower Bridge as these places are located within north and north-east London.

Thames - Blackwall Police Station

The head of the Thames River Police was shown in 1844 as Mr. James Christopher Evans who was the Superintendent and appointed in 1798[3]. Evans had considerable experience of the River Thames and of managing the River Police. He was assisted by 21 Inspectors. In the early days of the River Police the stations were shown as ships which were moored in strategic places. For example at Wapping in 1844 a floating station was located off Wapping stairs, the ship "Royalist" was shown moored off Somerset House, Strand Lane (although this was re-located eastwards later), and the "Scorpion" off the Folly House, Blackwall, in Poplar[4]. (Folly House was a famous Riverside Public tavern noted not only for its pleasure gardens but also for its famous resident and mistress of Charles II, Nell Gwynne who died in 1687. It stood between Stewart Street and the River Thames. Additionally the Thames Police shared the police station located at London Docks with "H" or Whitechapel Division. The station ship "Royalist" was leased from Mr. John Hards of Greenwich, Kent, and the Receiver paid for all outgoings. In July 1880 a mooring agreement was reached with the conservators of the River Thames who stipulated that the ship could be moored near the Saltings between Greenwich and Blackwall[5].

Records show that in 1844 there were seven Inspectors attached to Blackwall station. These were William Leonard who was promoted in 1837, George Webb, Richard White, Thomas Benjamin Walker, John Judge, George Maddox and Thomas Grimstone all promoted to Inspector in 1840[6].

In the early days of the Metropolitan police "H" Division sergeants and constables were under the direct supervision of the Inspectors of Thames Division[7]. This was a sensible step considering their origin and experience since they were formed thirty-one years before Peel's new model.

There were fifteen boats attached to Thames Division, eleven being kept for duty with four in reserve. These were rowing boats. By 1864 the strength of Thames Division was twenty-five Inspectors and 86 constables. In the intervening period there had been a change of ship at Blackwall with the "Royalist" having been moved from off Somerset House down to what was now considered to be an out of the way place for policing purposes off the Folly House, Blackwall[8]. The vessel was facetiously called the 'Abode of the Bliss' named after Inspector (Daddy) Bliss who resided there with six single constables[9]. John Bliss was the Inspector in charge, but it is doubtful that he lived in the vessel. Bliss was married and also had a son, which would have meant very cramped conditions for all on the floating station. In 1881 records show that he lived at 62, Brunswick Road, Bromley with his wife Maria and son William. Bliss was born in 1843 in London (Middlesex)[10].

On the next page is the hulk of the "Royalist" which was a designated police station with an Inspector in charge[11]. Records show that in 1873 it was situated off Strand Lane[12]. The Constables of Thames division were divided into four watches each of six hours duration, thereby ensuring a boat came in to the station every two hours and allowing for a fresh crew to take their place out on patrol [13].

Blackwall Police Station
Pierhead, Blackwall, London.
1875 - 1894

In November 1875 District Superintendent A.C. Howard proposed a new location for the floating station at the Pierhead, Blackwall, located at the west entrance of the east India Dock Wall Road. This site afforded good access for a land or water approach and also gave a complete view down Bugsbys Reach and again up Blackwall Road to Greenwich[14]. The call sign of the station was Romeo Tango (RT)[15].

In 1877 Inspector 1st Class Wootton was shown in charge of the Royalist assisted by Inspectors 2nd Class George Roberts and Thomas Pridmore[16].

Blackwall Police Station
19, Coldharbour Lane, London E14
1894 – present day

The 2nd Class Inspectors were in fact sergeants. It appears that efforts to re-locate the station came to nothing and little was done until 1887 when a number of new sites were proposed. A site located at 19, Coldharbour Lane, E14 was purchased freehold in May

1891 at a cost of £4,000. Blackwell (sic) was designated as a receiving house or mortuary for dead bodies taken from the Thames[17].

A new station called Thames Blackwall was built on the site together with four sets of married quarters. It was taken into service on 4th February 1895[18]. In 1894 the "Royalist" was taken out of service when the new Blackwall station became operational[19].

Lodging costs for the married Inspector was assessed at 5/6d per week whilst the three married Constables each paid 3/- weekly. At the location beside Browns Wharf, the jetty belonged to the Thames Conservancy, and the Receiver of the Metropolitan Police had to pay £1 per year for the privilege of mooring a coal hulk there[20].

In 1912 a national dock and transport strike severely tested the resolve of the police in London. As the photograph shows convoys leaving the docks had to be escorted by large numbers of police many

London Police escorting goods from the dock-yards during the 1912 Dock Strike

of who were brought in from outside the Borough to help. The police displayed an even-tempered attitude and earned the respect of the striking workers.

By 1924 the Port of London Authority had taken over leasing the mooring and control of the Jetty. Under the agreement the annual rental of the mooring still cost £1 per year, but use of the Jetty amounted to £4. 4s 0d per year. A clause in the agreement stipulated that if the PLA, who were the conservators of the jetty, gave notice in writing to the Metropolitan Police for the jetty's removal, and then the Receiver would ensure this was done. Furthermore rental of £1 per year was also charged by the PLA for piles and a boom, which were on licence from the conservators[21].

This photograph below was taken in 1909 at Blackwall Police Station shows nine constables and two sergeants, with the senior sergeant having 4 bars to his stripes. The Thames Division uniform was different from normal Metropolitan Police issue uniforms, because the type of duty was not normal foot duty. In those days the launches were not all motorised

A group of Thames Police pictured at Blackwall Police Station around 1909

and getting about on the Thames often relied on rowing everywhere. The waterproof short coats and trousers, rather than the normal police duty issue full length great coat, kept the police officers dry whilst rowing and protected them from inclement weather in the open boats.

Thames – Wapping Police Station.

Wapping Police Station was the Headquarters of the Thames Division, and was opened on the site of the present station in 1798[22]. At the station as well as a Police Department there was also a Judicial Department all under the control of a resident Magistrate Captain John Harriott. The Thames River Police were soon heralded as extremely good at their job, earning praise from merchants and ship owners alike. By 1800 they received statutory authority, and were frequently called upon to assist other law enforcement officers in their duties.

In 1839, some ten years after the commencement of the Metropolitan Police the Thames River Police were absorbed into the London Police, and the Judicial Department became the Thames Police Court. The first Officer in charge of the River Police was Superintendent James Evans who completed fifty years unbroken service when he retired on pension in 1848[23]. Evans had joined in 1798 as an assistant surveyor. He handed over command to his son Superintendent John Christopher Evans. Charles Dickens noted that a picture of James Evans hung in the charge room of the station[24].

By 1844 the court had moved near to Arbour Square, Stepney where two magistrates sat daily, except for weekends, from 10am until 5pm. Records show that the magistrates at Thames Police Court were Mr. William Ballantine of 89, Cadogan Place, off Eaton Square, and William J. Broderip of 2, Raymond Buildings, Grays Inn. The clerk was Edward William Symonds. Thames Police Court boundaries were fixed by order of the Council dated 10th December 1842, and included all in the Eastern entrance of the London Docks, north side of the dock area to Fox's Lane, High Street Shadwell, Ratcliff Highway, Cannon Street, Cannon Street Road,Whitechapel Road, Mile End Road, Grove Road, Eastern Counties Railway, along it to the River Lea, to River Thames and back to the eastern entrance of the London Docks[25].

On 9th January 1843 a letter from the Home Office to the Receiver recommended that the lease to the station should be extended and a new police station established on the site[26]. In 1844 the established Thames Division strength of Inspectors was twenty-one with nine posted to Wapping Police Station. These included William Judge appointed 1817, John Gaskin appointed 1826, William Isbester appointed 1827, Joshua Judge promoted to Inspector in 1831, James Christopher Evans, Charles Henry Falconer, and Thomas Fox all appointed in 1833. John Joseph Lewis and James Robert White were appointed in 1834[27].

Later a system of 1st and 2nd class Inspectors were introduced as only Inspectors were legally able to board boats and inspect their contents. The 2nd Class Inspector wore the badge of rank for a sergeant, i.e. three chevrons on each forearm. 3rd class Inspectors were also introduced at some later stage.

In 1863 the lease was renewed costing £100 per annum instead of the previous sum of £80 for a term of either fourteen or twenty one years. The strength of the Division was shown as 111 officers of mixed rank, which included seventeen Inspectors (second class) who were employed in the boats. The Division kept some fifteen boats, eleven being in use with four kept in reserve[28].

Land was leased from the Governors of Bridewell in 1867 on which to build the new station at Wapping. The lease was set for sixty years from

Christmas 1867 expiring at Christmas 1927. The Receiver had to pay the rates and costs of repair for the new station which included painting the inside of the station every seven years and the outside every three years. The Governors of Bridewell stipulated that the premises were to be insured for a sum of £3,000 annually[29]. The station included a Superintendent's Office, which was located on the first floor with a charge room, a reserve room, two cells and two water closets on the ground floor. In the basement were the shipwrights' office and two coal cellars. On the second floor was accommodation for one married Inspector who occupied two rooms with a third room downstairs on the ground floor for a weekly rent of 5/6d. There was also room for seventeen constables on both the first and second floors of the accompanying Section house. They paid one shilling per week rent. The station was occupied by the Police of Thames Division in January 1871 and had cost £3,490 to build[30]. In 1877 Inspector 1st Class Isaac Hill was shown in charge of the station assisted by Inspectors 2nd Class Charles Marler and William Robson[31]. More is mentioned of William Robson later.

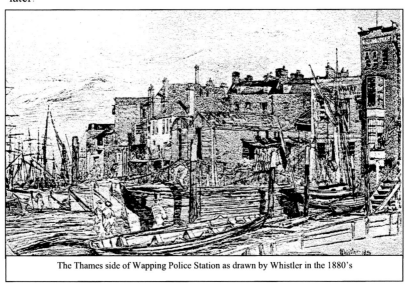
The Thames side of Wapping Police Station as drawn by Whistler in the 1880's

The print shown was sketched by Whistler the famous Victorian artist and shows the Thames at Wapping. It pictures the police station on the extreme right.

A report from the Surveyor prompted the need for a new pile and girders costing some £25. 10s in order to protect the police boats from barges drifting down on the ebb tide [32]. Suitable protection had been afforded to the station when Aberdeen Wharf was operating however now that the location had been vacated the boats and piles were no longer present leaving the location vulnerable.

On 1st November 1880 the Divisional Superintendent drew attention to the bad state of the foreshore at Wapping and the need

Wapping Police Station (Street side)
98, Wapping High Street, London E1 9NE.
1871 – Present day

for repairs. A barge load of shingle was purchased for £14. 10s and the cost of repair was £4. A granite causeway was built in October 1883 for

Wapping Police Station (Thameside)
98, Wapping High Street, London E1 9NE.
1871 – Present day

the sum of £25 in order to facilitate the launching of the boats[33].

In 1881 Constable William Snell, a 28 year old from Margate in Kent, was a resident of the section house at High Street Thames Police Station[34]. Constable Snell was to find fame later in 1884 when he was shot in the stomach by an armed burglar in Hoxton. By April 1885 the increased use of firearms by burglars led to authority for police to be armed with revolvers[35].

Also in 1881, Inspector 2nd Class William Robson lived at Wapping Police Station with his wife, and records showed the address to be 255, High Street, Wapping[36]. Tragically Robson gave his life for the job he loved. He was accidentally drowned in 1884 when his police boat was hit by a steam tug whilst visiting river patrols at Charlton[37]. Robson is remembered in the Metropolitan Police Roll of Honour[38].

In May 1888, the premises adjacent to the station were leased for use as a boathouse. Accommodation was provided for one married Inspector at a cost of 5s. 6d per week and one married constable for a weekly rent of 3s. The freehold for the station and the boathouse was purchased later in April 1891 for the sum of £8,290[39]. Records show that in 1888, Superintendent George Skeats was in charge of the Division assisted by forty nine Inspectors, (only) four sergeants and 607 constables[40].

Wapping Police Station was given the designated call sign Tango Alpha (TA)[41].

In 1904 the Superintendent of Thames Division reported to the Commissioner about the unsuitability of the current station, accommodation and workshops at Wapping, and suggested that a new more modern station should be erected. This was agreed and by March 1907 plans for a new station were accepted and tenders invited for building the new station. The bid by Messrs. Lawrence and Sons was accepted, and by August demolition of the old police station had started. The station, section house, married quarters and administration section were ready for occupation by 28th February 1910. The section house was built to house twenty-seven single men at a weekly rent of 1s, whilst the two sets of married quarters attracted rental of 9s. 6d and 7s. 6d respectively per week[42].

Constable 212 Howe
Thames Division

The picture at left shows Constable 212 Thames Division Howe in his uniform. Constable Howe joined the service with warrant number 96885 on the 17th May 1909. He was originally posted to 'H' division as 425 but transferred to Thames Division on 13th June 1912. He was promoted on 18th March 1916 when he became Sergeant 12 of the 4th Division Chatham Dockyard Police. Howe left the Dockyard Police on 9th October 1922 when he was posted to 'K' Division. He then became a Station Sergeant on 29th June 1923.

When World War Two broke out he was retained as a pensioner and then further pensioned on 25th September 1945. There is a great difference in type, style and make up of this uniform compared to the standard Metropolitan style. The flat cap shows an anchor badge with chinstrap up. The number of the constable is clearly shown on the lapels of the greatcoat he is wearing. Note also that he is wearing a collar (detachable) and tie. Today, in order to avoid being strangled with their own ties, Metropolitan Police officers wear detachable ties.

On 27th April 1920 a Bill called the Metropolitan Police Order Confirmation Act 1920 was passed in Parliament allowing the compulsory purchase of 102, High Street, Wapping to allow the station to be enlarged and improved. This property was located adjacent to the station and belonged to the Bridewell and Bethlehem Royal Hospital. The freehold was purchased for the sum of £5,605 on 5th January 1921[43].

The standard river police rowing boat was called a 'Galley', and they were in use from 1789 until 1925. These open clinker built boats were 8.2 metres long and carried a surveyor or Inspector in the stern who operated the rudder strings whilst three oarsmen rowed the craft[44]. The men were out in all weathers and all too often literally worked to death[45].The rowing boat was replaced in 1925 by engine powered patrol boats[46].

Station Sergeant 5 Porter
Thames Divison

The rare picture shows Station Sergeant 5/83458 Albert Ernest Porter of Thames Division, who joined the Metropolitan Police in 1898. The Station Sergeants wore four bars instead of three. He is shown with his three medals, the 1898 Jubilee Medal, the 1902 Coronation Medal and the 1911 Coronation Medal. Porter became a sergeant in September 1908 and was pensioned in 1924 after 26 years service. Porter retired as a Station Sergeant. Porter received his pension for 29 years and died on 12th March 1953.

On 25th March 1922 a licence was issued from the Port of London Authority which authorised rental of eleven single piles, seven double piles, booms, a causeway, a slipway, a gridiron and campshedding. Also included were a raft, an overhanging runway, and an overhanging girder together with two overhanging windows. This cost the Receiver £15 rent per annum. On 29th September 1923 a further licence was issued from the Port of London Authority to place six life saving chains on an iron ladder on the river frontage at an annual rental of £1[47].

Wapping has always been the headquarters for Thames Division. At various times the Division has been supervised by a variety of ranks. For example in 1937 Chief Inspector J. Brown was the officer in charge,[48] however twenty years later an officer two ranks senior headed the Thames Division. In 1957 Chief Superintendent C. L. McDonough GM commanded the Division with Superintendent H. Morley being responsible for the station and its patrols[49]. Thames formed part of No. 3 District, which also included the divisions of 'E', 'G', 'H', 'J' and 'K' Divisions. The District Headquarters was located at Macnaghten Section House, 55 Judd Street, WC1. Commander H. J. Evans was in charge together with Deputy Commander W. C. Batson[50] (see also Barking and Dagenham for further information).

It was felt that as the Divisional Headquarters for Thames Division more land would be needed in the future to further improve the facilities at the station. Accordingly two parcels of land were acquired, the first being the freehold site of the Morocco and Eagle Sufferance Wharves 82-84, Wapping High Street. This was purchased for the sum of £53,500 in February 1965. This purchase was intended primarily for the construction of a new boat repair yard. The second purchase occurred when the freehold interest of the old Aberdeen Wharf 94-96, Wapping High Street became available for the sum of £50,000. Plans had been laid for the complete rebuilding of Wapping Police Station scheduled to commence in 1971-2 and this second parcel of land was required in order to complete the task[51].

However in 1978 radical policies re-think in respect of Thames Division occurred, and together with substantial financial cutbacks, it was decided not to re-build the new station.

Wapping Police Station is now a grade II listed building because of its architectural importance and it cannot be demolished. The pontoon on the river is used to land the twenty or more bodies a year, which are pulled from the fifty-four mile stretch of the Thames between Staines and Dartford. Waterloo Pier had also been used to land dead bodies, however public concern at this site was deemed to be too disturbing so the practice ended. Whilst the station does have cells they are considered unsuitable for the detention of prisoners so they are transferred to Whitechapel Police Station.

The station is still in use today for parading of police officers and the housing of boats[52]. The call sign of the station is shown as Uniform Delta (UD)[53]. In 2002 Wapping Police Station was shown as closed to the public[54] although prisoners are taken to other land based stations.

---

[1] Colquhoun, P.(1875) A Treatise of the Police of the Metropolis
[2] Richardson, A. (1957) Nick of the River. Harrap, London
[3] Sleigh, A. W. (1844) The Police and Constabulary List 1844. Parker, Furnival and Parker, London.
[4] Ibid.
[5] Metropolitan Police Surveyors Records (undated)
[6] Sleigh, A. W. (1844) The Police and Constabulary List 1844. Parker, Furnival and Parker, London.
[7] John Back Archive (1975) The Metropolitan Police Museum, Charlton
[8] Budworth, G. (1997) The River Beat. Historical Publications, London.
[9] Ibid.
[10] Census records 1881

[11] Metropolitan Police General Orders 1873
[12] Ibid
[13] Budworth, G. (1997) The River Beat. Historical Publications, London.
[14] John Back Archive (1975) The Metropolitan Police Museum, Charlton
[15] Metropolitan Police General Orders 1893
[16] Post Office London Directory 1877
[17] Dickens Dictionary of London (1888) Moretonhampstead, Devon pp132 –133
[18] Metropolitan Police Surveyors records (undated)
[19] Budworth, G. (1997) The River Beat. Historical Publications, London.
[20] Metropolitan Police Surveyors records (undated)
[21] Ibid
[22] John Back Archive (1975) The Metropolitan Police Museum, Charlton
[23] Fido, M. and Skinner, S. (1999) The Official Encyclopedia of Scotland Yard. Virgin Press.
[24] ibid p79/80
[25] Sleigh, A. W. (1844) The Police and Constabulary List 1844. Parker, Furnival and Parker, London.
[26] Ibid
[27] Sleigh, A. W. (1844) The Police and Constabulary List 1844. Parker, Furnival and Parker, London.
[28] John Back Archive (1975) The Metropolitan Police Museum, Charlton
[29] Metropolitan Police Surveyors records (undated)
[30] John Back Archive (1975) The Metropolitan Police Museum, Charlton
[31] Post Office London Directory 1877
[32] Metropolitan Police Internal Report dated 1878
[33] John Back Archive (1975) The Metropolitan Police Museum, Charlton
[34] Census records 1881
[35] Gould, R and Waldron, M. (1986) London's Armed police. Arms and Armour press, London
[36] Metropolitan Police Orders dated 20th June 1884
[37] Fido, M. and Skinner, S. (1999) The Official Encyclopedia of Scotland Yard. Virgin Press.
[38] A tribute to police officers who died in service in the form of a roll of honour has recently been compiled and updated as part of a research project by Sergeant Anthony Rae, Lancashire Constabulary (formerly of the Metropolitan Police).
[39] Metropolitan Police Surveyors records (undated)
[40] Kelly London Directory 1888
[41] Metropolitan Police General Orders 1893
[42] John Back Archive (1975) The Metropolitan Police Museum, Charlton
[43] Metropolitan Police Surveyors records (undated)
[44] ibid
[45] ibid
[46] Fido, M. and Skinner, S. (1999) The Official Encyclopedia of Scotland Yard. Virgin Press.
[47] Op. cit (Surveyors records)
[48] The Police and Constabulary Almanac 1937
[49] The Police and Constabulary Almanac 1957
[50] Ibid
[51] John Back Archive (1975) The Metropolitan Police Museum, Charlton
[52] The Police and Constabulary Almanac 2001
[53] Ibid
[54] http:www.met.police.uk/contact/phone.htm dated 23.03.02

Chapter Thirteen

The London Borough of Tower Hamlets

Tower Hamlets is one of the smallest boroughs in London. The River Thames forms the southern boundary of the borough with eight miles of river frontage, and to the west lies the City of London.

In earlier times, the area between the River Lea and the Tower of London became a charge of the Constable of the Tower, and in time the hamlets and small villages contained therein became known as the Tower Hamlets. In the 1830's, the Borough of Tower Hamlets was formed to cover these seventeen hamlets and parishes situated east of the City of London.

In 1899, as the population increased, and the flood prevention work along the River Thames meant more land for housing to be built[1]. The parishes became independent Boroughs of Stepney, Poplar and Bethnal Green. These boroughs later merged to become the London Borough of Tower Hamlets in 1965.

The area has seen constant changes. In the seventeenth and eighteenth century the Huguenots from France settled there bringing their silk weaving skills. Poverty in eighteenth century Ireland brought in labourers who built the docks. Later Jewish families became traders in the area. More recently the Bangladeshi settlers have contributed to the richness of life in the borough[2].

Policing this part of east London has not been an easy task since most of London's commercial trade came up and down the River Thames. The ships unloaded at docks, which stretched from Stepney and Tower Bridge in the west, to Limehouse, and the Isle of Dogs in the east. Smaller ships transferred cargoes to warehouses along small rivers like the River Lea. Where there were docks, wharves and warehouses there was crime. Detecting and preventing crime helped to establish London's police as one of the best in the world.

The Thames Division was formed in 1798 to combat the high levels of crime on the river. High volumes of commercial trade created ever increasing opportunities for crime with the Thames Division, the Dockyard Police and the Metropolitan Police left not only to police the river, but also the docks, bonded warehouses and wharves. Police history has shown that tact and forbearance are required in good measure to police sensitive situations not only in London itself but also in dockland areas where from time to time different disputes occur such as dock strikes, industrial action and demonstrations.

The stations represented in the Borough of Tower Hamlets are Commercial Street, Leman Street, Arbour Square, Shadwell, Limehouse, Bow, Poplar, Isle of Dogs, Thames Blackwall, Thames Wapping and Bethnal Green.

Originally some of the stations were located on "K" or Stepney Division, however boundary changes over the years together with the growth of east London and the Metropolitan Police have made revision necessary. Therefore, on occasions, stations have alternated between "G", "H" "N" and "K" Divisions. Police Divisions tended to be formed radiating from the centre of London and being wedge shaped. This often meant that a central inner London station was the headquarters for the division although this was not the case in later years. The map below highlights the east end boroughs in 1925 showing Leman Street Police Station as the Divisional Headquarters.

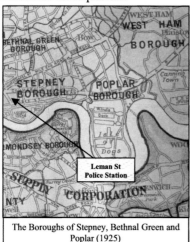

The Boroughs of Stepney, Bethnal Green and Poplar (1925)

The first officer in charge of "H" or Whitechapel Division was the unfortunate Superintendent D. Herring who took command from 10th February 1830 until he died a little over a year later in June 1830 [3]. The post of Superintendent was an unlucky one at this time as the incoming officer in charge, also died whilst in charge. He was at the station from July 1831 until March 1835[4].

By 1888 such was the expansion of the Metropolitan Police that the Division boasted thirty Inspectors, forty four Sergeants and 473 Constables. Superintendent Thomas Arnold was the officer in charge, and was located at the headquarters at Leman Street, Whitechapel[5].

These days there are two divisions within the Borough of Tower Hamlets. They are 1) Limehouse comprising of Bow, Poplar, Limehouse and the

Isle of Dogs, and 2) Whitechapel which was formed in 1994 with the amalgamation of Bethnal Green and Leman Street Divisions.

Arbour Square Police Station and Thames Police Court

This station was perhaps one of the more important stations of London's East End.

In 1840 it was decided to remove Thames Police Court from Wapping Police Station, and a search was made to find a suitable location not far away. On 17th July 1841 the Home Office approved a request from the Receiver of the Metropolitan Police to purchase the leasehold of a site in the Commercial Road, E1 owned by the Mercers Company[6]. This was located at Arbour Street, Stepney just north of Commercial Road. The site was to be used to build a court with a police station attached. The 61 year lease cost £25 per annum and commenced on the 25th of March 1841. A loan had been secured from the University Life Company by the Receiver for the sum of £4986. 0s. 6d with which to build the new police station. This attracted an annual charge of £311. 12s. 6d[7]. The documents do not state for how long the loan was secured.

The new Arbour Square Police Station, together with stables, was built on the site at a cost of £4,143. On the first floor of the station accommodation was provided for nineteen constables, whilst above the stables three rooms were set aside for the married sergeant and his family.

Instructions had been passed from the Home Secretary directing the Commissioner of the Metropolis to move Thames Police Court to the new building which had been built in Arbour Square, Stepney[8]. Thames Court commenced business in December 1842[9]. The address of the new Thames Court was Arbour Street East[10], Stepney and the station next door became known as Arbour Square Police Station. This was a station of sufficient importance to be supervised by an Inspector[11].

Records show that there were two courts in operation in 1844 in the east end of London - Stepney Street and Thames Court. Stepney Street, which had been instituted in November 1840, was headed by the principle magistrate George Chapple Norton[12].

In 1844 the Superintendent in charge of Arbour Square Police Station was Edward Young who had been promoted in 1836. Superintendent Young was head of the Division and was assisted in his supervisory duties by two Inspectors William R. Garde, promoted in 1832 and Anthony Rutt who was promoted in 1837[13].

Arbour Square Police Station
East Arbour Street, London, E1
1889 – 1923

In 1844 two magistrates sat daily, except for weekends, from 10am until 5pm. Records show that the magistrates at Thames Police Court were William Ballantine of 89, Cadogan Place off Eaton Square, and William J. Broderip of 2, Raymond Buildings, Grays Inn. The clerk was Edward William Symonds. Thames Police Court boundaries were fixed by order of the Council dated 10th December 1842, and included the Eastern entrance of the London Docks, to Fox's lane, High Street Shadwell, Ratcliff Highway, Cannon Street, Cannon Street Road, Whitechapel Road, Mile End Road, Grove Road, and along the Eastern Counties Railway to the River Lea, then to the River Thames and back to the eastern entrance of the London Docks[14].

In 1864 the police station strength at Arbour Square, Stepney, was 3 Inspectors fifteen sergeants and 120 constables. One Inspector, five sergeants and fifty constables remained at the station as 'A' Division

Reserve on standby for emergency use. Two sergeants and 24 constables worked the day shift whilst four sergeants and 42 constables worked night duty[15].

Records showed Arbour Square Police Station as becoming the Divisional station on "K" or Stepney Division. Boundary alterations in 1880 transferred a section of "K" Division, including Arbour Square and the whole of Shadwell Sub-Division, located south of the Mile End Road, to "H" or Whitechapel Division. In effect this meant the transfer in strength of nine Inspectors, seventeen sergeants and 157 constables. Although Bow Police Station was the Divisional station for "K" or Stepney Division the name and status were altered to Bow Division which now included Arbour Square and Shadwell. The cost of these boundary alterations involved an expenditure of £135, which the Home Office paid for[16].

Superintendent Thomas Arnold, Divisional Superintendent of 'H' Division for 18 years

Superintendent Thomas Arnold (shown left) resided at 14A, Arbour Square East with his wife Mary and six children[17]. Superintendent Arnold was the Divisional Superintendent from 14th November 1874 until 31st January 1893 when he retired on pension[18].

As the area developed and new streets and houses were built, the address of the station also changed and in 1884 it was recorded as Arbour Street East, Stepney[19]. On 4th August 1888 the Home Office authorised the Receiver to spend £7,500 to purchase the freehold for the Police Court and Station from the Mercers Company. The transactions for the purchase of both were completed in March 1889 at a cost of £7,350. Like the station the address of the Police Court also changed and was shown as Charles Street, Stepney[20]. Not only was the Receiver responsible for the purchase of the court building he was also required to pay the yearly rates.

This picture below shows the daily prison van collecting prisoners from Arbour Square Police Court for transportation to Holloway, Pentonville, Brixton and Wandsworth Prisons. It was taken about 1912 and shows a sergeant and constable helping with prisoner security.

Police horse drawn van collecting prisoners from the Thames Court for transportation to prison

In November 1920 building work was authorised to up-grade the court and police station. Whilst alterations to the police station were being carried out, police business was transferred to the Court building which was designated a temporary police station. The cost of the work amounted to £66,000. The police station came into service on 22nd December 1923 and the court was finished in January 1925. On 13th October 1930 Arbour Square and Shadwell sub-Divisions were amalgamated making the latter a sectional station of Arbour Square which retained its Sub-Divisional status[21].

Arbour Square became the Divisional Headquarters for "H" Division in 1934. It was extensively re-furbished again in 1936[22]. It was shown as having seven sets of married quarters, but was reduced to six to accommodate the administrative

Bomb damage at Arbour Square Police Station 1944

functions of its newly acquired Divisional standing.

On the 19th July 1944 Arbour Square Police station was badly damaged by a V1 flying bomb which injured some 18 people[23]. As a consequence the administrative functions were transferred to Shadwell Police Station in King David Lane (latterly a police section house) although an office was maintained at the station to deal with public enquiries. Six sets of married quarters had to be vacated. This was one of ten police stations badly damaged.

The Divisional Superintendent transferred his office to Leman Street Police Station. Three months later on 9th October 1944, the station was re-opened, although with reduced status as a Sub-Division, and the temporary station at Shadwell was closed at the same time. Leman Street station retained Divisional Headquarters status until July 1947 when it was transferred to Arbour Square once more until the new Leman Street station was opened in March 1970.

The 1965 Local Authority boundary revisions created the London Borough of Tower Hamlets within which Arbour Square was designated a sub-divisional station of "H" Division with its sectional station being Bow Road Police Station.

Arbour Square Police Station
East Arbour Street, London E1 OPU
1923 (rebuilt 1944) - 1999

The picture on the previous page shows Arbour Square substantially rebuilt and extended. In 1999 the station was still a designated charging station for prisoners, however it had limited public opening hours from 6am until 10pm daily[24].

During re-organisation in 1986 all the former divisions which were known as Districts reverted back to the title Division. This meant that Leman Street Division on which Arbour Square had sub-divisional status became a division of 2 District, with the District Headquarters being above the station at Leman Street.

The station was closed to the public in 1999.

Bethnal Green Police Station

The history of Bethnal Green and its division is an interesting if not complex example, because planners made errors when considering how the local area was going to be policed. Records show permission was granted to build a police station on a plot of land at 243 Bethnal Green Road, in December 1860. The freehold to this land was purchased in 1860 for £1400, and the construction of the station cost £2,660.

When the station was built it was a fine example of a Victorian police

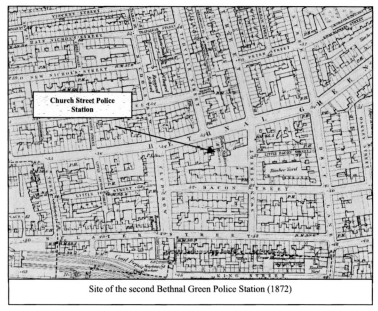

Site of the second Bethnal Green Police Station (1872)

station house which could provide living accommodation for fourteen single constables who resided in the section house. Additionally the station also provided quarters for a married constable and his family who were allocated three rooms, and a married Inspector and his family who resided in four rooms. The Inspector was probably the chief officer in charge of the station.

In 1868 reference was made to the purchase of a portion of freehold land and the cost of building a police station for £9000 at 458, Bethnal Green Road. The sale was finalised in 1869. According to records Bethnal Green was shown as a station on "K" Division with a strength of one Inspector, nine sergeants and 66 constables[25].

However, the building of such a station did present rather a problem as there appears to have been two police stations in Bethnal Green albeit they were on different divisions[26]. The orders stated "The police of "H" Division are to take up and occupy the new police station at Church Street Bethnal Green on the 9th January" [27]. This is strange as Church Street is the Shoreditch end of Bethnal Green whilst the other station is located near the junction with the (Great) Cambridge Road at the other end of the Bethnal Green Road. Research indicates that there was a station at the Church Street site because the "K" Divisional Superintendent makes mention of the fact in his Divisional account published in the Commissioners Annual Report of 1871. The Bethnal Green Road of today was only half its length in 1860, with the Shoreditch end being called Church Street. The Church Street Police Station was located on the south side of the road opposite Turville Street, between Club row and Swan Street[28]. Superintendent White said;

"A new station has been built, and is now occupied, situated in Church Street, Shoreditch. This is very commodious and much enhances the comfort of the men"[29].

Therefore not only were there two police stations in Bethnal Green in 1871, but they were situated along the same road and were within one mile of each other. This was not the only planning error because Hoxton Police Station (on 'N' Division[30]) was situated just round the corner from the Church Street station. In 1873 Bethnal Green was designated a station with an Inspector in charge[31].

A revision of the divisional boundaries took place in 1886 altering the status of Bethnal Green Police Station to Divisional Headquarters responsible for Bethnal Green, Dalston, Hackney, Leytonstone, Woodford, Wanstead, Loughton, Chigwell and Barkingside. Supervision by the Superintendent from Bethnal Green was essential and this explains the presence of a stable at the rear of the station for lodging the horse, as this was the preferred mode of transport at the time. The officer in charge of the station in 1881 was Inspector William Quigley. He resided at the station with his wife Sophia[32]. The Divisional Superintendent in 1888 was James Keating and he had control over 38 Inspectors, 56 Sergeants and 522 constables – a total 612 officers [33].

In February 1894 the new station at Bethnal Green was completed and opened for business[34]. A section house also opened at the same time and had accommodation for twenty four single men, and one set of married quarters for the Inspector[35]. In 1917 an administration section was

Bethnal Green Police Station
458, Bethnal Green Road, London E2
1894- 1995

completed at the new police station and was occupied in June of the same year. It appears a third set of married quarters was added with two sets of accommodation.

The records show that Bethnal Green Police Station was located at 458, Bethnal Green Road, and it consisted of a station, and a section house together with three sets of quarters. The section house is shown to occupy a site at the rear, of the station and it would appear that there was also a stable at the rear[36].

Bethnal Green lost its Headquarters status when in 1933 it became a sectional station of Bow Police Station after being transferred from "J" to "H" Divisions. During the Second World War an entrance was made in the yard of the police station to provide access to an air raid shelter belonging to the British United Shoe Machinery Company. The entrance was blocked up in 1948.

The Aliens Registration office was located on Bethnal Green Police Station area at Ainsley Street, Bethnal Green E2 and it remained there until 1951 when it moved to Piccadilly Place, W1. The office dealt with foreign seamen deserters.

Local Authority Boundary revisions in 1965 meant that Bethnal Green became a sectional station to Commercial Street sub-Division with Arbour Square as the Divisional Headquarters, however by 1967 sub-

Bethnal Green Police Station
12, Victoria Park Square, Tower Hamlets, London E2 9NZ
1995 – present day

Divisional status was resumed when Leman Street Police Station shut for rebuilding. By this stage there were signs that the old station was no longer suitable for modern day policing and plans were made to build a new modern station.

There is a detached police office located at 25, Brick Lane, London E1 6PU which is open to the public Sunday to Fridays 10am until 6pm[37].

In January 1994 the Divisions of Leman Street and Bethnal Green merged to become Whitechapel Division, without any revision of boundaries. In November 1995 both stations at Leman Street and Bethnal Green closed permanently and all officers and functions transferred to the new station located at 12, Victoria Park Square, London, E2 9NZ. The new station retained Bethnal Green as its title with the code letters "HT" as its call sign[38].

In 2002 the records showed the name of the station as Bethnal Green – Tower Hamlets Borough Headquarters. The station is open 24 hours a day 7 days a week[39].

Bow Road Police Station

In 1845 a rented station and section house were located in Devons Lane, Bromley (by Bow). The building was owned by Mr. C. J. Robbins of High Street, Bromley who rented the property annually to the Receiver of the Police. It consisted of an old brick and slate building with a charge room and two cells. At the rear was a small yard. It was given up in 1860 and no longer used for police purposes.

Bow Police Station
Lamp

Details were published that Bow was a designated station of "K" or Stepney Division[40]. Prior to this records show that on 8th October 1831 "H" or Stepney Division had two stations, probably both old watch houses, located at 8, Wentworth Place and Newby Place, near Poplar Church[41]. Section houses to house single policemen were shown located at Arbour Square, Devons Lane, Bromley by Bow and in Three Colt Street.

In 1840 Bow Police Station was used as a charging station for stations on "K" Division, and officers were authorised to cross the Divisional boundary from Stratford and Leytonstone stations in order to bring their prisoners for processing to appear at the Petty Sessions sitting at Lambeth Street Police Court off Commercial Road.

In 1859 the Receiver of the Metropolitan Police leased land in the Bow Road for ninety years from the Rev'd G. J. Driffield, Rector of Bow. A ground rent of £20 per year was payable on the land with a further £8 per year payable on land located at the rear of the station. Its exact position was 116b, Bow Road E3 immediately opposite Fairfield Road. The station was built in 1860 at a cost of £2,294. 4s 9d and insured for £1500 at the Law Office by the Receiver. Accommodation for thirteen constables was provided on the second floor, whilst the married Inspector resided in three rooms on the first floor[42].

Records show that in 1862 Bow Police Station was situated at the back of the High Street opposite Bow Railway Station and Fairfield Road. It was flanked by three public houses namely the Bowry's Arms, the Bird in Hand and the Sailmakers Arms. Another station called Mile End Old Town was also shown on "K" Division in a place called Hickfield not far from the Workhouse in a road we know today as Devons Road[43].

In 1865 the Receiver purchased freehold land in the Mile End Road, not far from Bow Police Station, for the purposes of building a section house specifically for single constables. The land and dwelling cost £2500 and comprised of basement, ground, first and second floors. In the basement were washing, cleaning and boot rooms, and a kitchen locker room and coal cellar. The ground floor housed a library, a mess room and two further locker rooms. There was space for 22 single officers who paid 1s per week rent.

Bow Road Police Station
1, Bow Road, Bromley-by-Bow, London. E3.
1860 - 1903

During 1880 there was a boundary revision of the Divisions of "G", "H", "K", and "Y"[44]. It stipulated that Bow was to become the new Divisional station for "K" Division and that this status had now been removed from the previous Divisional headquarters of Stepney. The division of Stepney was now transferred from "K" to "H" Divisions. Records show that in 1881 the Divisional Superintendent George Turner resided not far from Bow Police Station at 19, Tomlins Grove where he lived with his wife and three children. Turner became Divisional Superintendent in June 1876 and retired on pension in October 1887. The address of the station in 1881 was 1, Bow Road, Bromley, London. Records show there were thirteen single officers living above the station[45].

The address of the new station was published in 1884 as being Bow Road, Bromley-by-Bow. Even today the station can still be seen, as there is a preservation order on the building. In 1887 alterations were made to the station which included the building of new cells at a total cost of £895[46].

Occasionally an event takes place about which both police and public should feel rightly proud. Such an event took place on Bow sub-Division on 29th August 1894. Its officers, friends and acquaintances gathered at

Bow Road Police Station
111, Bow Road, Bow, London E.
1903-1999.

the Bromley Vestry Hall to commemorate the heroism of four members of the public who had rendered assistance to the police when they had had violent prisoners. The gathering was presided over by the Magistrate Mr. W. Hunter who, at the request of Sub Divisional Inspector Causby, wished to present Mr. Arthur Chambers, Mr. J. Sobey, Mr. J. D.Collins and Mr. D. P. Collins with ivory handled Malacca walking sticks complete with inscribed silver collars as a token of their appreciation. Superintendent Wells made a speech and then presented the gifts amid vigorous applause. It is always nice for police officers to know that policing by consent means that they can rely on members of the public in time of difficulty[47].

The Metropolitan Police reviewed its building stock in the early 1900's and considered that Bow Police Station was no longer suitable for modern day policing. They viewed a number of sites for the new station and found a suitable freehold site for a station being offered by Lord Tredegar at 111, 113, 115 and 117, Bow Road at the corner of Addington Road, Bow, E. Home Office approval was given for the purchase and accordingly a new station was completed for occupation on 20th July 1903.

The station was built with a section house to accommodate forty single police officers who were required to pay rent of 1/- per week each. There was also room for a married Inspector, who paid rent of 5/6d per week, and one married constable paying 3/- rent per week.

This picture shows an Edwardian constable smartly dressed for his photograph probably taken before a ceremonial event because he is wearing white gloves. Notice the leather truncheon holder attached to his belt on the outside of his uniform. Such an overt display of force was considered unacceptable so later uniform trousers were made to take a truncheon down the right leg out of sight.

Edwardian constable with truncheon

In 1915 new married quarters and a section house were built in Violet Road, Bow Common. The section house was built to house sixty unmarried officers. Additionally there were a set of married quarters and a room for one unmarried sergeant.

In 1938 the stable block at the rear of the station was completed. These stables were the largest in the Force at the time. The stables could house twenty horses although there were only about fourteen mounted officers. In 1968 the Mounted Branch at Bow had an establishment of one Inspector, one Station Sergeant and 12 Constables[48].

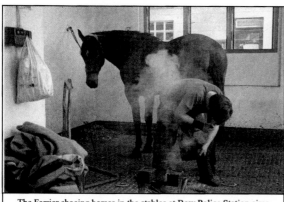

The Farrier shoeing horses in the stables at Bow Police Station circa 1970

There was also a full time farrier, Thomas Melody who was responsible for the fully fitted forge. The farrier was responsible for shoeing up to sixty horses a month[49].

The station suffered a direct hit by a German bomb during the Second World War. The damage was quickly repaired and the station returned to full operational duties. The stable block was emptied and the horses were housed elsewhere temporarily in case the glass roof collapsed after the attacks.

During the 1933 re-organisation Bow was transferred from "K" or East Ham Division to "H" or Whitechapel Division.

The police boundary changes of 1965, in line with Local Authority Boundary revisions, saw the transfer of Bow as designated sectional station of Arbour Square Sub-Division.

In 2002 the 99 year old police station at Bow appeared empty and boarded up, but records show that it has limited opening times to the public. It is open between 10am to 6pm Monday to Saturday[50].

Commercial Street Police Station

The first Commercial Street Police Station was a watch house situated in Spital Square at the junction with Lamb Street, and behind St. Mary's Church. This was known as Spitalfields Watch House because it covered that Area[51]. It was probably an original watch house handed over in 1829 but was still in use in 1862. It was usual to post two Inspectors to each station, one being responsible for taking charges, complaints and calls for assistance in the station whilst the other would supervise the constables and sergeants on their beats[52]. The two Inspectors were Joseph Lewis (promoted to Inspector in 1835) and Henry Harris (promoted to Inspector in 1836)[53]. Inspector Lewis was the senior of the two and was in charge of the station. This station was the divisional headquarters and housed the Superintendent.

A site was purchased for the police in 1874 at the corner of Fleur de Lis Street and Commercial Street. A large new police station was planned, built and ready for business by March 1876[54]. The payment for weekly lodging at the station for one inspector was 5s 6d, one sergeant was 4s, and 50 constables at 1s. The cost of one shilling a week rent for single constables had remained the same amount since it was instituted in 1829[55].

In 1881 there were 48 constables resident in the section house part of the station which at the time of recording also held five prisoners[56]. Also lodged at the station was a hard working detective who was suddenly thrust into the public eye during the controversial serial murder inquiry involving 'Jack the Ripper'. He was Fredrick George Aberline who lived at the station with his wife Emma who was ten years his junior. Aberline was from Blandford in Dorset and when he came to London he met and married Emma who was born in Islington. From 1878 until 1887 Aberline was a local Inspector on 'H' Division, and during that time he was responsible for investigating a number of gruesome murders in the east end of London. Aberline was promoted in 1887 to Inspector 1st class and to Detective Chief Inspector in 1890. He retired on pension in 1890, and went to work for the Pinkerton Detective Agency in the USA[57].

Police Orders in 1884 show the address of the police station as 160, Commercial Street, Shoreditch[58]. This was a large building which occupied an odd shaped corner plot. Officers who worked at the station gave it the fond nickname, 'Comical Street', which perhaps was an indication of the good humour required to work there.

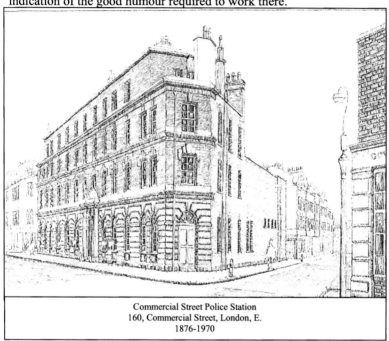

Commercial Street Police Station
160, Commercial Street, London, E.
1876-1970

At the eastern boundary of the ground was Sydney Street which became famous in 1911 when armed police and soldiers laid siege to a house. The story is well known. Three City of London Police Officers had been killed by Russian Revolutionaries who were disturbed whilst robbing a jewellers in Houndsditch in the City. The gang escaped and hid in the upper floor of 100 Sydney Street. A detachment of the Scots Guards laid small arms fire into the building after Detectives knocked at the door causing Detective Sergeant Ben Leeson to be shot in the chest. The building caught fire and all inside perished. A number of firearms and charred bodies were later recovered. Soon afterwards the service funerals of the three City of London Police Officers – Sergeants Bentley and Tucker and Constable Choat took place[59].

In 1907 the accommodation at the premises was altered to give two sets of married quarters and room for 39 unmarried men[60].

By November 1911 the building had been enlarged to accommodate up to 100 single men, still paying rent at 1s per week. These living quarters at the station were known as Commercial Street Section House[61], but in 1912 it was renamed Aldgate Section House[62].

In 1964 Commercial Street rejoined 'H' Division and became a sub-division of Leman Street[63].

Detective Sergeant Leeson who was shot by the conspirators

In 1967 staff had to move from Leman Street (HD) as the old station was being pulled down. The operational staff moved temporarily to Commercial Street. Bethnal Green and Commercial Street Divisions amalgamated. In 1968 the Special Constabulary on 'H' Division totalled sixty officers of all ranks. Woman Special Sergeant Miss M. R. Mounce was stationed at Commercial Street. She was in charge of the detachment of constables[64].

The station remained operational until March 1970 when a new police station was opened at 74, Leman Street, E.1.

Isle of Dogs Police Station

Prior to the introduction of the new Police the Isle of Dogs was patrolled by the Bow Street Horse Patrol from its station at Maryland Point near Stratford in London. The Parish Watchmen also patrolled the Isle of Dogs, although in winter the approaches to the "Island" were often impassable. The watchmen were situated at the watch house in Newby Place near Poplar Church.

In May 1863 the Home Office approved the leasing of a site on which to build a new police station on the Isle of Dogs. This was the first station to be built on the Isle of Dogs. The site was located at 126, Manchester Road, and was situated at the southern end of the Isle of Dogs. It was leased for 79 years from the Commissioners of Greenwich Hospital. The Receiver was required to pay ground rent on the land amounting to £18 per year. A new station was built on the site at a cost of £1500. 19s. 6d and comprised a ground and 1st floor. On the ground floor there was an Inspector's office, a reserve room, a charge room, a mess room, a cleaning room, a clothing room, a scullery and a drying room. There were also three cells, three water closets and two coal cellars. The first floor provided accommodation for eleven single constables in two rooms, a married constable who had two rooms and a married Inspector who had three rooms. The Receiver obtained £31. 4s per year rent for providing the rooms on the premises[65].

Records show that in May 1865 the new police station was located, and occupied, in the interior district of "K" Division. There were three cells for prisoners[66].

Isle of Dogs Police Station
126, Manchester Road, Poplar, London
1864 - 1973

Policing the dock area was undertaken by a number of different police forces. The West India Dock Company Police were set up in 1802 when the docks first opened, followed later in 1838 by the East India Dock Police. In 1871 the Great Eastern Railway Police were responsible for crime with the opening of the Millwall Docks Line to Glengall Grove and its later extension to North Greenwich (Island Gardens).

In 1881 records show that the station address was 126, Manchester Road, Poplar, London. The Inspector in charge was Thomas L. Proctor who resided there with his wife. Constable Smith also lived at the station with his wife and son. There were six single constables also in residence[67]. In 1909 both the Dock Police Forces were amalgamated to form part of the Port of London Authority Police. In 1923 the Great Eastern Railway Police were later absorbed into the London and North-Eastern Railway Police but were completely withdrawn after the general strike of 1926 when the North Greenwich line was closed.

In 1899 the Home Office gave their approval for the freehold purchase of the police station on the Isle of Dogs which was purchased for £600 in September 1899[68].

Isle of Dogs Police Office
240A, West Ferry Road, London. E14
1973- 2002

In June 1933 as part of general boundary revisions to ensure economy and efficiency, the Isle of Dogs was transferred to "H" or Whitechapel Division from "K" or East Ham Division[69].

Limehouse Division, on which the Isle of Dogs police is located, has always been famous for its public houses. These include places like the 'City Arms' the 'Vulcan' the 'Magnet and Dewdrop' the 'Tooke Arms' and the 'Watermans Arms'. Police stations were often sited near public houses and the latter was located behind the Isle of Dogs Police Station in Saunderness Road[70].

In 1960 the Island Police Station appears to have been relegated to the status of police office with the issue of an order instructing that the station should be closed from the hours of 10pm-6am (night duty). A telephone connection was maintained from the office with its sub-Divisional station at Limehouse where all calls were routed.

Further boundary changes in 1965, which occurred as a result of Local Authority revisions, established the Isle of Dogs (HI) as a Sectional Station of Limehouse Sub-Division (HH) within the newly formed London Borough of Tower Hamlets. The night closure order was rescinded as from Monday 16th May 1966.

By now the Isle of Dogs Police Station had outlived its

Isle of Dogs Police Station
Manchester Road, Isle of Dogs, London E14 3BN
2002 – present day

usefulness. The Receiver looked around for another suitable site on which to build a new station. Between 1963 and 1974 no less than three separate parcels of land were purchased in the vicinity, but Government cutbacks meant that none could be built on in the foreseeable future. Accordingly a temporary police office, in portakabins, was constructed on the former Westwoods site at 240A, West Ferry Road, E14, and it became operational on Friday 26th October 1973.

The old station was demolished to make way for the George Green Centre.

A new station was built on the Isle of Dogs in 2002. The address was shown as Manchester Road, Isle of Dogs, London E14 3BN. The station is open between 10am to 6pm Mondays to Fridays[71].

Leman Street Police Station

The police stations of the East End of London have always held significant importance in policing history. Most areas had a watch house except Whitechapel which had two, this being a consequence of its infamous reputation. One police station or watch office was located in Lambeth Street, Whitechapel (now Crowder Street) some fifty yards from the junction with the Highway, and not far from Leman Street[72]. It had been there since 1792. Two other watch houses were taken over by police in the East End of London. These were Denmark Street Watch House in St. George's E. and Chapel Yard, Spitalfields.

St Georges Watch House
Denmark Street, London E.
Pre 1829 -

Lambeth Street Watch House had been set up together with six constables from Thames Division, who were employed by a Magistrate. Lambeth Street Police Court, Whitechapel was set up by Order of Council on 10th November 1840 to hear charges as a Petty Sessional court. Another police watch house was located in Wellclose Square.

In 1844 policing of "H" or Whitechapel Division was policed from the old watch house situated in Chapel Yard, Spitalfields, which had been leased for 40 years in 1840 from the Rev'd C. Wheeler. It was a station with two cells. The Receiver was required to pay all taxes and rates, although the

Wellclose Watch House
Wellclose Square, London E.
Pre 1829

provision of insurance is recorded as not being needed.

The Chapel Yard Watch House was the oldest of the watch houses and was located near the site of the present post office in Whitechurch Lane in the yard of Whitechapel Church[73]. It was leased for 40 years in 1840 from the Rev'd C. Wheeler. It had a ground, first and ground floor with two cells. Annual rent was £11. 14s. payable to the Parish Authorities. The building only remained in service until 1880. It was shown as a station on "H" Division and it housed seven married constables who had two rooms each paying a total £55.18s rent annually[74].

When studying police orders from 1829 the name Watch House was used, later it becomes Police House, then Police Office and even later, by 1840 Police Station. It was called Police Station to avoid any confusion with Police Courts which were sometimes known as Police Offices[75].

This station served as the divisional headquarters for some time. The officer in charge of the division was William F. Pierse, who had been promoted to the rank of Superintendent on 6th March 1835. He was assisted by Joseph Lewis and Henry Harris who were both Inspectors[76]. He remained as Superintendent until his death in 1846, when Superintendent W. Medlicott took over. Medlicott remained until 3rd February 1849 when he was disciplined, reduced in rank to Inspector and transferred to "A" Division[77]. The rules for each rank were strict and discipline was harsh. In those days there was no right of appeal even if the officer had been unfairly treated.

The Metropolitan Police took over the old watch house site located in Denmark Street, Ratcliffe Highway in 1829 for £11. 14s annual rent, and used the building until a new station (called Leman Street Police Station) was built in 1847 in Goodmans Fields near Mansell Street, E1. The old watch house was entrusted to the Receiver of the Metropolitan Police by Act of Parliament. The freehold to Denmark Street Watch House was purchased July 1885 at a cost of £120. The building had a ground and first floor with two cells[78]. The officer in charge of the station was Inspector John Donigan who had been promoted to Inspector in 1841[79].

Records show that Superintendent J. Stead took over the Division in 1849 assisted by four Inspectors. The oldest serving on the Division was Henry Harris (in 1844 he was attached to Chapel Yard, Spitalfields), then Daniel Forbes, Thomas Ellis and William Miller[80]. They were all shown as located at Leman Street Police Station in Goodmans Field. By 1855 the senior Divisional Inspector was William Miller with four new inspectors George Marsh, Albert Gernon, Henry Barny and Philip Brine[81].

In published records Leman Street was designated the Headquarters station of "H" or Whitechapel Division, with other stations at Chapel Yard and London Docks[82].

In 1870 records show "H" or Whitechapel Division having 273 personnel consisting of one Superintendent, six Inspectors, twenty five Sergeants and 241 constables. The Division had seven officers posted to detective duties. The area covered 1.08 square miles[83]. In 1881 the station held 53 single constables, and the records also show there were six prisoners in the cells[84].

The address of Leman Street Police Station was published in orders in 1884 as 76, Leman Street, Whitechapel, although strictly speaking its address should be 74-78, Leman Street, Whitechapel E1.

Records also show that during 1886 the Home Office authorized the purchase of freehold land, formally known as the Garrick Theatre site, for the sum of £2,000. This site adjoined the old police station. A decision had been made to rebuild the station. Furthermore the Metropolitan Police purchased 16 Tenter Street, E1 in 1887.

A temporary police station was brought into operation at 64, Leman Street during the re-building process on the 27th March 1890. The new station was built by 1891, and occupation and police business commenced there in March. Demolition of the old theatre was entrusted to Mr. Base who salvaged materials from the Old Garrick at a cost of £66. 15s paid to the Receiver[85].

Early records also show that there was a police station located a short distance from the section house on the corner of Mile End Road and Stepney Green[86] although details appear sparse. Mile End Road Police Station was situated at 102, Mile End Road, and was a police section house, although the census refers to the building as being a police station.

The building may have been used as a police office except the occupants are referred to as borders. Sergeant Joseph Roskelly from Sampson in Cornwall was unmarried and was resident at the section house although it was a designated constable station [87]. There were nineteen other residents at the section house[88].

In 1881 the Inspector residing at Leman Street Police Station at the time was Adam Marsh who lived there with his wife and family[89].

In 1891 Sergeant Hugh Fanning was the senior officer in charge. He was aged 35 years, came from Ireland and was accompanied by sixteen single residents[90].

The Metropolitan Police Property Records of 1912 show that an ambulance shelter was located

Leman Street Police Station
76, Leman Street, London. E.
1891 – 1967

outside the Royal Mint, which was situated opposite the Tower of London in Royal Mint Street. The shelter was on land belonging to the London Borough of Stepney which required no rental from the police.

The Royal Mint had its own police guard which in 1876 consisted of one sergeant and six constables. In 1881 Sergeant William Durrant resided in Royal Mint House Entrance Gate with his wife and five children[91]. By the turn of the century there were two Sergeants and ten constables. The sergeants supervised the police constables, four on day duty whilst two patrolled at night[92].

One of the responsibilities of the Superintendent in charge of the division was to provide officers to police the Royal Mint. This 1907 postcard shows the complete compliment on the steps outside the Royal Mint building. The Royal Mint guard were Metropolitan Police officers from "H" Division attached to Leman Street Police Station. The station at the

Royal Mint was fitted with a telephone which had a direct line to Leman

Royal Mint Police of 'H' Division circa 1906

Street Police Station. There is the same constable present in both the photograph of the band and the Royal Mint Police. Seated second right next to the band sergeant is PC 243 H with a chest full of medals. He is located in the back row of the royal mint card situated third from the right. One of his medals is the distinctive Kedeve star which meant that he saw service in Egypt in the 1880's.

This is a photograph of the "H" Division Police band located at Leman

The 'H' Division Police Band circa 1913

Street Police Station 74 Leman Street, London, E. The two senior officers in the middle are the only police officers wearing their duty flat hats whilst all the rest have special Bandsman's hats and badges. Many police officers in bands learnt to play instruments in the services before they joined the police. The picture was taken about 1913.

In January 1919 after being demobbed from the Seaforth Highlanders, Peter (Jock) Beveridge joined the Metropolitan Police[93]. Originating from Fife in Scotland Beveridge later became a celebrated detective. After eight weeks training at 'Eagle Hut' in the Strand he was posted to Leman Street[94]. Beveridge resided at the section house with 98 other single officers. He remembers being advised to keep his food locker secured, although he considered this advice a little unnecessary, but soon found out that when someone ran short they would help themselves[95]. On each floor of the section house there were a number of cubicles with wooden walls which stopped about two feet from the ceiling. In each cubicle there was an iron bedstead, a hard chair and a steel locker with a few shelves for clothes. 'At intervals down the corridor gas lamps spluttered so that only certain cubicles were reasonably well lighted'[96].

By now Leman Street was a divisional station with a section house located in Tenter Street at the back of the station together with 7 sets of married quarters. In August 1947 Leman Street lost its divisional status when Arbour Square became the Headquarters for "H" Division. In the review of police and local authority boundaries in 1965 Leman Street was shown as a Sub-Divisional station situated in the London Borough of Tower Hamlets.

Leman Street Police Station
74, Leman Street, London, E.
1970 - 1995

In the late 1960's a new station for Leman Street was planned. The cost of building a new station was estimated at £400,000. On 9th December 1967 Leman Street Police Station was closed and its police officers were transferred. Building work commenced and meanwhile the area was policed from Commercial Street and

Bethnal Green Police Stations.

Doubtless the stations strength was distributed at the other two stations during re-building work. Bethnal Green Police Station assumed Sub-Divisional status during this process. The new station was completed and ready for occupation at 6am on the 9th March 1970 when all staff were transferred back. The station code was published as "HD" and the telegraphic code was revised to the letter "H".

In 1974 the Irish Republican Army left a bomb at the Tower of London resulting in one fatality and a number of people were injured. Between the 24th January 1986 and 15th February 1987 there was a protracted Industrial Dispute at the News International Building in Wapping. The police played a prominent part in keeping the peace. The dispute was manned by police 24 hours a day and aid from other divisions were directed from the purpose built operations room at Leman Street Police Station.

On 12th October 1992 Sector or Geographic Policing commenced at Leman Street. This was a new form of policing which involved consulting the public to assess policing priorities.

On Tuesday 7th November 1995 Leman Street Police Station closed and its officers and business were transferred to a new building. Simultaneously Bethnal Green Police Station situated at 458, Bethnal Green Road, also closed and policing of both stations transferred to the new purpose built station at 12, Victoria Park Square, London, E2 9NZ. Both stations amalgamated into Whitechapel Division although the new station retained the name Bethnal Green Police Station, and its station code became "HT". On 17th May 1996 the Commissioner Sir Paul Condon QPM (now Lord) officially opened the new police station.

Limehouse Police Station

Records show that a watch office became the first police station in the area and was located not far from Limehouse in Newby Place, Poplar next to Poplar Church (see Poplar Police Station). The station at Newby Place was shown located on "K" or Stepney Division. The Divisional Headquarters for "K" Division were situated at Arbour Square.

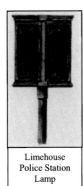

Limehouse
Police Station
Lamp

A new 'K' Division Section House was opened in East India Dock Road in May 1869 for occupation by single police officers[97].

Limehouse Police Station
15, Piggot Street, Limehouse,
London. E.
1879 - 1897

The first police station in Limehouse was opened in April 1879[98] and was located at 15, Piggot Street, Limehouse on "K" Division. Instructions stated that occupation of the new station should be taken up immediately. Piggot Street is located at the bottom of Burdett Road and Commercial Road (A13). Land had been leased on 11th August 1878 from Mr. Henry Spicker of Laummas House, Hackney Common, London E. at a cost of £32 per year. The lease was variable for 7, 14 or 21 years. The house was altered for police purposes at a cost of £304 19s and was reported fit for occupation in 1879.

On the ground floor was a charge room, a reserve room, a kitchen, a scullery, two cells and two water closets. The first and second floors contained living accommodation for police officers. The lodging assessment for those fortunate enough to receive subsidised housing was shown as one married sergeant at 3/9d and one married constable at 2/6d per week. Augmentation of the station strength was published at the same time and was set to increase by four 3rd Class Inspectors, one sergeant and three constables[99]. At 10 Piggott Street lived Inspector Thomas Reid, his wife Emily and six children. Reid had been born in Ireland in 1845. Constable George Wayman, his wife and two children occupied rooms above the station together with Police Divisional Surgeon Robert Kemp and his wife Sarah[100].

In April 1886 the Home Office approved the purchase of a freehold site, known as the "Cooperage", in West India Dock Road, Limehouse on which to build a police station. The site was purchased in 1887 and at the same time an adjacent property at 7, Birchfield Street was also purchased. The cost of building the new station was shown as £4,250, and its address was 27, West India Dock Road, E and it included a section house.

The Birchfield Street site was recorded as having one set of married quarters. The new station was ready for occupation in May 1889 and had Sub-Divisional status.

On 28th May 1897, just a day after the opening of the new Limehouse Police Station, there was the grand opening of the Blackwall Tunnel. The police were required to make arrangements for the tunnel opening, however this was marred by an unfortunate accident to Superintendent. Beard (A Division), who sustained a fractured arm caused by being

Limehouse Police Station
27, West India Dock Road, London, E.
1897- 1940

thrown from his horse during the event[101]. In October 1897 Constable Beveridge (K), who was a Limehouse Police Officer [102] was singled out for his bravery. It was recorded that he was presented with a marble clock, bronze ornaments, and a purse of money by the inhabitants of Limehouse in recognition of his courageous conduct in stopping two runaway horses a few weeks before, and thereby preventing what might have been a most serious accident.[103]

With the opening of the new station came a change in the boundaries. Poplar, Limehouse and Isle of Dogs section become Limehouse Sub-Division. During further re-organisation in 1933 Limehouse, Poplar, Bow and the Isle of Dogs stations were transferred from "K" or East Ham Division to "H" or Whitechapel Division.

Plans were made during the 1930's to build, on the existing site a new police station and section house (Harold Scott Section House) which would hold 130 single officers and several sets of married quarters. The freehold purchase of 29, West India Dock Road (a dilapidated old cottage) was completed on 26th September 1935 at a cost of £200. Further freehold purchases were made; 31-37 West India Dock Road and 1, 3 and 5 Birchfield Street. The houses at 33-37, West India Dock Road were adapted to become the temporary police station during building work. Because of the outbreak of war in 1939 part of the building work was left incomplete, however there was sufficient completed work for administrative business to commence on Saturday 10th August 1940. The station and section house were completed after the war. In 1958 Superintendent Swinden (co-author), as a young constable, lived in the section house for the first few months of his service, whilst stationed at West Ham Police Station. He then moved to Normal Kendall Section House at the rear of East Ham Police Station. This was his official home for the next four years.

In 1931 records show that Limehouse was the Sub-Divisional

Limehouse Police Station
27, West India Dock Road, Limehouse, London, E.
1940 – present day

Headquarters for "K" or Bow Division to which the Divisional Superintendent was attached.

The revision of boundaries in 1965 designated Limehouse Police Station (HH) to remain as a Sub-Divisional station with both Poplar (HP) and the Isle of Dogs (HI) stations to become sectional stations. All were shown located in the new London Borough of Tower Hamlets.

In 2002 the station address was shown as 29, West India Dock Road, Limehouse, E14 8EZ. It is open 24 hours a day 7 days a week[104].

Poplar Police Station

The first police station in Poplar belonged to the Parish Authorities and was situated on the west side of Newby Place, Poplar (next to Poplar Church) and opposite Montague Place not far from the entrance to the Blackwall Tunnel and the Isle of Dogs. The introduction of the new Police in 1829 saw many of these old stations handed over to the Metropolitan Police for them to use. The address was shown as 1, Church Papage, whilst next door at no. 2 was a section house with eight rooms for single constables. The premises at 1-4 were leased from 1840 for 40 years from Mr. Beckwish of 9, Lad Lane.

In 1844 Poplar Police Station at Newby Place was shown on "K" or Stepney Division, and one of the first Inspectors in charge was Charles May who had been appointed in 1839. Boundary revisions were published in police orders restating that Poplar Police Station was to remain located on "K" or Stepney Division[105].

In 1863 young William Henry Keens joined the police at Poplar. He assisted other officers to recover bodies from the River Thames when the Princess Alice sank off Blackwell Point. Constable Keens served in the force for 25 years and when he retired the ratepayers publicly presented him with a clock and a purse of gold. It was not unusual for there to be an advertisement placed in the local paper asking the public to subscribe to the testimonial of a retiring officer. Constable Keens went on to receive his police pension for 47 years, until 1935 when he died aged 91 years, whilst living in Grundy Street, Poplar. Very few officers manage to draw pension for many more years than they served in the Force[106].

In June 1868 buildings had been leased to the Metropolitan Police at 193 and 195, East India (Dock) Road, Poplar for the purposes of carrying on the business of a police station. The station was originally called East India Road Police Station. It was also sometimes referred to as Susannah Street Police Station. The station consisted of a basement, a ground floor and a first floor. On the ground floor there was a charge room, five cells, a day room, a library and four water closets whilst in the basement there were five rooms including a drying room, a mess room, a bathroom, and there were also three coal sheds. Located in the yard was a two stall stable.

The Receiver insured the station against loss or damage amounting to £1800 per year. In 1869 the station was altered, at a cost of £1343 with the permission of the owner. The relationship between the owner Mrs Simons and the police soured resulting in a rather strange course of events and recourse to litigation on the part of the owner.

The police station business, including noise and constant activity had been the cause of trouble and nuisance between the police and the owner. Mrs. Simons was not happy with her tenants and she sued them in the High Court. Under the terms of the lease the Lessee (the police) should do nothing which might cause the Lessor (Mrs Simons) any nuisance, annoyance, damage or disturbance, and if done this would amount to a breach of the covenant. The Lessor applied for a notice to eject the police from the station. It appears this situation arose because Mrs. Simons was no longer satisfied with the terms and conditions of the original lease.

Poplar Police Station
191-193, East India Dock Road, Poplar, London. E.
1897- 1971

The owner probably felt insufficiently compensated for the supply of this prime accommodation and felt she could obtain a better deal with new tenants.

The police ever fearful of the consequences of publicity arising from the court action attempted to settle the matter out of court. Negotiations commenced resulting in an out of court agreement. The action was finally settled with the police surrendering the present lease and replacing it with a fresh one costing £50 per year. All costs were borne by the police. The police felt they had headed off a significant problem because if the owner had won the case the court was empowered to eject the police from the station forthwith. Considerable embarrassment was avoided in this instance although later the police would encounter the difficult Mrs Simons again.

Protracted negotiations to secure the freehold for the station from Mrs Simons commenced in 1891. After a lengthy process the freehold was eventually secured on 26th June 1892 at a cost of £2,000. The records show that these drawn out negotiations included a threat by the police to take out a compulsory purchase order on the land in order to secure it. In 1873 records show Poplar to be a station connected by wire to Scotland Yard and also in the command of an Inspector[107]. In 1881 there were eleven single constables in residence together with Sergeant Joseph Plummer, his wife and daughter[108].

The address of the station was published in official police orders on 20th June 1884 as 195, East India Dock Road, Poplar. The station became a sectional station of Limehouse Sub-Division after re-organisation and a change of divisional name. (Limehouse was transferred from "K" or Stepney Division to "K" East Ham Division). In 1888 Poplar Police Station was shown as a receiving house for drowned or dead bodies. Equipment for dragging the Thames including a hand cart (ambulance) was often kept at public houses near canals or on the Thames[109].

On 23rd April 1897 the Home Office authorised the Receiver to accept the lowest tender to build a new police station and section house on the site of the old station. At this stage negotiations secured the leasehold of premises next door to the old station 191-193, East India Dock Road, Poplar. The successful builders were Messrs. Willmott & Son who secured the contract for £9,985. They commenced building the station and completed the administrative section and married quarters next door at 193, East India Dock Road for occupation in March 1899.

The section house was occupied in March 1899. It had space for twenty one single men who paid 1/- per week each for rent. The rent for the married quarters cost 5/6d per week and instructions stated that it was for use by a married Inspector.

Records also show that the leasehold for 68A, East India Dock Road, Poplar had been secured as the Superintendent's residence, from the leaseholder Mr. C. J. Anderson of 26, Lower North Street, Poplar from 25th March 1918 for an annual rental of £60. The police property manifest records that contracts were exchanged for transfer of the lease on 18th October 1929 to Dr. Fisher costing £400.

In 1933 Poplar was transferred from "K" or East Ham to "H" or Whitechapel Division. The freehold to 191-193, East India Dock Road, Poplar was secured and was purchased in January 1960 for £10,500. A review of policing demands had been completed entitled the "Dixon Report" This concluded that Poplar Police Station should be extended, however the work was never completed.

Poplar Police Office
2, Market Way, Crisp Street, E14
1975 – present day.

The Local Authority boundary reviews of 1965 located Poplar (HP) as a Sectional station of Limehouse (HH) Sub-Division, which was situated in the new borough of Tower Hamlets. A review of "H" Division on 1st January 1970 reduced the status of Poplar to that of a police office. In November 1971 Poplar Police Office was shut and boarded up. All police functions were transferred to Limehouse Police Station. The local population did not like to see their station close and in 1973 pressure was brought on the police at Limehouse to re-open the old station. Concern had been expressed from both the residents and stallholders of the nearby Crisp Street market that the nearest police station was some three miles away at Limehouse.

On market days the increase in visitors caused public order and crime problems which were not easily solved locally. Agreement was reached that a police presence should be kept in Poplar but the old police station was considered unsuitable. Negotiations were made to lease an empty shop from the Greater London Council at 2, Market Way, Crisp Street, E14 at an annual rent of £1,050. Arrangements were made to convert the shop into a police office, and this was opened in May 1975. The shop/office is still open and serving the needs of the local area.

In 2002 the office address was 2 Market Way, Poplar, E14 8ET and opening times vary. The station is open on market days Tuesdays and Thursdays from 8.30am until 2pm, and, on every other Saturday from 9am until 4pm[110].

Shadwell Police Station

Shadwell Police Station
King David Lane j/w Juniper Street, London, E1
1850 - 1908

Shadwell is situated in the Parish of St. Paul within the Borough of Stepney[111]. In 1848 negotiations commenced for the lease of a corner site in King David Lane, Shadwell, next to St. Pauls Leather Works in Juniper Street (later Juniper Road) owned by the Trustees to the Shadwell Estate. The 64 year lease commenced at Christmas 1848 and expired in 1912. The terms included that rates taxes and repairs were the responsibility of the Receiver who should also insure the property for four-fifths its value. The annual ground rent was £21[112].

A new station was built in 1850 at a cost of £1790, but within five years three more cells were added at a cost of £694.10s. The premises were insured at the Law Office for £1200[113]. In 1873 Shadwell Police Station was considered important enough to be designated as under the Supervision of an Inspector, and was linked to the Commissioner's Office

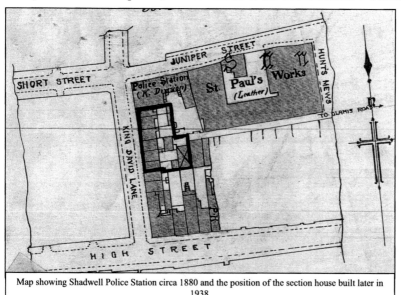

Map showing Shadwell Police Station circa 1880 and the position of the section house built later in 1938

by means of an electric telegraph.[114].

Shadwell was a station located on "K" Division, however by July 1880 boundary revisions meant that it was transferred to "H" Division[115]. The station was home to one married Inspector who paid 5s per week rent for three rooms, one married constable who had two rooms and paid weekly rent of 3s and thirteen constables who resided in cubicles in rooms which held between five and eight to a room[116].

In 1881 Constable Charles Thorndell and his wife Louisa occupied the two rooms. There were seven prisoners in the station at the time these records were made. The Inspector in charge of the station was John Le Cocq who resided there with his wife Catherine. Catherine was ten years older than her husband. Inspector Le Cocq was aged 35 years having been born in Alderney in the Channel Islands[117]. In 1885 the cells to the station were revamped at a cost of £694[118]. The health of those working at the station was a primary concern particularly amongst senior officers. A review of the drainage system raised further concerns regarding disease and led to a complete upgrading of the water and other drains costing £513 in 1896[119]. The freehold to the site was purchased in February 1889 for £1,1777 from the Estate of Lady Glamis, a relative of the late Queen Elizabeth, the Queen Mother.

In 1881 there were thirteen single constables resident at the station[120]. In March 1896 Inspector Smith of 'R' Division was promoted to Sub Divisional Inspector in charge of Shadwell Police Station[121]. Inspector Smith had replaced Sub Divisional Inspector Payne[122] who had been at the station for about three years. There were five inspectors posted to the station[123] and the Sub Divisional Inspector was the most senior of them all.

A further purchase of surrounding land at a cost of £2,500 from the same estate in 1905 meant that the old station could be demolished and a new one built in its place[124]. The station was situated between 9 and 19, King David Lane[125] although police records show the address as 10-24 King David Lane[126].

Shadwell Police Station
10-24, King David Lane, London, E1
1908 - 1933

There were four stations on 'H' Division in 1907. These were 1) Leman Street, Whitechapel, 2) Commercial Street, Shoreditch, 3) Stepney, East Arbour Street and 4) Shadwell, King David Lane[127].

A huge new police station (shown on the previous page) was built at a cost of £12,668 and opened in December 1908. There was residential accommodation for two married officers and 36 unmarried men[128]. Shadwell Police Station had been an important station serving the area of Wapping and Shadwell.

On the ground floor of the station there was a large Inspector's office, CID office, telegraph room, charge room, matron's room and ten cells. There were six male cells and three cells specifically for women. The last cell was an association cell or 'drunk tank' which could house up to ten drunken and rowdy prisoners at a time. In the basement was a parade room where the constables would be paraded by the sergeant. This would involve a formal inspection to see if the officers were clean and tidy. They also needed to produce their appointments, which included their notebook, truncheon and whistle. Often the Inspector on duty would supervise the parade of men coming on duty. Any officer who was not correctly dressed or equipped would be disciplined. In the basement was a Mess room or Canteen where the constables and other officers could

King David Lane (Moylan) Section House 2002

prepare their meals and refreshments etc. As the station had a large number of single officers resident a library and recreation room were included. The recreation room even had a skittle alley which provided a source of amusement and competition amongst the men[129].

Shadwell Police Station was closed for police purposes in 1933[130], although the section house had closed in 1931[131]. A large new section house suitable for 60 single police officers[132] was erected in 1938[133]. Shadwell Police Station was closed as a result of a large-scale divisional re-organisation implemented by the Commissioner Lord Trenchard in the 1930's. It was felt that the nearby stations of Leman Street and Limehouse could absorb the additional area and workload without any problems. The new accommodation for single men (which also included a flat) was built taking up part of the station yard and six residences in King David Lane[134]. This Section House was initially called Shadwell Section House, however it was later re-named Moylan House in memory of a previous Receiver of the Metropolitan Police.

In September 1971 the Section House was improved, and it would appear the flat was converted into single accommodation as six extra single rooms were built. Residents were moved to other accommodation while the building works were being carried out. Lifts were put in (or upgraded) to all floors during the building works[135]. There was a small yard with room for ten car parking places. It remained in service with the address of 10, King David Lane, London E1. until it became no longer suitable for police purposes and was sold.

In September 1993, as part of the scheme to dispose of properties to generate much needed income, Moylan House was sold to Mount Anville Construction Company, Elmscote House, Rickmansworth for £462,500[136].

Today the site belongs to London University and is used as accommodation for students.

---

[1] Tower Hamlets official guide
[2] The Municipal Year Book 2000 Newham Books, and Public Services Directory Vol.2.
[3] Commissioners Annual Report 1830
[4] Commissioners Annual Report 1835
[5] Commissioners Annual Report 1888
[6] John Back Archive (1975) The Metropolitan Police Museum, Charlton
[7] Metropolitan Police Surveyors Records
[8] John Back Archive (1975) The Metropolitan Police Museum, Charlton
[9] The Police and Constabulary List 1844 , Parker, Furnivall and Parker, Military Library Whitehall

[10] The names of streets and numbers of addresses in the area changed from time to time. The court and the station have been given differing addresses like Arbour Square, East, Arbour Street or East Arbour Square.

[11] Metropolitan Police General Orders 1873

[12] The Police and Constabulary List 1844 , Parker, Furnivall and Parker, Military Library Whitehall

[13] .Ibid

[14] Ibid

[15] Metropolitan Police Orders dated 11th January 1864

[16] Metropolitan Police Surveyors Records

[17] PRO Census Records 1881

[18] Metropolitan Police Service Records, The Metropolitan Police Museum, Charlton

[19] Metropolitan Police Orders dated 20th June 1884

[20] Ibid

[21] John Back Archive (1975) The Metropolitan Police Museum, Charlton

[22] Police Stations – erection dates The Metropolitan Police Museum, Charlton

[23] Howgrave-Graham, H.M (1947) The Metropolitan Police at War. HMSO

[24] Police and Constabulary Almanac 1998

[25] Metropolitan Police Orders dated January 1864

[26] Ordnance Survey Map London Sheet 51 Shoreditch 1872

[27] Metropolitan Police Orders dated 6th January 1871

[28] Ordnance Survey Map London Sheet 51 Shoreditch 1872

[29] Commissioners Annual Report 1871

[30] Ordnance Survey Map London Sheet 51 Shoreditch 1872

[31] Metropolitan Police General Orders 1873

[32] PRO Census Records 1881

[33] Dickens Dictionary of London (1888) Moretonhampstead, Devon pp197-99

[34] Metropolitan Police Orders dated 7th February 1894

[35] ibid

[36] Metropolitan Police Surveyors Records 1924

[37] hhtp:www.met.police.uk/contact/phone.htm accessed 23.03.02

[38] Metropolitan Police Orders dated January 1994

[39] hhtp:www.met.police.uk/contact/phone.htm accessed 23.03.02

[40] Metropolitan Police Orders dated 11th January 1864

[41] Metropolitan Police Surveyors Records

[42] Metropolitan Police Property Book

[43] Ordnance Survey Maps 1862

[44] Metropolitan Police Orders dated 15th May 1880

[45] PRO Census Records 1881

[46] Metropolitan Police Property Book

[47] The Police Review Magazine August 1894

[48] The 'H' Division Handbook 1968/69

[49] ibid

[50] hhtp:www.met.police.uk/contact/phone.htm accessed 23.03.02

[51] The 'H' Division Handbook 1968/69

[52] Metropolitan Police General Orders 1829

[53] The Police and Constabulary List 1844. Furnivall, parker and Furnivall, London.

[54] Metropolitan Police Orders dated 23rd March 1876

[55] Metropolitan Police General Orders 1829

[56] PRO Census Records 1881

[57] Begg, Fido and Skinner (1999) Jack the Ripper A – Z p8

[58] Metropolitan Police Orders dated 20th June 1884

[59] The Siege of Sydney Street is well known and detailed accounts are found in 'Londons Armed Police' by Gould, R and Waldren, M. (1986) and Scotland Yards Casebook by Lock, J. (1993)

[60] Metropolitan Police Orders dated 5th January 1907

[61] Metropolitan Police Orders dated 11th November 1911

[62] Metropolitan Police Orders dated 17th August 1912

[63] The 'H' Division Handbook 1968/69

[64] ibid

[65] Metropolitan Police Surveyors Records (undated)

[66] Metropolitan Police Orders dated 9th May 1865
[67] PRO Census Records 1881
[68] John Back Archive (1975) The Metropolitan Police Museum, Charlton
[69] Ibid
[70] The 'H' Division Handbook 1968/69
[71] hhtp:www.met.police.uk/contact/phone.htm accessed 23.03.02
[72] The 'H' Division Handbook 1968/69
[73] ibid
[74] Metropolitan Police Surveyors Records
[75] The 'H' Division Handbook 1968/69
[76] The Police and Constabulary List 1844 , Parker, Furnivall and Parker, Military Library Whitehall.
[77] Metropolitan Police Service Records
[78] Metropolitan Police Surveyors Records
[79] The Police and Constabulary List 1844. Parker Furnivall and Parker, London
[80] Police Office London Directory 1849
[81] Kelly's directory 1855
[82] Metropolitan Police Orders dated 11th January 1864
[83] Metropolitan Police Commissioners Annual Report to the Home Secretary
[84] PRO Census Records 1881
[85] John Back Archive (1975) The Metropolitan Police Museum, Charlton.
[86] Ramsey W. G. (1999) The East End (Then and now) Basildon, Essex. P 218
[87] Metropolitan General Orders 1873
[88] PRO Census Records 1881
[89] ibid
[90] PRO Census Records 1891
[91] ibid
[92] Metropolitan Police orders dated 9th February 1876 and Metropolitan Police General Orders 1893
[93] Beveridge, P. (1957) Inside the CID. Evans Brothers, London.
[94] ibid
[95] ibid.
[96] ibid.
[97] Metropolitan Police Orders dated 13th May 1869
[98] Metropolitan Police Orders dated 16th April 1879
[99] Metropolitan Police Orders dated 16th April 1879
[100] PRO Census Records 1881
[101] The Police Review and Parade Gossip May 1897
[102] This is not the same Constable Beveridge who was posted to Leman Street Police Station in 1919.
[103] The Police Review and Parade Gossip October 1897
[104] hhtp:www.met.police.uk/contact/phone.htm accessed 23.03.02
[105] Metropolitan Police Orders dated 11th January 1864
[106] East End News 30th April 1930
[107] Metropolitan Police General Orders 1873
[108] PRO Census Records 1881
[109] Dickens Dictionary of London (1888) Moretonhampstead, Devon pp132 –133
[109] T.A.Critichley in The History of the Police of England and Wales 1967 Constable publications. p42.
[109] Dickens Dictionary of London (1888) Moretonhampstead, Devon pp132 –133
[109] ibid pp197-99
[110] hhtp:www.met.police.uk/contact/phone.htm accessed 23.03.02
[111] Metropolitan Police Surveyors Records p62
[112] Metropolitan Police Surveyors Records (undated)
[113] ibid
[114] Metropolitan Police General Orders 1873
[115] The 'H' Division Handbook 1968/69.
[116] Metropolitan Police Surveyors Records (undated)
[117] PRO Census Records 1881
[118] Metropolitan Police Surveyors Records p62
[119] Ibid
[120] PRO Census Records 1881
[121] The Police Review and Parade Gossip dated 27th March 1896

[122] The Police Review and Parade Gossip dated 11th December 1893
[123] ibid
[124] Op cit Census Records 1881
[125] PRO Census Records 1881
[126] Metropolitan Police Surveyors Records (undated)
[127] Kirchner's Almanac 1907
[128] Metropolitan Police Orders dated 10th December 1908
[129] ibid
[130] Brown, B. (1998) 'H' Division 1830 - 1899
[131] Metropolitan Police Orders dated 2nd March 1931
[132] Metropolitan Police Surveyors Records, LB364
[133] Metropolitan Police Orders dated 29th December 1938
[134] Land Registry for Shadwell Tithe No. 102204
[135] Metropolitan Police Surveyors referencing notes 19th February 1973
[136] Metropolitan Police Surveyors Records, LB364

Chapter Fourteen

The London Borough of Waltham Forest

Five London boroughs surround the London Borough of Waltham Forest. To the west there are Enfield, Haringey and Hackney. Redbridge and the River Lea border the eastern boundary with Newham to the south. The County of Essex lies to the north. The London Borough of Waltham Forest was created in 1965 by the amalgamation of the boroughs of Chingford, Leyton and Walthamstow[1].

The stations located within the London Borough of Waltham Forest are Chingford (JC) Leyton (JL) Leytonstone (JS) and Walthamstow (JW).

Chingford Police Station

Chingford Police Station has had a long and chequered career. In 1837 the Bow Street Horse Patrol operated locally being based at Enfield and Loughton with responsibility for patrolling Chingford. The Horse Patrol was integrated into 'N' Division of the Metropolitan Police in 1839[2]. Chingford was allocated two constables from Waltham Abbey from a strength of four sergeants and 13 constables[3].

Chingford Police Station Lamp

Records tell us that on 31st December 1864 the Commissioner directed, with immediate effect, the Divisional Superintendent for "N" or Islington Division, in co-operation with the Metropolitan Police Surveyor, to make every effort to find a suitable site for the location and building of a new police station at Chingford. Before this time Chingford was policed from Sun Street Police Station, Waltham Abbey. Police officers usually worked from their homes and were scattered about the parish. In 1873 the station was designated a constable only station[4].

In 1874 a memorandum from the Commissioner of Police to the Receiver[5] requested a report from the police surveyor on the suitability of a plot of land owned by Mr. Charles Alcock. The land available was on the hill at Chingford, not far from the railway station. This land fronted the highway, behind the old Lockup, and had a side road. It was available for sale at £250. The surveyor commented that it was most suitable in every way for the building of a police station. The Commissioner recommended to the Home Office in January 1875 that the land should be purchased with a view to building a police station on the site. The Home Office duly approved this and the freehold was secured in June of the same year[6].

There appears to have been no urgency to build a station at the location because the site remained vacant until 1887, except perhaps for the "old watch house" and the stable built in 1881. The stable was added at a cost of £495 in order to stable the horse ridden by the Divisional Superintendent. The horse was used to inspect the division and the Superintendent had to travel from Islington to the Divisional Headquarters station located some distance away. "N" or Islington Division stretched even further out to Loughton and Waltham Abbey making the job of supervision by the Superintendent a difficult and arduous task. A married sergeant resided above the stables occupying five rooms at a weekly cost of 4/- rent.

In May 1882 the police at Chingford were present when Queen Victoria opened up Epping Forest to the people of London. By 1871 the Corporation of London had purchased some six thousand acres of forest land, which whilst private in nature, came within the newly constituted Epping Forest Act 1878 allowing access by the public. The Queen arrived at Chingford Railway Station by train and was conveyed by carriage to High Beach where she planted a sapling oak, which did not survive. Apparently seventeen Divisions supplied officers to police the event with 1529 police officers involved in ensuring the security of the Queen during her visit. The three and a half mile route from Chingford Station by way of Rangers Road, Fairmead, had police officers at intervals of between two and twenty yards. It was estimated that half a million people welcomed the Queen to the forest with ten thousand of them being officially entertained by the Lord Mayor of London at temporary accommodation set up on Queen's Green. The Queen arrived late at 4.05pm and returned to Windsor at 5.30pm. This was a costly affair for the Police Commissioner as the Secretary of State instructed the Receiver to give the officers employed on the Queen's visit an extra days pay [7].

With the formation of "J" or Bethnal Green Division Chingford was re-affirmed as remaining on "N" or Islington Division[8].

Permission was granted by the Home Office to build a new police station on the hill at Chingford in 1886. The building work commenced in 1887. The new station cost £1,869 and was completed for occupation in March 1888 [9]. With the building of a new station came the authorisation of an increase in staff and an alteration in the boundary for the station. The enhancement included two Divisional Inspectors and two Sub-Inspectors. The boundaries of Enfield Highway and Walthamstow were altered in consequence of the opening of the new station.

The Police and the Fire Brigade usually worked together at the scenes of fires. If a police officer rendered assistance to the Fire Brigade at the scene of a fire he could receive a cash reward[10]. In 1900 there was a fire in Station Road and Constable Wiggins, attached to Chingford Police Station, gave assistance to the Brigade. On reporting a fire to the Brigade the reward was ten shillings, whilst rendering assistance was a further five shillings which he claimed.

At the beginning of this section the dedicated lamp of Chingford is shown. The practice of placing police lamps outside police stations originates from Westminster City Council in the early part of the 19th century. The council specifically ordered the police to put a gas lamp outside their stations to identify them. The practice of surrounding the gas lamps in blue glass was established by Police Orders in 1861 when Superintendents were required to surround the external gas lamps on at least three sides. The blue lamp at Bow Street was removed on the instructions of Queen Victoria who did not like to see the lamp on her way to the Opera[11].

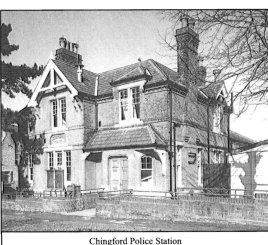

Chingford Police Station
Kings Head Hill, Chingford, Essex
1888 –1977

An incident, which attracted significant attention in Chingford in 1912, was the mysterious death of a local councillor and member of the Stock Exchange, Mr. Piers

N. Holmes. Chingford Station Sergeant Edward Maber was assigned to investigate the matter and visited the scene of the suspicious death at Chingford Lodge now re-named "Kilgreana" at Chingford Green. He found the deceased in bed holding a five-chambered revolver, and from this he concluded that Mr. Holmes had taken his own life. Ultimately suicide was the verdict of the Coroner, and in those days it was a criminal offence for someone to take or attempt to take his/her own life [12].

During the First World War Mr. R. Bullock OBE was the Divisional Commander of the Chingford Special Constabulary. In 1917 Police Sergeant Francis Breed was shown as the officer in charge of the station with a compliment of 38 constables. He served until 1922 [13].

In 1924 an additional strip of land was purchased for £160 at the rear of the station. As a consequence of this purchase the station was enlarged to ensure greater efficiency. In 1930 a change occurred in how fires should be notified to the particular emergency service. Previously notifications by the public had been given to the police, but now this responsibility passed to the local fire brigade, bypassing the police. This system altered on 21st July when the new fire station, which had been built in the Ridgeway next to the Town Hall, took over responsibility for fire warnings [14].

Metropolitan Police Box
circa 1955

In 1932, as part of the Force re-organisation, Chingford was transferred from Walthamstow Sub-Division to Enfield Highway Sub-Division. A further status change a year later transferred Chingford to "J" or Hackney Division, but kept it as a sectional station of Walthamstow Sub-Division [15].

During the mid 1930`s police telephone boxes appeared at major traffic junctions in Chingford. They were originally made of concrete painted blue and contained a single telephone which was connected by secure private line to Walthamstow Police Station. The picture at left shows a Special sergeant making notes inside one of the police boxes. In the 1960's this type of police box was made famous by the television series "Dr. Who" which used a police box as a 'tardis' space ship.

During the mid 1930's Chingford Police received its first motorised transport; a police car, for patrolling the Walthamstow and Chingford area.

Between 1860 and 1938 a hand ambulance was used at most police stations to transport ill, injured or drunken people. The "barrow", as it was called, was a heavy three-wheeled vehicle and was purpose made for the Metropolitan Police. The ambulance on Chingford Division was situated behind the police box on the corner of New Road opposite the Prince Albert[16].

During the 1965 boundary changes there was no change in status or responsibility, except that the new Division was located with the London Borough of Waltham Forest.

Towards the end of the 1950's and early 1960's the Metropolitan Police began to modernise by making officers more mobile. Previously pedal cycles and patrol motor cycles had been used. The motor cycles were usually a single 500cc Triumph twin, Norton 500c or BSA Bantam solo motor cycle. They were allocated to individual stations. The Metropolitan Police issued the Velocette LE light motor cycle, a water-cooled 198cc motor bike from 1959 to police stations for the purpose of speedier response to calls for assistance. Some of the "Noddy" motor cycles, as they were called, were fitted with a Force radio transmitter so that they could remain in contact with the station or New Scotland Yard. They lasted until the early 1970's when they were withdrawn[17].

Personal radios and unit beat "Panda" cars were issued to Chingford Division in 1968. The Panda's were Morris Minor 1000cc saloon motor vehicles and were issued to replace the ageing "Noddy" bike. With the advent of the personal radio, which was issued to each officer on duty outside the station, came the demise of the police telephone box. Mobile communications meant that the fixed telephone boxes could be removed, as they were now out of date. They were phased out over a period of time[18].

Chingford Police Station was extended in 1971/2 although it was still woefully inadequate for its task. The police considered building a new station soon after the extension was completed. Tenders were invited for a four-storey building of reinforced concrete pillars surrounded by brickwork and blocks. Costain's won the contract and authority was granted at a cost of £700,000, however final completion cost the police some £200,000 more. It was built with a basement and for further vertical extension later if necessary. [19]. The building took two years to build, but on completion was surrounded in controversy. Speculation had indicated that the re-organisation of the Metropolitan Police District might have meant that Chingford lose its police station, however in reality this was not the case.

Waltham Forest (Chingford) Police Station
Kings Head Hill, Chingford, E4 7EA
1977 – present day

On completion of the new building Chingford replaced Walthamstow as the Sub-Divisional headquarters. The new station became operational on 10th January 1977 but was officially opened by the Minister of State for the Home Office, Lord Harris of Greenwich on Friday 23rd September 1977. On the following two days the station was open to the public and many visitors took the opportunity to look around the station.

On 29th November 1991 Sergeant Alan King was stabbed to death in Higham Hill Road, E17 when he went to apprehend a suspect[20]. The killer was captured, later convicted of his murder and sentenced to life imprisonment. A monument was unveiled by the Film Director Michael Winner of the Police Memorial Trust during a ceremony as a tribute to Sergeant King at the place where he gave his life.

In 1999 Chingford Police Station was renamed Waltham Forest Police Station, and became the Borough Headquarters. The newly appointed Borough Commander and administrative staff were re-located to the station. The station is still operational and is open to the public 24 hours a day 7 days a week.[21].

Leyton Police Station

Lea Bridge Road Police Station was the title of the first station in the Leyton area. It was situated on the site of the current multi-storey Police Section House, which still stands today, located on the north side of the main road about half a mile south of the Bakers Arms at the junction with Shrubland Road. In the early days it was often referred to as Walthamstow Police Station, even though it was in Leyton[22].

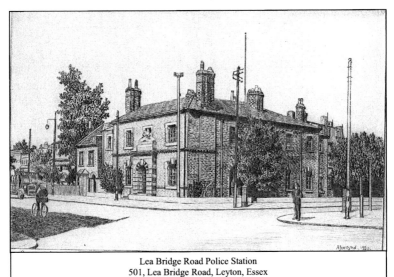

Lea Bridge Road Police Station
501, Lea Bridge Road, Leyton, Essex
1861 – 1955

343

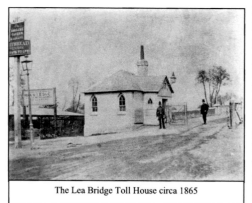

In 1867 the Receiver of the Metropolitan Police purchased a freehold parcel of land in the Lea Bridge Road at a cost of £620. In november 1868 the new police station at 501, Lea Bridge Road opened at a cost of £4,139. This was a brick built station house with a ground and first floor. The ground floor consisted of a charge room, a day room, a mess room, a brush room, a wash room scullery, a drying room, four cells, four stalls (stables), three water closets and four coal sheds. The first floor provided accommodation for ten single constables paying 1/- per week rent, one single constable paying 3/- per week, one married sergeant paying 5/6d per week and 1 married Inspector paying 5/6d per week rent. [23]

The Lea Bridge Toll House circa 1865

The picture above shows Lea Bridge Toll House situated near the Anglers Public House about 1865. The constable was posted to the toll from Lea Bridge Road Police Station to assist the toll keeper to ensure that the necessary tolls were paid.

In 1871 Lea Bridge Road Police Station was shown situated in an area

Leyton Police Station
215, Francis Road, Leyton, E.
1891 – 1940

known as Leyton Street and was one of the more important and substantial stations in the area[24]. In 1881 the Inspector in charge of the station was Henry Craggs who resided there with his large family. He had two daughters and three sons. Inspector Craggs was from Chelsea, London and at the time was aged 35 years. His wife Sarah was aged 38 years and came from Brighton in Sussex. Also resident at the station was Constable John Cook, his wife Ann and their son. There were also ten single constables living at the station[25].

The formation of "J" or Bethnal Green Division in 1886 encompassed part of Lea Bridge Road sub-division. There was no station at Leyton and policing of the division operated from either Leytonstone (Harrow Green) or Lea Bridge Road stations. In 1894 the officer in charge of the station was shown as Station Sergeant Henry Pratchett. [26] Located next door to the police station was a station cottage (seen to the left of the picture). This was occupied by a serving police officer William Denford and his family.[27]

In 1887 freehold land was purchased at a cost of £420, on which to build a new station. The Home Office approved the purchase in Francis Road, Leyton, at the corner of Morley Road. The station was built at a cost of £4,355 and was ready for occupation in January 1891 [28]. It included section house accommodation for fifteen single men. The building was a two storey brick built station house. Leyton Police Station was a Sub-divisional station of Wanstead Section.

Leyton Police Station
Retirement circa 1900

The picture on the previous page shows a retirement at Leyton Police Station between 1898 and 1901. The recipient is shown with his presents - a beautiful mantle clock, which is flanked by flowerpots. Police officers served for 25 years before they were eligible for a pension, and only a very few stayed after this time.

Police officers bonded together in many ways. Not only did they work together they also lived and played together. Senior officers were concerned that single police officers would develop bad habits if they were not kept occupied. Competitive sports were encouraged, whether it was football, rugby or cricket. Each station had a variety of sports teams. Leyton had a reputation for having a good swimming team which was helped by having a municipal pool not far away.

The successful Life Saving Team from Leyton Police Station in 1904

The above group is the Life Saving Class of Leyton Swimming Club taken in 1904. These are the successful medallion holders with their medals shown in the centre. The back row comprises of Constable 509J Budd, Constable 607J Waters, Constable 258J Ping, Constable 553J Boyling, Sergeant 78J Allen (Hon. Sec.), Constable 299J Mapeley, Constable 560J Hopker, Front left to right, Constable 97J Barker, Mr.T.

Minett (non police instructor) Mr. W. Wire (non police instructor) and Constable 364J Palmer.

Once the new station had been built the Lea Bridge Road site was rebuilt to provide accommodation for more single police officers. The new Section House at Lea Bridge Road was occupied in April 1908, and provided accommodation for twenty-six unmarried men at 1s. per week.[29]

It appears that Lea Bridge Road Police Station was re-opened in February 1913 after refurbishment and included two sets of married quarters[30].

Up until July 1927 there was no Leyton division as such, because its status was as a sectional station to Wanstead Sub-Division. Records show the status of both stations were altered - Wanstead became a sectional station whilst Leyton was enhanced to Sub-Division. Accordingly Sub-Divisional Inspector Farrell was transferred to Leyton from Wanstead to take up supervisory duties [31].

The photograph taken in the yard at Leyton shows Constable 509J/84134 Ernest Budd on the left. He had joined the Metropolitan Police on 20th June 1898 and retired on 24th June 1923 (25 years service). It would seem he remained at Leyton Police Station for some time – probably all his service. The picture features Constable Budd, together with the Station

Setting off the maroons in the yard at Leyton Police Station to commemorate the end of WW1

Inspector (in flat hat) and another Constable. The Inspector is setting off the maroons as a mark that peace had been signed in 1918. Constable Budd is also shown in the retirement group photograph shown previously in this section, as the fifth from the left in the back row.

In August 1927 the section house was converted into two sets of married quarters [32]. On re-organisation in 1933 Leyton remained a Sub-Divisional station but with Leytonstone as the sectional station. The address of the station was published as 215 Francis Road, Leyton. Leyton station and area were located on "J" Division with Hackney Police Station being the Divisional Headquarters. Lea Bridge Road Police Station was closed in August 1933[33].

By 1939 the station required rebuilding, as it was no longer adequate for policing purposes. The premises were vacated on Sunday 26th March 1939 and personnel were transferred to the previously closed Lea Bridge Road Police Station situated at 501, Lea Bridge Road. The old station was demolished and a new much bigger one was built in its place.

There were a number of problems with the building of the new station. The site was "V" shaped with Francis Road and Morley Road forming an acute angle. Furthermore the station had to be three times larger than it was previously. To overcome these problems the Architect Julian Leathart FRIBA designed the intersection of the two wings by curving the frontage rather than slicing off the corner. He included a large lower ground floor and designed in the fenestration of the top floor, which tends

Leyton Police Station
215, Francis Road, Leyton E10 6NJ
1940 – present day

to give the impression of a two-floored building. The coming of war meant that late Air Raid Precautions had to be designed into the building.

The cells were built to have natural light with exterior glass bricks forming part of the external walls. The general contractors were Messrs. Pitchers Ltd. of 57, Ashburton Grove, N7.

The new station was quickly built and was ready for occupation in August 1940[34]. Lea Bridge Road Police Station had served the area well, having previously been an "N" Division station covering Walthamstow and Leyton from 1868 to 1904. In later years Lea Bridge Road Police Station became married quarters as well as a Section House. It was then demolished and a new multi-storey Police Section House built in its place and called Lea Bridge Road Section House.

There has always been a number of mysteries concerning the station at Leyton. Firstly, why was a station built with no licensed premises in its vicinity? This is usually a pre-requisite e.g. Stoke Newington was built between two public houses. The second question relates to why the current Leyton Police Station has no Blue lamp outside when the old station had? The third and perhaps most perplexing question was why was the station built in such an out of the way place in a quiet side street and not in the main High Street?

In the early 1900's various Editors of local papers called the siting of the original station 'as in the wilderness' and its location has caused much anger and frustration. Rumours - which have absolutely no factual basis whatsoever give the reasons for siting as follows; Land was bequested to the Receiver which stipulated that only a police station could be built and no other building. This raised interesting possibilities that perhaps the benefactor was concerned at the lack of police presence in the area or perhaps the donor just liked the police. The answers to these problems we will perhaps never be known[35]. What tends to

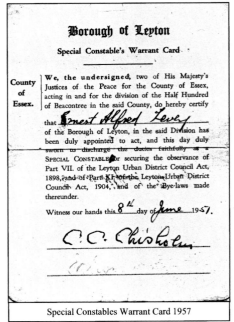

Special Constables Warrant Card 1957

dispel this theory is that Metropolitan Police Surveyors records show the various amounts of money paid for the site and building.

Special constables have always provided a support function to the regular police. They hold the Office of Constable and Special Constables are sworn into service by Justices of the Peace or Magistrates within the area they police, and are provided with a Warrant card like the one shown above – as proof of that office. In the example Ernest Alfred Levey was sworn in by two Justices in the district of Beacontree, in the county of Essex.

In 1963 further re-organisation and restructuring of the London Boroughs filtered through to police re-organisations in 1965. Part of Local Government boundary revisions identified Leyton within the London Borough of Waltham Forest. Furthermore the station was upgraded to Divisional Headquarters for "J" Division replacing Hackney Police Station[36].

As from 1st April 1965 the telegraphic code for Leyton became Juliet Delta (JD), located within the London Borough of Waltham Forest.

In 1969, Leyton Police Station became the Headquarters for 'J' Division, moving from Hackney. This was a popular move, and placed Commanders in charge of the old Divisions which were re-named Districts[37].

In 1975 a new station at Chigwell (Brook Parade) was built to accommodate headquarters functions and these were transferred. In 1986 Leyton and Leytonstone formed the new Leyton division.

In 1999 under the latest re-structuring arrangements and re-organisation of the Metropolitan Police, individual Borough Commanders replaced the 3 Area Headquarters management structure, which was abolished. The new Borough Commanders (now Chief Superintendents) took up their, posts and today Leyton remains within the London Borough of Waltham Forest, although the Borough Police Headquarters moved to Chingford.

In 2002 Leyton Police Station is open to the public 24 hours a day, 7 days a week and is situated at 215 Francis Road, London E10 6NJ[38].

Leytonstone Police Station

Situated on a main route out of London to Colchester was a small hamlet called Leyton Stone. About mid way between Maryland Point (near Stratford) and Leyton Stone travelling East was located the tiny village of Salts Green (1777), later re-named Harrow Green on account of a nearby Inn called Le Harrow [39].

Before 1872 the area of Walthamstow and Low Leyton was policed from Lea Bridge Road Police Station. Police records make reference to the building of a new station at Leytonstone, although originally the name of the new station was Harrow Green Police Station [40].

The police sought a suitable house in the Harrow Green area to use as a police station. In 1878 they found a suitable house called Maria Cottage, in Harrow Green, Leytonstone which could be leased for the purpose. An agreement was reached with the owners to lease the house initially for seven years, but with options for fourteen or twenty-one years, if necessary. Leytonstone (Harrow Green) station was occupied by police and shown located on "N" Division with a call sign of Lima Echo (LE) [41].

The lease to the station was terminated in 1892 after 14 years when it was retained on an annual basis. The station at Harrow Green (Leytonstone) was small by today's standards but it included a charge room, a reserve

Harrow Green Police Station
High Road, Harrow Green, Leytonstone.
1878 – 1913

room, two coal sheds, two cells and a water closet. It was a place where constables paraded for duty and prisoners were charged for court. It was located on the west side of the Leytonstone Road just south of Cathall Road, Harrow Green.

As far back as the mid 1880's the police decided that because of local expansion in population that a larger more suitable premises should be sought. The local people were happy with the location of the station, and a row brewed up over police plans to close the local station and re-site it some distance away.

The editors of several local papers joined in the argument by stating that,

> 'We do not know if the police authorities are still determined to persevere in their utterly mad project in doing away with Harrow Green Police Station and placing one in the wilderness. We should fancy the condemnation of the whole intelligent public... blundering...preposterous notion... silly and gigantic muddle at Harrow Green'[42]

The wilderness referred to by the papers was a small plot of land three quarters of a mile away off the High Road, Leyton, situated in what some observers described as 'the better class residential area of Leyton'.[43]

On the completion of the new Leyton Police Station built at 215, Francis Road, Leyton the former building was re-opened as married quarters for a police officer at a weekly rental of 2/-. In 1892 instructions were issued to re-open the station as a result of strong local representation. Accordingly force instructions stated that Harrow Green (Leytonstone) re-opened on 9th May 1892. With the formation of a new division "J" or Bethnal Green Division, Leytonstone was transferred from "N" to "J" Division[44].

Soon the area of Leytonstone became a popular location for people and

this caused a significant increase in population. By 1908 concern was expressed as to the suitability of the old station and its ability to cope with the pressure of the increase in inhabitants.

This is the station lamp that greets visitors to the station at Leytonstone. Except for Bow Street, which had a clear lamp - police station lamps are traditionally blue and come in a variety of shapes and sizes.

Leytonstone Police
Station Lamp

Accordingly permission was given to purchase a

parcel of land located at 470, High Road, Leytonstone with sufficient space for a back entrance in Cobden Road. The freehold was secured in 1908. Accordingly a new station was built on the site and opened in February 1913 [45]. It also included two sets of married quarters. Rent for one set of quarters was shown as 8/6d per week, whilst the other set cost 8/- per week.

Leytonstone had an ambulance shelter which was located at a public house called the "Old Red Lion" at 640, High Road, Leytonstone. Mr. E. W. Greenwood is shown as being the person responsible for the said

Leytonstone Police Station
470, High Road Leytonstone, E11 3EH
1913 – present day

shelter[46], which probably housed a wooden two wheeled cart known as a hand ambulance. Locating an ambulance at such a place appears to have assisted police officers conveying drunken persons back to the police station. This facility was withdrawn on 13th August 1929.

In 1931 Leytonstone was shown as still located on "J" Division but Hackney had superseded Bethnal Green as the Divisional headquarters. Re-organisation in 1965 made Leytonstone (JS) a sectional station of Leyton Sub-Division.

In the early 1960's concern had been expressed at senior level regarding the effectiveness of police to fight crime and deal with disorder. The solution to this dilemma was to 'form a squad' of suitable constables, sergeants and Inspectors. The name of this squad was the Special Patrol Group (SPG). The SPG were organised throughout the Metropolitan

Constable (later Inspector) David Leonard Donaldson

Police District in 1961[47]. The SPG were a centrally based highly mobile unit introduced to combat serious crime which could not be dealt with by Divisions due to increasing shortages in manpower[48]. Leytonstone was considered a suitable station to house one of the new mobile patrols.

The picture at left shows Constable 161281 David Leonard Donaldson who transferred from 'C' Division in March 1973 to A8(2) Department – the SPG and Leytonstone Station[49]. It was during this period with the SPG that Constable 563 CO Donaldson found a skill in detecting crime because he became a Temporary Detective Constable in March 1975 and a Detective Constable in 1978

where he was posted to Bow Police Station. He successfully studied for the promotion exam and became a sergeant in October 1979 when he returned to uniform duties. Sergeant Donaldson stayed in uniform for a year and transferred back to detective duties as a Detective Sergeant 2nd Class, from Kentish Town to Barkingside Police station. He was twice commended by the Commissioner for the Metropolis. He became a uniform Inspector in June 1990 and ended his distinguished career in 1996 after returning to the CID having been seconded to the recently formed National Criminal Intelligence Service (NCIS) in 1993[50].

Daily our police act with courage and bravery. One officer attached to Leyton Police Station was Constable John Barrett who in July 1965 kept observation on a stolen mini saloon car with false number plates in Drayton Road, Leytonstone. On seeing a person return to the vehicle he challenged him, however the driver ignored the officers warning and tried to knock down the officer as he attempted to make an arrest. The officer jumped on the bonnet of the vehicle as it sped through the back streets of Leytonstone. It crashed after travelling some distance severely injuring the officer. The driver decamped leaving the officer lying injured on the road, however Constable Barrett was able to direct other officers to the suspect who was hiding nearby. Later at the Old Bailey the driver was imprisoned for a variety of offences including grievous bodily harm, theft of a number of motor vehicles and marine equipment from Southampton. Constable Barrett was commended for his bravery at the Old Bailey by His Honour Judge Griffith-Jones and later he was awarded the British Empire Medal for Gallantry. The picture right shows Constable Barrett being awarded his medal by Field Marshall Earl Alexander of Tunis.

Constable John Barrett receiving his British Empire Medal from Field Marshall Earl Alexander of Tunis in 1966

British Empire and Police Long Service Medals

The British Empire Medal (at left) is shown together with Constable Barrett's Police Long Service and Good Conduct Medal which is received after 22½ years unblemished service. The Queen usually awards the Gallantry medals but wrote to Constable Barrett apologising for not being able to on this occasion[51].

In 1998 Leytonstone Police Station was no longer a charging station but was open to the public[52]. The opening times show that the station little more than police office and is open Mondays to Fridays from 9am until 5pm[53].

Walthamstow Police Station

In 1829 the general area of Walthamstow was patrolled by the Metropolitan Police Horse patrol. A building of brick and slate with six rooms had been leased from Mr. Leberty of the Castle Inn, Walthamstow for a rent of £17 per annum. This building was used to house the officer and his family and also to stable the horse.

Walthamstow Police Station Lamp

In 1840 the police officers moved into premises at Vestry House, Church End, Walthamstow[54] (this building is now the Vestry museum). This was a two storey building made of brown stock brick and had been constructed in 1730 (and extended in 1756) by order of the Vestry[55]. The extension provided extra room for the large number of paupers in Walthamstow at the time. It was this space that was used by the police from 1841 until 1870 when the police were transferred to Lea Bridge Road[56].

There were four sergeants, seventeen constables and one mounted constable. The Station Inspector from Enfield Highway Police Station supervised them – some distance away[57].

The station below provided accommodation for a single internal cell in which to house one prisoner, whilst outside there was a lock-up attached to the east wall of the building[58]. In 1864 the Commissioner approved the transfer of Walthamstow to 'N' or Islington Division[59] and the employment of Police Sergeant 57 'N' Turner on station duties at the police station [60]. Even today the lock up can still be seen complete with Victorian graffiti written on the walls by the prisoners[61].

Walthamstow Police Station
Vestry House, Church End, Walthamstow, London.
1840 – 1868

However, these premises were not ideal for police use and a new building was opened in November 1868 [62] in Lea Bridge Road on the corner of Shrubland Road. Once vacated the old station building was taken over for use as an armoury by the Walthamstow Volunteers[63]. In 1886 Bethnal Green took over as the Headquarters station for 'N' Division[64].

In August 1889 the Home Office sanctioned the purchase of a plot of land at the junction of Clay Street (Forest Road) and Greenleaf Road, Walthamstow as suitable for a police station. The freehold site was obtained for the sum of £435 [65]. It opened for business in December 1892 [66].

From December 1898 until December 1906 various communications were received from 'The overseers of the poor of the Parish of Walthamstow', 'Walthamstow Urban District Council' and certain individuals complaining of the shortage of police in the area. In 1891 there were seventy officers of all ranks performing duty in the parish. In December 1892 the Superintendent requested a further augmentation of two sergeants and 22 constables to add to his overworked officers at the station, however only five more constables were granted[67]. In 1899 the strength had risen to ninety officers [68].

Walthamstow Police Station
360, Forest Road, Walthamstow E.
1892- to 1941 (then re-furbished)

This was the station built in 1892 however it was substantially reconstructed in 1941.

There had been a population explosion during that period and the numbers had risen from 46,000 to an estimated 80,000 persons in 1899. Many new houses were built during this period and newcomers were attracted to the area by the twenty-minute train service journey to London. Fares were cheap and the Great Eastern Railway issued workmen's return tickets to London at 0004 hours for 2d. and then up until 0800 hours for 4d [69].

In 1907 the station was connected to the public telephone network[70]. In 1929 a motor van was delivered to the station – the first police transport for the area[71].

Just prior to the 1939-1945 World War it was decided to re-construct the Station on the original site purchased in 1890. The new station at 360, Forest Road, Walthamstow, E.17. was built for the sum of £26,815 and building work was completed in 1941 [72]. In effect the size of the station was doubled to its right with the building of a new entrance hall and gabled extrusion. Walthamstow division suffered only one casualty during the war when Constable 620 'J' Bentley was killed during an enemy air attack in March 1941[73].

Walthamstow Police Station
360, Forest Road, Walthamstow E 17 5JQ.
1892 - (refurbished 1941) to present day

A variety of additional requirements brought on by the onset of war caused a certain amount of disruption at the station. The addition of Air raid sirens, a certain amount of target hardening and the building of a cleansing centre connected to Air Raid precaution measures meant that the contract to re-build the station could not be completed until 1943[74].

In 1971 more space was required for the increase in the numbers of police officers, however it was decided that re-building Chingford Police Station was a better option[75]. In 1977 Walthamstow transferred its divisional offices to Chingford[76] when it became a sectional station[77].

In 2002 to help them police the busy Walthamstow Town Centre which

Walthamstow Town Police Office
193 High Street, Walthamstow
2002

boasted the longest street market in Europe, a purpose built police office was set up at 193, High Street, Walthamstow and it is open most days [78]. The opening hours are 9.30am until 5.30pm Monday to Saturday[79]. The station is staffed by one sergeant, seven permanent constables and five other constables drawn from the core relief team[80].

The office does not have cells or interview facilities, but the unit makes a large number of arrests each year and these prisoners are taken to the nearest police station for processing[81]. The market area is covered by a number of closed-circuit television cameras in an effort to stamp out crime through the Walthamstow Retail Anti-Crime Partnership.

---

[1] Municipal Year Book 2000 and Public Services Directory Vol. 2 Newman Books (1999) and publicity literature of the London Borough of Waltham Forest.
[2] Elliot, B (1992) History of the Police Stations of 'J' Division 1886 –1986 p5
[3] ibid p5
[4] Metropolitan Police General Orders 1873
[5] Metropolitan Police Commissioners Memorandum dated 15th December 1874
[6] Elliot, B (1992) History of the Police Stations of 'J' Division 1886 –1986 p5
[7] Metropolitan Police Orders dated 23rd May 1882.
[8] Metropolitan Police Orders 26th June 1886
[9] Metropolitan Police Orders 12th March 1889

[10] Rider, G. (1987) Chingford Police – Law and Order 1504 - 1987
[11] Fido, M and Skinner, K. (1999) The Encyclopedia of New Scotland Yard. Virgin Press p24
[12] Rider, G. (1987) Chingford Police – Law and Order 1504 - 1987
[13] Ibid and Reay, Col. W. T. (1920) 'The Specials' Billings, Guildford, Surrey P71
[14] Back, J. (1975) The Metropolitan Police Museum, Charlton
[15] Metropolitan Police Orders dated May 1932
[16] Metropolitan Police Surveyors Records
[17] Rider, G. (1987) Chingford Police – Law and Order 1504 - 1987
[18] Ibid
[19] Ramsey W. G. (1986) Epping Forest then and now. p86
[20] Mead, B. (undated) Welcome pack Chingford Division
[21] http://www.met.police.uk/contact/phone.htm dated 06.05.02
[22] Mead, B. (undated) Welcome pack Chingford Division
[23] Metropolitan Police General Orders November 1868
[24] The Metropolitan Police Annual Report for 1871
[25] PRO Census Records 1881
[26] Kelly's Directory 1894
[27] Ibid
[28] Metropolitan Police Orders dated January 1891
[29] Metropolitan Police Orders dated 27th April 1908
[30] Metropolitan Police Orders dated February 1913
[31] Metropolitan Police Orders dated 20th July 1927
[32] Metropolitan Police Surveyors Records
[33] Metropolitan Police Orders dated 27th July 1933
[34] Metropolitan Police Orders dated August 1940
[35] Leyton Police Station cited in Three District Magazine (1960)
[36] Back, J. (1975) The Metropolitan Police Museum, Charlton
[37] Fido, M and Skinner, K. (1999) The Encyclopedia of New Scotland Yard. Virgin Press p277
[38] http://www.met.police.uk/contact/phone.htm dated 06.05.02
[39] Ramsey, G (1997) The East End –then and now. Heronsgate, Basildon , Essex p 368
[40] Metropolitan Police Orders dated 20th November 1872
[41] Metropolitan Police General Orders 1893
[42] Express and Independent November 27th 1886
[43] Leathart, J. R. (1941) Leyton Police station cited in 'The Builder' January 3rd.
[44] Metropolitan Police Orders dated 22nd July 1886
[45] Metropolitan Police Orders dated March 1913
[46] The Metropolitan Police Surveyors records dated 1924
[47] Fido, M and Skinner, K. (1999) The Encyclopedia of New Scotland Yard. Virgin Press p252
[48] Ibid
[49] Metropolitan Police Service Records (undated)
[50] Ibid
[51] Personal correspondence of Mr John Barrett BEM.
[52] The Police and Constabulary Almanac 1998
[53] http://www.met.police.uk/contact/phone.htm dated 06.05.02
[54] Elliot, B (1992) History of the Police Stations of 'J' Division 1886 –1986 p11
[55] http://www.lbwf.gov.uk/leisure/vestry/vest_hist.stm dated 06.05.02
[56] http://www.lbwf.gov.uk/leisure/vestry/vest_hist.stm dated 06.05.02
[57] Mead, B. (undated) Welcome pack Chingford Division
[58] Elliot, B (1992) History of the Police Stations of 'J' Division 1886 –1986 p11
[59] Mead, B. (undated) Welcome pack Chingford Division
[60] Metropolitan Police Orders dated 27th April 1864
[61] http://www.lbwf.gov.uk/leisure/vestry/vest_hist.stm dated 06.05.02
[62] Metropolitan Police Orders dated 5th November 1868
[63] http://www.lbwf.gov.uk/leisure/vestry/vest_hist.stm dated 06.05.02
[64] Mead, B. (undated) Welcome pack Chingford Division
[65] Back.J (1975) Metropolitan Police Museum, Charlton
[66] Metropolitan Police Orders dated 24thDecember 1892
[67] Mead, B. (undated) Welcome pack Chingford Division
[68] Back.J (1975) Metropolitan Police Museum, Charlton

[69] Elliot, B. (1992) History of the Police Stations of 'J' Division 1886 - 1986

[70] Mead, B. (undated) Welcome pack Chingford Division

[71] Ibid

[72] Back, J. (1975) Metropolitan Police Museum, Charlton

[73] Mead, B. (undated) Welcome pack Chingford Division

[74] Ibid

[75] Ibid

[76] Ibid also Back, J. (1975) Metropolitan Police Museum, Charlton

[77] Metropolitan Police Orders dated 7th January 1977

[78] http://www.met.police.uk/police/mps/walthamforest/market.htm dated 06.05.02

[79] ibid

[80] ibid

[81] ibid

Appendix

POLICE OFFICERS MENTIONED IN THIS BOOK

Name	Rank	Date	Chapter
ADAMS Wilfred John	Constable	1936	Barking & Dagenham
ABBEY William	Sub-Divisional Inspector	1929	Haringey
ABERLINE Frederick George	Detective Chief Inspector	1890	Tower Hamlets
AGGS	Inspector	1844	Camden
ALLEN	Sergeant	1904	Waltham Forest
ALLEN George	Inspector	1890	Barking & Dagenham
ALMOND Dave	Superintendent	1998	Newham
ARCHER Charles	Constable	1881	Havering
ARNOLD Edmund	Inspector	1877	Camden
ARNOLD Thomas	Superintendent	1888	Tower Hamlets
ASH J.T	Chief Inspector (Specials)	1914	Camden
ASKEW Austin	Sub Divisional Inspector	1902	Hackney
AUBYN George	Constable	1897	Islington
AUNGER Henry	Inspector	1877	Camden
AXTEN	Station Inspector	1922	Haringey
AYLAND Edwin	Constable	1836	Hackney
AYLETT T.W.C.	Superintendent	1937	Newham
AYRE A.	Constable(Specials)	1916	Enfield
BACON	A/Sergeant	1864	Haringey
BALDWIN James	Constable	1898	Hackney
BARKER	Constable	1904	Waltham Forest
BARNARD James	Constable	1840	Havering
BARNES A.	Sub-Divisional Inspector	1938	Newham
BARNY Henry	Inspector	1855	Tower Hamlets
BARRATT A.L.	Superintendent	1957	Redbridge
BARRETT John	Constable	1965	Waltham Forest
BATEMAN	Constable	1898	Newham
BATSON Walter C	Deputy Commander	1953	Barking & Dagenham/Thames
BEAN Thomas	Constable	1851	Newham
BEANEY M.	Constable(Specials)	1916	Enfield
BEARD	Superintendent	1897	Tower Hamlets
BEASLEY	Constable	1901	Havering
BELL Edward	Inspector	1835	Camden
BENTLEY	Sergeant	1911	Tower Hamlets
BENTLEY	Constable	1941	Waltham Forest
BEVERIDGE	Constable	1897	Tower Hamlets
BEVERIDGE	Constable	1897	Tower Hamlets
BILLERS George	Inspector	1840	Camden
BIRDSEYE Jonathon	Constable	1851	Havering
BLAKELOCK Keith	Constable	1985	Haringey
BLISS John	Inspector	1881	Thames
BOOKSON Frank	Inspector	1910	Newham
BOREHAM Isaac	Constable	1881	Havering
BOWLES Gilbert Humphrey	Commandant	1937	Haringey
BOYES E	Constable(Specials)	1916	Enfield
BOYLING	Constable	1904	Waltham Forest
BRADFORD Sir Edward	Commissioner	1890	Islington/Newham

BRAILEY C.	Sub-Divisional Inspector	1920	Newham
BREED F.	Sergeant	1917	Waltham Forest
BREWER	Constable	1896	Islington
BRIDGE Sir John	Commissioner	1894	Islington
BRINE Philip	Inspector	1855	Tower Hamlets
BRISTOWE F.S.	Inspector(Specials)	1916	Camden
BROKENSHIRE	Chief Superintendent	1969	Enfield
BROWN Ivan L.A.	Chief Superintendent	1992	Newham
BROWN J.	Chief Inspector	1937	Thames
BROWN Lawrence	Constable	1990	Hackney
BUCKINGHAM E.	Constable(Specials)	1916	Enfield
BUCKPITT	Sub Inspector(Specials)	1916	Enfield
BUDD Ernest	Constable	1904	Waltham Forest
BULLOCK R.	Divisional Commander (Specials)	1914	Waltham Forest
BUTFOY Abia	Constable	1846	Barking & Dagenham
CANTER K.	Corporal(Specials)	1916	Enfield
CARLIN Francis	Constable	1881	Camden
CARLIN Francis	Detective Superintendent	1890	Camden
CARR George	Inspector	1881	Haringey
CARSON Cornelious	Superintendent	1957	Hackney
CARTER John	Superintendent	1840	Camden
CASTLE H.W.	Assistant Commander (Specials)	1914	Redbridge
CAUSBY	Sub Divisional Inspector	1894	Tower Hamlets
CHECKLEY Richard	Inspector	1855	Camden
CHOAT	Constable	1911	Tower Hamlets
CLACKETT Sidney Charles	Constable	1937	Newham
CLARE Albert	Constable	1937	Epping Forest
CLARK George	Constable	1846	Barking & Dagenham
CLARK Leonard	Inspector	1941	Islington
CLARKE Frederick Ernest	Constable	1944	Haringey
CLARKE Harry	Station Sergeant	1898	Epping Forest
CLARKE William James	Inspector	1922	Haringey
CLEMENT William	Inspector	1855	Camden
CLIFFORD John	Chief Inspector	1877	Camden
COLE George	Constable	1882	Hackney
COLEMAN Benjamin	Constable	1881	Newham
CONDON Sir Paul (now Lord)	Commissioner	1996	Tower Hamlets
CONNELL Patrick	Constable	1897	Haringey
COOK John	Inspector	1877	Camden
COOK John	Constable	1881	Waltham Forest
COOK William	Constable	1901	Barking & Dagenham
COOPER Thomas J.	Inspector	1885	Havering
COOPER William D.	Inspector	1844	Hackney
COPE	Constable	1938	Hackney
COPSEY Joseph	Constable	1841	Havering
COUCHER	Chief Inspector (Specials)	1937	Haringey
COULSON	Superintendent	1844	Havering
COUSINS William	Constable	1861	Havering
COWARD James	Inspector	1850	Hackney
COX Charles	Constable	1961	Newham
CRACKNELL	Constable	1841	Havering
CRAGGS Henry	Inspector	1881	Waltham Forest
CREASEY John	Constable	1881	Redbridge

CROSS	Chief Inspector (Specials)	1914	Camden
CROWLEY J.	Sub-Divisional Inspector	1933	Newham
CRUISE George	Inspector	1877	Camden
CURRY John	Station Sergeant	1941	Islington
DANES James	Constable	1861	Havering
DANIELS E.	Constable (Specials)	1916	Enfield
DAVIES Joseph	Inspector	1897	Islington
DAVIS Edward	Superintendent	1840	Havering
DAWS Ebenezer	Constable	1851	Newham
DE MAID William	Inspector	1877	Camden
DEATH Joseph	Inspector	1888	Newham
DENLOW Charles	Constable	1881	Hackney
DENNIS William	Constable	1861	Havering
DICKINSON	Chief Superintendent	1980	Enfield
DICKSON James	Inspector	1890	Redbridge
DIGBY George	Constable	1861	Havering
DIXON Thomas	Inspector	1890	Barking & Dagenham
DONALDSON David Leonard	Constable (later Inspector)	1990	Waltham Forest
DREW	Constable	1886	Havering
DUDLEY Gregory	Inspector	1840	Camden
DUDMAN George	Station Inspector	1881	Hackney
DUNN William	War Reserve Constable	1940	Redbridge
DURGAN Edward	Inspector	1855	Camden
DURLEY John	Inspector	1881	Barking & Dagenham
DURRANT William	Sergeant	1881	Tower Hamlets
DUTCHESS James	Inspector	1877	Camden
EFFORD Charles Victor	Constable	1920	Islington
ELLIOTT Bryn	Constable	1987/1993	Epping Forest/Redbridge
ELLIS Thomas	Inspector	1849	Tower Hamlets
ELMES E.	Constable	1990	Enfield
ELPHICK Horace	Inspector	1927	Haringey
EMERSON John	Constable	1836	Redbridge
EMMERY George	Constable	1881	Havering
EMSLEY Ernest George	Constable	1944	Hackney
ENGLAND Leslie	Constable	1961	Newham
EVANS James Christopher	Inspector (later Superintendent)	1833/1844	Thames
EVAN John Christopher	Superintendent	1848	Thames
EVANS H.J.	Commander	1958	Thames
EVERFIELD.A.	Constable(Specials)	1916	Enfield
FAIR William	Constable	1833	Redbridge
FALCONER Charles Henry	Inspector	1833	Thames
FANNING Hugh	Sergeant	1891	Tower Hamlets
FARRELL	Sub Divisional Inspector	1927	Waltham Forest
FARROW James	Sergeant	1881	Havering
FARROW Jepthah	A/Sergeant	1876	Epping Forest
FERRETT Arthur	Inspector	1910	Newham
FITT William E	Superintendent	1912	Hackney/Redbridge
FORBES Daniel	Inspector	1849	Tower Hamlets
FORD	Inspector	1898	Hackney
FOWLER James	Constable	1843	Havering
FOX Thomas	Inspector	1833	Thames
FOXALL Frederick George	Superintendent	1850	Camden
FREE Benjamin	Constable	1881	Havering

FULLER Uriah	Constable	1843	Havering
GARDE William R.	Inspector	1832	Tower Hamlets
GARDENER	Constable	1867	Redbridge
GARDINER. D.	Constable(Specials)	1916	Enfield
GARNER David	Constable	1884	Hackney
GASKIN John	Inspector	1826	Thames
GATESBY	Sergeant	1860	Camden
GAY Isaac	Constable	1851	Newham
GERNON Albert	Inspector	1855	Tower Hamlets
GIBSON	Sergeant	1890	Redbridge
GIBSON MacAlan	Sub Divisional Inspector	1941	Islington
GILBY George	Inspector	1877	Camden
GILLETT William	Superintendent	1835	Hackney
GILLIES John	Inspector	1890	Redbridge
GILPIN William	Inspector	1861	Havering
GOLDER John	Inspector	1881	Camden
GOLDING Eccles	Inspector	1881	Newham
GOSLING C.	Constable(Specials)	1916	Enfield
GOULD	Inspector	1873	Camden
GRANTHAM	Constable	1830	Camden
GREEN	Constable	1897	Hackney
GREEN	Superintendent	1864	Epping Forest
GREEN R.	Sergeant(Specials)	1916	Enfield
GREEN W.F.	Superintendent	1871	Barking & Dagenham
GREENHOFF George	Constable	1917	Newham
GREENHOFF Edward	Constable	1955	Newham
GREENWOOD Dr.E.Climpson	Chief Inspector (Specials)	1914	Camden
GREENWOOD William	Superintendent	1845	Camden
GRIMSTONE Thomas	Inspector	1840	Thames
GRIMWOOD William	Superintendent	1832	Camden
GROVES Thomas	Inspector	1890	Redbridge
GURNEY Eddie	Constable	1967	Barking & Dagenham
GUTTERIDGE George	Constable	1927	Havering
HALFORD Henry J	Constable	1915	Enfield
HAMMOND	Superintendent	1894	Islington
HANKERVILLE	Sergeant	1898	Epping Forest
HANNANT S	Superintendent	1856	Camden
HARDING John	Inspector	1910	Newham
HARRINGTON Charles	Constable	1881	Havering
HARRINGTON William	Constable	1861	Havering
HARRIS Henry	Inspector	1835	Tower Hamlets
HARRISON John	Sergeant	1845	Enfield
HARVARD Roger	Inspector	1855	Camden
HAVERS	Constable	1922	Havering
HAYDON John	Inspector	1840	Havering
HAYNES William	Constable	1896	Islington
HEAD George	Inspector	1881	Enfield
HEMS David James	Sergeant	1970	Hackney
HENRY Sir Edward	Commissioner	1910	Camden/Haringey
HERRING D.	Superintendent	1830	Tower Hamlets
HILL George	Constable	1898	Newham
HILL Isaac	Inspector	1877	Thames
HILL Thomas	Inspector	1938	Redbridge

HINDS Albert	War Reserve Constable	1841	Epping Forest
HISTED G	Constable	???	Enfield
HITCHCOCK	Station Sergeant	1936	Hackney
HODGE J.R.	Constable (Specials)	1918	Camden
HOPKER	Constable	1904	Waltham Forest
HOPKINS Henry	Inspector	1881	Enfield
HOWARD A.C.	Superintendent	1875	Thames
HOWE	Constable	1867	Redbridge
HOWE	Constable	1909	Thames
HOWIE	Superintendent	1859	Epping Forest
HOWIE Daniel	Inspector	1845	Hackney
HOWLETT H.E.	Chief Superintendent	1957	Redbridge
HOWLETT W.T.J.	Superintendent	1916	Havering
HUCK Charles Henry	War Reserve Constable	1940	Islington
HUGHES Nevil	Constable	1967	Barking & Dagenham
HUNT	Chief Superintendent	1969	Enfield
HUNT Charles	Superintendent	1888	Islington
HUNT Robert	Assistant Commissioner	1992	Newham
HUNTLEY William J	Superintendent	1888	Camden
HUTCHINS Frederick	Sergeant	1961	Newham
HUTCHINGS G. S.	Constable	1896	Islington
HYDE	Detective Inspector	1922	Havering
IMBERT Sir Peter (now Lord)	Commissioner	1990	Enfield/Islington/Newham
ISBESTER William	Inspector	1827	Thames
JAMES Alfred Charles	Constable	1930	Epping Forest
JENKINS	Inspector	1878	Hackney
JERBURGH-BONSEY H.	Assistant Commandant	1919	Hackney
JOHNSON George	Constable	1861	Havering
JOHNSON James	Superintendent	1840	Islington
JOHNSON M.	Sergeant(Specials)	1916	Enfield
JOHNSTON James	Superintendent	1845	Hackney
JORDAN Dora	Constable	1918	Havering
JORDAN Samuel	Constable	1941	Epping Forest
JOSLIN Fred	Constable	1919	Havering
JOYCE	Constable	1894	Islington
JUDGE Joshua	Inspector	1831	Thames
JUDGE William	Inspector	1817	Thames
JUDGE John	Inspector	1840	Thames
KAYE K.	Constable(Specials)	1916	Enfield
KEATING James	Superintendent	1888	Tower Hamlets
KEENS William Henry	Constable	1863	Tower Hamlets
KEIL Frederick Henry	Sergeant	1952	Hackney
KENDALL Sir Norman	Assistant Commissioner	1940	Newham
KENNEDY John	Constable	1867	Haringey
KENNISON	Constable (later Inspector)	1972	Islington
KENTS Robert	Constable	1960	Epping Forest
KILLEN Tom	War Reserve Constable	1941	Islington
KING	Inspector	1894	Haringey
KING Alan	Sergeant	1991	Waltham Forest
KING William	Constable	1861	Havering
KIRBY	A/Sergeant	1864	Enfield
KNIGHT C.	Constable(Specials)	1916	Enfield
LAMB Thomas	Inspector	1881	Barking & Dagenham

LAMBERT F.	Constable	1841	Havering
LANKTREE	Inspector	1908	Newham
LAZELL Alfred	Constable	1881	Havering
Le COCQ	Inspector	1881	Tower Hamlets
LEE Charles Richard	Detective Sergeant	1918	Hackney
LEES George	Constable	1898	Hackney
LEESON Ben	Detective Sergeant	1911	Tower Hamlets
LEONARD William	Inspector	1840	Thames
LEVEY Ernest Alfred	Special Constable	1951	Waltham Forest
LEVICK	Chief Inspector (Specials)	1914	Camden
LEWIS John Joseph	Inspector	1834/1835	Thames/Tower Hamlets
LITTLE N.	Constable(Specials)	1916	Enfield
LOCK Samuel	Constable	1950	Haringey
LOCKWOOD Arnold	Chief Superintendent	1960	Barking & Dagenham
LOVETT Charles	Constable	1851	Newham
LOXTON	Superintendent	1864	Camden
LUCAS	Sergeant	1867	Redbridge
MABER Edward	Station Sergeant	1912	Waltham Forest
MACKAY A.	Constable(Specials)	1916	Enfield
MACKAY Nina	Constable	1997	Redbridge
MACKAY Sidney	Chief Superintendent	1995	Redbridge
MacKINNON	Chief Superintendent	1968	Enfield
MADDOX George	Inspector	1840	Thames
MAHER Thomas E.	Inspector	1881	Enfield
MANNING James	Constable	1861	Havering
MANNING John M	Sergeant	1851	Newham
MAPELEY	Constable	1904	Waltham Forest
MARKHAM Edward	Chief Superintendent	1984	Enfield
MARLER Charles	Inspector	1877	Thames
MARLOW John	Constable	1836	Redbridge
MARSH Adam	Inspector	1881	Tower Hamlets
MARSH George	Inspector	1855	Tower Hamlets
MARSINGALE	Superintendent	1841	Havering
MARTIN	Chief Superintendent	1980	Enfield
MASON Arthur	Inspector	1874	Newham
MASON	Sub Divisional Inspector	1900	Islington
MAUDE Henry	Inspector	1841	Camden
MAY Charles	Inspector	1844	Tower Hamlets
MAY James Brian	Constable	1967	Haringey
MAYNE Sir Richard	Commissioner	1849	Camden
MAZETTI Bertie	Constable(Specials)	1941	Haringey
McDONOUGH C.L.	Chief Superintendent	1957	Thames
McFADDEN	Superintendent	1894/1896	Hackney/Islington
McFADDEN Alexander	Constable	1861	Havering
McGOWAN Patrick	Constable	1898	Hackney
McLEAN Capt. J.R.	Commander	1914	Redbridge
McLEAN Geoffrey	Assistant Commissioner	1990	Enfield
McNEE Sir David	Commissioner	1981	Newham
MEDLICOTT W.	Superintendent	1849	Tower Hamlets
MEE William	Inspector	1877	Camden
MELLISH Joseph	Inspector	1850	Hackney
MERCHANT W.J.	Superintendent	1960	Barking & Dagenham
MILLER	Inspector	1898	Camden

MILLER William	Inspector	1855	Tower Hamlets
MOORE John	Constable	1897	Islington
MOORE A.	Sergeant(Specials)	1916	Enfield
MOORE John	Constable	1851	Newham
MORLEY H.	Superintendent	1957	Thames
MORRIS	Chief Superintendent	1976	Enfield
MORTLOCK	Sergeant	1894	Haringey
MOULAND E.	Constable(Specials)	1916	Enfield
MOUNCE M.R.	Woman Sergeant(Specials)	1968	Tower Hamlets
MOUNT John	Constable	1881	Havering
MOUNTIFIELD	Sub Divisional Inspector	1897	Haringey/Islington
MULVANY John Michael	Divisional Superintendent	1911	Early Days of Policing
MURRAY	Inspector	1901	Newham
M'KELVIE	Constable	1899	Islington
NEAN	Sub Divisional Inspector	1894	Hackney
NEWMAN	Constable	1909	Haringey
NEWMAN Sir Kenneth	Commissioner	1986	Hackney/Islington
NEWMAN Ernest	Constable	1897	Haringey
O'CONNOR Michael	Chief Superintendent	1989	Enfield
ODELL William	Chief Inspector	1877	Camden
OSGOOD	Inspector	1898	Hackney
OVERY	Inspector	1878	Hackney
PACEY	Sub-Divisional Inspector	1919	Camden
PALIN S.A.	Superintendent	1960	Haringey
PALMER	Constable	1904	Waltham Forest
PARKER Henry	Inspector	1881	Hackney
PARSLOW James	Constable	1861	Havering
PARSON J.	Sub-Divisional Inspector	1921	Newham
PARSONS	Sergeant	1864	Enfield
PARSONS	Chief Inspector	1894	Hackney
PARSONS William	Sergeant	1846	Barking & Dagenham
PASCOE John	Inspector	1850	Hackney
PAWSEY Philip	Inspector	1961	Newham
PEARCE	Superintendent	1929	Hackney
PEARCE Nicholas	Superintendent	1846	Barking & Dagenham
PEARCE Roger	Chief Superintendent	1992	Enfield
PEARMAN William	Inspector	1894	Redbridge
PERNULL .S.	Constable(Specials)	1916	Enfield
PHILLIPS	Sergeant	1867	Redbridge
PICKARD E.	Constable(Specials)	1916	Enfield
PICKETT Thomas Robert	War Reserve Constable	1940	Hackney
PIERSE William F.	Superintendent	1835	Tower Hamlets
PING	Constable	1904	Waltham Forest
PIPE Henry	Sub Divisional Inspector	1897	Newham
PIPES	Constable	1894	Islington
PLUMMER Joseph	Sergeant	1881	Tower Hamlets
POCOCK James H.	Inspector	1896	Islington
POPE Richard	Inspector	1877	Camden
PORTER Albert Ernest	Station Sergeant	1902	Thames
POYNTZ Major	Chief Constable	1885	Havering
PRATCHETT Henry	Station Sergeant	1894	Waltham Forest
PRIDMORE Thomas	Inspector	1877	Thames
PROCTOR Thomas L.	Inspector	1881	Tower Hamlets

QUIGLEY K.	Inspector	1895	Newham
QUIGLEY William	Inspector	1881	Tower Hamlets
RAWLEY John	Inspector	1835	Camden
RAWLINGS William	Constable	1919	Camden
READ M.	Constable(Specials)	1916	Enfield
REDGEWELL	Chief Superintendent	1981	Newham
REID Thomas	Inspector	1881	Tower Hamlets
RICHARDS W.H.	Constable	1940	Enfield
RICHARDSON	Inspector	1846	Barking & Dagenham
RICHARDSON Joseph Ernest	Constable	1928	Hackney
RICHARDSON William	Inspector	1844	Barking & Dagenham
RIDLEY Albert	Constable	1861	Havering
ROBBINS Peter	Chief Superintendent	2001	Hackney
ROBERTS George	Inspector	1877	Thames
ROBERTSON Alexander	Inspector	1933	Epping Forest
ROBINSON John	Constable	1845	Camden
ROBSON William	Inspector	1877	Thames
ROLFE George	Inspector	1890	Redbridge
ROOKS William	Inspector	1890	Newham
ROSEN James	Constable	1941	Islington
ROSKELLY Joseph	Sergeant	1873	Tower Hamlets
RUFF	Sub Divisional Inspector	1897	Islington
RUSSELL Leonard	Constable	1904	Haringey
RUTT Anthony	Inspector	1837	Tower Hamlets
SANDERS John	Constable	1851	Newham
SAUNDERS Thomas	Inspector	1890	Redbridge
SAWYER A	Sub-Divisional Inspector	1929	Newham
SAWYER William Rivers	Constable	1874	Haringey
SCOTT	Sub-Inspector (Specials)	1914	Camden
SEARLE Graheme	Chief Superintendent	1992	Enfield
SHERLOCK William J	Superintendent	1888	Hackney
SIMMONDS John	Inspector	1910	Newham
SIMMONS	Inspector	1885	Havering
SIMS-KIRBY J.L.	Superintendent	1957	Haringey
SIMSON R.A.	Commander (Specials)	1914	Camden
SKEATS George	Superintendent	1888	Thames
SKENE William	Superintendent	1829/1832	Camden
SMITH	Constable	1856	Early Days of Policing
SMITH John George	Cadet (later Inspector)	1965	Havering
SNELL William	Constable (later sergeant)	1881/1884	Thames/Hackney
SOLMAN David	Superintendent	1992	Newham
SOMERSET Raglan	Assistant Chief Constable	1885	Havering
SPALDING William	Constable	1881	Havering
STANLEY Alick	Detective Sergeant	1941	Islington
STANTON	Constable	1900	Islington
STEAD J.	Superintendent	1849	Tower Hamlets
STEGGLES Richard	Superintendent	1888	Camden
STEVENS Sir John	Commissioner	2002	Havering
STRATFORD Frederick	Sergeant	1874	Barking & Dagenham
STURGEON Henry	Sergeant	1872	Epping Forest
STYLES James	Sergeant	1937	Epping Forest
SUMMERS Raymond Henry	Constable	1958	Islington
SWINDEN David Reginald	Superintendent	1992	Islington/Newham/Tower Hamlets

TARLTON Edward	Inspector	1850	Hackney
THATCHER George	Inspector	1850	Hackney
THOMAS	Inspector	1909	Haringey
THOMPSON	Sub-Divisional Inspector	1890	Newham
THOMPSON A.	Sub-Divisional Inspector	1923	Newham
THOMPSON A.H.	Chief Superintendent	1957	Newham
THOMSON James J	Superintendent	1877	Camden
THORNDELL Charles	Constable	1881	Tower Hamlets
THORNTON	Chief Superintendent	1979	Enfield
THORPE	Sub Divisional Inspector	1898	Hackney
TIMMINS H.	Superintendent	1957	Newham
TITCOMBE H.	Inspector	1895	Newham
TOLFIELD E.	Constable(Specials)	1916	Enfield
TOMLIN Major M. OBE	Chief Constable	1929	Hackney
TONGE John	Inspector	1844	Hackney
TOTTERDELL George H.	Detective Superintendent	1950	Havering
TRENCHARD (Lord)	Commissioner	1930	Tower Hamlets
TUCKER	Sergeant	1911	Tower Hamlets
TURNER	Sergeant	1864	Waltham Forest
TURNER George	Superintendent	1855/1881	Newham/Tower Hamlets
TYLER	Constable	1909	Haringey
UNDERWOOD William	Superintendent	1831	Hackney
VARNEY Eric	Station Sergeant	1972	Enfield
VARRONE Mark	Inspector	1881	Newham
VINCENT Barry	Superintendent	1992	Enfield/Newham
WALCH John	Constable	1851	Newham
WALKER	Superintendent	1872	Enfield
WALKER Thomas Benjamin	Inspector	1840	Thames
WALLACE Alexander	Sub Divisional Inspector	1897	Redbridge
WALTERS	Special Constable	1881	Redbridge
WAPLING George	Constable	1881	Havering
WARE James	Inspector	1890	Redbridge
WATERS	Constable	1904	Waltham Forest
WATERS Phillip	Constable	1995	Redbridge
WATSON	Superintendent	1998	Enfield
WATSON	Superintendent	1998	Enfield
WATTS	Sub-Divisional Inspector	1943	Newham
WEBB	A/Superintendent	1865	Haringey
WEBB J.	Constable	1886	Havering
WEBB George	Inspector	1840	Thames
WELHAM Leslie	Constable	1933	Epping Forest
WELLS	Superintendent	1894	Tower Hamlets
WELLS Creswell	Superintendent	1897	Redbridge
WEST G.	Sergeant(Specials)	1916	Enfield
WHARTON	Superintendent	1960	Islington
WHARTON COLLARD C	Assistant Commander (Specials)	1914	Camden
WHEELER A.	Constable(Specials)	1916	Enfield
WHITE	Inspector	1936	Hackney
WHITE Richard	Inspector	1840	Thames
WHITE A.	Constable(Specials)	1916	Enfield
WHITE James Robert	Inspector	1834	Thames
WHITE William	Inspector	1874	Newham
WIGGINS	Constable	1900	Waltham Forest

WILKES Edward	Inspector	1881	Islington
WILLIAMS	Chief Superintendent	1986	Enfield
WILTSHIRE	Sergeant	1898	Hackney
WINSHIP Peter	Assistant Commissioner	1990	Enfield
WOOD Henry	Chief Inspector	1877	Camden
WOODGATE J.	Sergeant	1985	Havering
WOODHOUSE	Inspector (Specials)	1937	Haringey
WOOTTON	Inspector	1877	Thames
WORELS Edward	Superintendent	1877	Camden/Haringey
YALDEN William	Chief Inspector (Specials)	1926	Haringey
YEO Albert	Detective Inspector	1910	Newham
YOUNG A. KPM	Detective Constable	1915	Camden
YOUNG Edward	Superintendent	1836	Tower Hamlets